VERY COLLECTED POEMS

SELECTED OTHER BOOKS BY RON PADGETT

In Advance of the Broken Arm
Bean Spasms, with Ted Berrigan and Joe Brainard
Great Balls of Fire
The Adventures of Mr. and Mrs. Jim and Ron, with Jim Dine
Toujours l'amour
Tulsa Kid
Triangles in the Afternoon
The Big Something
Blood Work: Selected Prose
Ted: A Personal Memoir of Ted Berrigan
New & Selected Poems
Creative Reading
Albanian Diary
The Straight Line: Writing on Poetry and Poets
Poems I Guess I Wrote
Oklahoma Tough: My Father, King of the Tulsa Bootleggers
You Never Know
Joe: A Memoir of Joe Brainard
If I Were You (collaborations)
How to Be Perfect
How Long
Collected Poems
Alone and Not Alone
Big Cabin
Dot

TRANSLATIONS

The Poet Assassinated and Other Stories by Guillaume Apollinaire
Dialogues with Marcel Duchamp by Pierre Cabanne
Complete Poems by Blaise Cendrars
Complete Fiction by Serge Fauchereau, with John Ashbery
The Poems of A.O. Barnabooth by Valery Larbaud, with Bill Zavatsky
Prose Poems by Pierre Reverdy
Flash Cards by Yu Jian, with Wang Ping
Pink Dust
Dick: A Memoir of Dick Gallup

VERY COLLECTED POEMS

RON PADGETT

COFFEE HOUSE PRESS
MINNEAPOLIS 2025

Cover design by Mel Nigro and Ron Padgett
Book design by Coffee House Press and Bookmobile

Coffee House Press books are available to the trade through our primary distributor, Consortium Book Sales & Distribution, cbsd.com or (800) 283-3572. For personal orders, catalogs, or other information, write to info@coffeehousepress.org.

Coffee House Press is a nonprofit literary publishing house. Support from private foundations, corporate giving programs, government programs, and generous individuals helps make the publication of our books possible. We gratefully acknowledge their support in detail in the back of this book.

LIBRARY OF CONGRESS CATALOGING-IN-PUBLICATION DATA

Names: Padgett, Ron, author.
Title: Very collected poems / Ron Padgett.
Description: Minneapolis: Coffee House Press, 2025. | Includes indexes.
Identifiers: LCCN 2025021257 (print) | LCCN 2025021258 (ebook) |
ISBN 9781566897433 paperback | ISBN 9781566897440 epub
Subjects: LCGFT: Poetry
Classification: LCC PS3566.A32 V47 2025 (print) | LCC PS3566.A32 (ebook)
LC record available at https://lccn.loc.gov/2025021257
LC ebook record

PRINTED IN THE UNITED STATES OF AMERICA

32 31 30 29 28 27 26 25 1 2 3 4 5 6 7 8

VERY COLLECTED POEMS

Table of Contents

IN ADVANCE OF THE BROKEN ARM (1964)

from GREAT BALLS OF FIRE (1969)

TOUJOURS L'AMOUR (1976)

TRIANGLES IN THE AFTERNOON (1979)

THE BIG SOMETHING (1990)

POEM AND OTHER POEMS: UNCOLLECTED (1960-2004)

ALONE AND NOT ALONE (2015)

IN ADVANCE OF THE BROKEN ARM

Wind

Now it is over and everyone knew it
The bad grass surrendered in unison and with much emotion
The long-awaited became despised
Everyone got tired and concluded that phase

Reports followed, causing intrusions
In the old-timers. Others go off for refreshment
The distrustful student prefers German popular songs,
A language which he does not understand

But now there is the tremendous reassurance of being
At the dinner table and tense, a stalwart melody
Tromping to its fluorescent conclusion.
This you find unimaginable, that rent should be suddenly so high
Up there in the cupola, the gauze
The tiny excitement of the generator
The note you read without even looking at it
Going back where you lose your hands you bask
Whitewash vistas a voice that finally remembers
Hedges that were once formidable
You watch and are horrified to be a part of it

The booth puts you out for miles this speedometer
The "fertile lowlands" you chalk it up in orange
And again a brush applies the proper lascivious colors
The postcard making it "right" instead of wrong

Rome

The people begin to get on to you
But with a deft wrist you erase their heads.
The next scene goes on to include you:
There you are, kicking
Some kindly nun in the shins! Then the brush,
Its carefully chosen colors, paste and you shine
Forth from the page with your face.

Now you and I look at you during the meal;
The spoon was inserted in the bowl of soup
Before everything
Gets naturalistic again and a tree
Grows quietly beside you. Then "shorts,
The unnoticed removal of newsreels and lots of auto accidents.
This made us very popular.

Then the people began to get on to "you" again,
But as always, the Dwarf rushes in with his foil
And fends them away, keeping you safe.
I cannot be the dwarf, for I am many dwarfs,
Chopping and sawing at wood in this forest you grow around me
And whistling a tune to the words of "Signal Failure."

To a Berry

I came to you as two friends
But you escaped down the secret stairway
Known only to yourself and a few members
Of the family. Strange report, now, of the Queen
Alone in his chamber, scratching her head.
I thought I ought to. But no, you wanted table napkins,
Men telling lies in boats, pastilles and other
Things that generally looked up. "Ha ha!"
Said Richard, laughing over the death of his beloved.

Those who say that they served me
Most loyally did; to them this lemonade.
But now what? Goatherds flocking
The suburb with airs, while a lady most white
And fair inspects the small hole in her stockyard.
Alas! The wax museum be the whistle!

Clap clap. Ugh. Two cigarettes
In a finger, erasing discussion. Better the wet rain
And dire pneumonia than all this vase fame! Out, out
The empire thumbs, and all through California
Trees fell in a demonstration of heraldic boredom!
On the cold beach three clams
Refuse to mention it, which saw them. There now,

Everything is in the air except the air itself!
Hmmm. Time to set the French horns on edge,
Discouraging the zeros which now swoop down
To strafe us. If only I hadn't eaten so much.
Well, all's well in a world of corduroy.
The king slapped his forehead in disgust. Checking the sun,
Our flak spun up again, only to burst
With joy in the clear blue flaming zeps.

Distracted by the funeral procession, the twin
Bumped into himself. "Gosh, I'm sorry,
But I just can't give out information of that nature."
Following a glass of goat's milk, the guest of honor
Was just led to the next course of the peach-colored cottage;
But a hand tiptoed through the rose gardens
And, seizing the brush, begins to paint out the entire
Scene with brilliant white.

The Ems Dispatch

Opening up a mud duck
The sin of the hearth had made him handsome
Don't ever give me what continues to be the tan arm of the hero
As identical, these sums and the chance to disappear
By including the chamois
Though that's a fine mess, I wist
Titles, etc. 2. Two Veins.   followed, pursued, sought after
But the curse now
Laid you down in the patient tent
Where there are men, there are no men
Just what I wanted (lie) perfect (lie)
I cared for the boy's drawing of the horse to get going
Then the lovely shin quest
Into the untracked signal gun, flowers, birthdays, sonnets
Put the hot, sweet breath of your breath against mine enemy
Come with me the nurse ferocity
Streets streets and less equal streets
The sails being torn to pieces in the upstairs part
But in a few moments
Without themes space or the invisible table message
Under the legs "far" into the night our hut
Its flaming gates
And the invitation to commit bibliography
The proffered hand
Guessed we're on to each other
The lice looked up in astonishment
Didn't explain the available cardboard murder
Going on into the mail covered with rust and the box
The great shoe prediction sigh clock
No doubt about it the neighbor thought it over
The extra put on its countenance and clicked on off
Let my dog sleep
On the altar of girlhood
But polish around it, observing the priority of the bump
The close call packed away and sniffing at the edge

The Blind Dog of Venice

The tartar sauce lesson was misunderstood
By those who didn't even want to miss it.
Just in the nick of time the knob came forth with Kleenex,
The cow licked its way into our foreheads.
We responded with great tonsils, though we were soon
To forget that the angel of logic
Is not logic, and that the power of a personal
Hair is more aware than unusual.
This was the choir boy's dead.
Everyone moved up a row.

Later you beat me to a pulp magazine
Which I desired most fiercely, in thus wise
To far errands o'er the earth.
In the domino stand we committed the sin of homework
To drift up against the door and dream
Of a dog who would dream of a circle which draws a dream around us.
Then your long, leather smile consoled me
As far as the potbellied stove, in which had been placed
Our name, address, and age.
The delivery boy turned away from the door in despair,
His a fruitful mission!

What could we have been left out of?
Did it fall among the positive dominos? A vicious
Song leaped out of the frying pan.
The result is more high and low Latin, these letters
I am getting to and from you through our new past, since now
The mist is getting bigger
Over the sarsaparilla-colored pond and the searchlights
Which are getting cut down through the trees
Reveal the gentleman lawn reclining in a gesture of crassness.

Somnambulism

I come out of you in big
deep goshes   "Hi, toe!"
you know that story   told you and told on
you sang out
of sheer right (left)   mine was the middle one
between the other two someone was there   I
then the hammer   let us out
you cried   play cry   and I can can
you?   how to avoid the grimacing yoyo metaphor

then
the alpine refreshment of pine drinks   up you
didn't urge   I urged   everyone urged   but you
collecting the hammer and all
night cigarettes   kept flying   out of your   pockets
you came into focus from "I may I might I my my me"

then I took your place
in bed   it was worn   a little
bug sank down   on my arm
            holding the shadow of a dot!   quivers   foots
hills they diminished with spraying   beads broke
on your head   they buffed
you up   and asked yourself to fall together
did but "didn't"   they was plumb put

            zing!   out

now geared up for the encore
you enlarged   drinking cocoa   plopped down
"a real card or you that began saying   "I sound.

the last in angel, mountain and Franz Lizst . . ."

One Cent

Out of the bright upholstery of a face
A breath death breath at me that's going on?
Whoa! Strung up
Something on every side
Of an effort portent
A swine some grit a Tibetan ox
Fingering a trigger light
Breeze in a heavy wind
Where mine entrance to its outside is
Sunny and cold today, high in the twenties,
Fair tonight with twenty-one pieces of snow. Then
One igloo dawned on me hard. Ouch!
There were twelve of them men there
Eight ash trays and five puffs of smoke!

But now who uncovers a sign
In a white tornado friend
Just yodels the abbreviation of a state of going on
In California, though when the future poems
Of Keats write better
In your wrong, real, and solitary pants come on
And go right away to smithereens, back
In a jiffy to the miniature lady friend.

White Coffee

None biggest quiet
Bone over bones   a tether
Now we are back to front   cockily
The seconds pile up against the trees
Drove us into the northern part   it was hot
Our toes were hollow   then religious   then warm fizzle
Sunk back   the hand of the handball
Certain tight exploding jets
No more fearful loud
A sheriff was asking us to stop rotating again

Now these are not ours but are
Some effigy bruise   flip   inching to the cap
The crowd soon to begin booing in delight but
A steamer gauge held them back   they were hot   they urged

You gave them a mundane nickel   I
Backstage everything was glowing and pulsing
The water tap "facts"   an accumulation of gravity

Stop that the blackboard, anti-
More all
You supplicated for a mere water pretense
The southern clime was not fond of you nor you
So a dash
A colon a vertibra and an explosion of pills kept going
Until the middle part could be colored in

But who there of those we knew could
They had opera, chevrons, earned keep and hard
Noodles
There was no room on the outside only
A humble mint

But ferns though sloppy would suffice
You were always disappearing into heaven or slunk
Get up rumple
Of serious danger
On account of the flat white bull's eye
"A feeling good with no shaft or foot infection"

You did not tell me you were in Mexico
With me
We cut off our arms with you in them
You raved consecutively up the host
His sneakers in sight of the striped pole

We only looked black because we were
Of the family of the good teeth
Learning the lesson of the oat and the bump
Nothing was continuing like that might have
Out of those zzzzzing piazzas
The heinous sleeper hold

Please come back head heart and the rainy day
I have been saving until the end

The Life of M.

The true test of a man is a bunt. So kiss me!
O please come back to me! Then go away . . .
I only like you for a long time.
And then: "The gaucho is coming!"

The old room back in you
Or a complicated object by a pond
Weren't exactly "piled up"
But a tall short masculine kept starting to go

There's nothing in this box
Or the one in it but what's there?
Brown old arithmetic, a stopwatch,
A wrist and some h.........n.
Put them back. They are good for you.

No! They aren't! For they still love
Though the toe has been
But off the bumper crop of fumes.
Besides, the gaucho is almost here.

Via Air

Headlights are following a car whose headlights are turned off
Lies a mile long like collisions
That never daunt the Singing Killer

These old roads have been run over before
They ran all over the road
It was wet
My slippers plunging into the dark
Something was running by the running board
Symbol.
With a gasp you expired through the desert
I poured nickels and dimes out the window
And you burst into a new kind of wrong tick

Further ahead was a hill through which
There were the lights of the town we could see
Behind us a sudden storm of envelopes dictators
Special regimens and indications of hives
A several numb skull handed us an ordinary finger
Which popped
Into a series of whinneys on our parts

But your chair was sleekest
That never went
But to creeks and severe rustic manipulations
Spy-glasses and a chalk drawing of a ravine in it
To gather us back
To the continuing rip of the destination
That was not ours yours

The Left Half of 1816

Out of the other thermos jug its fifteen-foot-high letters
Air masses were moving to the north
Some lips said there was much ventilation
Then a series of oinks and growls
Made by beautiful young girls
It never sounded like anything

The spade experience was simulated
By dogs and gophers
Out on the west coast it's already on the move
My left arm feels it
The exact thrill of arriving on a dot
Which is being photographed
There was a specific flash of lightning in my pants
The old-fashioned birds asked to see it

Let's warm up the simian pianola
The female birds spoke of honey shacks
Our hair stood up for its own chore of enthusiasm
Then the enthusiasm went camping
It was wonderful

I spoke seven languages of the contact winds
My name is Freddy
Please disregard the kiss emblem I enjoy

The desk is gone and the harpy
Especially if you're young and "all the time"
Got pulled together

Some pans went down causing on the softball's brother
Sparks were coming from my toes

(Fauntleroy business)
About then a series of stupid joys came out of a mouth

But I don't even like Hawaiians
Though rectitude (in secret) knocks me out
Having no slow desire to inflict the golden mental joke
Said the freaks of history

After the Broken Arm

From point A a wind is blowing to point B
Which is here, where the pebble is only a mountain.
If truly heaven and earth are out there
Why is that man waving his arms around,
Gesturing to the word "lightning" written on the clouds
That surround and disguise his feet?

If you say the right word in New York City
Nothing will happen in New York City;
But out in the fabulous dry horror of the west
A beautiful girl named Sibyl will burst
In by the open window breathless
And settle for an imaginary glass of something.
But now her name is no longer Sibyl—it's Herman,
Yearning for point B.

Dispatch this note to our hero at once.

The Four Flying and Singing Assassins

Today that girl has one face saying 36 things at once
With her exploding teeth
But why does there have to be a particular number of cigarettes
In her mouth?   as if rhetoric
Somehow depended on the kind of tapestry one is standing in front of

Chester the King stood on the pale yellow veranda
Of his summer palace, watching himself smoke
And thinking up interesting lies

Then back in the city palace he sits down at his desk
For a long afternoon of history in the making

In his art museum six dwarfs are standing before a blot of orange
They have custom-made pencils and small pink tablets
What they really want to do is stand before the red gash

When it is time for night to come after a cigarette
He is going to decide which of the 36 faces
To save from the electric chair

I'd Give You My Seat If I Were Here

The shadows these flowers are making on each other
The wild and sleepy eyes they make
Are being thrown against the notion *de voyager*
By fingers that are not silver or blue and they point

This keeps happening for eleven months.
But tonight she's in her grave at the bottom of the sea,
Leaving us at that.

If I could tell you why
The delicious crunch of feathers
Through fifteen heads of yours
Can encourage and surround
Then there would be no need for this needle in my head
Or the electricity that is not really mine.

Though it is only real,
My dream to raise no curtain on the other stage
That isn't there, but there
Under the breeze of a handkerchief
That is brushing against the temple you will find
On either side of your head—

And you know and you know.

from
GREAT BALLS OF FIRE

Detach, Invading

Oh humming all and
Then a something from above came rooting
And tooting onto the sprayers
Profaning in the console morning
Of the pointing afternoon
Back to dawn by police word to sprinkle it
Over the lotions that ever change
On locks
Of German, room, and perforate
To sprinkle I say
On the grinding slot of rye
And the bandage that falls down
On the slots as they exude their gas
And the rabbit lingers that pushes it

To blot the lumber
Like a gradually hard mode
All bring and forehead in the starry grab
That pulverizes
And its slivers
Off bending down the thrown gulp
In funny threes
So the old fat flies toward the brain
And a dent on brilliance

The large pig at which the intense cones beat
Wishes O you and O me
O cough release! a rosy bar
Whose mist rarifies even the strokers
Where to go
Strapping, apricot

After Reverdy

I would never have wanted to see your sad face again
Your cheeks and your windy hair
I went all across the country
Under this humid woodpecker
Day and night
Under the sun and the rain

Now we are face to face again
What does one say to my face

Once I rested up against a tree
So long
I got stuck to it
That kind of love is terrible

Nothing in That Drawer

Nothing in that drawer.
Nothing in that drawer.
Nothing in that drawer.
Nothing in that drawer.
Nothing in that drawer.
Nothing in that drawer.
Nothing in that drawer.
Nothing in that drawer.
Nothing in that drawer.
Nothing in that drawer.
Nothing in that drawer.
Nothing in that drawer.
Nothing in that drawer.
Nothing in that drawer.

Body English

Say something about still life.
At daybreak the sun rises—
Read out its highfalutin mess
Which is terror to the idiot
And the non-idiot alike, cut into
As we are on our trip to the water construction
Whose finish is a somersault
Done by a dark and angry rabbit.
But we listen with a valve open
Occupied with magnetic stacks
The blabbermouth responds to.
For it takes nerve to beat oneself
About the jaws—it takes, in fact,
Like a sudden phooey! illumination!
The thought centers shoot out
Through doors that open
Onto hideous lovers. . . .
The detective comes into all this
And goes to sleep.
Lamps go
By in the night a dress brought.

The beak that discolors the apple
The teacher imagines
Is the same that reads your letters on the sly
Only to find that they were
Pecked out by a canary,
One shooting downward.

Shooting and cussing are pleasures
Ripped from the loudest
Lawyer in the world you call Casanova,
He whose rump is tickled by a tie

Riddled with buckshot.
Which brings me to guns:
There is a gun in this world—one
Limb is glue, the other tree—
That makes us all philosophers on seats,
Hateful tendency!
It's true we use our muscles
Being friendly
But at the same time we clear the range.

One thinks of the world as a hungry bird
Where fingers fly making a thing go.
Another applauds from his saddle
And rakes in the ancient chips
Father and brother knew.
It's Hallowe'en, was.

*

At least a pie is resting
On an ink pad. A pianist weeps
And jumps up. A confession is
Paddling its way up on high
Where he can't stand up. It grips him.
A button sails coolly toward his coward.
Who fails again!

But these vitamins that issue
From the back pocket covered with flowers
Cause a modest applause,
Yes ha ha!
One in a bottle that flies to a cripple—
Him and a gnat's bristle
Topping the mad alive book!

Pulling and straining,
You went out into the wrong snow
To measure like a mad fool.
Matches flare in the crevices

According to law
And die.
A snob in a skirt rolls past.
The panorama, which is growing truly vast,
Now reveals the lowest kind of person
And his peculiar trained weakness:
Adios. A detective comes in
And goes to sleep. He is
Unique.

Except at Night

Seurat and Gris do meet
Walking down the street.
How do you do, Seurat,
Says Gris, and How do you do,
Says Seurat, too.

A Careless Ape

The real reason I'm not you

Gillyflowers Buttercups Black-Eyed Susan

Is that I don't have your parts

plus some other little white buggers

However, we are friends

My God! My God!

And this is good

Mallarmé was a careless ape
In the writing of his work *Un Coup de dés*

Sunshine pages ziggedy black and red ants locked in mortal combat

He unwittingly made some letters and words larger than others
Francis Ponge Fresca and Wayne
Emerge from a pasteboard box with their hands held high

and placed them at enlarged parts of the pages

very strange

202 CALO
DOG FOOD

As I said before I'm in pretty poor shape

Someone a bee a baby a can of food

is screaming at me

We are so stupid we do not even know this

This, I guess,

is my abiding problem
Others more transient swoosh by

It's a stupendously terrifying huge grotesque Flower Dog

knocked out all night through mist and rain
knocking my head softly against the bed weeping and crying

Madonna!

Wayne, you're a sweet boy if only
How can we arrange everything so that everything is great?
If only we could all live in contentment as you do
Some of the time

Unlike you
we live in perpetual torment and pain

Are you okay?

I am not only okay I'm in perfectly stupendous shape

In fact

I am the excellent Alfred North Whitehead

buveur de l'opium chaste et doux

Drawn aside like music to show the notes glittering quietly below

16 November 1964

As this morning seemed special when I woke up
I decided, as is my custom, to go for a refreshing walk
In the street. Preparing myself for the unexpected, I
Combed my hair and generally made ready. I was ready.
In the hall outside my door the lady from down the hall
Shouted my name to get my attention. I waited
As she came down the hall with a newspaper in her hand.
I expected the worst. On the other hand, one can never tell
What mystery might spring up from the most commonplace,
For example, the lady and her newspaper. She wanted
To show me a headline which must have disturbed her,
Because her hands trembled as she read to me, "FIREMEN CHOP
THEIR WAY THROUGH SHED." I thanked the lady
And started toward the stairs when I realized that
The headline she had read me was rather astonishing.
I went back inside and wrote it down. Then down

In the street a suspicious-looking fellow approached me
And gave me a handbill, which, had not one of its words
Caught my eye, would have been quickly disposed of.
The word was "they"; it appeared once in the sentence,
"Do you realize that *they* are undermining your existence?"
I was puzzled by the fact that the word *they* should be italicized,
And the more I thought about it, the more it fascinated me.
Now, I have a small blue notebook which I carry with me
At all times, in case of any emergencies,
Such as the one I have just mentioned. I opened my book
To "T" and wrote down the word.
Well, my walk hadn't gotten along very far until
I remembered how close to the park I live, and how rarely
I go there. So picking up my stride and finally passing
A handsome girl, I reached the stone wall which bounds the park.
Ah, the red park! Where as a child I remember I had

Done so many things. . . . But that was in the dim past. . . .
Right in the middle of my reveries I felt someone
Looking at me and, turning, I was face to face with a very old man,
Who, without saying one word, gave me a small white card
With hands on it. Underneath the rows of hands
The card read: "I AM A DEAF MUTE. I SELL THIS CARD TO MAKE
A LIVING. COULD YOU HELP? THANK YOU."
The old man did not take his eyes
Off me as I fished around in my pocket, and even after
I had dropped some coins into his limp hand, he stood there
Looking at me. How embarrassing it is when someone watches you
Put your hand into your pocket!
The old man finally shuffled away with my second donation.
I don't know why, but I was so upset that I had to sit down.
I disregarded the rain that never seemed to go away
From that bench, because I was so upset. A few moments
Later my senses came back to me and I found a small white card
In my hands, and its curious rows. Then I remembered
That their language is called "finger talk." The thought
Of talking fingers, so to speak, so thrilled me that the words
"Finger talk" went into my notebook, under "they." "Who knows,"
I said to myself, "by the end of the day I may have written a poem!"
"Now is no time to worry about poetry," my stomach chided me,
And I made my way out of the park, generally enjoying the air.

At one of the numerous lunch counters which dot our city
I ordered my lunch. The place was busy with people in a hurry,
And I knew I would have to wait for my order to arrive, and then
It would probably be the wrong thing or cold. To pass the time
I glanced through the two-page menu, which bore
On the title page the word "MENU."
Then it was that what had been happening to me all day,
This sudden illumination of the trivial, happened again.
Menu! How mundane, yet how miraculous! I wrote it down,
Under "M." It made my fourth entry, and I hoped for many more,
Since I have a great desire to write a long, beautiful poem,

Though I have nothing against short poems. But sometimes
I feel as if short poems are sort of a hoax, don't you?
Well, to get on, I finished the lunch, which was not
So bad as I had anticipated, and I once again met the air

With a light step. My next step? Who knows! I was full of vim! Vinegar!
It so happened that a young mother was strolling her little daughter
And that a small book dropped from the mother's handbag.
I went to fetch the book with every intention of returning
It to its proper owner, when I noticed the title and began
To think about it. The title was "THE PLUM, THE PRUNE, AND THE APRICOT."
Had this story once held me enchanted as a child? The last
Sentence seemed so familiar: "Forbidden pleasures leave a bitter taste."
It was all I could do to keep myself from bursting into tears,
And only the thought of recording this sentence, so mysterious
In its familiarity, prevented me from doing just that.
I slipped the book into my pocket, like a long-lost memento.
The experiences of this day, so exciting and wonderful, were still
Rather tiring, so I went into a theater to see a movie and to rest
My eyes. The movie was very boring and I soon left.
Back in my apartment I managed a small dinner, in. "TV DINNER"
Began to attract me, but when I went to write it down I hesitated:
The modern poet must be discriminating.

So now I sit in the kitchen writing in you, diary, a soda bottle
In my hand. "You are like me, soda bottle," I just said,
Shaking it and making it fizz. There must be something in a soda bottle
That we can understand, though I don't know what. Just as there must be
Something of value, to someone, in my blue notebook. I open my book
To see the four lines I have written down during the day, in those spare
moments of inspiration:

This offers us the stale air of the balcony
Of the future which you don't want or can,
Blue, marigolds, the sum of all that you love in him,
Where is it?

Birches

When I see birches
I think of nothing
But when I see a girl
Throw away her hair and brains
I think of birches and I see them
One could do worse than see birches

Some Bombs

after Reverdy

1.

One goes by like some oafs
On the K way the laminators along gents and lays you
The wagon turns on the roulette melee

Hair knights dress themselves in night
Moats which go by fount brutes

I ray you stop me pour the garter outdoors
Aw fond eel you all a quill train which darts
I ray you whar's sedans
Latrine key imports news and is Mobile in the vent

On intends

On Intends Creek
-cest a "whyso?" of the newt
The montage swallows a toot
Twos "suh" key oinks purrs the butt
Gene Autry sleeps

I'll send the Lautréamont coat, "Do, Monday
Awnglish Dan's a true key at the frond paws
One east tents with sin alley-oop
The sill is fond

And a pea-tit galosh dresses itself oh bored Walter by the sea

2.

I'll nudge sir the mount blank
And one goose clock son sedans

Josquin has a procession of gins in black Dis End

The curs broil a neck-green few
A mince hombre author of *Sack Cur*
Says Monty Martyr
The lune foams a quintet
Rondeau comes your figure

O tempts these flames plus Ardennes
And Desnos jures
Shack a petty toilet
They ramps
Lash Larue is black and the sill Clare

A sullen hominy veils the hut
Analogues robe Blanche
The loaned hand is a dim haunch

One sort of that maize sends vocabulary
One is gay
A bomb ear trembles in core of the knee

The plus Grant champ do mowed is in reverse
And debates coo her
Elves divulge and plow Sir Key who is past saying
The ensign manacle eats depasturized

Fund of the hombre you remoo
At home Monty tits anew
The solenoid saps you he on his hilt
Caws "one Sulla quoit pus commerce fit"

Me nudity

A home marches the suit and divan
The sane is la-la
And one intends on the Oh to clack paws
The rest sea pass Dan the rest turret Donne you we

3.

The pied quarts of Chevrolets trim blent Sir her eyes on
The memo leg's knee asserts me with coo
Monday is a tent soused with covered fur
The fen beings brillo like the years

One of the arms pour rear
And a cur pours more rear

The General et an old monster
Sand's civil habits
A Black blight a bone Blake blight at the fair
Ah a member of the fame isle
Says Louie Key a prissy toot he row is my parasol

The cur is a pre-sound without a rage where Lou too urns without fins

Blue as a hurry
Monty "The Soup" Godzilla
His figuring is a Negro Roy decorated with my soft age

He purrs Rye Anne

Chase the salvages
The music mews
New sums try and I sew O mildew
Where's Alley Ooops
The plays here ate Mort author of *News*

4.

Isle yards means Key peasant
Kill cue chose the pass in the vent
Troy's tea (rooftop) teas De Moins ballerina cent
Malasia par tint I found D train
Your river pace attempts
May's a pong my sentiment

A man is a tomb
Kill coon sort of ate Nesbit's rent tree
O sank he him the lamb pest is two juries halloo May

Dance the newt
Souse the P. Louie
Ate 10 franks do tax he

The numerous tom bee "hallo"

El Paso invents the bush of gout
The tru
Kill gout
The pen drool key bat dances the maize on is come a cur
The isle has dice monuments where Lon foods rat et her milly hair
"Ew!" to hear kill coon

There now there's a pig

A no ear chat files on Sir Nigeria

And desk chins!
This chins Cousin Crane's minds less a gents

La looney is fat I guess of gartering the newt
Ellie is a party
And I vase my meter
"The portie no me suitee dee rainee nor the fen beings!"

I pry pour and moo the con's sea urge do, by Dis
Celery you too vice
Blah hurries won bash floor
Don's lovie I am Surrey I am Tojo ours levee bastard

The temperature was basted
I neighed "Run fast"

An hombre glistened in tree cur ate your din
I Surrey lying in Kore demand matin'

Sir the trot tore
Desk vice ages flow tent ah bass dance the drooly yard

5.

My dog sag knee
Jet Chris
A Vic
Lee rig knee of old Roys is finite
The rivets is a jam bone
Lewd
Key pinned play fond
Ate the sender of ton cigars
Continent toot the loom hair

O day two our do shimmy
Less armrests sign it
The solenoid ass askin'
In 's England lispins
And cooks "keep off" Dan's the priory who meed

The sore where indoor mitt the prim hair chat haunt
Epée ivory
Mess mine rests moose pen dent la
And the "See Hell" may soot ten
See Hell lava mess yours toots the matins

Ma man roughest on mot-
An apple breath pal pits sang a lot
Do sang "Versailles the Paper Boulevard"
Lucre nekkid rye hen

March the attachés' gizzard does Mary
Enter Rousseau noise key vaunt flues loin
A bout Monday where Lon mat tin
Brzeska fought any or less gouts he sang key coo lent of moan cur
  which Lon Rin Tin
A clay iron dances as sure sonny la gin rail

6.

Lee bid on the pet role
And the brute
Celery kill the party writ

A marionette skin till
Dance the newt

The tramp way tray (rooftop) ee you knee my load I dance sez Ruse
Ate a Chevrolet the loom hair
The utensils sell key passes by the party hair
Sez jukes are tombs sit the ray isle
You 'n' rat faculty tiff purse honey Dis skinned
A rampart
They trey in my cur ate messmates see sore tson ten retarred

I food raise for ire the boot detest soul ears
I food raise salve rays sick of two pence decept reamer boy age Gene
  Autry
Their hair the Autrys

Isles send Von invite. Ills taunt lazy
Acorn do trot tore
Ate the puppy key sordid a foe is decibel
Dance the fit rind
Tea did it bounce sore

Lash Larue is Rio Grande and Tristan comma a bully fardle

Words to Joe Ceravolo

I think tonight I am beginning to understand some impulses
That a friend of mine Joe Ceravolo seems to have been having
And which others have certainly had
Which makes no difference
But which might make him seem terribly silly for a while
And which if I'm right I'm beginning to feel myself
About now and therefore sympathize with
It's a cheap sympathy when you have to come about it like this
But who cares

Listen, Joe Ceravolo
You're O.K.

Falling in Love in Spain or Mexico

A handsome young man and a veiled woman enter. They stroll slowly across the stage, pausing from time to time, so that their entrance coincides with the first spoken word and their exit the last.

JOSE: I am happy to meet you. My name is José Gómez Carillo. What is your name? This is my wife. I like your daughter very much. I think your sister is beautiful. Are you familiar with the U.S.? Have you been to New York? Your city is very interesting. I think so. I don't think so. Here is a picture of my wife. Your daughter is very beautiful. She sings very well. You dance very well. Do you speak English? Do you like American movies? Do you read books in English? Do you like to swim? To drive a car? To play tennis? Golf? Dance? Do you like American music? May I invite you to dance? I like to play tennis. Will you drive? Do you live here? What is your address? Your phone number? I am here for four days. Two weeks. One month only. Would you like a cigarette? A glass of wine? Anything? Help yourself. To your health! With best regards. Many happy returns! Congratulations! With best wishes! Merry Christmas! My sincere sympathy. Good luck! When can I see you again? I think you are beautiful. I like you very much. Do you like me? May I see you tomorrow? May I see you this evening? Here is a present for you. I love you. Will you marry me?

GIRL: *(She lifts and throws back her veil, revealing her face, which is extraordinarily beautiful.)* Yes!

THE END

Autumn's Day

Rilke walks toward a dime. I saw.
It was very great. But now
His shadow is fast upon the sundials.
How then can the winds remind
The shadows it is late?

"Who has no home cannot build now,"
Said Rilke to a grasshopper.

Little grasshopper,
You must waken, read, write long letters, and
Wander restlessly when leaves are blown.

Y . . r D . . k

It w.s c....h f.r t..m to go b..k to t.e h...e
T..y h.d r..d a...t it

I am s.....g d..n to w...e y.u
A...t t..s a.d a...t b....e he d..d
He l...s on h.s o.n f....r a.d s.n

It t..k f..r of t..m to c...y in t.e s......s
F..m t.e s...l s..t g...n p..d
T.ec....g w.s t......e

T.e i.e c..e w..n he w.s w.....g f.r it

It c.....s i....f n..t me
C....g b..k t.....h t.e g....d
D....y c........s
B...k p..e of w.....g
S...e t...e is n.....g b.......l in t.e w.y

T.o w..n f...r w.s c......g t.e w...e
T..t d..t t..t m....r
N.t to c..e b..k w.....d a.d s...n in as...y

V.....e a...e in t.h d........g
O..e u........d we d.......d
T...h it g...s no p......e as d..s w.....r

On t.e s....l b......n b...d
L....s a.........g in t.e h...s
T.e t...g we i........d as a b....e
Or t.o f....s of r.d in t.e t...s
(He w.s w.....g to it)

C.n be k..t in p.....s a.d n.t d.......d k..p
G...g o.f a.y m....t
K..p t..m o.f

To k..p in m..d on a p...h d...g t.e r..n?
No m..e t..n o.....g o...s y....r h..d to l...h
No m..e o.......e to it t..n to a b...n d.g

Poulain

An orange and blue box of Poulain chocolate
Is what I think of often
As I sit just outside the late afternoon sunlight—
I see it in another light
Sitting on a brown oak or something table,
Maybe a white kitchen one,
And when I reach out for it
My hand touches it
And I pick it up

Mister Horse

Mmmm
I get up and am seized by the present
Whose presence is
As a roof fits on a house whose car in the garage
Backs out
And in the back seat
Childhood is normal but the scaffolding thrown up around
The road is built with an insane logic
Which is at once its interest and its uselessness
Save as torment

Not an example is a loose nail here
One I caught my sleeve on
But I've moved
Up to the floor all in blue
And the décor is stunning in its vacuity
As if the air were suddenly sucked out
By a passing machine
The one we ride and operate
With our hands and feet

So the landscape turns out to be a dial
Of stars and numbers
No less fascinating than the cold pair of scissors
That cut the shirt you are now wearing
The starry one of water
In the quickly deflating evening

Evening is so small these days
It's the size of a green pea
The small expensive kind
That come in a silver can
That rolls for a long time
Decorated with a fleur-de-lis

Which is the sole bud in the sky at the moment
Other times
You'd have the flower in your buttonhole
Its center round and packed with goodness
Like the yellow of a sunny-side-up egg

But the egg is exempt
From nature's clumsy machinery
It is something very much like your own heart
A lady drops on the way home
On the sidewalk in some small town in Arizona
Where it fries secretly
And is then whisked away by a tumbleweed
Or eaten by a horse
The same one I feel as if I mentioned a moment ago

I would like to devote my special attention
To this horse
Let me tell you about it
It can jump a bush a small one
It is the kindest horse in the world
That is why it is the subject of so many thoughts
That is why it bites both the apple and you
And why when the blinders are put on
It weeps

And with good reason!
For now it is a mere piece of glossy paper
The only furniture in this room
Whose blue it takes on
And whose flower has gone a terrible green
Under the influence of the hard light
Whose manipulations increase
In proportion to the scales they're laid against

Yes, I'm afraid today's just a chart
Plowing through a stormy sea
But the horse is still here!
He's at F-3
And is marked with a blue and green dot
The green a concession to the plant world
Whose proper domain
Is growing on the living
This sort of radiant fungus
You noticed in the last picture I sent you

I didn't think you'd see it
Since the photograph was not of me even
Though at first my thoughts filled it with me
I sent it as a compensation
For the money I owe you
And whose astonishing presence neither
Of us will ever really know
We have been short-changed by the modern world
But at least we got a receipt

Maybe we'd better keep it
Since nature is so expensive
And day pops up like a big number inside a cash register
Perhaps I'd better forget about the forest and the hills
And the balls that lie there covered with pins

These are the same pins I stuck in you
To wish you a speedy recovery
And to hint that you need no longer pursue the rain
With your magnificent intelligence
Which is sparkling and fizzing loudly
Across these many years to me

But now I really must be going
The horse is getting restless and no wonder
I gave him only a piece of paper to eat today
By the way
He's just a mule
But I don't think that will make any difference
To him in the long run
Also I hope that you won't mind
If I send him to visit you sometime

Homage to Max Jacob

Good-bye sting and all my columbines
In the tower which looks out gently
Their yo-yo plumage on the cold bomb shoulder
            Good-bye sting.

Good-bye house and its little blue roofs
Where such a friend in all seasons
To see us again made some money
            Good-bye house.

Good-bye line of hay in pigs
Near the clock! O! how often I hurt myself
That you know me like an apartment
            Good-bye line!

Good-bye lamb grease! hands carrying arteries
On the well-varnished little park mirror
Of white barricades the color of diapers
            Good-bye lamb grease!

Good-bye verges calves and planks
And on the sting of our black flying boat
Our servant with her white hair-do
            Good-bye verges.

Good-bye my clear oval river
Good-bye mountain! Good-bye cherry trees!
It is you who are my cap and tale
            Not Paris.

A Man Saw a Ball of Gold

A man saw a ball of gold in the sky;
He climbed for it,
And eventually he achieved it—
It was gold.

Now this is the strange part:
When the man went to the earth
And looked again,
Lo, there was the ball of gold.
Now this is the strange part:
It was a ball of gold.
Ay, by the heavens, it was a ball of gold.

To Francis Sauf Que

1.

You think of everything:
Modern silence, where I go back continually
To you, as does everyone, it seems. . . .

2.

We are getting younger, perhaps

3.

I "hate you hate you

4.

The man walks under the house
In the Renaissance, the plum etc.

5.

More data, adversity is like walking
In the sun which is shining on you
In bed, where you are with her,
"everything like that"

6.

Now I love you again because of these roosters

7.

Yours is topography to me in my dim head. I'm sorry, the virgins.

8.

This color, orange, tries to remind me of you,
Orange slice

9.

And you are

10.

Sometimes I leaped at the wrong time
Or right time, this made you who shall receive
This scarlet rose with some sort of greatness happy

11.

I thought so, so you changed your fasteners.
I think I hate you more than anyone else.

12.

If only you knew how to ignore me

13.

Then symbolism gets a model today,
But you didn't believe in that, its flaxen gray—
And neither does the porch
More than these worth taking notes on

14.

I didn't hear you when you all did it

15.

I will kill you

17.

To envisage your doom (it), and,
"Get with it, kid"

18.

To be plucked at exactly 2:10 in the morning

19.

They faded en masse onto the yearbook,
The shoelace through six years of catatonia,
Of Gérard Labrunie and this

20.

So whose shadow is this, yours or mine? and why
Are there two of us here instead?

When I Think More of My Own Future Than of Myself

Coming out of the bathroom
That one has to go down the stairs one-half flight
Out a door into an elevated courtyard
Along a little balcony to get to
I often have the thought
"How sad it is that I must die"

I do not think this thought proceeds
From emerging from the bathroom
Though emerging from the bathroom
Can change one's thoughts
—Just as, since my college studies,
When the thought was made available to me,
I have never been able to make any sort of really reasonable connection
Between Love and Death

The Complete Works

The big black bear and the prowling panther lived near our beautiful school.
Irving received seven dollars for moving.
A rib hung from the marble bust of Robert Burns.
Alfred's friend lifted the tough fire.
Phyllis found the hand on the sofa.
Becky led the sob to the bakery.
Marian and Marvin were married in the month of May.
Maurice and Edmund tramped many miles over muddy rods.
Whittaker left the waffle under the wagon wheel.
Harvey proved that atomic particles are ugly.
Steve is suffering from severe oldness.
Mr. Thurston thwarted the plans of the three bugs.
The thirsty mouth took the broth and ran southward.
Ruthless Judy threw the red thimble through the door of the thatched cottage.
We criticized the wound and swatted it around.
They went bathing in the other broth.
Ruth saw a beautiful moth on the white sloth.
Toot! Toot! Thump! Thump! Theo is tooting the horn and Tim is thumping the table.
Tin is a soft, lustrous metal which becomes brittle when heard.
Edgar divided the dainties among the fiends.
Dick wept farther and further into the dense wood.
Then Dan did the daring deed.
Gilbert left his hat, coat, and foot in the boat.
The artist bought tiny paint.
Ottawa, the capital of Canada, is situated in Ontario on the Ottawa River.
Put these beans and peas on your back.
The thieves took Sylvia's vacation.
Baby's rubber ball bounced into the world.
Steve drove twelve snails into the sieve.
The fawn jumped the fence and found the forest.
Rufus put the rash into the refrigerator.
Strive to remove that vine from the shelves.

Rob tumbled from the ranch and fell into a berry.
Elizabeth and Alberta sobbed when they read *Black Beauty.*
Maples, hemlocks, and elms grew on Mr. Miller's forearms.
Martin promised Mother he would come with Tom.
The wood was watching the woodcutter.
Mrs. Mather soothed the withered loaf.
The thoughtless teamster turned himself into Third Street.
Theodora placed the thick pimple on her thumb.
Martha took the wreath from her box.
Beth thought Ruth's fourth toot came through slowly.
The brothers cut the heat with a scythe.
Their mother gave each of them a fart.
Tom threw the thorny stick into Teddy's steak.
Did the bath save Fanny and her brothers?
Wilbert and Herbert walked to the tulip in the heart of the forest.
Mr. Dunn drove directly to the dent.
The timid deer turned his lifted head, gazed toward the meadow, and listened.
That cold December day Douglas waded through deep drifts to the drug.
Then Father placed Paul in the park.
We voted to remove evil and vice from the aged.
The visitor viewed the duck in the valley.
Frieda frightened the leaf by telephoning the officer.
Did the horse whinny when he neared the arf?
The wizard waved his wand underneath the weeping.
The servant left the shove on the walk.
Thelma and Theodore yanked the studious youth.
The author thought Nathan less and less.
But Kenneth found the heat in the path.
The silver scythe fell into the seething pool.
Moths gathered on their fathers.
The northern weather was severed.
Dawson made a pond for the ducks by damaging a ditch.
That day they drove the north wind into town.
The maiden found the plant trodding its way into the ground.
The stick was sighted near the table.
Three silver thumbs stood there on the shelf.

A red cross stepped from the bus and entered the hospital.
St. Augustine is the coldest man in the United States.
Later the valet put five cravats into the waltz.
Mr. Porter presented the diplomas to the pups.
The wee whistler wailed when he was wheeled away.
Mr. Nicholson and Lester saw the works at Syracuse.
John gave ten dimes for the meat and nine cents for the meat.
We saw the month on Theodor's new spring suit.
Did the frogs leap, thus making rips on the pond?
The Arab beckoned the man to the cur.
Walter wheeled the wheelbarrow full of wild followers.
Columbus sailed away from pain.
The snowmen looked at pictures from their frozen youth.
Jack jumped when he heard the huge gnat.
Julia washed the dish and put it on herself.
Brother and sister were hardening in the garden.
Robert Bruce learned the lesson of perversity from a spider.
Mrs. Moore will hire Mr. Ayre to imagine the sheep.
We could hear the roar more distinctly as we drew the shore.
Oranges and fruit grow in Florida.
Arnold knelt beside the vat of chili.
Did the careless driver puncture the corner store?
Harry likes breathing but Rebecca prefers Brussels.
Health is better than health.
The halleluja rejoiced at the hurrah.
The steam was leaking in the rain.
La Salle and his hand explored Louisiana.
Kenneth's curiosity caused him to kick the cake again.
The truck broke down and wept.
Cora's uncle took a picture of the country.
On Christmas Eve crawled down the chimney.
Thomas brushed his face.
The engine watched the huge machine crush the pebble.
Eliza sold six zuzu snaps to Ezra.
Lucretia wished to become an illusion.
The car crashed into the sandman and pushed him over.

Papa found a law in the umbrella.
Duncan was listening to the wrong nightingale.
"Yes! Yes!" shouted the mouth from the yacht.
Jim injured his wrist when he slapped the hill.
Emmet and Elliot enjoyed the mayor's chest.
Mrs. Swan gave Oliver a dollar for doing "odd" jobs.
A drop of ink dropped on the college.
The jacket ran along the bank.
The unusual seizure of the Parisian gown caused great confusion.
Richard tilted the merchant toward Mars.
The fragrance of sweet peas was wafted to the piazza.
Did the allusion to the event destroy the Hoosier's composure?
The Missouri River is a tribute to the Mississippi.
The tire felt better when it had rested.
Edward addressed the envelope with sharp tones.
But the man drank the brook and saved his son.
After dinner Pearl and her mother walked on their sweaters for two hours.
Rare, red raspberries grow in their raving.
The whistle was heard over the hustle and bustle of the meat.
The wealth dwelt in a belt.
Then on Saturday Grandpa planted the rash.
He said, "Sound the last in angel, mountain, and ruin."
So Henrietta had money for lunch.
Harvey and Horace hid the hammer in the cut.
The roof leaked and the boys were damaged.
Dick lugged the heavy leg to the doctor.
"Quack quack," said the duck to the quadruped.
Six pecks of history were in the bag.
The quiet had started in quest of the quail.
Leaning against the gate was a rag.
The courteous cloak called a cab for the colonel.
Soon we were to learn that Lucy and Rose were part apple.
The ex-clown thrust his throbbing thumb into the slave.
Clarice makes delicious ice.
Trailing vines and large trees, we grow in the tropics.
The South Atlantic Ocean is east of North America.

The wind piled up around our house.
Did Eleanor enter the boat and erase the farther shore?
On Wednesday Helen and Harry entertained an idea.
You fill out the yellow metal questionnaire.
Frank sang to the ground when he turned his ankle on the riverbank.
The youth longed to try his strength by swimming the length of his tan.
The sick musician made a quick rip in his physician.
The drugs weighed exactly ounces.
The carpenter fasted with screws.
Meanwhile Quentin inquired the whereabouts of the question.
The beggar thanked Nancy for the pun.
The heroine wore a satin dress and a coral neck.
Even so, in the spring wens come to this meadow.
The Eighteenth Amendment prohibits the selling of beverages.
Robert McDuffy gave his father away in a fit of generosity.
Eleanor Ross tossed the ball into the feces.
A gust of wind sent Ben's hat into lust.
That chair is upstairs in the bare room.
The toy child destroyed the adjoining room.
A tall boy stood up in the state of Montana.
A severe storm sent the vessel against the beep.
The lucid explanation subdued the ears of the multitude.
But Archibald argued with Harvey about the quality of the khaki arf.
The goose looked at the pillows in the brook.
Earl hurled the burning captain to the curb.
The literary cricket praised the poem.
One morning Claude saw a yawn walking alone by the wall.
Papa drove the car into the father.
The cadet saluted the Ten Commandments.
Nora saw a white organ in the window.
O it was terrible!
The hungry monkey finished off several nuts.
The brook ran on through Mr. Woolsey's food.
Look! Look! A pussy by the brook!
The organist laughed when the choir rebelled.
The three millennia then approached the bone.

Margaret gave the hungry god some meat.
The Wicks sent the box of wax to the monks by express.
The foreigner examined the ruined Latin.
Green moss and gray lichens grew on its old hoof.
Christopher laughed at the cranberries through the gate.
The eloquent lecturer requested the head to sing.
Listen to the restless wind in the Europeans.
At last at dusk the brisk skate returned.

Jet Plane

Flies across sky

Buckets

Of rain
hit the buildings
but we in our apartments
are kept dry by the buildings they're in

the rain is rolling off the buildings
and bouncing off
and the roofs keep the rain from getting us wet

the ceiling is not letting any water in

it goes spat spat spat
on the windowledge
trying to get in

the windowpane is streaked with rain
trying to come in

to go everywhere
to make everything wet

I am lying in my bed
head near the window

aware of all this
thinking How Great

We Win

You Again

I think I'm smoking too much too many cigarettes
And with a sore throat coming on why don't I
Get to bed watch a string
Of late movies there're some pretty good ones on
Tonight the apartment is colder than
Usual when it's usually verging on broiling   if I were
A lobster I wouldn't be getting a sore throat and certainly
Wouldn't be smoking and cigarettes are so high
In New York   an odd situation   in Vermont
I'm going to stop smoking even
Though I love to smoke like a
Turk in Tulsa the cigarettes are cheaper and Dick
Is smoking them up   pretty soon he'll be back
To enjoy the luxury of smoking as opposed to the habit
I ought to read Cendrars but
He makes me want to smoke and squint and hit
Someone in the heart as you've hit me
Every day this week and I'm glad I don't drink so there

Ode to the Astronauts

O astronauts!
You have flown higher than our dear Dante!
His light is as a flashlight to yours
That is the sun of our solar system!
The Arno was his to walk over
While to you it is less than a tear!
And while Virgil stands at the door
Moving his ugly fingers,
You are pushing the bright new shiny buttons of your machine!

Ode ai Astronauti/ O astronauti!/ Siete volati più in alto del nostro caro Dante!/ La sua luce è come una lampadina tascabile di fronte alla tua/ Che è il sole del nostro sistema solare!/ L'Arno era il suo da attraversare/ Mentre per voi è meno d'una lacrima!/ E mentre Virgilio sosta alla porta/ Movendosi le dita brutte/ Voi maneggiate le lucide maniglie della vostra macchina!

Ode to the Futurist Painters and Poets

Futurist painters and poets!
You are finished!
The youth of modern Italy no longer listen to your horrible shrieks!
Marinetti, your *parole in libertà* were just a gibberish of stupid thinking!
Boccioni, you died young and we do not hate you, though we do not love you, either.
Papini, your Christ was recently buried in Milan under a heap of Fiats!
Gino Severini, you thought you were smart by living in Paris and associating with the Cubists, but you were only deceiving yourself and your fellows. . . .
I know you are dead and I weep
But that does not change your absurd notions of life and art!
You, Futurists, thought the airplane and telephone so wonderful! Ha!
Tomorrow an Italian will walk on the moon
And the day after, Italian youth will live on the sun—
O great flashlight! sun, greater than Dante's light or Boccaccio's flickering candle,
You shine down on the graves of those who are now dead forever, the Futurist painters and poets!

Ode ai Poeti e Pittori Futuristi/ Poeti e pittori futuristi!/ Voi siete finiti!/ La gioventù dell'Italia non ascolta più le vostre grida orribili!/ Marinetti, le tue *parole in libertà* erano soltanto balorde stupidità!/ Boccioni, tu sei morto giovane e non ti odiamo anche se non ti vogliamo bene./ Papini, il tuo Cristo è stato da poco sepolto a Milano sotto un mucchio di Fiat!/ Gino Severini, tu ti credevi furbo recandoti a Parigi e legandoti ai cubisti, ma ti ingannavi te stesso ed i tuoi colleghi e basta. . . ./ So che sei morto e piango,/ Ma ciò non cambia le vostre assurde idee sulla vita e sull'arte!/ Voi, futuristi, credevate meraviglioso l'aeroplano e il telefono! Pah!/ Domani un italiano passeggerà sulla luna e l'indomani la gioventù italiana si troverà sul sole—/ O grande lampadina tascabile! sole, più grande della luce di Dante o della candela scintillante del Boccaccio,/ Tu illumini le tombe di loro che ora sono morti per sempre, i poeti e pittori futuristi!

Fiat Ode

Fiat!
You have freed us from our dusty dreadful past
In which Boccaccio,
Though he is often very funny,
Has kept us locked up in the old-fashioned rooms
Of his long *Decameron*!
Fiat! we ride in you
Past the graves of the early Tuscan lyric poets
Not even knowing where they are
And not even caring very much
Because they are dead!

Ode alla Fiat/ Fiat!/ Tu ci hai liberati dal nostro passato pauroso ed antiquato,/ nel quale il Boccaccio,/ benchè spesso sia molto divertente,/ ci ha tenuti rinchiusi nelle camere antiquate del suo lungo *Decamerone*!/ Fiat! noi passeggiamo con voi/ davanti alle tombe dei dugentisti toscani/ non sapendo nemmeno dove essi siano/ e non curandoci poi gran che/ perchè essi siano morti!

Ode to Giuseppe Ungaretti

D.C. Italian sphinx semi-divine! fled from Egypt's sizzling figs in your
nineteenth year!
To the banks of the Tiber
You, Giuseppe, have sat like a stupendous hoary battery these fifty years!
Sending forth energy from the electrode and anode of your nose!
You knew the fizzing terror of the First World War and the double terrors
of the Second!
Literary movements you have—bah!—brushed them under your
intelligence with a broom!
And they died of electrocution!
For you are greater than movements—or movement!
(Even though it was your pleasure to visit New York in 1965)
You did not leave us, you could not!
For you are covered with the olives of desire for Italy
Where the olive trees bend toward your boat as you return, as on a magnet!
The shoelaces of the boot come unlaced and reach out for you, Italy's
greatest twentieth-century poet!

Ode a Giuseppe Ungaretti/ Sfinge italiana semi-divina di corrente diretta! fuggito dai fichi scottanti d'Egitto a diciannove anni!/ Alle sponde del Tevere/ Tu, Giuseppe, sei rimasto come una stupenda pila candida per cinquant'anni!/ Emettendo l'energia dal anodo e dal elletrodo del tuo naso!/ Tu conoscevi il terrore frizzante della prima guerra mondiale ed i terrori raddoppiati della seconda!/ I movimenti letterari tu li hai—pah!—spazzati sotto la tua intelligenza con una scopa!/ E sono morti per l'elettricità!/ Perchè tu sei più grande dei movimenti—del movimento stesso!/ (Benchè sia stato il tuo desiderio di recarti a New York nel 1965)/ Non ci hai lasciati—non potevi!/ Perchè tu sei coperto dagli ulivi di desiderio per l'Italia/ dove gli ulivi si piegano verso la nave al tuo ritorno come verso una calamita!/ I lacci dello stivale si slegano e si stendono a te, il più grande poeta italiano del ventesimo secolo!

Ode to Mussolini

Mussolini, we do not want your brain in our country!
It reeks of the hateful Fascism of the '30s
And which still persists!
Though we respect your wife and understand her desire to have your
complete remains,
We do not want it here!
The Smithsonian Institution in Washington
Is a better resting place
For the hideous gray contents of your skull!

Ode a Mussolini/ Mussolini, noi non vogliamo il tuo cervello nel nostro Paese!/ Esso puzza del Fascio odioso degli anni trenta il che perdura ancora!/ Anche se noi rispettiamo la tua moglie e capiamo il suo desiderio di avere le tue spoglie intere,/ il tuo cervello non lo vogliamo qui!/ All'Istituto Smithsonian di Washington troverà riposo migliore il contenuto grigio e orrendo del tuo teschio!

The Sandwich Man

The funny thing is that he's reading a paper
As if with his throat
With the bottom half folded neatly under his chin
Which is, incidentally, clean-shaven
As he strolls absently toward us, toting a sewing machine
On the front
With delicate little gold lines curling and swaying below a white
    spool in the afternoon
A dog barks—well, arf! you pull the cord attached to the monastery
Bell that rings utterly somewhere else
Perhaps the cord is ringing
And you are a Russian
In some hideously small town
Or worst of all
You're listening to the story behind the bell
A history whose rugged but removed features
Resemble those of the sandwich man
Not the one that wandered off into the swamp
Cuffs filled with wind
And was never seen again
But this new one who overestimates his duty by teaching
School in a place that has as students
At best only a bunch of heavily panting dogs
Seated in rows of wooden and iron desks linked
Like slaves on a dismal galley, the Ship of Genius
Sailing for some points known and a few unknown
Caring little about either, huffing away
Toward the horizon destroyed by other students . . . *estudianti*

One of these others, the head, is in fact the Infanta,
In reality only a very intelligent little girl
But beyond the immense corrugated brook we know of as this earth
Covered with raving, a constellation in the shape of a bullet—

She always did love the sound of a ricochet—and I too
Can hear it often, at night, before I go to sleep
In my nose
                    In Spain, ah
In Spain there are the prune fields and the dark
Beauty of a prune now lowers a shade
Past the sewing machine, over which blow long, regular waves of dust particles
In one of which a medium-sized boy in white sandals is peddling up to
Offer you a worried rose

Rose . . . but I know nothing of this rose
Although I will draw it for you in words if you wish
Clockwise beginning at noon on the outer rim
On the first petal is a cave and the second a squiggle
The third a proper noun or else a common noun beginning a sentence
Or perhaps a noun capitalized for no reason at all, for God's sake!

Japan! Penitentiary!
That's what we want!
To move and dance
With strangers, people we don't know
With lines and circles going through us
Who are the landscape

Whose clouds are really toots from the nearby factory
I love so much, the steam factory, making steam
For people to fall down on and permit their bodies to vibrate
Occasionally a straw hat is flung through the factory window
And sails spinning into the water

It is night

A dog barks outside the window
Either that or the window's silent in the dog
—You'll say I'm playing the overture
And finale off against each other, after all

There's no other way to locate the middle,
Which is more elusive than it might seem:
The fifty-yard line does escape
The gridiron, extending itself through
Both grandstands, through you and me, plus
A parking lot now indistinguishable from the fog, backyards, dreams,
    washing . . .
And the large peanut that has come to stand for something
    beautiful and intelligent
In short, civilization.
"No so!" says a man in striped pants wheeled in out of the moonlight.
"You think this only because you associate this object with yourselves
    . . . which is okay by me. . . ."
He was wheeled out and chucked over the balcony
Into the magnolia bushes.

At dawn, I find one other example, though nearly driven away
By the dust on it:
You are, say, six feet tall
Or six feet long,
In the first instance you are an active human being other than a baby
In the second you are either a very large baby or
A corpse or perhaps a bed-ridden invalid or
Two yardsticks placed end to end. What your six feet
Would be were you tilted at a 45-degree angle
I do not know
Doubtless a census taker's nightmare, in which bent
Horrible monsters jump out and bite him.

The next step is to know that this fuzzy angle is true in your heart
But not to know what happens to it
When it leaves there, flowers gushing out.
It appears in Amsterdam always
City of extension cords
And ladies with boxes of rubber bands and
A truly horrible music washing the streets rushing below the pigeons

That now seem to be following him as sure as iron
Follows a crook

I don't think I can stand it! the birds
Are swooping down in and out of a large design yes!
A police car is pulling itself together
In the skies, its headlights on now
Bearing down on the sandwich man, still reading,
Whose next step puts him behind
Us as we turn ourselves around to see his other board
And the horrible license plate on it

Le Mouvement de César Franck

On a laissé des raisins secs

Quelle que soit la raison, le spectacle qu'ils présentent est digne d'admiration

En même temps, dans les jardins, le soir commence

En effet, d'immenses forêts couvrent déjà la contrée

Les mains de la reine passaient successivement sur diverses seigneurs

A gauche de l'avenue d'Iéna

On change de pantalons. Très bien. Pour moi

Si je penche vers le palais de l'Industrie

Le soleil tombé derrière des tours roses et blanches, j'y

Goute une paix profonde.

Un kiosque à musique

S'éleva

Loin du mouvement de César Franck   où je me promène

Auteur d'une histoire féconde

En triangles d'asphalte

Around Paris

Everything in Paris is round.
First is the city itself
Intersected by an arc—
Which is a division of a circle—
Which is the Seine.
Then the well-known spokes
Around the Arch of Triumph.
The café table tops are round as well
As the coasters (and many of the ash trays)
That sit upon them. Looking up, the cafés themselves
Their names at least, are round.
Over there for instance is La Ronde, La Coupole, Le Dôme, La Rotonde
And others.
Only the beautiful Closerie des Lilas escapes our classification
And still remains in Paris.
The lilac, is it round?
People here do a lot of sitting around
As in the Luxembourg Gardens
Where the toy sailboats go round the artificial pond.
They do this.
Last but not least—and how natural!
Are the paintings of Robert Delaunay
Called *The Windows*
In which Paris is seen
As lots of circles.

The Statue of a Libertine

I've chosen this title not only because I like it
But also because it embodies the kind of miniature grandness
A toy instrument has, or powerful dwarf, half sinister
Half pleasure and unexplained

Now I address the statue

Lips that were once as volatile
As similes spoken by an insane person
Who resembled the carving of an irrational human being
But one endowed with such sweetness the pockets are
Blown to bits through their emptiness,

There is no margin of doubt to this reverse
Power, it moves back immediately, a Leonardo's square
You start back from—it extends a confusing,
Buffered metric scale of being
Toward the deep green velvet
That makes sleep possible
Near the gravel smitten with the gloam's evocative power—
These unintentionally horrible memories cling like peaches to the walls
Of the streets where stilettos whiz swiftly toward an incorrect mansion,
    probably

Not very pleasant thoughts
MOVE TOO QUICKLY

What's happening is that we're pawning especially
The vegetation
                        Watch it   There was a first light of print
Then suddenly my view of things
Either enlarges or contracts incredibly
And all I can see is the two of us, you

With your long dark hair, me looking at your hair against the screen
In this small kitchen with its yellow and white curtains
Shot into place with light
And everything else is gone forever
If it does nothing else, this feeling, at least
It relieves my temporal worries
And then it dawns on you: you're looking at the background
For every painting you've ever seen!
It's a kitchen exactly like this one
Containing the orange juice and two dozen eggs
And the coffee pot, the electric
One Tessie and I posed on either side of just before our trip to Rome
We went flying over Rome in a giant aspirin
We didn't see much but were free from headache
(This on a postcard home)
Moving up I thought I'd have the aspirin turn to powder
Which would fall on the city—the echo
I didn't answer because not answering is one of the luxuries
We have here, if we have a phone. . . .
But enough of this, my head

The sun is now going up and down so fast I can hardly keep track of what day today is—it's the next day, in fact, though it shouldn't be: I'm wearing the same clothes, smoking the same cigarette, the temperature is the cigarette. There is less darkness outside, though;

Unfortunately, I can't seem to fit it into any reasonable sequence—
                    one hundred fashionable yachts burning
Remind me of a Blaise Cendrars poem about yachts
I translated in Paris
A few minutes before seeing a young girl break
Down and cry in the Boulevard St-Germain. Thomas Hardy
Was with her but didn't seem to notice she was sobbing horribly and
I felt like pushing both of them into the traffic light
My bus had stopped at

2

Higher up, the wrist assumes a puffiness
Not unlike a pajama leg stuffed with hundred-dollar bills
But a dramatic resolution is passed
Into the extended index finger whose rushing
Detonates the very tip

The Farmer's Head

At that instant there came a crash more terrific than any that had preceded it, and the whole place glared with intense light. Everyone was momentarily stunned, and when they recovered their senses, Ernest, looking toward the farmhouse, saw a sheet of flame coming from the farmer's head.

"Fire! Fire!" she shouted. "Your head is afire! It's been struck by lightning!"

"By gum! So it has!" yelled the farmer. "It's blazing!"

He was rapidly shouting this as he ran from the barn.

Tone Arm

The clouds go rolling over
The rooftops of the 17th-
18th- or 19th-century buildings—
They are really rolling

You people of the future
How I hate you
You are alive and I'm not
I don't care whether you read my poetry or not

1

The diamond is real—
See how it cusses over the pheasant
A kind of test lad
Who kicked the elevated man on the bag of light
When just ahead a kind of gold foil geometry
Was spread across a time lapse of London

The results of that experiment came later
Since now you know its diction
Just up here come here

The thin family will die out
When the swans on the ornamental lake
Are signalled
By the French Revolution

Sentence the tattered bucket spinning of the tree

What's all this talk about
Law and order

I wish you would go stick your head up your own butt
As well as your hands, feet, midriff, and other parts
I'm sick of you you turd-faced queer

Well

This town ain't very big at sundown
And the other Henry is approaching
The dusky ski
Which is penetrating your heart at this moment

For what is art but a bauble
On the breast of Time
Or the lady that gives you the time

I'd like to cough on the breast
Of the lady who gives me the time
Arta longa vita brevis

It's a codpiece that I brought along this here vitamin boat
Where you and I
The two of us
Can dilly and dally the whole day through
With naught a thought
But of me and of you
Trouble is
You are a sullen dart

I warned you
You should never have come
But now that you're here I may as well tell you everything
About the orb
A man saw a ball of gold

Later

What is this anyway
But a sort of alchemy of the mouse
Who enters and exits from
His little house

New York, March 8 (RP)—
This will be man's greatest accomplishment
Hand in the old night

up the de Kooning

Whose sullen felicitation now emits
A sort of deafening knob
You turn to get to an "in"
Sign

I salute you, jigsaw critters of the Northwest
But please leave this wafer to another
Dram in the presence of a craw

After a fashion
All breathed easier
Through their own noses
Your nose for instance

I've seen many a ruble in my day
But none so fugitive as this one
You have offered me
As a consolation for being the local
Anesthetic of "I warned you, Brett"

You may wish to lock me out of your life forever
Or to live as a lock lives
On the bean of understanding
A mole's destruction of the weathery facts

We all pretend are true—
By the way, signore, they are all true

By the sea
I remember you when I met you
There by the stately sea, the sea
That is both stately and wholly of itself
Your wings resembled arms
Your beak was as if a woman's mouth
Or a man's that resembled an entire woman
Now I understand that you were a man
Dressed as a bird
One wishes to Ernst upon
To feel the nitrogen and mustard guts
                                        . . . . ah!
Your muscles are bands of steel! and your beak
Emits a country-and-western-style song

Go away, glib cur
You were not made for poesy
You aspire, how shall I say, too much?

Token

2

I used to know a song about a hamper
It went
"On a large sock, O. . . ."

The rind of Borneo
Is absolutely zero zero
An étude!

Adjourn the cup is pure

Is it perfect if I rip off your sandals
And bring them to you
A dress retreating
Through a forest fire makes another whole sense

Unfortunately and I'm sorry
I forgot the star of the show
I can see it all now

3

Some showdowns are shaping up
And if the definitions are just
Step the other way
Avoiding the good car

the crude limbs of history
a bunch of shit
deftly!

I was just walking in the street in a short-sleeve shirt
This man passes me going the other way
He was going the other way!

Everything
Needs an intermission
Since in these days here and there
There's not much
One can get many little pleasures from

Wood
Fire
Air
Water

Not that I mind going up
In this ace of hearts

He pulled out his giant prick etc.

He?
Who?

Who did?

Some people came to visit me in prison
They said I was going to pieces
But the person they came to be
Took the rest of the stickers away *(He hands them to her.)*

I suppose we're worth more these days
Pulling out our giant pricks
My friend Joe Brainard wants to sell his body to a medical school

I feel the whole world shaking
Something must be going on
One never knew, dear, oh dear
The shortness of your answers
Would contribute to this sergeant feeling of sadness
That tugs at my ears
On the clean spring days that are going on around me
My mother, my father, and my friends

4

Let's take a string quartet
Playing one of Beethoven's compositions
We may explain it as the scratching
Of a horse's hair against a cat's gut;
Or we may explain it as the mind
Of a genius soaring up to an infinite
Horse's hair scratching against an infinite cat's gut

5

Hasten the chinchilla
For tonight you die

Only a clever ruse extends the wastebasket
Wise men are said to keep
The weather makes no difference is pure information
Rain banging the toes

6

A red car rolls out.
You are the closely pursued prey of a pack of cards,
Or a parcel of fish.
You are, in fact, a slip
Of the tongue drifting to the point of no return.
But you do return this time
As a child trampled by a rabbit.
A red hat burns in the feces about
Which you are led toward an object
Made of ropes and spikes—an instrument.
And you are also the one who lies thirsting near
The edge of the cog, yet cannot reach it with your mouth
Then you hit the dust off the record
Changing everything.

7

What modern poetry needs
Is a good beating
It is the love call of the gorilla
And a knob is born stunningly

On the affirmative plaza
Huge crowds affirm
An affirming machine

There is indeed money in the tummy
Though wisecracks split the ocean

Throwing up a bad leather pellet
You reach for a vegetable
The train is accountably wrecking
But I know
I'll never bring back that awful stick again
To beat you mercifully
Grandma

8

In its own little place near the obviously phony barn
The spirit evaporates like wise cows before a farmer
In the dawn decorated with mist
Warming up
The day's delicate experiences
Death waits at the end of the trail
And he's boss
O who will lay him out with a good right cross
(Religion, do your part)

I wish (toot toot) to eat it and make beautiful music
Together sometime but not right now
You can have your old city environment, though
With its words on boulevards
I want to walk on a wounded leg in fine weather

9

One makes mistakes in order to appear
Before the human race does

Another poop scene: the last
We see of you
Is this pathetic little figure selling olives

Why do you attack the door, aggressive penny?
Because the scissors you left behind
Snip narcotically at a small thing in a cup

Or
The painter's name was interesting—to be precise,
Rather interesting.

10

You have a lovely name-calling instinct
Though some say you stink
Or so you think
Ted to the high heavens
For even the gravest accents trip occasionally
Through fields of wheat, slaw, and a third
Where desolation's grape snuggles closer to
Desolation's other grapes, forming
An excellent, a piercing arrangement

As they do
So do we
These squeeks emerge from scissor-holes
Causing a gentle motion in the eardrums

No, I have nothing to declare
But your country is beautiful
It wishes to stay here

Poinsettia ravages automobile
Subjecting it to summer's gentle torture

The taxi is beautiful because it is open at all hours
Said George Washington Carver
Whose head shall be separated from his body forever more

He went to Chicago in a taxi
Not the Chicago of Sandburg
But the Chicago of tissue and how to get there
Am I disturbing you?
It's wonderful, splendid!
To put one's foot in a Wednesday night rape
You see I am bored
In fact, I am short of money
Here comes winter's dim claw (balance)

II

Batten down the hatches boys I'm having an idea!
It was cold, very cold. . . .
(What is a house
But a bunch of hints thrown
In and out a window?
This suggests that history
O infinite hints!
Has sometime in its past
Caught up with itself
Come by itself
Passé
Is now only an imitation of itself
Like a car
Driving toward itself in the rain
Developing its own misty personality
Only to be photographed from behind
As we all eventually are.

In other words a house
I suppose
May as well be a horse's ass
Breaking the visible chains of logic.

12

Outside my window is preparing for the darkness
That broke my mother's heart—
For you kiss a pair of lips only to realize,
Later, that it was a single lip, in fact
The Blarney Stone. . . . You see how lucky you really are
Though the bicycle part is over
The fence first. The size of the buildings
You step over is of no importance
Since the buildings brought their own sky,
One you enjoyed but preferred to run
Like a funny baby into

13

The Jews like to eat
The Italians like to eat
The Irish like to drink
The Germans like to think
The French, they like to swim
And sink and swim
MY ANIMALS

14

For one brings everything to a bear
In a crucial moment
On a silver platter—or better yet
A silver spoon whose engraving tells
Of a future

The bear holds a jerking fish in his dumb paw;
In fact, he is standing on his hind legs, and
Judging from this equally bad drawing,

The legs of other bears as well.
That's what it's always been, hasn't it?
From book to bed to book
With nothing but perfect holes between,
Spaces to be filled in later
Or simply brought out as in invisible ink
As the case may be, as
A hammer is brought down as you move toward the bed
A book in one hand a book in the other
Both feet moving, one then the other.
Yes, something is moving toward the bed
As surely as day and night flip through one another
Like a ball.
What might be
Is of no concern to me—
You see I have neither tooth nor brain in my head,
Which love conspires
To relieve you of.

15

He went for an empty holster.
A short circuit was blamed.
It was a musical score.
Try the packet.
And his pants—that's France.

16

Socrates was a mutt, this is generally not known
But understood at some hilarious fork
For a few years! oh
Then watch the ducks peck at gunpowder on the dental walks
Where we pace so as not to upset the tipping lake

Now the ducks are picketing the island
We can get to
The hills (those hills) pose instead and offer themselves
We climb the hellish peanut
Now the ducks are standing in a white surface
The grassy edges rise to music's flown cough
Now the ducks tear the water's surface off
The telling ducks
The park is moving out
Now the ducks cornered in sunset are really burning up
Now the ducks assault the night they're turning away from

O but we could throw down sects
And step on it

17

Sir
Will you please keep going to the bathroom you do it magnificently
Which reminds me
Of this place, this time, you and me
We're back!
We are eating terrific amounts of food
Food food
So we can go to the bathroom good good good

You're weak I'm not
Your
Energy gone down someone else's cheek's rosy sheet
I'm quite comfortable here
In my motorized chair
That was crated by mistake
Those tears could take you miles up
To the rosy heavens we thought so wonderful just a little while ago
Don't I know it

I can't help it Louis, Louis Pasteur
Deft chemist of manure
It's back again that pastille you hated so

18

The genitals run amock
Sliding in and out and around one another
And here I have two beautiful young girls in this room
Both of whom I am going to fuck unmercifully
These girls that skim along a beach of money

Let's say we look
Into this box and
See two ladies talking
With one another. Each
Is standing on a beach.
The lady on the left. . . .

Several peaceful girls come running down the beach
But the letters they are fly away
Like gentle, harmless farts

Those girls I spoke of there
Were hit only here and there
With bright patches of color
They had no bodies
Please do not think of them as the products of a vivid imagination

Right now I just happen to be looking at the Atlantic Ocean
Or at least a part of it
Please to box with me on the beach?

The white pellet passes under the monster
Decorating the fence
Down the fence goes the pellet

Then becomes the pellet of distance
Which is what it always was anyway

Old kinds of geometry are strafing the beach
In search of this famous belly
Perhaps it is the pellet they are searching for
Or the hole made in the sky
By the pellet bye and bye

If I had the world's great grease extinct beside me now
I could at last kill
The people who go out and drop carelessly into the holes
Of the white pinball machine
They tally, yes
But without the ho!
And when you add up the scores
Generosity erases them
After all

19

In guarded spasms you broke the ruler
Vanishing 7
Good heavens! was said

The fact broke the cigarette too
And that mad us
Or the other version of the clink at Columbia University

The clink that falls fiery off the bridge
Over the large canyon
The climate that day was contest though
Crowds disperse. Girls bleed in the great calm

20

You select something small like a pimple
And quick as a wink that's all there is
In a world of moles, pores, hairs and other
Indications are made
Who made them?
Not you, certainly, but the lonely pimple
On its journey to the tip of the nose
Which is its destiny

The blemish you see
Is a stage unto itself
And also around itself
One on which you perform
For you are smaller than the smallest pimple
When smoke goes rushing over the vase

When the vase goes rushing over the ocean
I'll be rushing with it
Toward native lands
To take a shower along with me
Dismantling the atmosphere with my hands

21

Sings

When the cows and the leaves begin to fall
They fall like falsehood

Just as coffee comes from the brains
Well-behaved elephants pass

Sandpaper toughens the holes
The dialogues of Plato rage in the pre-dawn

The wind shows off
The cows fall again

The bus goes pitching over Kansas
Joe is reading
I am asleep

I wired the violets

*

A contact lens drifts above the cervix
And it's not a bad idea

You work in a highly visible bowl

22

"I'm coaching in the orange groves
Near the snow fields of my heart"
Is an example of a kind of poetry
I wish to discuss here. It is not
Simply great poetry nor is it simply
Great sentiment, it is both.

23

You go on as a taxicab keeping still to this music
Me, I do my homework

Hashish go
Under your dress . . . at the dining room table
All suspect.
And you tsk
The Pied Piper, 6 foot 4.

—Classic January black—
Prince P. broke the light on the porch
Where used to run and play the glass figure
That is no more!

24

I am shaving in the distance
The nights come and pass by
Come and pass by
There is a tremendous nature here
Where I am
A shirt is here, too

The Haunted House

Put a coin on the doorstep. Gears begin
to whirr—light above door flashes.

Slowly the door swings open. A ghostly
figure steals out—and covers the coin.

Suddenly the ghost takes the coin and
fades back into the house.

Remembrance of Things Past

I'm afraid Father's hair is slightly cancelled
In three general areas:
First in the town,
Then the in-between,
And finally the second town.
For it is difficult and not even necessary to decide
Where he is
For he sits enthroned in himself
Before a flowery screen
Reading the completely white newspaper.
Son is playing with a watering can,
A white disc, a sabre, and probably earlier
A blue bag. The sabre is held up in his right hand.
Yes, son, you may play with the sabre
Only please do not disturb me with it in any way,
Or disturb me in any other way either.
I wish to read,
To read this newspaper,
Or . . . do I wish to sleep?
Now that Father has gone to sleep
Faster than any human ever,
I may show you, O observer!
This disc which is a tambourine,
I may use my left hand to strike this match,
Apply it to and set fire to the newspaper.
The blue bag. . . .
Ah! you little son of a bitch,
Down before me as you are on one knee,
Kneeling, what have you done?
You've set fire to my newspaper,
Woke me up, bothered me in a vicious manner,
And generally done something you shouldn't have.
The blue bag. . . .

Must I open my arms and tilt my head forgivingly
When you say you will never do it again?
You see out of the corner of your eye
That my newspaper has stopped burning
And lies where I dropped it, half covering the blue bag
Near the tambourine,
Far from the cancellation which has become
In the manner of a painting a work of art.

December

I will sleep
in my little cup

Poem for Joan Inglis on Her Birthday

As he stood saying good-bye
to the small, empty stage
on which he had played
the happiest scene of his life,
he noticed that
the mirror was reflecting
the counter, and that
a thin streak of light showed at the top
of the door behind it. At
the same moment the wind
swept down the street again,
ripping a board
from the wall across the way,
rising
to hurricane violence
as it howled past
and in the mirror he saw the door
behind the counter burst its catch
and swing inward,
revealing the widening oblong of the inner room,
the bedpost with a bright blue coat and a tie
hanging over it, the corner
of the dressing-table and a
small, darkly shaded lamp.

Joe Brainard's Painting *Bingo*

I suffer when I sit next to Joe Brainard's painting *Bingo*

I could have made that line into a whole stanza

I suffer
When I sit
Next to Joe
Brainard's painting
Bingo

Or I could change the line arrangement

I suffer when I sit

That sounds like hemorrhoids
I don't know anything about hemorrhoids
Such as if it hurts to sit when you have them
If so I must not have them
Because it doesn't hurt me to sit
I probably sit about 8/15 of my life

Also I don't suffer
When I sit next to Joe Brainard

Actually I don't even suffer
When I sit next to his painting *Bingo*
Or for that matter any of his paintings

In fact I didn't originally say
I suffer when I sit next to Joe Brainard's painting *Bingo*
My wife said it
In response to something I had said
About another painting of his
She had misunderstood what I had said

Wonderful Things

Anne, who are dead   and whom I loved in a rather asinine fashion
I think of you often

buveur de l'opium chaste et doux
Yes I think of you
with very little in mind

as if I had become a helpless moron

Watching zany chirping birds

That inhabit the air

And often ride our radio waves

So I've been sleeping lately with no clothes on
The floor   which is very early   considering the floor
Is made of birds and they are flying and I am
Upsidedown and ain't it great to be great!!

Seriously I have this mental (smuh) illness

which causes me to do things

on and away

Straight for the edge

Of a manicured fingernail
Where it is deep and dark   and green   and silent

Where I may go at will
And sit down and tap
                                        My forehead against the sunset

Where he takes off the uniform
And we see he is God

God get out of here

And he runs off chirping and chuckling into his hand

And that is a wonderful thing

                                        . . . a tuba that is a meadowful of bluebells
is a wonderful thing

                    and that's what I want to do

Tell you wonderful things

Reading Reverdy

The wind that went through the head left it plural.

*

The half-erased words on the wall of bread.

*

Someone is grinding the color of ears.

*

She looks like and at her.

*

A child draws a man and the earth
Is covered with snow.

*

He comes down out of the night
When the hills fall.

*

The line part of you goes out to infinity.

*

I get up on top of an inhuman voice.

Strawberries in Mexico

At 14th Street and First Avenue
Is a bank and in the bank the sexiest teller of all time
Next to her the greatest thing about today
Is today itself
Through which I go up
To buy books

They float by under a bluer sky
The girls uptown
Quiet, pampered
The sum of all that's terrible in women
And much of the best

And the old men go by holding small packages
In a trance
So rich even *they* can't believe it

I think it's a red, white, and blue letter day for them too
You see, Con Ed's smokestacks *are* beautiful
The way Queens is
And horses: from a pleasant distance

Or a fleet of turkeys
Stuffed in a spotless window
In two days they'll be sweating in ovens
Thinking, "How did I ever get in a fix like this?"

Light pouring over buildings far away

Up here when someone shouts "Hey!"
In the street you know that they aren't going to kill you
They're yelling to a friend of theirs named Hey
John David Hey, perhaps

And the garbage goes out
In big white billowy plastic bags tied at the top
And even the people go out in them
Some are waiting now
At the bus stop (for a nonexistent bus)
And I thought it was garbage!
It's so pretty!

If you're classless or modern
You can have fun by
Walking into a high-class antique store
So the stately old snob at the desk will ask
In eternity
"You're going where?"
You get to answer, "Up."

I like these old pricks
If you have an extra hair in the breeze
Their eyes pop out
And then recede way back
As if to say, "That person is on . . . dope!"
They're very correct

But they're not in my shoes
In front of a Dubuffet a circus that shines through
A window in a bright all-yellow building
The window is my eye
And Frank O'Hara is the building
I'm thinking about him like mad today
(As anyone familiar with his poetry will tell)
And about the way Madison Avenue really
Does go to heaven
And turns around and comes back, disappointed

Because up here you can look down on the janitor
Or pity him

And rent a cloud-colored Bentley and
Architecture's so wonderful!
Why don't I notice it more often?
And the young girls and boys but especially the young girls
Are drifting away from school
In blue and white wool
Wrapped in fur

Are they French? They're speaking French!
And they aren't looking for things to throw
Skirts sliding up the legs of girls who can't keep from grinning
Under beautiful soft brown American eyes
At the whole world
Which includes their Plain Jane girlfriends
She even smiled at me!
I have about as much chance of fucking her as the girl at the bank
But I stride along, a terrifying god
Raunchy
A little one-day-old beard
And good grief I really did forget to brush my teeth this morning
They're turning red with embarrassment
Or is that blood
I've been drinking—I ordered a black coffee
Miss

And then a black policeman comes in
Unbuttoning his uniform at the warmish soda fountain
While I pull the fleece over my teeth
And stare innocently at the books I've bought
One a book with a drawing
By Apollinaire called *Les Fraises au Mexique*
Strawberries in Mexico
But when I open the book to that page
It's just a very blue sky I'm looking at

Detach, Invading

Oh humming all and
Then a something from above came rooting
And tooting onto the sprayers
Profaning in the console morning
Of the pointing afternoon
Back to dawn by police word to sprinkle it
Over the lotions that ever change
On locks
Of German, room, and perforate
To sprinkle I say
On the grinding slot of rye
And the bandage that falls down
On the slots as they exude their gas
And the rabbit lingers that pushes it

To blot the lumber
Like a gradually hard mode
All bring and forehead in the starry grab
That pulverizes
And its slivers
Off bending down the thrown gulp
In funny threes
So the old fat flies toward the brain
And a dent on brilliance

The large pig at which the intense cones beat
Wishes O you and O me
O cough release! a rosy bar
Whose mist rarifies even the strokers
Where to go
Strapping, apricot

TOUJOURS L'AMOUR

Post-Publication Blues

My first book of poems
has just been published.
It is over there on the table
lying there on the table, where
it is lying. It has
a beautiful cover and design.
The publishers spent a lot of money
on it and devoted many
man- and woman-hours to it.
The bookstores are ordering copies.
Unfortunately I am a very bad poet and
the book is no good.

Ode to Stupidity

I

Duh . . . I . . . uh . . .
I bet you never heard of Huntz Hall!
Huntz, he was a heck of a guy!
He had two eyes, in his head!
And a mouth, under them!
And some other stuff, like you know
Ears and stuff, but the best
Was his brains, boy did that guy
Have brains! I saw him do great stuff
One day in the movie theater, he
Was on the screen with his friend Leo
And they were in trouble and Huntz
Got them out of this trouble and
Ever since then I've been a changed man.
You might describe it as a pivotal experience
In my personal life, crucial, at any rate.
The jaws of a big pair of pliers
Are gripping the edge of my desk—
I have learned how to make them do this!
And when I go out into the street
My leg is special—just one leg, I
haven't learned to make two legs special.

2

Dawn breaks over the sprawling metropolis,
You drink a glass of beer at three o'clock,
Friends come and they go, the post office
Refuses a package, girls lie down
And are fucked by huge turtles, a voice is heard,
The dictionary is opened to page 387
By a young man who pores over the entry
"Hermetic": eye wanders to "heroic":
"Fix'd is the Term to all the Race of Earth,
And such the hard Condition of our Birth"
And a green and orange carton is discarded.
Perception and cognition arrange these bits and pieces
Into a recognizable pattern which, associated
With feelings, forms a continuity
Which is our life. Yes, there are jagged
Edges here and there, huge spaces
Ripped out by intruding gizmos wielded
By gigantic Skeezixes who come to fix gigantic gizmos,
But generally it is more like the River Thames,
Smoothly flowing, punctuated by boats
Where people raise their smiling faces and wave
To you, women overheard yesterday
Who said today would be cold and it is warm,
You thought you would feel bad this morning
And you do not but the street
Looks chewed up, people lose their footing,
Their mouths open in surprise as they slip and fall,
Perhaps some old person will break their hip!
So you examine the street, write a letter,
Organize a march, run for Congress, lead
A revolution, are stood before a firing squad
Without a cigarette dangling between your lips!
They didn't even give you a cigarette!
No cigarette!!

And as a final mockery to your ideals,
The assassins are smoking four cigarettes each,
Billows of smoke pouring from their faces,
Vision obscured, so that when their rifles
Expel the bullets, chickens
Fall from the sky, 39 cents per pound!
And you are liberated by a band of compadres
In white pajamas who then melt back
Into the wall some bullets had knocked chips from,
Liberated too from your social conscience
Or love of country, but still a wounded figure
Who hides back up in the hills, counting the days
Before he will sprout wings, like Hermes',
And fly with his message through space and time.

Poem

Funny, I hear
Frank O'Hara's
voice tonight in my head—
i.e. when I
think in words
he's saying them
or his tone
is in them.
I'm glad
I heard him
when he was alive
and I'm glad I can
hear him now
and not be sorry,
just have it all here,
the way Jimmy,
stark naked with rose petals
stuck to his body,
said, "Have you seen
Frank? I heard
he's in town tonight."

Sweet Pea

You are sweeter than the sweet pea
that climbs high and blooms
in early summer, mixed colors
pink, purple, blue and red;
few flowers have the charm
you have, and few flowers
have the charm of the Sweet William,
but you have more charm
than the Sweet William, the Perfection
even. The Sunset Cosmos
flames in orange and scarlet:
you are more beautiful than the Sunset Cosmos.
The Mammoth Yellow Mum is more beautiful
than the Sunset Cosmos and you
are more beautiful than the Mum,
you are more astounding than
super racy glads, assorted
colors, every color imaginable.
When I'm with you
terrific colors exist
unknown to the super gladiolus,
colors the Sonny Boy or Azure Blue,
the Climbing Crimson Glory or riotous Color Carnival
or the happy Swiss Giant Pansy
never attain, though they fly
upward through their hybrid generations
madly seeking the brilliance that is yours,
the brilliance Morning Glories strive
to equal in their matinal wide-awakeness,
the Pearly Gates opening to trumpet,
the Wedding Bells announcing, the Moonflower
glowing ethereal in its suave fragrance,
the Heavenly Blue—there is no flower

quite so blue as Heavenly Blue, its blue
reflected in the heavens
where light comes from, and when
I realize all the light
that goes to make a flower
I realize how much has gone
into making you whose presence is more
to me than all the heaven's blue.

For you are more spectacular than Champagne Bubbles
flown from Iceland, more amazing than the Presto
appearing at a magician's fingertips and more gracious
than the Petunia, the Pinwheel spinning,
the Blue Mist drifting in bliss, Victory
flying high, Plum Purple heavy and sensual,
the wild throw-up-your-hands Elite Mixture,
the gorgeous foaming red ambiance of the Warrior, the
enormous blossoms of the Cream Whiz, the
funny snobbism of the Tiffany, more
sociable than phlox, Twinkle or Dwarf Star,
more absolutely engaging than the primrose
in its distant suggestiveness,
blooming in shade. The fantastic big blooms
of Oriental Poppies draw wild visions
from the brain, but you are wilder and
more visionary than the Poppy, shooting
higher with brilliant trail, like the Rocket
Snap, the magnificent tall hybrids, or the
Bright Butterflies flying, crazy and excited,
the Madame Butterfly with its aplomb,
the sobs of the Little Duffer. You are more
beautiful than the Little Duffer. You are
more alert than the zinnia, more
mysterious than Lipstick, deeper than the
deep lavender of Dream Zinnias where Blue
Magic flies, greater than the Great Scot on

a background of pretty Rosy Morn, adjusting
its petals like vain Fluffy Ruffles, goofier
than Knockout Mums and more of a knockout than
Goofy, quicker than Blue Blazing Ageratum, more
majestic in gloom than the dark vibrating blue of Lamartine
Delphiniums, more persistent in memory than Woody Woodpecker
that blooms with a tremendous announcement, darker
and more passionately terrifying than the Giant Señorita,
warmer than Big Smile, more marvelous and
punctual than Marvel-of-Peru Four O'Clocks,
whiter than the white gardenia that leans
over the piano, like Oscar singing to Love Song
whose light pink blends into the Glitters,
and for me you are even more dazzling than
the most exaggerated memory of a Junior Prom:
you are more than all of these, it is
as if I were to take five hundred
handfuls of every kind of flower,
fling them into the air and see
them bloom immediately there.

You are forever with me
as if my just being alive were enough
to surround me with the silver flames
of massive dahlias, cool and sexual
as Promise, the red blur of The
Cardinal perched on perfect stems
and then gone, the intriguing comic strip sexuality
of Kidd's Climax, the blasé bare shoulder
of New Look or Variety Girl, the moonlight
that shines down on D-Day. These are all
so beautiful! Blue Smoke over Albert
Schweitzer, Whirligig and Little Nemo, Visual
Illusion and Forever, Loves Me Loves Me Not,
Reynaldo Hahn and Equal Sign, Mahayana and
Angry Bumpkin, Out to Lunch, Magic Flute

and Dream Boat, Sunshine
and White Friendship, the quiescent
sentiment of Afterglow and
the yearning for the Infinite that is
in Bright Star—you are my Bright Star,
brighter than Superlative and fresher
than Baby's Breath, when it has just bloomed
and its pretty little flowers sigh
in delicate profusion, nodding gently in the air,
white in June and July. In June and July
is where I am when I'm with you,
the middle of the year, when looking back
and then ahead to the same amount of days
means everything is in perfect balance,
you do not know if you are happy or sad,
who or where you are, you are
like the Senator Dirksen Marigold
now that the Senator is dead—he has
become a flower.

You are not a flower, thank my lucky stars,
you are a woman, a girl, a moving
body of beauty, you are mine for nothing and
for no reason: the rain falls, the trees
stretch and yawn, the flowers fly
up out of the ground and burst
in zany gladness, constant as those lucky
stars I bless, bless for having you.

Poema del City

I live in the city.
It's a tough life,
often unpleasant, sometimes
downright awful. But it has what
we call its compensations.

To kill a roach, for example,
is to my mind not pleasant
but it does develop one's reflexes.
Wham!
and that's that.
Sometimes, though, the battered roach
will haul itself onto broken legs and,
wildly waving its bent antennae,
stagger off into the darkness

to warn the others, who live in the shadow
of the great waterfall in their little teepees.
Behind them rise the gleaming brown and blue mass
of the Grand Tetons, topped with white snow
that blushes, come dawn, and glows, come dusk.
Silent gray wisps rise from the smouldering campfires.

Poema del City 2

A light chill on the knees
& I sneeze
up late, alone, in my house, winter
rain against the window and glittering there
in the constant light from stoops across the street
cars hiss down from one moment to
the next hour: in an hour
I'll be asleep. Wrapped
in new sheets and old quilts
with my wife warm beside me and my son
asleep in the next room, I'll
be so comfortable and dreamy,
so happy I'm not terribly damaged or dying yet
but sailing, secure, secret and all
those other peaceful s's fading
like warm taillights down a long landscape
with no moon at all.
                              Ah, it's sweet,
this living, to make you cry, or rise
& sneeze, and douse the light.

Cut Shadows

We sell
cut shadows

Come in and see us

You can buy the cut shadow
of anything

A flower?

There
you have the shadow

of a cut flower

Baby Rollin

There are certain things that
Once you get them in your mind
You can't ever get them out

Just such a one
Is Baby Rollin
Paris 1966

Every day I would go down the avenue
And see this store
Baby Rollin

Why baby in France?

Then a mental picture of Rich Rollins
Third baseman for the Minnesota Twins

Poem

I don't know
I may not be much
Be a mess
Personality no good
All surface no inner strength
Poetry not any good
This poem not any good
I might die an old man
Scribbler of trash
Forgotten paper-scratcher
But I'll tell you this
I really love to lay around on my ass
Totally watching television

The Most Beautiful Girl I Have Ever Seen

Ulp,
I turned my searing eyeballs onto that flaming image
of a perfection so great, so far beyond flawless,
where values blend to participate
in an impossibly real curvature of space
that everything flown away millions of years ago
and returned millions of years hence
is here now
with her with you
never to be forgotten ever
as long as you live which is forever

Forever in her face with skin so white
and hair so black and smoke curling at the edges
Forever in those long graceful limbs that move so well together
Forever in that lovely doghouse we will live in
I puffing a corncob pipe and she over the Electrolux
with two yellow clouds in the future and a free ride
on the flying donkey to Mexico
where little old señoritas will grab their faces and cry
Caramba! Never have I seen such beauty as is this girl,
Never such perfection under the earth's sky!
and they will swivel their dark eyes on her male companion
and they will say

Double
Caramba! Holy Shit! Who is this skinny unathletic male
who walks by her side
saltshakers in his hands?
And I will hurl the saltshakers into the dust
and shout, "Go away, depressing hags!
Back to your depressing hovels!" and the sun

will set on Vera Cruz which we will have by then
cleverly escaped: the same sunset occurring over the earth in. . . .
No,

no. Why go on with this drivel. Sian Ballen,
sister of Kate who was my student,
hello, lovely creature,
and goddamn the fucking fate that laced our shoes
and then tied knots in them,
leading you out the other night with your friends,
and me home alone to my wife and son, two
people also beyond my understanding in their incredible beauty. (Or
something like that!)

I paused here and put away the typewriter,
thought of kitchen and of food and thought,
Why stop now? Why not go on and see what's there
beyond the will to "understand" oneself or anything?
It's simple: I met this girl tonight and felt this thing,
came back home, sat down confused and excited,
typed some words and felt my syntax slip
into long limber cadences that led me into not
much of anything: you read book to page 397 and die,
you didn't get to finish! Those last revealing pages
left unread perhaps some future monkey trained
in the art of our tongue will read and understand
and visit your grave with the book to read them down
a tube to where you lie beneath the ground
watching the screen and brushing concepts off the bed
onto the long, long, long river that flows from the heart straight out
into the terribly live and beating heart of the single person
who at a single moment meant more to you than anything else,
silly poet! Silly to say such silly things,

silly to spill such words insignificant in the entire universe
where a Spinoza is drifting, where a Los Tres Hermanos is also
drifting with their musical instruments, where a Girl Scout is
drifting in a green dress,
where all the spirits of the past are floating along behind the sky
sucked down to fit your frame you rise up through
to find them in the sky sucked down on her,
two skies touching and floating, darkening

Poetic License

This license certifies
That Ron Padgett may tell whatever lies
His heart desires
Until it expires

Three Little Poems

I call you on
the 'phone &
we chat, but
the way tele
is missing from
'phone is the
way it makes me
feel, wishing
the rest of
you were here.

In literature and song
love is often expressed
in the imagery of
weather. For example,
"Now that we are one
Clouds won't hide our sun.
There'll be blue skies . . .
etc." Partly cloudy
and cool today, high
around fifty, mostly
cloudy tonight and tomorrow.

4:50 and dark
already? Everyone
wants to be
beautiful but
few are. 4:51
and darker.

Homage to Franz Schubert

I saw the lovely sky, blue and bright.
If only I were a little bird
Inwardly firm, so I might
Delight myself with lovely sights.

The huntsman's out to kill us who pecked at his fruit.
How clearly the moonlight speaks to me:
You will find the right words
To gaze on the earth from a dazzling height!

What can be the real difference?
Difference?
O fate, O sad duty,
O mankind, O life, what does it mean?
They grumble toward heaven,
But ah, who will lay me in it?
Being already up there
In the deep, deep grave
Of the stars.

How wan the moon, how dim the stars
Passed over from the world:
The sky is so clear.
Then gallop boldly through the night!

Though the wood stretch out deep and dense
Far over land and sea we watch
And when the earth is young again
Only a shadow yet remains behind.

So long as I am in powerful motion,
Up and down mountains, in and out of forests,
It draws me more strongly down to you.
We are both mighty wanderers

For everything is as it was then—
The sky endlessly outstretched
Like your moonlight through space,
Inspiring me for my travels.

So I walk on in the dark,
In wild troughs and lofty crests,
Where I walked by her side,
I on earth, you in the sky
And earth and sky have vanished from me.

Over their heads eternity still circles.
Here it billows up, there swoops down,
Rock rolled upon rock,
But I am nowhere, alas!

I look with longing,
Climb boldly, sing merrily,
Breathe the holy air,
Until God, in heaven's pure light,
Did not know one thing from another!

To eat, drink, and be glad,
Ecstatic and rip-roaring with joy,
And smile and think
In metallic harmonies
From Western cradle to Eastern grave,
In the grave so peaceful, so cool!
The grave rather damp and musty.
In the forest, the forest, they bury me,
Gentle ebb and high tide deep in my heart.
Please follow the imagery:
A boat swims on the mirror of the waves,
The waves rustle
At the blue of the waves
In the sky
And my passing is enveloped in overwhelming splendor.
It rushes on with gentle quivering,
Breaks old Saturn's scythe in two
And so easily avoids all misery.

And when we exchange kisses,
Your majesty,
Who have achieved sweet dreams
When the mighty tempests roar
And beddy-bye time disappears into the Meridian,
I will run my Cadillac   flaming
Over a cliff but
Where? Where?

Brainstorm

Spring comes
and you with it
I come to you in the springtime of my life
you are great
I am great
but we are not great
because there is no we
There is you out there
and there is me in here
and between us
a fulcrum
lifting us

an us of beauty
an us *dont je suis absent*

or *vous* I don't remember which
I am absentminded
my mind is wonderful
so is your body
stiff, aerial, renovated
in front of some stars
that rags fly from
sideways and insanely

Wilson '57

A terrific blast:
stately white columns sunk in deep fog
and the face of Miss Sheehan enshrined in soft focus
above a crisp Mr. Elstner at his neat desk, ready to work,
shadow flashed onto the wall,
his face a living reprimand; then
Miss Helen G. Lee, Miss Giffert, Mrs. (!) Craig, class
counselors all, their old ladies' forties mashed curls
shimmering in studio light, their expressions a mixture
of benevolent understanding and acerb malevolence.
One day Larry Bennett stood up in Social Studies
and said in his soprano voice, "Miss Lee,
I think you are stupid." I'll never remember
the bland faces of the Office Workers, glued
to their typewriters but friendly withal. Here troops
of individuals are scattered over the steps, standing,
others sedately seated, some in contrapposto poses,
others caught yawning, surprised, blinking, blank,
utterly frozen, hardened in Revlon. "You've been
a very nice student—good luck! Mrs. Plunkett"
whom students called "The Frog"
to commemorate her hideous face.
Rex Stith, unjustly renamed Stiff, is casually friendly
and elected President. Bill Vanburkleo, more athletic
but less executive, achieves the Vice-Presidency.
Marilyn Rider is sitting on a white slab, Treasurer.
Her triumph over a strange ugliness culminates in tragedy:
she later dies of cancer at the age of 17, mother of one. And
then, really just the most popular person in the school,
Gini Wyant, whose older brother had been Class President,
whose sisters had been Secretaries and Treasurers,
she too is elected and photographed with a smile
slashed into her features. And here is the School Council,

a group of tiny people inside a photograph cropped
to resemble a blob; everyone is staring down:
I believe they are praying, or searching their laps
Waterloo Sunset
The Basketball Champs have suited up to shoot baskets.
Walter Lipke is blocking a shot. He once asked me if
my father were a bootlegger. "It's important," he said.
The girls in blue and green gym suits have won
the Volleyball Championship. Once again I examine their legs.
Who's she? She's really cute, with a sweet, open smile.
Dismal assemblages of children engaged in Activities:
Red Cross, that collected so many nickels to furnish boxes
sent to foreign countries where bemused natives
gaped at their contents; Orchestra, strident fart-blasts
and sawing bows which, like Frankenstein, recreate the cries
of a tortured being; Band, with its no-nonsense march tunes,
plus Assistants in Homemaking—these girls are busy
baking, reading recipes, and opening the cabinet—
and Library, zealous demons engaged in research,
employing the Dewey Decimal System,
and Stagecraft, those tall, silent, capable boys
who operated the movie projectors, and Cafeteria,
a small group of poverty-stricken children
obliged to suffer the humiliation
of being forced to wash their classmates' dishes,
scrape the disgusting leftovers into a sack or hole:
these children are clearly spiritually deformed at this point.
Facing them, in a tactless stroke of layout, is Leader Corps,
young men and ladies superior in athletics and leadership
who supervise the younger children. There I am,
pretending to be an athlete. At least I had the sense
to avoid Glee Club, where crazed music teachers
led the way up stylized mountains of song
into even more majestic sonorities.
The Yearbook Staff, More Staff, and Committee seem relaxed
and genuine. One of them is Madelyn Grove, a tall and lovely

gray-eyed beauty who spoke so softly
no one ever heard a thing she said
and didn't care, she was so pretty. She jerked
me off in the lobby of the Hotel Hilton in Chicago
in a dream two weeks ago. And then,
beginning with Jayne Adair, pages of rows of faces
framed in squares. Jayne was pretty cute; her father
owned Adair Typewriter Co., where everything
was expensive. Larry Bennett, who studied calculus, rode
a motorcycle and, five years later, fell from a six-story building
after scaling its façade. I saw him three years after that
in an air-conditioned car with his father. I shouted, "Hey,
Larry!" He didn't hear me. I guess the air-conditioning
was too loud. And John David Berry, who had played third
base for the Kendall Thunderbirds, where
I was shortstop. Incredible Dot Bottenhead,
whose vast forehead and wild eyes
express her astonishment at being six and a half feet tall, half-
witted, the No. 1 laughingstock of the school.
Next to her is G. Craig Bolon, left-handed, awkward,
brilliant, but who never beat me at chess,
not once! He usually conceded
by throwing the chessboard against the ceiling.
John Christoffersen, enormously strong, who liked
to hit his friends in the groin, to "scraunch" them, and
Fred Clare, who studied calculus and whose father disliked me
because my father *was* a bootlegger. Mr. Clare
succumbed to a heart attack a few years back. Tom Cox,
so "oriental" as to be invisible, and attractive Howard Crain,
whose mother owned and operated Aloha Flower Shop,
Jo Crider, whom I kissed once, for some reason,
and Howard Cunningham, my best friend in grade school,
and Bill Cupps, my best friend in junior high,
Fred Daily who looks like Larry Rivers, Lyle
Davis who played right field for the Kendall Thunderbirds,
with his face of the hick, and Judy DeCamp,

oddly civilized and vaguely not unpopular, and
Tommy Dempsey. I pause here
for Tommy Dempsey. One foot tall, chubby, hair
cut by a lawnmower, teeth jagged, wheezing,
a voice like bedsprings, irascible, ornery, irritatingly happy,
the object of absolutely everyone's contempt,
I give him to you, world, Mr. Tommy Dempsey!
And Ted Duncan, who set the school on fire
lighting a cigarette in a wardrobe full of costumes;
Carolyn Duck, confident, comfortable, sexy,
but now that I remember her, not really very sexy.
Donnie Emerson, thin, dry, brittle, intelligent
and worse than contemptible; Michael Eoff,
pronounced "Oaf" but invariably "E-off" by gym coaches,
short, overweight a little, deeply embarrassed to undress
in gym and have his name disfigured day after day,
actually a bright boy whose shyness kept him away
from everyone. Diana Finn ("nniF")
whose boyish sociability made her popular with boys,
and Kay Finn, whom I never noticed until now: she's
very pretty. I must have mistaken her delicacy for weakness.
Jim Funkhauser, known as "Fuckhouse,"
and Warren Gandall, a smart aleck
who once sneeringly told me he'd give me a quarter
for a "blowjob." I didn't know what a "blowjob" was.
Gandall had, it so happened, an enormous cock, but
I guess he figured it was worth only a quarter. Money
values have changed. Right near is Charles Godbold *(sic)*
who also had a giant cock. Further down
I locate Sam Graber, who
came to the school new in the ninth grade and whom
I befriended, only to have him steal my girl, the asshole!
Oh, lovely Madelyn Grove again. She has such lovely eyes.
Here with pudgy eyes is Charles Hargrove, whose father
taught at the local university. I told Hargrove
about Plato in the school lobby one morning, and

here's Hilary Henneke, whose father, coincidentally,
was heap-big President of the University.
Hilary had been to London, Paris, and Tyler, Texas, and
her sophistication (that is, her tolerance of our boorishness)
put her in a class by herself, so to speak.
Here's Phil Hull, who had a paper route
and legs like a grasshopper, and Gary Hunt, whose father
embezzled funds and lived next door to my grandmother.
"It just killed Gary when his father went to jail," she said.
Roger Johns, one of the real studs, who passed out in Metal
Class because his best friend had hit him in the balls,
just horsing around, and Tom Lieser, a good friend
of mine who studied calculus, invented "leg spasms"
and was the most wacky person at Wilson.
Next to him is Viva Lillard,
who had been my girlfriend in the fifth grade
and with whom I had had a passionate and interesting romance.
She was a lovely girl and I'll bet she still is.
In fact I'd call her up if I knew her number.
Viva, if you're reading this, call me: area code 212,
local number 477-4472. Lynn McClaskey, whom I loved
madly and who kissed Sam Graber on New Year's Eve.
Here's Jimmy Meredith, who was getting handsome,
known simply as "Meredith," and Gary Meske, well
over six feet tall at age 14, who led our basketball team
to victory by getting 107 rebounds in every game,
and the great Leon Mooney, weighing in at well over 275 pounds also at age 14, and who lived a block away, and whom I actually liked! He ran the mile in a little over twenty minutes. The coach used to praise him, saying, "Look at Mooney here—he gives it all he's got!"
And Charles Morton, a plumber's son
I believed to be very wicked, and who was, no doubt,
and Yvonne Mullen, whom I believed to be very wicked
and wasn't, I'm sure, and here is a cross-eyed girl
named Mary Helen Niemeyer;

John Orth, with the reserved manner of a Librarian, and,
wearing the expression of a person
who has just been informed
that he has won a million dollars
and the right to be immortal,
Ronnie Padgett,
wearing a red and white checked shirt and a crew cut,
followed by Anita Page, better looking here than she was,
and Jimmy Pommeroy, who was so modest, slow, and kindly
that everyone took him for the imbecile that he was.
I love this picture of Melanie Puryear:
red lipstick, real blonde hair, doo-wop,
a sultry Elvis Presley smile, and a sensational signature
flaming beside her face. She was one of the school Dream Boats,
who not three years earlier had claimed she loved me.
These other faces, hundreds
of them, facing out, boys with hair like swirling ice cream
and girls so ordinary that I simply cannot believe it.
Ah, but here's David Shreve, as proper as Clifton Webb,
colorful Norma Tandy, who liked my eyebrows, Lee Tatum
whom I despised for no reason, and Linda Thomas,
the first girl who ever "gave" me an erection,
without knowing it, of course. We were dancing a fox trot
near the end of the ninth grade; her thigh. . . .
And Jimmy VanBuren, whose father died in his sleep
of a heart attack, and Jimmy became
the head of the family, shed not a tear, moved
to Massachusetts; Howard West, who hid his chips
under the table when he played poker, who
joined the Air Force and rode through the air in a jet;
Jim Wise who fell in a hole; Lynn Yelton,
whom a few years later I would find attractive, too late, alas.
Twelve people entered school too late in the year
to have their pictures included. And then

Ronnie
You're a
real neat guy.
It's really been nice
knowing you these
3 years. Even though
you are going to Central
I will still see you sometimes.
Good luck at Central and
always. Your're a real brain boy.
Have fun at Central.
Loads of Luck Always,
Lynn McClaskey
P.S. Have
fun in Latin
next year! Keep up your great
smash!!!

Sides

Women.
It is 1973.
I am going on 31.
I find women less attractive sexually than I did five years ago.
At the same time I feel more sympathetic toward them:
I look into their eyes, so sad sometimes, sometimes not,
And I sigh, "Oh."
I see breasts, beautiful breasts advancing, ass, lovely ass, cunt, incredible, boing!
I sense lovely arms lightly tanned, ears pierced and sparkles, knees one then the other, hair with its warm smell, stunning to Baudelaire, and real
Human hands, each with its personality, its particular dexterity,
I see these living contours, and others, wildly voluptuous or oddly flat and unidentifiable,
And I look into the eyes and sigh.

It's not embarrassing to be sentimental
When the sentiment equals
Seeing things just as they are here now.
It is late and in late spring with cool air and quiet
in the room and outside in the street by the building I live in.
A car goes by
disappearing, no trace left, as if
it entered a slit in matter and is gone forever
with the slit then entering the slit. . . .

Brain, shake out thy water, dog-like. Intelligence,
send thy cool breeze to ruffle this field of weeds.
A bull rampages in the field, kicking those little weeds
with his sharp hooves. Tough on the weeds! Scene
freezes: bull snorting eternally in the weed-field.
I reactivate the bull, he jerks forward, freezes again,

as if to say, "No more, Padgett. I'll not perform
in your damned poem!" I notice the ring shining in his nose

And at the same time I'm aware of some shining tightness in my skull,
self-consciousness in writing about it, now floods
of terror: here
now me in room writing New York 1973 me just this and
nothing else! Is that, is that it?
Is this the thing
you've been going to think about so long?
This the menacing idea peripheral to your fancy?
More menacing because of its "purity"—it gives no images.
Simply the idea,
a concept perfect because it fits physical reality
so as to be more than synonymous: it is coincidental,
the glove turning out to be the hand which in turn had turned inside
    out to be the glove.
Hmm. This sequence of ideas is so interesting
That I am flushed with pride, which damages my contemplation,
Like the wonderful hit of pride I got
when my teacher handed back a paper with A, Excellent, 100 or even
    Very Good with the Very underlined:
a sensation remarkably, in fact astonishingly similar to eating,
placing the chunk of sweet cold watermelon in your mouth, yum! yum!
Divine obliteration! You just blow
your fuses, like coming sexually,
when you really are sent flying out,
I mean wahoo utterly blasted out on some infinite flying carpet
    unrolling along that forever flow of power
and in a sense you never return: the larger part of you comes back
but that self coming in that moment goes on and on
the way I sometimes think that everything goes on forever in everyone,
Still standing in the doorway to Mother's bedroom saying half-asleep,
"Mommy, I peed the bed again,"
so chagrined, and then so pleased
with those nice fresh sheets, so sweet and clean,

and my mother never complaining! Agghhh!
Was she a secret saint?
When it came to changing wet sheets in the middle of the night
she was everything the most exacting definition of Charity could require.
It's odd, to think of that person, of whom
I know little, 1,500 miles away asleep
as I write this, though
it's even odder to think that odd. Odd.
Normal. Odd. Normal. Two words,
defused as concepts, become Ed and Norma, move
to a large town in Uruguay and forever
is such a lovely word, like Ed and Norma's hearts linked
through time, also with its cruel side, Death, which
I can't reconcile myself to. Ouf,
Comme diraient les français, no wait, don't hide
behind another language! Your own is camouflage enough.
Stick with Death, deep thinker. I slammed
two doughnuts on the highway up in Dunkirk, N.Y.
suddenly remembering my personal extinction,
which didn't help the doughnuts. They got
all lopsided. It's such an incredible thing,
I should just throw this typewriter out the fucking window,
keys bent sideways, man with eyes bent sideways, walk out the door sideways, price tags on sideways, piano music of Lizst sideways, nepotism sideways, the beard of Bluebeard sideways, trisected angle sideways, sinus headache sideways, Happy New Year sideways, mademoiselle sideways, a marathon sideways, Seidenbach's sideways, a crying child sideways, a laughing child the other way sideways, an idea being on its side!
Side on its side! Ides of March on your hide! I'd hide in Hyde Park with Mr. Hyde on the Ides by your side, inside your duck-billed blabbermouth spatter-bladder! And nanny-goat eat this can!

O Poetry, who leads us away and brings us back,
tell Grandmother her tomato plants are doing fine and her grandson
is riding a Hershey bar (Note to people living in 97th century:

Hershey bar is a geometric system whereby nanny-goat eats this can).
(As I write this, a parallel poem is being written in my head,
then crumpled and tossed into darkness
where it seethes silently, bursts into flame: my feet tingle, which is the other poem bursting into flame.
As you, reader, do

because you are the poem that bursts into flame,
then bursts again, and bursts, and with this bursting
a mosquito bit me

Sonnet

Lights in daytime indoors make outside
less real until night
falls. Night is falling now, 6
p.m., March 26, 1972, Vermont, USA:
too late for tea and too early for dinner,
reminiscent of the Windsor Diner
on US 5 today: shining silver with red
trim perched over an abyss. Risk
your life for a hamburger? With
mayonnaise and tomato? Outside now
the snow is blue with purple rips,
brown snags, tufts of gray and green
twigs reaching toward treehood. Pretty
soon dark, dinner, smoke, and lights out.

The Music Lesson

I would like to tell you a story.
My little wife suggested that I tell you this story
because she received such pleasure from it,
and I such pleasure in the telling.

Once there was a musical note.
It had a thin black stem, a black bulbous dot
on its side at the bottom, and on top a
single line jetting back. The note
lived in a universe whose time was equal
to its space: one could move through
this world by staying put and waiting
until enough time had passed to be somewhere
else.

    There was also in this world
a metronome which served as overseer
of the time-space continuum, a regulator
of the so to speak *basso continuo* of existence.
The metronome was unaware that he in turn
was overseen by a higher power, a man
named Wolfgang Amadeus Mozart. Mozart
was a child who had the physical appearance
of a genius, so that when he appeared
in public great sheets of light ripped
from his presence and flew away. One such
sheet wrapped itself around a bird so
that the bird was shot through with
this light.

            The villagers noticed a bright
object in the sky at night, moving about
unlike stars or moon or other celestial bodies,
and they soon created stories to explain
this phenomenon. You see, they were unable
to see Mozart: he had been dead

for more than 200 years. But his death was the kind
that remains over the years that pass,
not under them. He was buried in the sky,
and if you'll recall what I told you
about the time-space continuum you'll understand
just what I mean. Anyway,
one explanation of the gliding brightness
in the night sky was that some electricity
from a bolt of lightning had been captured
inside an idea which had lost the mind
it came from. Others felt that some sticks
had caught fire.
Neither of these theories was true, although
the sticks idea is interesting: the bird
could die, decompose, fertilize a small tree
and go into the limbs which then
would fall or be torn from the tree,
set alight and cast into the air.
The second movement of the arm that cast them,
the downward movement, the arm
attached to the body of Mozart
as he composed his Serenade No. 11,
the downward movement, I say, terminates
in a delicate flutter of the wrist and fingers,
and the cuckoo bird alights on a branch.
It sits there for a moment, sensing.
Once again the arm rises. The bird pours forth
a song which the Japanese felt sounded
like *hototogisu,* which is Japanese
for "cuckoo," whereas we think it sounds
like "cuckoo." The fact that both cultures
are correct illustrates my point
about the time-space continuum.
Actually the *hototogisu* and cuckoo are
different birds, but I equate them
to demonstrate a point. But back to our story.

First let me explain that the villagers'
first explanation, of electricity trapped
inside an idea which had lost the mind it came from,
would have been true had they not carelessly
sought to explain everything by electricity.
"Electricity" was a word they used
at random, a catch-all meaning virtually nothing.
Electrical concepts had permeated their religion
the way atoms permeated matter in the twentieth century:
so small as to be everything
once you got the idea. The idea
the villagers had was correct insofar
as they linked the mysterious noctural illumination
to a mental being, to, of course,
none other than Mozart. He is in
this room with me right now, not
figuratively speaking: he quite
literally is in this room, his real physical person.
He is signing a contract which will
grant me all rights to his works past,
present, and future. Actually this is a part
of the story I should have reserved for later,
and about how he is deaf, dumb, blind, and paralyzed
from the toes up. Yes, time has taken
its dreadful toll of the great composer, even.
Think of the men who dragged great stones
over vast deserts, only to hurl them
into deep chasms! Great stones
which diminish in size as they fall,
clattering like small hailstones
as they hit the canyon floor, where Handel
scoops them into a basket. Back
in his cave he affixes stems to them;
if only he had a staff to place them on!
Instead he must fling them into the air
and watch them increase in size, only
to fall back. Of course some notes did

continue to rise from time to time:
The Harmonious Blacksmith is one example,
notes that go so high up they become planets.
Incidentally, the planets of the solar system,
arranged on a circular staff around the sun,
form the basis of Couperin's *Pièces
de Clavecin,* but perceived as
the "music of the spheres" not in two dimensions
but in three: this "natural" music being
more complete than "written" music,
which is flat, pardon the pun. The great beauty
of man's "written" music consists in its complete removal
from anything we think of as "real," in fact
it is very much like the word "real" itself:
once said it becomes utterly without meaning.
But this digression goes on too long: my story
concerns the single and remarkable meeting of
Wolfgang Amadeus Mozart (1756–1791) and George Frideric Handel
(1685–1759).
You will notice that Mozart was three when Handel died,
or so musical history tells us. The truth
of the matter is that Handel did not die
until the autumn of 1786, when he not only
met the young Mozart but actually
collaborated with him on an operetta in one act,
Bastien und Bastienne, K. 50, a piece commissioned
by Dr. Anton Mesmer, the discoverer of animal magnetism.
Mesmer was a perverted homosexual who attempted
to use his discovery for evil ends:
he tried to hypnotize pretty young Viennese boys.
He was successful in the case of Mozart, in fact
Mozart wrote his part of *Bastien und Bastienne*
under hypnosis. Handel was of course a notorious
homosexual in his own time, but was well
beyond his prime by 1768. He refused to submit
to hypnotic suggestion and in fact was unaware
that the young Mozart was "in Mesmer's power."

The premiere of *Bastien und Bastienne* took place
in the open-air theater of Mesmer's house
in the suburbs of Vienna, with Mesmer directing
the production and playing Bastienne. In
his perversity he cast the by then ancient
Anna Maria Strada del Po, the exceptionally ugly
opera star whom Londoners had nicknamed "The Pig,"
in the role of Bastien. Colas was played
by a someone who drifted back
into the forever mists of the Unknown.
    Mesmer, an insanely jealous man, suspecting
that Handel was about to steal his young lover,
devised a monstrous plan which culminated
in having Handel bound and gagged, carted
onto the stage near the end of the sixth scene,
and as Bastienne sang

O Lust, O Lust
Für die entflammte Brust!

O Joy! O Joy!
For the burning breast!

he set fire to the venerable composer.
The light-hearted pastoral continued
with no one's taking notice: Mozart under
hypnosis, Anna Maria Strada del Po a hopeless
senile and opium addict, and the audience
a bizarre group of statuary assembled
by Mesmer from all over the world.

I have ants in my pants

and they are wearing pants

and there are little tiny ants in those pants

Isn’t that odd?

Radio

In the magic realm
of the *Arabian Nights*
Aladdin rubbed his lamp
to evoke fabulous genii
who performed remarkable feats.
Today we have only to turn
a small knob on a piece of furniture
and out of the aether comes
Rudy Vallee with his brilliant array of entertainers,
Wayne King's dance rhythms,
good old Cap'n Henry's Showboat troupe,
Grand Opera,
"The March of Time" with its stirring dramatizations
of important news events,
and plaintive Irish ballads sung
as only John McCormack can.

And now our radios offer an even greater thrill,
for we can tune in stations on the other side of the world
almost as easily as we can get our local ones.
Daventry (England), Sweden,
Moscow, Morocco,
Java, each
with its characteristic program,
come to us with a turn of the dial!

If you would listen to the world,
see that your new radio is "all-wave,"
meaning
that it will pick up American stations on long wave lengths
and foreign stations on short waves,
as well as police calls, airplanes, and signals from ships at sea.
There is one appropriately named model called

"The Globe Trotter." On its large
dial is a miniature map of the world
surrounded by battleships.
And if, in the whole wide world,
you find no program
to satisfy your mood,
there are Globe Trotters equipped with phonographs.

Another all-wave radio, as if to emphasize
the ease
with which
far-distant stations can be heard,
is equipped with remote control.
This means dials
are set in a small end table standing conveniently
beside your easy chair where you doze over the funnies,
and from here you control the radio at the other end of the room,
or even in an adjacent room. A
distinctive feature of this radio is an inclined
sounding board which deflects the
sound upward and increases
its clarity and brilliancy.

Although tuning in on foreign stations is exciting,
many of us are quite as content to be unable
to understand the words of the Metropolitan Opera in New York
as those of La Scala in Milan, Italy. It is quite likely that
United States broadcasting schedules
are better suited to our waking hours.

There are many devices on the newer radios
which enhance our enjoyment of these programs.
We appreciate automatic volume control,
keeping the sound evenly regulated
so that it does not suddenly screech at us.
We approve of tone control,

which balances upper and lower registers
and regulates pitch to suit our taste.
And if our ear is not sufficiently acute
to tell us when we have the precise point
on the dial for perfect reception,
we can have a convenient marker to indicate it
for us.

The reduction in size of radio mechanisms
without any loss in good performance
is an important technological advance.
No longer are they "the bigger the better."
Now the 5- or 6-tube set equals or even
excels the 7- or 8-tube set of two years ago.

A new compact portable radio
serves two purposes: it can be carried
from home into the automobile
where it serves as an armrest.
Your arm is tired.
Some persons prefer the small radios
even when price is not a consideration.
They are compact, require no floor space,
and come in smart, simple styles, and
they appeal to Mom and Dad, who have one
large living room model and wish to shoo
Bub and Sis off to listen to their favorite shows,
each in his or her room listening.

Perhaps the most engaging of the little radios
are those of special design: one model stands
hardly 8 inches tall, with unusually charming cases
of red, blue, or green Florentine leather, gilt-tooled.
Others are in stunning white calfskin,
to fill the need for white accessories.
One modern small model of shining black

has lacquer trim, and another is in sleek
gray hardwood, aluminum-banded, to suit the modern mode.

Women who want radios to fit carefully planned period
rooms will appreciate the period
cabinets now available, authentic in style
and of the finest woods and craftsmanship.
What,
for example,
could be more suitable for an early American living room
than a sturdy maple hutch,
admirable for an end table,
and concealing a radio of standard make.
Another attractive maple piece is a bookcase
with radio set in the closed shelf.
Open shelves hold pottery or glass or books.
Secretaries and Governor Winthrop
desks are also excellent pieces to hold radios.
Usually the radio panel
is placed behind a small door
in the middle of the rank of pigeonholes,
and until this door is opened
the desk gives no hint of its dual purpose.

But whether you are modern-minded in your furnishings
or prefer the traditional pieces,
you will find a radio to suit your taste.
You will select your new radio
for its appearance as well as its performance,
and you will take satisfaction in the manner
in which it at first harmonizes and then transforms
the furnishings of your home.

2.

Dick Rowland stepped on Sarah Page's foot
and she lets out a scream.
Rowland, a 19-year-old bootblack,
flees the elevator. Sarah Page, a 17-year-old part-time
elevator operator in the Drexel Building,
and divorcée attending business college,
tells those who rush to her aid that
he had assaulted her.
Later that afternoon two black police officers
arrest Rowland at his home and take him
first to the City Jail, then the County Jail.
That evening's *Tulsa Tribune* carries a small story
of the alleged assault, and rumors of rape
spread through town. By 4 p.m.
Commissioner of Police J. M. Adkinson reports to Sheriff McCullough
that there's talk of lynching Rowland.
Others confirm this report. Rumor of a lynching
reaches "Little Africa," where Tulsa's 15,000 Negroes live.
Blacks phone Sheriff McCullough to offer their services
to protect Rowland from a lynch mob.
(Less than a year before, in July of 1920,
Roy Belton, a white man accused of murdering a cab driver,
was taken from the Tulsa County Jail and lynched.
Witnesses stated that local police officers
had directed traffic at the lynching. The presence of a strong
and active Klan in Tulsa added to the fear of a lynching.)
By 9 p.m. about 400 white men have gathered outside the jail.
At 9:15 word reaches Little Africa
that the mob had stormed the jail.
About 25 armed blacks drive to the jail and find
this rumor to be untrue. They leave,
but soon return with about 50 more armed blacks.
Sheriff McCullough persuades them to leave
and a white man tries to disarm a black.

A shot is fired.
According to the sheriff, "All hell breaks loose,"
firing from both sides. Twelve fall dead,
2 black and 10 white.
Pitched and running gun battles rage
around the County Jail at Sixth and Boulder
and spread from there. Whites break into
pawnshops, hardware and sporting goods stores
to loot for guns, ammunition and what-have-you.
The fighting continues, groups of men surging through the streets,
excited, angry and terrified, unreal.
By midnight the blacks are forced to fall back
to Little Africa. One-half block (North Cincinnati
between Archer and the Frisco Railroad)
composed of Negro pool halls, whorehouses, and restaurants
bursts into flame. The blacks fall further back,
as far as North Greenwood, the main business street of Little Africa.

The fighting abates somewhat during the early morning hours
of Wednesday, June 1st, but sporadic shots are heard
throughout the night. The Final edition of the *Tulsa World* proclaims,
"Two Whites Dead in Race Riot." An Extra edition appears with
"New Battles Now In Progress." About 5 a.m.
10,000 white men (and Mexicans) assault Little Africa—
the total white population of Tulsa is 57,000, 7,000
of whom were in uniform for World War I—using small arms,
rifles, shotguns, machine guns, and 6 airplanes
for reconnaissance. The *World* brings out a Second Extra!
"Many More Whites Are Shot." By this time
many blacks have fled town or are in hiding
with their white employers. The white army
rolls through "Niggertown," killing the black men they see,
looting houses and businesses and dousing them with kerosene.
One eyewitness said, "Cars began to drive slowly
along our street. Cars driven by the sort of men
who wear their caps backward, the visors down their necks."

The Fire Department and National Guard are powerless
against the mob. The fires rage all morning:
800 stores and homes burned to the ground,
the business district of Little Africa completely destroyed.
Later that morning the last black stronghold,
the 40-day-old Mount Zion Baptist Church,
is overrun and burned to the ground.
At noon martial law is declared. "State Troops
In Charge," declares the *World* in its Third Extra.
National Guard reinforcements arrive
from Oklahoma City, Muskogee, Bartlesville, and Wagoner.
The Guard barricades Little Africa, disarms
blacks and whites, and herds blacks into compounds;
by evening there are 6,000 of them
in Convention Hall, McNulty ballpark at 11th and Elgin,
and out at the County Fair Grounds. Dr. A. C. Jackson,
a highly respected black physician
who had defended his home and family with a rifle,
surrenders to the Guard and is conducted to an internment camp;
on the way he is shot and killed by a sniper.
The Frisco Railroad removes its porters from trains
to Tulsa, while passenger trains leaving town
are jammed with blacks. Others leave by car or on foot,
some stay in hiding up in the Osage Hills.
Civic groups come to the aid of the homeless:
Red Cross, Humane Society, the YMCA, and YWCA,
with food, clothing, medical attention, and information.
The *Tulsa Tribune* comes out with a strong editorial
condemning the lawless element, white and black,
but articles convey an undertow of public opinion:
"Martial Law Halts Race War" "Nine Whites and 68 Blacks
Slain in Race War" "Trains Held Up; Negroes Ordered Off"
"White Woman Shot 6 Times By Sniper" "Barney Cleaver,
Negro Officer, Remains On Duty" "Civic Workers Care
For Negroes Held In Concentration Camps" "Girl Attacked
By Negro Not At Home Today" "Fire Fighters Are Helpless;

Flames Raging" "Blacks Carry Belongings As They Vacate."
One story relates how an old black woman
had given her "Bible records" to a National Guardsman.

The next morning the exaggerated headline reads, "Dead
Estimated At 100; City Is Quiet." Blacks are slowly released from camps
if their employers vouch for them, and they wear
yellow armbands to signify their harmlessness.
The city promises reparations for damages.
A Board of Estimates is formed.
The responsible white community is shocked, ashamed, and angry.
On Friday martial law is lifted at 3 p.m.
One hundred members of the American Legion are sworn in
as special police officers to keep the peace.
There are rumors of truckloads of black bodies
dumped in the Arkansas River.
A grand jury is to be called to "probe the rioting."
The *World* carries an article in which
"Negro Deputy Sheriff Blames Black Dope-Head
For Inciting His Race Into Rioting Here." Barney
Cleaver describes Will Robinson not only as a "dope-head"
but also as an "all-round bad Negro."
A city board moves to rezone the area near the Frisco tracks
where black families had lived,
changing it into an industrial and warehouse area
and forming, in effect, a wall between white and black communities.
The new "Niggertown" is to be rebuilt, to have, in fact,
its own police station (until 1945).
Many blacks have fled Tulsa forever:
young hotheads and "radicals" on one side
and professional people, community builders on the other.

On June 5th the flood in Pueblo, Colorado
is splashed across the headlines.
The *Tribune* will not rehash the story of the race riots
for the next fifty years.

The Story of Saint-Pol-Roux

Saint-Pol-Roux was a French poet. His name, Saint-Pol-Roux, suggests that he was made a saint by the Church. This is true to an extent: the Church did make him a saint, but long after he got his name.

He grew up in the north of France. He was so ordinary that there is no trace of his existence until the year of 1910, when he married Ilga Rasmussen, daughter of the famed explorer. Although Saint-Pol-Roux was only 30 at the time of his marriage, he had the appearance of a man 75 or 80 years old. This is the man we think of when we think of Saint-Pol-Roux. Bearded, tall, gaunt, long white hair flowing over his shoulders, his thin but powerful body concealed beneath a flowing white robe, at the bottom of which protruded two large feet in hand-made sandals. So he appeared at his wedding: the way God does when he resembles Rabindranath Tagore.

Nine months later Ilga Saint-Pol-Roux gave birth to a baby girl, but died doing so. The blonde, blue-eyed baby, named Christa, grew up out in the country with her father. They lived in a dream world, like Heidi, and bright yellow birds landed on their heads. She was a beautiful child and her father wrote many beautiful poems during this period, which lasted until World War II.

By this time Christa was 15, no longer a girl but not yet a woman. Then one night the Germans attacked their village and the surrounding countryside. They broke down the door and knocked down Saint-Pol-Roux and took his daughter outside, where many Nazis raped her before the very eyes of her father. Then they stabbed her in the chest and set fire to the cottage.

When Saint-Pol-Roux regained consciousness, he found the mutilated body of his daughter near the charred remains of his house. All of his poems had gone up in smoke.

Voice

I have always laughed
when someone spoke of a young writer
"finding his voice." I took it
literally: had he lost his voice?
Had he thrown it and had it
not returned? Or perhaps they
were referring to his newspaper
The Village Voice? He's trying
to find his *Voice.*
                    What isn't
funny is that so many young writers
seem to have found this notion
credible: they set off in search
of their voice, as if it were
a single thing, a treasure
difficult to find but worth
the effort. I never thought
such a thing existed. Until
recently. Now I know it does.
I hope I never find mine. I
wish to remain a phony the rest of my life.

Little Remains

The tears of Lycergus germinated the cabbage

another record drops onto the turntable:
this time I do see the houseplants
and the box sits on the table.
Window
very unlike matchsticks, which,
with friction at their tips, appear at the tips
Of the lover's fingers as they rise
Across the darkness where
this stunning woman stares to the left.
She thinks
                    Lester Lanin
And his Orchestra have been explaining
How inevitable everything is in musical terms.
I think they are right. I think
I would like to (interruption) . . . bath, she said,
But little remains of Norman Bath.

Don't Forget

Great perceptions of the oceans and the plains,
contemplation of the biggest mountains in their ranges,
philosophies of snow at their tops and theologies of the clouds
that hang forever from their ears and send mist
into the atmosphere I breathe in
and out, a delicate moisture
that keeps my body supple so the mind can operate
in its various ways, suitable to higher perception
which gradually, like a car with a flat tire, rises
inch by inch, tilted in elevation and then
nothing like an automobile, nothing like a mentality,
the way heartbeat is translated into drama
and drama into an aftertaste or a memory
into a convulsion or a simile into a sledgehammer
that breaks your glass head off at the neck (fortunately
it was a toy head mounted by toy workmen on toy shoulders,
the real you having absconded into the great outdoors
where everything is big, three-dimensional, and life-size
when your life has grown as great as life can grow
and there's nothing left for death to know
about bringing you down again among cherry trees
where people clutch their hats and fight back tears
that fight back feelings that fight back and
drench the hats of these people, clustered
in a silent meditation on the most lamentable fragment
of what they always imagined was a philosophy.)
But it was more like a stage setting for a concept
in which various vectors entered through shafts in the ceiling
and rammed spears of light into the floorboards,
narrowly missing the table and its flames,
the houseshoes Father Time lent to Santa Claus,
the box in the corner under eighteen feet of dust,
the frozen cat smashed against the half-moon silhouette

and a mandolin heard in the distance, clear
and melodious as the young man playing it is unaware
that his fingers moving deftly over steel have us paralyzed
in a vision of something infinite tinged with nostalgia
for a past constructed entirely
of nerves and photographs, a world-picture as synthetic
as one's erroneous prediction of what "the future" will be like.
It will be like the future tense in grammar, special
potentiality in its fictitiousness, a powerful fairyland
that this very moment threatens to overwhelm an ant
who, sitting down to dinner, finds his porridge
growing green hair on its steaming surface and is terrified!
He shoots back from the table and rushes helter-skelter
into the darkened forest where we await him
in our amphitheater, eyes burning floodlights
that rake the arena of the present, a circular stadium
whose playing field bulges upward in an attempt
to become spherical and float free of its environs,
a shuttlecock free of its feathers and hence able to go on up.
For weren't we, I ask myself—bringing in another personality
to help me with this point—meant to keep going up,
I mean, like rockets with our fuses lit at birth,
weren't we meant to keep going, our heads leading
the way through matter like tremendously fast
bullets fired into outer space? Perhaps not. Perhaps
I will rise from this chair and go take a leak,
fix a sandwich, and let the energy drain back into my body,
my only body. Dear body, poor body, arms
that go from shoulders down to hands,
how did you get there, attached so? Legs, my ideas
are not inside you, what are you doing down there,
crossed at the ankles, and toes, come out of the shoes
and explain yourself! And of course the great
horrible enigma of the trunk, the miasmic viscera,
the hideous human heart, the gray spongy lungs,
made even more terrifying in color illustrations,

how can I learn to love my own liver? Ugh!
Fingernails are abstract, but the intestines? Ugh!
Knees are adorable, but the spinal cord? Ugh!
The funny bone is harmless, but the gall bladder? Ugh!
The lips are erotic, but the gums? Ugh!
Physical matter of the body, so diverse and generally unloved,
you are more confusing than the spirit,
which at least has a flame-like purity
to our concept of it. But couldn't I ask my voice box
to tell me what I fail to understand, command the tongue
to speak and ears to listen? Listen, ears! Open, mouth!
Speak, tongue, if you have anything to say!
"Mother. . . ." it whispers.
"Tomorrow. . . ." it adds.
"Aaaahh. . . ." it seems unsure.
"Leave me alone," it demands.

Louisiana Perch

Certain words disappear from a language:
their meanings become attenuated
grow antique, insanely remote or small,
vanish.
            Or become something else:
transport. Mac
the truck driver falls for a waitress
       where the water flows. The

great words are those without meaning:
   from   a   their   or
   Or   the   for a   the
   The   those

The rest are fragile, transitory
   like the waitress, a

beautiful slender young girl!
I love her! Want to
marry her! Have hamburgers!
Have hamburgers! Have hamburgers!

Gentlemen Prefer Carrots

I nearly went to sleep standing on a corner today.
The light turned green
People charged down into the street, arms
with bags and boxes
while I stood there disappearing.
And after dinner, forehead resting
on the table, I saw some gentlemen
eating carrots in a dining car
with a landscape whizzing past outside,
really fast trees and hills, varied sights
and views, and those carrots disappearing
into the eaters' mouths. I raised
my eyes: music on the machine,
light, and fall coming on.

Ladies and Gentlemen in Outer Space

Here is my philosophy:
Everything changes (the word "everything"
has just changed as the
word "change" has: it now
means "no change") so
quickly that it literally surpasses my belief,
charges right past it
like some of the giant
ideas in this area.
I had no beginning and I shall have
no end: the beam of light
stretches out before and behind
and I cook the vegetables
for a few minutes only,
the fewer the better. Butter
and serve. Here is my
philosophy: butter and serve.

Realizing

Walking briskly past Schrafft's
I saw Anne Kepler's face
smiling at me and raising her eyebrows:
How nice, she's
not dead, I can see her
later, I thought on my way to
a marvelous and touching extravaganza
of clowns dancers orchestras movies &c.,
the show ending with Muddy Waters
coming down into the audience next to me
to embrace Leadbelly and sing
"What a Gloomy Day in London"
so beautifully it brought tears to my eyes.
Later, walking down
into a moment in which
the light seemed to stop
in a way as familiar to itself as I am to myself, I
remembered my dream—
and realizing I was remembering pushed
me ahead into whatever else was going to happen,
my writing this, you reading

Tennyson Invincible

Where is the poem "Tennyson Invincible"
I've been wanting to write for almost two years?
It seems to exist
in a world continuous but not contiguous
with mine
like an alternative to an event:
I ate a larger bowl of cereal
this morning and wasn't killed by that speeding taxi!
Inside the taxi a passenger stares
glumly into the future
which the past absorbs as he
leads his life through it.
Pretty soon poof
No Nothing. A thousand
years pass. An animal
with a shiny white ball for a head
declames, through strange body vibrations,
"Tennyson Invincible." This
of course will not happen—
just a fantasy I had.

Air
Light
Energy
& Love
All so wonderful
To be a part of
& have them be
part you:
Light so sweet
& Air so mild
Energy so great
& Love so wild
& crazy when
it hits you
hard & All
at once & then
Is gone
& you with it.

But it comes back
you know
bigger & better
& harder than
ever before.
This is true
& I am here to
tell you so.

Poem

The insanely lyrical and majestic concerti
Of Archangelo Corelli
Are coming to me through two boxes
From a point far beyond the recording
Far beyond too the hand of Corelli
Existing in Italy
Existing in New York
As I am existing
With Opus 6 as a nervous system
And Time scattered through me like stars of nervous energy
Drifting out in all directions
Gone from wherever I was
Back to where I came from
This cold, dark, beautifully elevated afternoon

June 17, 1942

Pity me, Patty

Pity me, Mother

Pity me, Father and friends

Pity me, you who see me on the street and go by
And those of you whose eyes meet mine
Along a rod of vision
Then skid and break off

Replace that rod
And hit easily
The exclamation points on my head

I see them there!

like tears that fall from having had
ideas too happy or too sad

like last night
when the actors who had just done Molière
bowed at the end:
I wanted them to pity me too
as I had loved them

Pity me, an ape in cel[illegible]d

Look the word is blotted!

Pen, pity me too!

At least let me finish!

I want the pity to stream in from all nations

Diplomatic ambassadors arriving in limousines
with tears in their eyes. . . .

(The pen is running black ink
down my hand)

"My sincere sympathies, Ron,"
they say quietly and sincerely.
"We knew your former self well
And it was a fine self,
But time hath no mercy
And the bull phones and the elevated shoe
comes to a roaring halt"

I accept their sympathy. . . .
Is this too Mayakovskyish?

Can you hear me in the back?

The waterfall is not moving
because it is plural
and I saw a . . . can't think of anything to say . . .

I'm off my theme
lost the original impulse
which was about pity
wanting everyone to pity me
because I'm a miserable dumbbell

It's not pity I'm not giving in return!

Hell no!

I know you're out there

I know you're there
among flat drifts of rising smoke from my cigar

I mean

George sick in New York

Get better!

Know you feel horrible!

Dick, no postcard from me

makes you feel forgotten

Sorry!
Know you feel horrible!

Patty, with the weight of the world
on your shoulders
with all that like centuries of
sadness in you,
with all the shit I've given you
I know you feel horrible!

Burning alive
Ted, sorry for you
already flying out into what
really is the end of everything. . . .
I know I'm always reserved around you—
lock my heart up when you're around—
Sorry! I can't stop myself!
And I know it makes you feel bad. And

Oh Joan, who brings burning tears to my eyes and whom I love!

Tessie I love you and treat you awful! Wish I didn't and
you loved me! Pretty funny!

Michael, boiling in horror!
Anne crying in the supermarket!
Katie always fearing the worst! So fragile!
Larry sad beyond belief!
My poor father doomed forever to be unhappy
and my mother more unhappy than anyone
I've ever known
Two people who are me split in the past
More unhappy than anyone I have ever known
And then me a little baby
Born into a world blazing with madness
and trying to grow up "right"
but absolutely miserable every second,
my eyes filled to the brim with tears
that burn and flow over—bursting!
For my little Wayne
            my little boy
                    so beautiful
                         so beautiful
                              so innocent
                                   and so beautiful
          and born like me—just me all over!
walking as I walk
    and smiling and making a face
              or looking serious and introspective
    just like I did—

              you think I don't remember?

I'm only 28!
          It's only a few years back!
   I remember every fucking last detail!
Every time miserable

sobbing
throwing myself into absolute despair
Totally fucked! Ruined!
Forget it!

Well, who's left?
My grandparents?
Treated them like shit
and still do, but Noah's dead,

that nice man dead, oh

What the fuck

Raving maniacs are destroying the planet
and my grandfather is dead?
Shit!
And soon my father will be dead
and my mother will be laid in her grave
and then there'll be nothing between me

and the Great Unknown

I'll just be facing it

like a cold wind in your face

that blows from within

and then coming to an end

as this poem comes to an end

on

January 29, 1971

Two Vermont Sketches

Autumn in the country. I am sitting on the lawn. My wife comes up the road, hands full of beautiful leaves. As she goes by us and into the house, she gives our son a bright red and green maple leaf. He looks at it. "Leaf," I say. He looks at it. "Isn't it pretty?" Delicate spine glowing in green fading to yellow and burnt into deep red at the edges, early spring to late autumn in a capsule. "Isn't it pretty?" He looks at it, raises it high over his head, and smashes it into my face.

I am outside reading Whitehead. "But the body is part of the external world, continuous with it. In fact, it is just as much part of nature as anything else there—a river, or a mountain, or a cloud." I hear a noise up on the ridge to my left. The air is still. I do not like it that a bush is making its way toward me.

Big Bluejay Composition

Compositions in harmony

the sunlight rods over the Commuter's Spa
bluejay

oh

I don't want to go in
and watch Gene Tierney on TV moonlight

when the shadow of a doubt

tiptoes down the hall

crumpled tossed in wastebasket

Rainbow Colored Pencils made by Eberhard Faber
maker of Mongols

i.e. Children of Paradise

gray line wiggle

a large permanent flinch

just under the skin then

She turned to me - - - - - - - - - - in the flying starlight

in the in the

tiny (there are no straight lines in a curve) breeze

breeze curving

moonlight

when the m-moon shines
over the cow's shit

bzzzzzzzzzz

bzzzz

the square of the sum
of two . flashing . numbers from the now on bzzz

suddenly the onions replaced the onusphere

—to leon the counterpoint— and Tommie Vardeman
stuck his

head out the door a very old auto racer

gray wearing glasses

bluejay

sweet as stops

I catch my breath I cry (cont. p. 42)

of planetary music

heard in trance

well the figurine of the bluejay

½ in the dimensional side of God

the earth is still—

. . . stars . . . stars . . .

God is in a trance,
now's the time to compose a few immortal lines

re's the immortal paper?

e immortal brain? star

we go trot

trot-trot

past the abattoir

sliding 1968 sliding

---

under the beauty of

broken thunder

he goes over center

k-boom softness is northern

alert

alarming

the north,

le même nord où la mission Albert agonise maintenant
parmi les cristaux

that is the wild blue yonder

screwed onto a bolt from the blue

magnetic,

the pursuit of Hedonism emerges boink from unwrinkled clouds

while . . . trumpets . . . Haloed, long pause

from across the ocean long pause

came gunshot

a piece of rain fell and hit the horizon

Slowly I turned . . .

behind us loomed the awesome figure of the gigantic

baked enamel ape, which Professor Morrison had, with fanatical patience, constructed over the years.

A bluejay

Tennessee raised in the dark

to the highest power

Tennessee is the n it made

I have spoken

– – – –

I am speaking

like a sunset going down

behind

the rising dawn

to ♪ot mother,

Remember me in your semi-conscious prayers hit the brakes

when the dew is glistening on the bluejay

and I go walkie to nightmare school

and the refinery is blasting away

Process and Reality   on this damp, foolish evening

bl   here

the future
casts a pall bearer on the present—in the future the present
will be

a thing of the past   losing altitude

You shake

No

your head No

the smell of coffee on a morning the smell of hot coffee on a

winter's morning

the table is set in the breakfast room frost on the windows
sunlight

lock into which Mr. Morrison is inserting his key
floods the hardware store ⋀ the black-and-white cereal box
the porcelain

the fresh peaches the milk +

Now our mighty battleships will steam the bounding main

people jetting along

a symphony of tweets

the light of the Eternal Flame
clearly visible

from where you sit

in those great, golden heights no doggie
in the neighborhood

all the doggies have gone off to war to be male nurses

the moonlight on the earthquake

into which many doggies fell

plunged fiery and screaming

in their machines

. . .

gravely the Statue of Liberty

turned and faced the nation, finally!

a medium-sized flesh-colored male sexual organ extending

from its inner ear,

"The period in history termed Modern is now over" it said

—CLICK—

the bluejay fluttered on its shoulder

"Y-you'd b-b-better b-b-believe it!" it cried wildly

Crazy Otto

Tonight the
light is
right   on the angle of the
imagination

by whose grace

I imagine

but the direct object is crosshatched

as it hits the proverb

ageing alongside the

primrose path

you walk along whistling
very nonchalant

hands in overalls

sky yellow

over rows of radios

leading to Crystal City . . . .

There,

at Chrysler city everything is sparkles

driving wild by

wild magnetos

whose wires lead to the figure 8

behind which a dank but not lonely

Gutzon Borglum sits saying over and over

I-Love-You

only he says it in a tone of voice which implies that it is not he who loves you

and, well

Blue turns to gray

If the rate is being increased
to increase its heart rate, each
time the rate rises above a pre-
set level, the animal immediately

receives his first electricity.
At first, large increases in rate
get some electricity. As the
rate begins to catch up, progress-
sively larger increases are
needed to detonate the device

needed to detonate the device
Out on the breezeway

which gives continually onto

Great Smoking Mountains

a young man in suede

stares at a tangerine

The natives of Tangiers
are referred to as
Tangerines

tears
come from

behind his eyes and
spread in white sheets until they
spill over onto my cheekbones

down which they
stream leaving a
glistening
trail

a tiny panda runs down

The thin but swift winds in the upper layers of the breezeway
tugged on the trail at various levels. From a straight line
it became a question mark and finally,

your smile is not the thing lips make

It's a spiritual condition risen at the edges

dreams neither technicolor nor black & white

Light

a ray of light

a ray of light from the star Arcturus

must travel fo- forty years

before it hits us. The rays of light that launched the

spectacular lighting display at the opening of the World's Fair

of 1933 had left Arcturus forty years before—when the Chicago

a slow, blooming orgasm

World's Fair closed in 1893

Capital letters

come out suggests orgasm
too much

and slide up the runway

into the sky

All the SKY is gray

your edges break off and fly away

dip missing

the great heavy cables which rise

above my attention span

and the . . . . . .
. . . for going downstairs backward
is certainly not the same as going upstairs forward
and going sideways spinning

upward through clouds

rolling

Rolling n rolling

Progressively larger increases . . .

I Love You

each word increases squared

by the word before and the word after

Because you spoke to me in words

with an English countryside on
one side of them and

a televised stilt

on the other

Sonja Henie was born in Oslo, Norway

her body goes back and starts all over
on the end of your body

whose sunrise

glows in the dark

It is morning dark
rain etc. I am out running
down the great dotted line

that leads to born in Oslo, Norway, in 1913
and almost immediately put on ice skates by
her father, Wilhelm, a shopkeeper and European
cycling star

Wilhelm

peddling his 100 percent chrome flying piano

I can't get through to him He

is a foreigner

and you can't get through to a foreigner

by simply speaking your own language

slower and more clearly

You have to speak his language: in this case a vertical line

looks longer than a horizontal line

of equal length

&

– – – – –

Sooner or later all the clichés come true
They just wait around
Until truth catches up with them
They are not exactly untrue
They are only waiting for truth;
For instance, the idea that sooner or later all
The clichés come true
        ——expressed above——
Strikes me as not yet being true

                                        and if and when

                                                like Borglum

I say like Borglum I Love You

if it isn't true   it will be

as soon as the sodium

                is released at elevations above 50 miles

where it glows

under the action of sunlight after the sun has set
        on the earth's surface below

and as soon as it is

I'll be down there

on the earth's surface

capped by the bright soaring light

of the truth

gradually coming true

Ode to Clemens Laurrell

Immortal Clemens!

immortal in my mind
though when anyone's mind turns into mine
you may well wake up
in the arms of an autumn night
whose enormous blossoming is your entire body

Always so kind!
to me (so first I make a student
of the thing as it is
then one as it isn't
one idea on top of the other)

Mortal *and* immortal Clemens!

you who in 1961 were working in a plastic boat factory

I look back

see stars
out in the backyard
Mother mowing the lawn
at midnight

So great
to look back
at the way I used to look forward
to looking back

Old Mexico!

No shit!
my future me
a mirror I would gaze into
New Mexico
to see ahead of me
the person I was becoming
Mexico
the person
I am

Such surprise
morning is sending its dark blue
across the skies

And with the smell of exploding alcohol 33
watching the centuries
we catch strange and interesting figures
passing along the edge
of a land of sky-blue waters

Hose Nose
Chrome Dome
Mr. Absent Offenhauser
Skinny Jack Pinpoint
Hector L. Stormwindow

I hear a voice
in the darkness
it is the voice of Hector L. Stormwindow
wrapped in mystery followed by seventeen zeroes
like the top of a mountain
but very alluring
the austerity of its expression sailing
supreme blitz finagle

Hello Clemens
Listen

This is The Punk

I say

if you would go
to other
than where you are
you have only to stand still
permit

yourself to be carried away
& should you wish
to travel at a greater rate
you have to move through your ideas
in the manner of a pedestrian

Here comes a pedestrian now
your insane sister Eileen Brain
totally with a mind
her bathing suit shining
sprockets of moving pink
Wow!
and as I drew near
they leaped
over the side of
a bright idea
they had

So I lean back against the willows

just to be free again

just to embrace the fleeting image

of a monumental and disasterous chord

struck on a defective Omaha

Sky & clouds tearing apart at sunset

and the tones fading on waves

of rising melody

in the flowing geography of the sky

(   )

the rainbow resumes
its formal presence

over the colonnade

and a tremendous midnight is suffused
into the lemonade

and like a light
we go out

in a Studebaker convertible
to where the divine firmament
babbled down to the divided highway

– – – – – – – – – – – — – – – – – – – – – –

the car automatically
begins to go
when the machine is turned on
and the land moves

in daydreams at night

in my biggest sexual fantasia
the mugwump sighs in the afternoon

IDEAS AS SENSATIONS

Everything in the world preceded by
I think . . .

I think . . . it is the dawn
of a new morning
of which you have no memory
one with both
itself and nothing else
the way nothing and zero appear to be   to the non-existent eye
the same size
as they go up and down
in the shadow of

jump!

Wonder of Wonders

Tell Us, Josephine

The blue and white tie arrived at the man's neck through merchandising:
he walked up to a store window, reached in his pocket, and, inside,
completed the transaction.
Now, as he walks away, he exercises his body. It improves his health.
The blue and white stripes of the tie improve his appearance.
It improves his gray shirt, a palm tree improves a desolate landscape,
A desolate landscape improves empty space
And his spirits are improved, if cheerfulness is an improvement.
The eyes of his face now seem meaningful and happy to be so,
The smile that rides below the eyes reflects the moonlight
That glances off the roaring and shimmering dress of sequins,
Maroon sharks that flow down the body of the girl from Martinique,
The girl who smokes a cigarette, darkly, in his mind,
As he walks into the darkened room and waits for his eyes to catch up
with his past.

Dark red, almost black, the long sharp fingernails click against the varnish
smoke floats in waves on
And a lime grows cold against a cube
Of ice that couldn't remain solid. Cooler,
The air along the floor flows along legs of table and woman
Who shifts slowly in her chair to keep the blood evenly distributed—
She does not like her legs buzzing unpleasantly.
They rest here, then there, their surfaces smooth against the black silk
That sheathes her body. It is so dark in there!
And so quiet, only skin on silk, click of nails, tiny sequins crashing like
tiny cymbals for which we get tiny ears, and gentle zephyrs
In curls of smoke lifted from her lungs.
I don't think she has any thoughts!
I don't thi . . . the man in the blue and white tie appears in the doorway.
She moves her hand. The room bursts into flame.
Both die in the holocaust. Statues are erected in their honor:
Leaves fall from the trees. The sap rises. The sun rises.

Prices go up and people sit under the ground.
The ground rises. It has wings. It is an airplane.
After a while it levels off over the clouds, cruising at an altitude of 56,000 feet and a speed of 300 miles per hour.
You are alone on the plane: there is not even the pilot!
You have stolen the airplane, with no one to drive it, and now you must suffer the consequences.
But the first consequence is your pleasure at being alone up so high all silver and blue
Over pink and gray cloud patches that blur to orange wisps over there
And down to a rather artificial-looking purple beyond that.
Could that cloud be real, so purple?
Your attention is drawn to that cloud, how could it be so purple?
And then your spirit is drawn down to it, utterly riveted to that flowing shape, the intensity is aural, it is awful—O let me go, cloud!
And poof it parts gracefully and evaporates. . . .
Behind it the man and the girl from Martinique are parting and evaporating
And as they do your ignorance parts and evaporates and you remember: you are a pilot

from

TULSA KID

Lettera

Old typewriter,
when my Olympia got stolen
and I went to Europe
I found you
in the Galeries Lafayette,
with your French keyboard,
accent marks and Italian name:
and never thought of you in terms of olives
until tonight, lying in bed,
vague unregistered thises and thats
flitting through my head the way
my words have flitted through you
and out, and I thought back
to that Smith-Corona, used,
the executive office-model Olympia,
and its sidekick the big black ancient monster
with keys I had to bang and its table tipped
over bending the keys sideways
with the impact: my greatest poem!
Then, leaving them behind and buying
a portable Olympia on upper Broadway,
the one thieves stole
just before we sailed
and I've had you ever since,
through thick and thin,
changed a lot of ribbons, always black,
threading the inky cloth into its grooves,
cleaning and oiling the mechanism,
leaving you idle for months and then feeling
your soft touch again

The 26 Letters

by Oscar Ogg,
a history of what we call the
alphabet, face up on the desk
next to carbon paper and typing paper
and typewriter, keys "punched"
by fingers of me
the man sitting in this chair
in old gray and white robe
with big black buttons,
3:55 in the morning
with a head cold and a beard
and some tortoise-shell spectacles
attached to my head,
not a bad guy really,
a touch of Sad Sack tonight,
a bit of red and green tomorrow
with a long streak of blue into the future
with orange and black zigzags along the sides

Orange Man

I am orange
I am an orange man
Just like other men except I'm orange
Yes people stare at me
when I walk down the street
but one day I decided,
"Hell, I'll just have to ignore it!"
And ever since then
I've known several things:
1. that races are different,
2. that all people are beautiful in their way,
3. that this differentness is beautiful:
Look at the Chinese girl, her skin so smooth and
soft, her lips so soft, look at her overalls, her blue overalls
that hang on a hook at night;
look at the Watusi man, tall black supple flex,
sheer athleticity; look at the Swedish diplomat:
blond hair and brown suit, a handsome figure,
a civilized image developed against an urban backdrop;
look at the Moslem women in purdah—it must be great
to rip off their clothes and fuck them! And think
of them, so hidden all day, and riiip! they
are madly fucking and being fucked by Moslem men!
Think of the other various peoples of the world
ripping each other's clothes off and fucking,
everybody on earth fucking simultaneously
writhing and gyrating, moaning and crying, sobbing
screaming and shrieking and coming
in one vast radiation of orgasm!!!
Well, that's how I see mankind.

Mon Ame

My soul, that's what you are,
that's what I thought to myself,
or at least that's what I thought,
before the light changed
as you entered, skirts flaring
like arms tipped with hands that fly out
to welcome a special someone:
the war is over, tears come to your eyes,
and I am born.
I am the generation of 1946.
I swept over your land 22 years later
like a searchlight
that swept the skies for German bombers
and raked the leaves into small heaps
and burned them, the smell of autumn leaves
sent out in the air
to the window where Mrs. Higgenbottom
is kissing the butler, he is surprised
that the stately old *dame* has thrown her chubby arms
around him and is laying a massive kiss on his lips!
But soon lust bangs against the kitchen sink
and they fall on the tiles in an indestructible orgy!
("I am fucking Mrs. Higgenbottom!")
Mr. Higgenbottom is gliding through the landscape
in his chauffeur-driven Bentley automobile and smoking
a massive cigar with a perfect ash he taps
to topple governments, a bat of his eyelashes
and entire factories shudder and weep, the economy
is held in his throbbing grip!
South of the border hordes of Mexicans don't give a fuck!
But in "America"—ha! people read the newspapers
and rush to the soup lines: it is the Depression.
Thirty or so people fly through the air

before they hit the pavement
and two days later a man pauses on the streetcorner and drops a
gum wrapper, it is Juicy Fruit!
Forty years later I am chewing, it is Juicy Fruit!
And I am seeing your pretty face in my mind
as I stand on the corner, thinking,
"That's what you are, my soul."

Lemon Meringue

Do you think it is an easy thing
to make a tuna salad sandwich?
Shall I mash this pie in your face,
the face of God?
Yes, God came into my kitchen one afternoon,
as the sunlight slanted and laughed
and the leaves on the trees sang in unison
the little song of their jubilation,
and he looked out the window and said,
"Jesus, what a beautiful day!"
He took another bite of his tuna salad sandwich
and turned his hoary face to mine,
so close it made me uncomfortable:
our noses were touching, and suddenly he
let out a tremendous roar! that blew my hair back.
And knocked my chair over. God leaned
over the table and was frozen protractor
I could sight along to find the North Star,
still twinkling up there on the ceiling
that caves in like a broken record
of an avalanche proclaiming its greatness
to the surrounding waterfall, squirrels, pine
trees, rocks, deep, lichen, and the other stuff
found in Northern Arabia. Hey, wait a minute,
there ain't no waterfalls in Arabia!"

Stop and Go

I would like
to pause here
in the day's
occupation
to say
that I think
Harrap's
Standard French
and English
Dictionary
is a wonderful
book,
Echappez-vous!
Run away!
Edited by J. E.
Mansion M. A.

A Thank You to Henri Matisse

An orange lay on the table, similar to an orange ball,
on the patio that sparkled in afternoon sunlight,
the air crisp and vivid. Inside
the whitewashed villa, Henri Matisse
and his beard in the shade. He is old
but beautiful. The room has the furniture
he painted and it became his furniture.
Right now he is brushing in large areas of color,
the watercolor paint still wet. It is
one of his finest sketches, "Bathers,"
three nude female figures who seem
to have some ulterior motive for being
in the picture, whose tone is the blue
of the Big Blue, the Mediterranean.
Here and there colors twist in a pattern
reminiscent of dancing—and here
the young man's handsome profile was etched against
the mahogany mantle as he tapped his briarwood
against Lady Elchinham's head, spilling
ashes down her neck and shoulders.

Chocolate Milk

Oh God! It's great!
to have someone fix you
chocolate milk
and to appreciate their doing it!
Even as they stir it
in the kitchen
your mouth is going crazy
for the chocolate milk!
The wonderful chocolate milk!

Elegy to a William Burro

If you are suffering and unknown
there is always the possibility
that you are horrible

and if a jumper cable were attached to you
the sudden rush of power would be too much,
annihilating the unit it was meant to energize.

Many jumper cables gyrate over the land
attaching themselves to random trees
stray dogs jailbirds passing fancies,
each in its turn jolted into a higher and sometimes unfortunate
    format of being

Notice the chili dogs tearing into the growling stomachs
of executives too busy to realize the French
restaurant has been replaced by Arnaldo's Chili Dog Hut

Not that it matters: the food and service
are far superior now. Arnaldo himself
is an interesting chap. There are tiny sombreros
tattooed on his forehead. A few years ago
no one had ever heard of Arnaldo and look
at him now. King of the Chili Dog Chains.
It's true his spirit is still slapped
by religious anxiety, but on the other hand
he has tattooed a burro with a comic expression
of stubborn pride on its behind

and he has installed a cyclone fence around
his drive-in to secure it against the jumper cables;
every night he goes out and beats them off

with a stick. The moon rises with a smile
and "Guadalajara" emerges from the vibrating
prong inserted in his future and
all is calm, all is bright

Twins on Wrestling Team

Dave and Don Roberts, iden-
Dave and Don Roberts, iden-
tical twins from Iron Mountain,
Mich., are members of Michigan
State's wrestling team. Dave
wrestles at 123 pounds, Don at
115.

Song

Learning to write,
be a good person and get to heaven
are all the same thing,

but trying to do them all at once
is enough to drive you crazy

Problem

I wouldn't care if America slid into the ocean
The only problem is: which ocean?

Scouting Report

Señor, I have seen
the encampment of the fair-
skinned ones: they were
cleaning their windows with
a blue liquid in a
bottle, cleaning the windows
so nicely with this liquid
they called Windex

Little Crush on Jenny Dunbar

Into your life tonight
a girl of planetary beauty steps
for the second time ever
a girl you could fly over everything for
well almost
because you would have to fly over yourself
completely
that is be not just "another you"
but a different someone entirely
I wouldn't
not even for the astonishing perfection that is you

So let's say I bump
into your arm
going out the door
putting my hat on and
my elbow rises into your arm
That's enough and
Excuse me

With Lee Remick at Midnight

The lights shoot off the windows of the Plaza
and into the sky where they become stars.

Stars shine over the Playa de Toros
in Mexico, D.F.

We have a Washington, D.C.
We have such a thing as alternating current.

The current flows in one direction for a while
And then in the opposite, alternating rapidly thus.

I get up out of my chair and walk to one end of the room.
There I see a little statue of a friend, Tony Towle.

Hat, coat, muffler, and gloves appear on the statue
As the door closes overhead and the sky is black.

My hand reaches for the alarm clock in a dawn
Muddle-headed wha? and I settle into another level

Of being. I want to read Marx, *The Voyage of the Beagle,*
Jean-Jacques Rousseau and Thomas Jefferson, get out

Of bed and meet Bob by noon to have
Mousse au chocolat chez Schrafft's

And be back home in time to hear Fred Flintstone
Give out his mysterious "Yaba-daba-dooo!" wahoo,

As evening settles down in its glorious space
and I shoot down the slide and up, and out

The Impressionists

With a stick he paints the scene

leaves, shadows and sunlight,
an arbor, a nude woman
with a round belly and breasts
wicker chairs, the calm

father in the library polishing his shoes
with German grammar at his elbow
and a group of Italian singers
in his mind's picture

framed in ornate gilt.
Guilt, get it?
        Ruth Roman shot in the back!
And here come the angry miners!
their arms laden with huge chunks of gold
and their teeth shining through clouds
of gnats, great big ones
as big as your Radio City Music Hall

Reading Proust

I am aware of the volume,
the pages, their size and color
and their texture, with edges
and their words set in blocks
surrounded with margins,
And I am aware too of the meaning
of the words and sentences,
the majestic flotilla of the paragraphs
in the flow of the story—I recognize
the characters and remember them
from page to page, and I note
the art of the writing and the quality
of the author's mind, and I see him
writing his book, the words of which
I hear being read aloud to me
by a friend, whom I saw today
and who had stayed in my mind,
offering, while he was there, to perform
this service.

Literal oil flowed across

Then I went on reading

Not

I saw two boys chasing a ball
so small
they couldn't catch it

Everywhere they reached
it was not

And everywhere it was
they were not:

Larry Fagin 670 3128

The Unfinished

The present is terrifying
because it is irrevocable
and made of steel. That
is why a man is
in infinity
with comets and everything
facing the music of the spheres.
On each sphere is written
a different note, and there
are *an infinite number of them.*
See p. 212.
I personally hate music,
the way it enters my ears and I
leap over my bed ever
so sprightly, ever so lightly,
ever so . . . but hark!
All those humans come
pouring over the sound barrier:
Pretty soon Cousin Elvira rips
off her clothes and runs through
the woods, her arms
extended in rapture toward that dazed man,
for her a hero to yearn for,
a man among salt shakers,
and a damn good foreman.

The Day Grows Colder As It Goes into Its Little Metal Container

I sit by the fire station
and think of the stars wheeling
and dealing their pinpoints
and I say, to the Chief,
"Chief, what has happened
to the Indian? What has
happened to the majesty
of monarchy? What has happened to
Ritz soda crackers?" I now
see the alphabet has been
divided, half sent to the moon,
half to Times Square where
monstrously misspelled messages
mix 'mid the matinee mob,
and I say, "Would other things
be happening here, now, if
what is here now weren't here
now?" A small diamond
glitters in the forehead of
a waitress who is my father,
in Hampton Bays, now drifted,
like wood, onto an enormous mantelpiece.

The Magnificent Pilgrims

The sky shines through the pilgrim's hat
a blue sky
with white clouds rolling
the blue American sky
with white clouds rolling

A man gets on a piece of wood
and floats across the sea
where great timbers are waiting
and pine needles hit the ground
like musical notes spilled
from the hand of the Great Musician
in the treetops
Mr. Henry L. Sincere. I
somehow didn't mean that.
I wanted to hear the blue and green breeze
raised in the forest, gently,
to the roar of a lion
bursting into flames

flames sputtering in the campfire

Old Ned turns to Billy and says,
"Billy, pass the mustard."
This is mustard he will spread
on his hot dog—or
frankfurter?—in the yellow light
of the moon. "It's only a
paper moon," the song says.
I always believed that, I always
had to, do you hear me?
An ominous sound fills the chamber
in which only some ghosts

are messing around. They look
like sheets twisting in the air.
Then after a while they freeze
the way water does to make ice cubes,
little pieces of ice that go
into beverages, to melt and make
them cold. I drink such a beverage.
It's a Hawaiian punch. I am in Hawaii.
It's beautiful here.

Havana Heat Wave

Hot and muggers
slink and drool
in murky shadows:
they's cool,

Black shades
and silk shirt
with palm trees
like Burt

Lancaster
in *From*
Here to Eternity.
More glum

Than depressed,
steaming here
half dressed,
cold beer

In the box,
dreamy head
in Dreamsville.
Go to bed,

Go to sleep,
turn away,
ride the breeze
far away.

Disappearing Muffler

Little zones of cold
get mapped up against your
face when you're out
walking in one big cold zone

through which warm
pockets glide—these are cars—
when you were little
you were often inside a car
with the heater going
the outside moving by

now you are moving by on
the outside
a car goes by
white gas from your nose
over your shoulder
a disappearing muffler

Poem

I'm in the house.
It's nice out: warm
sun on cold snow.
First day of spring
or last of winter.
My legs run down
the stairs and out
the door, my top
half here typing

Hula

While I was writing my poem
Patty was doing the crossword puzzle
Hula was the word she got
Plus an all-expense paid trip to Hawaii

Now I live here all alone
A short fat figure made of gray stone
And as the flowers go past my door
I see their shadows move across the floor

The doughnut sings its pretty song
And so does sing the tellyvision
The purple martin flies for fun
The purple martin flies for fun

The purple martin flies for fun
Around the ego's solar system
Which hangs there like an illustration
That we are truly a great nation

Three Animals

THE BUTTERFLY

The butterfly flies up like pow
der to a woman's face
and drifts down
like a woman's face to pow
der

THE ELECTRIC EEL

The electric eel
slides through the water
forming different words as it goes
when it spells
"eel"
it lights up

THE GIRAFFE

The 2 f's
in giraffe
are like
2 giraffes
running through
the word giraffe

The 2 f's
run through giraffe
like 2 giraffes

Ars Prosetica

The novelist was writing a chapter of a novel
And having trouble describing a Haitian girl.
He decided to "throw in the towel."
The Haitian girl picked up the towel
And wrapped it around her body.
But it was time for her bath!
She took the towel and threw it back
To the novelist, who had long since risen
From her chair and left the room, so that
All that was left was a yellow towel,
Rumpled and disordered on the chair.

Bunchberries

How pretty the bunchberries are
and pleasant in sunlight
with their leaves an expanded
green echo of themselves
that came from the sky
this morning.

A rowboat is on the lake
voices carry over
with a dull thud of oar
and wind rising in
the trees over there

I think everything is
intimately connected
touches every other
existent thing simply
by existing also. I
breathe along the path.
You see what I mean.

I see what I mean
but when sent
the messages are
not what they were.
Shades of meaning
flee into the woods.
The woods are full
of meanings darting
in deep gloom. And
out in bright bursts.
Would that some

brightness would
flash through our
universe now so
difficult to understand.

A man is a log
who gets up off
the ground and
breathes. Funny
transformations
send up airy
structures: the
soul is way up there.
But the spirit
is somewhere.
Consciousness
proves something.
The tall grass
moves slightly,
blows away, the tall
log goes up in smoke.

I wish I could tell you
more, bring great
expressive power
to the language
through great power
of thought and intuition
and simple apprehension,
flatten and shine
to reflect what is here
for us without altering
its qualities. The sound
of the typewriter is
part of the afternoon

but one false word
destroys it.
The bunchberries will
still be pretty
but unavailable
to you if you are false.

Poem

The man said
Land ho
but instead
of a whole
continent
it
was only
an island.

Blue ocean
all around.

The natives
beating on coconuts
like crazy.

Sitting Duck

A man in his underpants I am
listening to the ball game on the radio
because it is summer and he is thrown out
at second base, dog is barking, why?
I feel like a fool, sometimes,
not knowing what to do
with myself. I look around
me, there is life which I melt into
like ideas that blend,
such as a man existing and
not existing at the same time.
It's certainly odd. I never noticed
that pipe before, here, on the table
in the library that does not exist
except in my wonderful imagination.
Outside is OK too. So why
not put them together
in some way that would enable you to see
who you are. It would be interesting and significant
in large black letters across the banner
that blazes from every forehead,
so good-bye. I'm going home now.
Thank you for a lovely such . . . er
. . . such a lovely evening.

Arch of Triumph

It certainly is a beautiful night
One of the most romantic I've ever seen
And I want to kiss your lips
Really kiss your lips: stars
are people who have leaped
into light. I am
spilling lemonade on my trousers.
Would you care for some lemonade?
I do wish you would have some.

Disgruntled Man

I brush the hair located on the right side of my head,
I brush it beautifully,
thinking of you. Then
I notice that the hair on the left side
is standing slightly higher than on the
right, and my head appears to be lopsided.
I don't want it to look that way.
So I begin to brush down the left side,
grimly, with a sense of
purpose devoid of pleasure
that drips down the well wall
toward some deep, dark, and cool pool
in which only peace is reflected.

Soon my head is in balance,
but it has become a head brushed for bad reasons
and I do not like the face I see.
A man disgruntled
with the way he brushed his hair.

Haiku

First: five syllables
Second: seven syllables
Third: five syllables

Art Works

Alex Katz, with his sharp taste in clothes, to design a pattern and fabric for pajamas. I would guess he would use silk. To be called "The Katz Pajamas."

*

Jasper Johns to design bathrooms using precious or semiprecious materials such as onyx, jade, and of course jasper.

*

Larry Poons to design spoons—espresso to ladles.

*

Larry Rivers to divert the flow of the St. Lawrence River in some way which will be useful and beautiful as well as religious in function: perhaps a cathedral made entirely of water (there is a Paris métro shop called Château d'Eau).

*

Jim Dine to design a roadside diner with a large neon sign saying DINE. Occasionally the N would flicker and go out, so that passing motorists would think that this sardonic command is related to the cemetery in which the diner is located.

Bad O'Hara Imitation

Palm trees and pyramids
on the boob tube:
Ptolemy (with the p)
is "upset": Cleopatra
is thirsty. We
mustn't give up!
And there they go
staggering across the desert
to some aimless violin music
over which a big blow
begins to . . . to blow.
Or the TV
on the blink? I
close my eyes. It's
all just too terrible!

The Unwobbling Jell-O

Every writer
transcribes his own reality.
His idea of how to write
probably sucks,
because it is boring
and unreal. But it is
his.
    Why
are some
better than others?
Why is Herrick or O'Hara
better than the feverish
rhymster in Del Monte, Pineapple, zap code 11111?

Here in the twenty-first century
we use only the number 1.
But we are welding
a large steel plus sign on
our "Building of Mathematics,"
now complete, ready for occupancy:
all those numbers and concepts
come running toward school,
but at some point they all slow
and fall into a deep sleep,
snoring audibly in the fields of arithmetic. . . .

Shh!
Do not wake their peaceful sleep!
Use stage whispers!
Get your money back!
Hurl tomatoes at the stage!

At this point a tall man with a pointed beard
stood up and stabbed the moderator
with his beard. The moderator
slumped into his chair, a glowing
blue key where his wound was.
This I could not understand!
I have studied fingerprinting
and general sleuthing, you know,
seeing where Mom keeps the kitchen money,
but otherwise I spend most of my time
in the pool hall, learnin' dirty words.

Clue

With the light undisturbed upon his pantleg,
its vertical stripes gray and suave,
his hair parted by a razor's edge,
the glistening intellect apparent in the face
so filled with itself
that gluttony takes on new meaning,
is brought into the psyche
glowing and radiant the way meaning should be
when it isn't in the papers
or in the clichés
that fit so neatly into one's language.

Edna had red lips
and she was an English teacher.
Twelve years down at the high school
and never once had a student made a pass at her.
She was disgusted.
She was almost disgusting,
but near the brink
something pulled us away
and we swerved into her fascination.

Yes, I was enamored of her.

I carried her into my dreams
and out again,
as a plane passing through clouds,
and the clouds trailed from her arms and legs
in one long sweeping rapture. . . .

But back to the pantleg. My God!
There is a shot!
A gunshot has rung out!

. . . The world's population rises
to its feet, gasping and groaning.
The red blood flows forth from every nation,
down the face, drips
off the tip of the nose,
stared at by crossed eyes,
onto the pantleg. Thud,
the murder weapon falls to the floor.
A gloved hand reaches for the doorknob.
It is the Easter Bunny!

Or a man dressed up in an Easter Bunny costume.
He is dead drunk, festive, gyroscopic.
"Where's that Carrot?" he slurs out.
Blue and yellow stars appear.
You are ten years old, earth-time.

Ode to Uncle Edgar

If bugs left a black line behind them
everywhere they went,
New York City would be a mass
of lines zigzagging back and forth
into a snarl.
                    The nose and mouth
of the man in the cartoon
form a snarl
in black ink
you can smell with your nose
and taste with your mouth,
ugh, snarl!
                    Uncle Edgar threw down the funnies
and stomped into the house. The afternoon
heat had gotten to him, he would
rage and froth and then go up to bed,
where he wrote in his diary,
the one we stole, remember?
The funny thing was that his diary
had just ordinary stuff in it,
no reflection of the stormy days we passed,
with flames leaping from our ears
and thermometers exploding in the hinterlands
with kangaroos lit up in the glare
and a pretty good feeling about how good
it was to be alive. So.
What do you want to talk about now?
I hate you,
because you never have any opinions on anything.
You just sit there chewing gum
and pretending you're William Bendix.
Well, you're not William Bendix!
I am William Bendix!

I didn't know how to tell you,
because I didn't know who you were
or how you got here, you were primordial,
you were black flames, you were a spirit creature,
and I kept running into fenceposts.
Every few steps I'd bang into another one.
I just didn't know what was going on.
And I never have understood that afternoon,
the time the tree bent down and spoke to me
just as I told you I loved you with all my heart,
and it was true, I do.
May I sit down now and watch the lemonade
in the sunset, with my serenity and my hunting horn,
O vivid dachshund!
O ancestry!

Silverware Attitudes, a Sketch

to my mother

Light beige, silver & gray
ladies sit in felt or plumed hats
in the department store tea room
1948
lady chatter
among floating veils
and silver shafts of light through powder blue
the pale green check
among clattering Depression ware and spoons
whose polished surfaces
reflect a fashionable moment
in the world's history

Sestina

Tonight
love
flies
through
blue
air.

Air
tonight,
blue
love
through
flies

flies!
(Air
through
tonight,
love
blue!)

Blue
flies
love
air
tonight.
Through,

through
blue
tonight
flies

air,
love.

Love,
through
air
blue
flies
tonight.

Tonight love flies
through blue air.

Questions and Answers

What is a question?
It is a sentence in an interrogative form
addressed to someone to get information in reply.
That is the answer to that question.
An answer is a spoken or written reply to a question.

Poem

Patty's big belly's
so soft, so round, so inviting,
where, like a pillow
on a bed, I
place my head:
deep gurgling!
human body!
human bodies!
I confess I don't care
that I don't understand:
it's too late at night
to understand anything.

Saturday

Once upon a time
when I was knee-
high to a gnat's bristle,
I'd go Saturday mornings up
to the Royal Theatre on 11th near Columbia in Tulsa
to see the double-featured battle of the then-great two Western stars,
Roy Rogers and Gene Autry.

Then Saturday
night out at the Fairgrounds
it was the "Battle of the Bands,"
Johnny Lee Wills and his band and
Leon McAuliffe and his band and
each band would play a number,
alternating all night.

Thing is, if you draw a dotted line
between Roy Rogers and Johnny Lee Wills and
one between Gene Autry and Leon McAuliffe . . .
and then lines between Rogers and McAuliffe and
Autry and Wills. . . .

Something or Other

The open-mouthed quail
while the closed-mouth stomp
along a runway of Declarations of Independence
and you burst into flight

and burst into song.
Oh, this person is going to die.

There is a separation
between life and death
where flowers grow

and that is where I want to go
this weekend,

to forget about my assignments
and my horn-rimmed glasses which fall repeatedly to the floor.
O give me the ambiguity of a table
resurrected from the tree
sawn down by a lantern-jawed fellow
named John, John Something or Other.

Blue Pickup

I have to go to the bathroom,
sort of. The electric lines
quiver in the afternoon.
The snow on the hill across
goes gray, its trees
a deeper green, sky white.
Then light yellow rolls across
right to left and branches
stand out, like . . . branches.
That's what they are. I'm
sitting at a wooden table
with a worried look on my
forehead. A jade
Ford just went by.
Several minutes pass.
Absolutely nothing happens.
Now a buff Plymouth and a long
silence. Soft russet
and fuzzy smoke drift
along the ridge where
birch and pine are deep
in mist. I think of Jimmy
Schuyler and the plastic weatherproofing
ripples in the windowframe.
All those branches are moving!
like power lines surging
with dark secrets, dark as
gunpowder, liquid as smoke
gliding down valleys,
itchy as a beard on a soft
breast. O soft breast!
O delicate soul! O
wait a minute. A blue
pickup whines past.

The Muse

Do you know about
the little feller with a bandage
on his image of himself,
later elevated in a statue
of an enormous bandage
in gray concrete
and with the stern, theoretical blessings
of Amédée Ozenfant?

And what about the chocolate, bread, and oranges
on the latticed patio
with bright slits of light
across the back and shoulders
of the most beautiful, sophisticated,

naive young woman you have ever seen?
She is lovely, she rises.
Her look falls into the very depths
of some swimming pool in your heart
and it takes your breath away.
It takes your breath away.

¡My Spinach!

My spinach runs over the land.
It flees the crimson tide,
brutal *padrones* who crack their cigars
over you and the night sky rumbles.

My spinach runs over the land.
It bangs on the poll booths
with dark green fists.
Inside, the young girls
are being raped by gorillas.

My spinach runs over the land.
It darts into the public library
to read the history in books.
The pages are hard to turn
and soon are covered with sand.

My spinach runs over the land.
It cries out, *"¡Liberación!"*
to the wind. Bits of the word
tear away into the wind. Bits
of word that later sunbathe
watching the crimson tide roll in.

19_

The tips of my fingers
& a band around my ankles
are cold tonight
it's cold outside
late fall and early winter
(November 9th)
air outside
cold, clear & stationary
it just sits outside
like the blue envelope
of an airmail letter
in the baggage hold of a jet
at 56,000 ft
its contents words
written on a piece of paper
from one person to another
the way winter is its own letter
to next winter, connected thus

Poem

No sir!
Trade places with an animal?
Have a muskrat read my books
while I scuttle through the woods in terror?

Ode to Horace

I was dancing with Matilda,
a big fat woman in a purple polka-dotted dress and a white bandana
with the straw in the loft flickering in the lantern light
and the fiddlers laid back into the softness of their exhaustion
and a chorus of cats on the fence yowling in the crescent moonlight,
then did I take this great fat woman
and squeeze her with all my might,
gritting my teeth with a grimace on my face and sweat beads on my
    visage and agony in my countenance,
squeeze her until the silver stars in heaven above
sent down their silver dust
to drape the ambiance with a veil of 'forties sleepiness,
O Horace!
I shall return to thee
when gentle snows have settled on my head
and I am catching pneumonia, can't you
shut that window you imbecile! Can't you see I'm freezing to death?!
I don't know why I even let you in the house!
The angry woman grasped at her throat
to keep control, and as she looked about the empty room
she heard nothing but the box of wooden dogfood
fall and hit the floor, its contents rattling.
Silence fell on the floor

and broke it into a jillion noisy little pieces
that exploded in revenge, even they
can seek their liberation!
                                        A zen monk
sits in zazen . . . a tremor of fear . . .
maybe that ten-ton truck will not run over him!
Of course there is no such truck where he is,
in a helicopter, but the truck is real
in his meditation. His face is mashed flat.

Silence falls on the moon
where a heterosexual is putting his foot for the first time in the
history of the universe!
But couldn't this have all happened before?
So?
We are just here, now, and the sooner we realize it
the more real it will be. "Give
me a regular coffee to go." A woman swivels
to hand you an unnaturally light container
in which some dark liquid has been deposited.
This will not do. You need religion.

Ode to God

I sincerely believe I am running toward the great house of God.
It is a large and stately mansion at the end of the avenue
lined with large blue and green lemons
squirting blood onto the nearby local enigma, a cage
in which sits a rubber effigy of Albert Einstein,
his hair wild waving rubber strands periodically attacked
by large electronic rubber bands. He came
not to condemn the world, but to buy a war bonnet
and place it on the head at the top of his body,
with nice shoes on his feet, too. But taking up
where we left off, sometimes the voltage will lag
or lead, creating a phase displacement between the waves.
Large plastic fishes float among the waves, asleep.
One of them is named "Grandpa," because he carries a cane
and is a fish most advanced in age. And a dolphin goes by
several inches from your nose, which is out of phase
with the rest of your face. Or perhaps the rest of your face
really had been assembled from various replacement parts:
composite you are designated. Which proves there is
a resurrection. Apollinaire died and the Eiffel Tower
rose before he did. It's all over, and

I'm having a little trouble
finding even the clouds that befuddle my feeble noodle,
like a man called Fudd, Elmer the given name,
could not even understand what country he was in.
He did not even have the sense to ask, politely,
of the cartoonist, "Excuse me, could you tell me
the name of this comic strip I am in, and after that,
the comic strip you are in?" The cartoonist is filled with rage,
he calls his compatriots and together
they rip that cartoon character limb from limb. . . .
But he lives on in the universe, his spirit

having changed the nature of everything, down
to the smallest nuclear dot; the dots are dancing
to the clarinet music of Harlem in the 'thirties.
They shook their bodies and rattled their bones
and when they rolled up seven it all clicked,
they understood, so clearly, that they were destined
to be blessed by God so as to win this $115.
That night you blew it on some dames, just blew
the living hell out of it, blasted it back to dots.

Symbols of Transformation

The yellows and creams
blaze a little brighter
when you get older;
the blue-gray of the office furniture
doesn't look so bad.
The details are different
because you are Grandma Moses:
the cows come right up
into your face and moo,
sunlight pours out of a large hole
and the trees are toothpicks
and it's okay like this, it's
a little
like staring at yourself
in a funhouse mirror: your body
has melted into your shoes
and your neck extends into a curve in time-space
and the flashbulb pops,
the graduates heave a sigh of relief
and their mortarboards
into the backseat.
Driving home, you watched
the streetlights flash on the seat covers
and when you pulled into the driveway
it wasn't Mom and Dad who got out of the car,
but two large goats.

"Now Hear This

A lady I know—now, you won't believe this—
can actually . . . uh, you see,
this dame's a contortionist and she"
snore. I think
that bald-headed imbecile's idea of
humor sucks. I crosshatch him
with slashing black lines. He smiles weakly
and fades into comic book history,
forever the same, Bugs McGee.
Back at the Civil War,
Colonel Robert E. Lee is waiting
at the levee, his chest thrust out,
his gray pantalooned leg pointed with light glints,
his ineffable self cloudy among wisps of glory.

1876

"To whom
Do I have the honor of speaking?
What is your name, sir?
Can you not reply?
Are you in some sort of distress?
Sir, I say, sir. . . ."

The wooden Indian stared straight ahead
With a fistful of cigars
And one in his mouth,
Smoke rising from the ash. . . .

"I say, sir,
What kind of cigar is that,
Exactly? It must be mighty good
For you to smoke it like that.
I sure would like to get me
One of those very fine cigars."

The Indian swivelled his rough eyes
Onto the gentleman in white
With white hat and white mustache
Curling out from beneath his nose
With those two mammoth nostrils
Like caves a foul wind blows from
With a blast of snot and a hail of boogers.

"White man," he said
With his terrible jaw moving,
"Go and move across the prairie
To the ocean where the great sun rises,
Go unto the very sea and plunge
Your head into the ground.

Then will be given unto you
A great vision, a blaze of red
Inside whose essence a revelation
Will spill out of the everlasting ketchup."

Hector Airways

The wing of the Berlioz airliner lifted an entire generation into the sky
and they stayed up there, transparent,
risible, quite large. And
Elda brought in the tea
and left again, her black and white
uniform disappearing through the evening shrubbery.
Where she was going
no man could tell, though the lonesome howl
of the buffalo could be heard among the skeletons,
and Abner spit in his sleep
onto his toe. In the morning he arose,
and on the third day he wept. Cried
bitter tears. Made lamentation unto the
milkshakes, and stuck straw into his
underwear. He made an admirable
haystack, sunset in the redness over
town, with the hardware store just closing,
the tools spiritual in their solitude.
It is night and America sleeps.
Everyone in America is asleep, like Bud and Mary Sue,
even Victor the dachshund is asleep,
with his funny eyes, ha ha!
Everyone, that is, except
a man in a gray flannel bathing suit,
his silhouette carved against the masonry
by a floodlight and
his eyes filled with smoke, the smoke
filled with dice
all rolling up snake-eyes.
Definitely a character
to keep in fiction so he won't actually
walk in your house some day
and ask for a room of his own.

What My Desk Said

"I don't know.
I don't know when my grain will shift.
Perhaps it will eventually reveal something
essential, such as how much canned
cherries sell for, the 16 oz. size,
or perhaps present us
with an image of a Christmas tree.
A tree glowing in an old-fashioned way,
the way they looked before fluorescent
and mercury vapor lamps. The light was creamy
and it made you feel good. Just sitting
in the grass under the trees and hearing
the stars in the trees as they shed
their lonely shafts of light.
These shafts are larger than anything
you are able to imagine, earthling.
So go back to the second grade,
you are in China, there is a prehistoric dust
on everything because it is in prehistory,
yes a prehistoric second-grade class.
All the students are little Chinese cave boys,
grunting and hurling rocks at one another,
their teacher a small red rock.
The students were so stupid
they did not distinguish between rock and man.
They were in very poor shape. A meteor shower
had driven them out of their minds
and into mine, where mint is growing,
and large cardboard boxes stand in the fields.
It is late afternoon. Inside every box
is the same refrigerator: the ice age
is coming. These refrigerators were sent
as a warning, by a very bizarre force,

one I do not quite understand. My brain is weak.
I am feeble. My electrons are nervous.
I open the electrons of my mouth and speak
to the raving populace. Below me
they stagger and sway like a mass of lunatics,
which is what most of them are,
human flutes with holes being jabbed into them,
ouch! A bar of sound
has banged off my top,
which is flat like the books of the humans."
This is what my desk said to me
as I sat and watched it. Then it said
goodnight and went to sleep.

March Slav

About 1:15
I looked out the window
and walked out the door
to where the snow had begun to fall.
For a while the flakes were thin.
They disappeared as they hit the ground.
Later they formed a light haze on the ground
but continued to disappear against the pavement.
As the temperature fell
the snow came down harder
though terribly soft
and thick, and quiet
and then thinned out
around 8 o'clock: by then
it lay in white lines along the tops of branches,
in patches on car tops and hoods,
in perfect quadrilaterals on lawns and roofs,
in fuzzy melting clusters on hats and heads,
some random bits in mustaches and beards.
It is pitch black out
with a steel blue undertone and some mercury
lights over there behind the railroad tracks.
Over my left shoulder the lamp shines down
on the grooves of Walter Gieseking
playing Mozart's complete music for solo piano.
The notes fall from the sheet music
onto the piano keys as easily
as a man breathing and smoking without thinking
as he looks at the snow come down
or words come up from out of the typewriter
and onto the page, O blancheur! which I guess
is now likely to be thought of as comparable to
you guessed it snow. I wish all this didn't tie in

so well. I'd prefer to have the snow
just fall outdoors, with me looking at it,
and you upstairs looking at it, and you
in your car behind windshield wipers looking,
the beams of light hitting the flakes with their own little stardom,
the old people who stare out the window
and say bah when it snows, as it is now, again;
the kids who go running outside with their tongues out
to catch the snow and roll in it and be made cold,
so they can come back in and stomp the floor
and lay their wet gloves by the fire;
the mayor who is about to be returned to private life
as he compares his fate to the snow, pristine and pure
one day and gone the next,
the snow that falls on the grave of, say, Walt Whitman,
or on the hands of Walter Gieseking, or
on the sheet of music dropped by the anxious girl
who adjusted her muffler at the stoplight
and went on across: the man who saw her drop the music
with something on his mind, and snow gathering on his head.
Soon it would melt, and there was always
the horrifying possibility that it would freeze there,
his head wearing a frozen cap of snow and ice
like the face of the earth
when it tilts forward to show you the Arctic Circle,
you who are your own cold blue white round self,
big snowball in space so pure,
perfect sphere secure in gravitational pull.

Poem

Little hairs
are growing
on the bottom part
of my face
from the ears
to the upper lip
all over the jaw
and down the neck:
it is a beard.

The wind blows
over the hill
where clouds
have sun behind
and through them.
Rain drips
from the roof
into puddles
on the ground.

That is all ye
need to know.

TRIANGLES IN THE AFTERNOON

Early Triangles

Can you feel the swell—
or is there one?—
of something vast & wonderful
coming over America?
Or is that just the glow
of lights from Montpelier?
I stood out in the woods
and spoke to the trees with their leaves,
and they answered back. They said,
"Jerome, Jerome,
return to your village."
I did so, and began
to lick postage stamps.
Red ones and green ones, some
with pink and yellow,
delicate triangles in the afternoon.

High Heels

I have a vision
in my head of Cubism
and Constructivism
in all their artistic purity
joined with a decorative attractiveness
that exceeds deliciousness,
even more to be desired
than becoming a milkman
in a white suit and hat
delivering milk to the back door
of a white frame house
on a street lined with elms
and being invited inside
by the curvaceous, translucent lady
of the house, not once
but many times, too many times,
perhaps, for later her husband
will be coming home
with a sledgehammer in his hand,
the pink hand with light blue fingernails, oh
you have colored the wrong picture!
You were to put the pink and blue
on the beachball on the next page.

Red Bendix

A red Bendix
belts out its great aria
into the afternoon's great area
little birds fly through
and around in, they
are blue and it is summer,
you lie in a white crib
with the sun on your face: this
is not a photograph, it is
not a memory, it is
something that really happened,
and when you see it that way
it is happening again
inside your mind. Inside your mind
the outside of your mind
seems very pleasant, but
as you home in on the center
it gets dark and there is
something there, something
utterly horrible!

The Story of Roscoe

Onward to a new personality, whoopee!
Give me some Cheez-Its in their red and yellow box,
their square orange selves inert inside the box. . . .
I salute them!
Especially the broken chips and desultory fragments
that lie sprinkled over the archeological ruins.
A painter is brushing in some white clouds
and the view is filled with steam. An
elderly gentleman from Scotland fought his way
through the dense fog, waving a cane.
Beside him stood a fantasy that was running down:
the image slowed and faded quietly. . . .
Night fell over Moonville,
a black wedge on which three large stars glimmered
and a crescent moon shone brightly
and the people of the little land stood up
squealing "Hosannah!" in their beds,
hundreds of nightcap tassels swaying in the breeze.

Yes, but must I trivialize
in this fashion,
must I bang the typewriter against your head,
O bust of Verisimilitude?
Must I crank the couches over the wall in one swift motion?
Must I join a football team
and score the winning touchdown?
Must I tear my hair out by its roots
and mail it to Havana, Cuba?
Must I gnaw on the bone of contention
that seesaws in the morning light?
Must I baffle my eternity into being
by unscrewing language from the wall?
Must I submit a self-addressed, stamped envelope?

Must I hurl Herbert Hoover
off the pier at Atlantic City?
"These are questions which are not easily answered, Roscoe.
Why don't you come sit down over here in the shade
And rest awhile, with the shade spread on the ground,
And birds that ride the branches in the gentle swaying,
And stay to dinner."
                                        The kindly old man laid his hand
on the ground and went into the house
where his wife was hiding. Roscoe slipped
into an ice cube and slid down an inclined plane
that had begun years ago and would finish in a few minutes,
for Fate had run out of carbon paper
and no more copies would be made today.
It was now or never, let me say it
was both now and never in which young Roscoe dreamed his dream,
and like the butterfly in the Zen parable
woke surrounded by flames: someone
had carelessly tossed a match onto the ground
and those darned leaves had caught fire.
The flames danced like extras in a Haitian film
that ends with a big green and yellow sunset trees
wave good-bye in and you leave the theater
no better or worse than you were, but not the same.

Cufflinks

I am brother to the frankfurter
Not brother literally of course
That would be silly
To propose myself as such
What I mean is metaphoric
I am brother to the frankfurter
I place the frankfurter on a plate
And it is gone and I am
One frankfurter larger

The frankfurter has fallen from heaven
Onto evil days
It rode serene in its clouds
It gave off light
It was universally admired
It was like Adam and Eve combined
But a great chicken entered the factory
And shook its body in outrage
Bellowing, "Why am I excluded? Why? Why?"
And it rammed its head through the factory roof
And aimed its beady eye at the heavens—
"Goodness!" cried the clouds tearing apart
And since then there has been a great chicken in the way of all this
So that now I am brother to the chicken too
Via the frankfurter

In Frankfort the Frankforters rise
And commit their terror-stricken deeds
And return to their homes in the evening and bolt the door
Against the plastic chickens
That stagger through the night there
Pecking and acting irrational

(I don't seem to have a very well thought-out philosophy,
in fact I have never made a sustained effort

to systematize my various fleeting ideas on the Big Issues.
Not that any such systemization would have to be an ultimate one,
in fact the first premise would disallow any such finality;
to set my ideas in order would simply allow me to see
how they look placed side by side one after the other:
they would, like optical illusions, change
before my "very" eyes. My not having done this
perplexes me and then sends me into a bona fide gloom:
perhaps I am as frivolous and idiotic as I say I am
when I wish my listener to insist on the opposite, which,
thanks to social form or a desire to please,
he does, she does
the laundry and billows of soft foam float out the door
onto the sidewalk and into the street. I think
to myself, "That's the cleanest the street's been
since it was liquid itself." The optimism required
for such an outré observation goes hand in hand
with the most Protestant—if you will—sense of propriety
which I possess to the extreme, while, paradoxically,
scorning Duty as a mechanistic ethos foisted on us
by fingers that wield lingering wisps of smoke only.
Making the best of it, stoical but efficient,
that's me, and efficient might mean one thing today
and another tomorrow because it's emotional as well as anything else
and this is commendable, come to think of it,
though dangerously near to opportunistic.
But right now I don't know where to take this line of thinking
and I'm thinking you might be getting bored with this first person.
Let me switch to an earlier train of thought involving the unconscious.
Everybody shares the unconscious whereas everybody isn't me, I
am my own particular self sitting here more isolated than I thought humanly
    possible—writing this poem has isolated me.
As for the unconscious, I have an inexhaustable source of images there.
                                                                                Donald
Duck flies through the trees under a sky of exploding dirigibles.
"My goodness," he squawks, "what a hostile environment!" Etc.
I can tune in so precisely to my own thoughts

that they are in perfect focus, no fuzz,
but I cannot for the life of me trace them
all the way back to their origin. So for me
they appear from what appears to be nowhere, a point
of origin that in effect does not exist.
I would like very much to be able to go
back through that point and into

nuts? Maybe I'd go nuts!
It's a challenge. One night walking home
from a poker game about 5 a.m.
I noticed a prostitute strolling along the other side
of the street. No one on the street but us. The sun
would rise in thirty minutes. She was
unbelievably attractive: sleek, slender, young, beautifully dressed
with a long wool skirt that buttoned up the front, and she was
chocolate. I found it hard to believe she was a whore
yet she was, unmistakably—a man in a car
pulled up to the curb and discussed some matters with her,
then drove away. I thought, "What if she approaches me?
How would I justify my refusal? No money? Tired?"
It was a challenge I couldn't meet. The heart
has so much courage and then some but no more.
I look into my heart from time to time. I am clever
but basically honest, actually a shy person
who's afraid of having his feelings hurt
or pride wounded, in other words a person
whose self-image, that of a minor, is essentially correct.
But I have a strongly developed sense of Beauty
and I am touched by Beauty when I sense it
though I feel I have never once been able to use an experience of Beauty
in my own attempts to create it: it's as if
I'm alone, no poetry or art ever existed, no
vast and dazzling vista of some foreign strand,
no uplifting experience communicated to me in any way,
as if the entire weight of the Cosmos

were on my fragile shoulders
and some powerful fingers were poised
above a Grand piano for a final, devastating chord.
I see the fingernails, clear and clean and fine
and the cufflinks: on them written in script
the word "cufflink."

But you never can tell
what might happen.
Jean-Baptiste Marie Alouette François-Jones
might be born any minute
to Mr. and Mrs. Arturo-Torres Helen Kafka
who are riding across the night sky
on shafts of silver light. Their
spurs jangle and glint like spurs
in the immensity of space. Is space
immense? Or is it vast?
Here today to discuss the question
is Mrs. Arturo-Torres Helen Kafka.
Madame, uh
where is she? She was sitting here
in this chair
uh
who took
that chair?
You will be italicized
like the tops of mountains that slowly crumble and slide
along the sides of their immensity: you
are far below, not yet italicized, watching the spectacle
with an excellent pair of Zeiss field glasses
which you stole from the Spanish ambassador this morning.
Consequently he was unable to locate his breakfast.
I mean, you might think it peculiar,
as indeed it is, I'll grant you that,
but the ambassador likes to have his breakfast
served on a tray several thousand yards from the villa,

so he can track it down like a wild animal
and blow it to pieces. So without the field glasses . . .
. . . meanwhile the broken rocks continued to fall
followed by night: you hear the great rocks
pounding out some symphony that would have sent
Bizet screaming up through the earth, for the darkness
is a metaphor for modern man's existential dilemma.
The first thing I think of in the morning is
"Good God, another day! Incredible!"
And I dive whistling a merry tune into my clothes
and burst onto the street with a radiant smile
and an irrepressible air of joy and exultant optimism.
Passersby mumble into their English muffins,
"Doesn't he know about modern man's existential dilemma?
Doesn't he realize the rocks are falling?" They turn
away and step into massive piles of dog dood.
Now they are really pissed off. Some leap right
out of their shoes and run down the street in their stockings.
The shoes scrape themselves off and plod onward
toward work. The elevator is filled with empty shoes.
All over the busy metropolis
the shoes are trodding, trodding,
they are leaving the offices and stores,
the tiny pink ones in kindergartens
and the clodhoppers at construction sites,
the terrifying white numbers stream from the hospitals,
the scuffed pumps from the thrift shop, plate-glass windows
kicked out by shoes escaping from the shoe store, all
heading along waves of force
to where a rock the size of a . . . what? ball?
is lying on the ground. Next to it
stands Mrs. Arturo-Torres Helen Kafka
as the shoes walk in and pile up
like goofy teenagers at a campus pep rally
forty years ago, about the time Mrs. Kafka
would have been a College Jill herself. Now

she gestures to the throng and they fall silent.
What will happen?
I don't know.
From a great green rent
in the sky a bright yellow bolt
of lightning strikes the stone
and when the smoke is fanned away
the shoelaces have come untied,
a massive spaghetti-like confusion
surrounds the serenity of the stone.
The stone is immobile.
It does not move.
It does not change.
It is not Chinese.
It is not mysterious.
It is not pretty.
It is not a stone.

Mrs. Kafka is growing restive,
she pokes it with a small manual thunderbolt,
breaking the point off,
leaving a broken yellow thunderbolt in her Mrs. Kafka hand,
the hand of the Statue of Liberty.
She turns her head to gaze
through the green and dark brown woods
where sunlight sets its shafts into the water
and rocks look happy with the water rolling
around and over their bald stationary heads.
Far along back up the stream
some trees dart into the darker woods
at the sound of an approaching human step.
You could not outrun a deer,
how do you expect to catch a tree?
Don't feel too bad, friend,
nature moves in mysterious and wonderful ways,
such as the boulder that crushed a stick last summer.

Or is that the right word, "stick?"
That is your code word.
                                        (A crowd
of onlookers approached the befuddled teenager.
"Speak!" they commanded.
"My name is Rodney Harlem, I live at 2254 Willow Drive
here in Beverly Hills, I have a sister, sane
enough to pass a driving test, who calls herself
Beverly Hills, and when the morning sunlight hits
Beverly Hills and Beverly oh Beverly
kiss me darling as I melt into the fading sunset
all red and orange and like rivers of good-bye
saying hello to our departing greeting. . . ."
Here the Club members grew restive. Benjamin Franklin
pounded on his knee and rose to speak.
It was as though all Philadelphia
were suddenly shrouded in silence.
Only the quill of the secretary
could be heard by a fly which had landed
on the head of Benjamin Franklin's daughter
who was the secretary. "Gentlemen,"
he began, and the members of the Philosophical Society
leaned forward and craned their necks,
"you resemble a flock of cranes
bursting into slow flames
across the wall of the Stork Club
in New York," and the volleys and salvos
of laughter that rocked the old brick cradle
of American tradition could be heard
all the way to the face of Ralph Waldo
Beverly, a stagehand
who barely spoke because his mouth has been removed
by a special process I am not at liberty
to disclose: liberty
is subject to wild variations.
It takes "longer" to walk down a new and interesting street.

It takes three times longer
to walk down two new and interesting streets, etc.
But when we sit at home alone facing the same view as ever
we might easily find ourselves free-floating toward
what we have the courage to call eternity. At other times
we forget all about the whole thing and zip
presto it's gone. The variousness of time
gives it an elusiveness that exceeds the mercurial
shifting of, well, just about anything you want to name.
Even great mountains change their height. And
planets in their distant, lovely flight. And
future-removing dynamite.
The French quote Heraclitus as saying, "On
ne se baigne pas deux fois dans la même fleuve,"
which translated literally reads, "One
does not bathe twice in the same river."
In English I have heard, "One
does not step twice in the same stream."
Let us examine the troubling discrepancy
between the French and Anglo-American interpretations,
without reference, damnit, to the Greek.
The Frenchman bathes while the Anglo-American steps,
the former in a river, the latter in a stream.
One is so useful, a participant, the
other so aesthetic, like a daintily turned ankle
placed just so by a passing cloud.
That cloud! Hey, cloud! It's
the cloud
that poets of the English language love.
It floats gray and free above
and below an all-pervading blue,
bright and perfectly extended, and
your brain is understanding:
my two-hundred-mile-long dark-haired reclining flying lady,
it was you I imaged as a youth,
trodding o'er hill and dale, striding

straight through mountains into math homework.
And dusting the venetian blinds.
The simplest problem consisted
of whether to buy paper with two
holes or three. I thought
people who bought two-ring paper were mad.
It fitted less neatly into one's notebook,
and if one hole tore loose, the entire sheet would slip out
and dangle in a most disagreeable way,
in need of ring reinforcers.
Yes, I went through school
inside a cardboard box: graduation
was your own present you burst out of

into what seemed an absolute liberation: you in socks,
the kitchen floors of the world suddenly waxed
and placed before you end to end, extending past the moon,
icebox doors flung open to light your way through space.

As the years passed, you found yourself
stopping for a midnight snack: Dagwood
sandwich here, cold chicken leg there.
Why is there no meal so satisfying as the midnight snack?
How is it that you can recognize
the chicken leg at midnight?
Because after years of reading Classics
of the Humanities and Philosophy, each
volume at exactly 72 degrees under a light rain,
you find they form a chicken leg
that left some distant planet the day you were born.

And they're off.
Small green horse is taking the lead
with blue and red horses in second,
black third and orange off to a poor start
with white left at the gate.

Into the near turn it's still green
followed closely by bed and red
with black moving up fast on the outside,
orange in fifth. Coming into the backstretch
it's red moving up fast on the outside, it's red
and green neck and neck, it's Christmas
it's red and green along the tablecloth,
red and green, with blue third and black
moving up. They're going into the far
turn with red leading by a head and green
second, black is moving up along the outside,
followed by white nine lengths back
and orange fifteen. Into the home turn it's
red by a length, green and black followed by
a pack of wolfhounds—get those dogs off the track!
The picture freezes here/
The camera draws back to reveal a man
beside the screen, hair cut short and a pointer
in his hand. "Nine out of ten dogs prefer
Doggy Dogfood. Tests show—" and here he tapped the screen
with his pointer—the screen fell to the
floor with an awful clatter. On it the track
was bent into unrecognizable shapes.
Picasso smiled and approached his canvas.
It is 1908. He will paint
a great picture. He will paint several. He will paint
paint paint! Many bad pictures also.
But the public will hail him as a genius,
an artistic genius who walks around in his underwear
with dark eyes that say everything and nothing.
It would be embarrassing to ask him what he means
by that look of his. I would like
to ask him a few questions. "Mr. Picasso,
excuse me. I know your time is precious
but our studio audience is wondering:
What's with the 'Ruiz'? Are you really as solid as you appear?

Did you ever learn enough French
to have any idea of what people were saying around you?
And why did you ruin the horse race???"
Eyes back to the screen—it is sixty-five
years later—it has been magically restored
and is suddenly set in motion! It's red
by a length, green and black are closing,
with . . . hey! orange and white have streaked
ahead in a blur, with blue, a gray blur,
even now with black and green and now with red,
it's the entire field moving neck and neck,
across the bright explosion
forming a stymie.
The judges study the photograph and knit
their brows with first-class yarn: those foreheads
will come in handy when winter comes.
But one has come loose, a thread is dangling.
One of the other judges notices it. Unconsciously
he reaches up and tugs at it, slowly unraveling the forehead
until nothing is left but
a bright idea in a bright emptiness,
a photo finish.

Sambo

Buddy, can you spare a
continent, like Africa,
where the natives
jitterbug around the trees
and turn into illustrations
in a children's book
(Hachette, 1933)

Postcard

It is not easy writing
someone a postcard.
The size and shape
of the card cut you
down to size, a
pygmy, with little pink
flowers on you; then
there is the picture
of, perhaps, a kangaroo
dressed in a tuxedo
in a violently blue room,
or maybe just a smoking
cigarette and a woman's
hand, and a woman's face,
and they rise to dance
into the sparkling evening
with bananas rhumbaing
on the veranda, darling.
Now what do you say to that?
How can your message
have anything to do with
that!
        But
you take pen in hand,
bend over the card,
and write, "Dear Kenward."

Ode to Poland

It is embarrassingly true
that you don't begin to die
until you begin to live,
embarrassing because it is a truism
uttered by big fat idiots.
I am a thin person, myself,

seeing the golden sunlight
of sunset radiant against red bricks
that appear quite ordinary, too,
lifting me out of my shoes and into some real
or imaginary sense of the Eternal

as I turn into the New First Avenue Bakery
where the girl is saying, "At home
our manners have to be perfect, I
have to set the table just so,"
the light on the buildings set just so

and Intellect extending its puny arms
toward some greatness of cognition—
only to have the proverbial bully
of Mystery kick sand in its face.

Back home I pound on the table,
knocking a lamp into the air sideways.
Straight lines appear in the air
around the lamp as it falls.
These are they.

Poem

When you get out of the shower
in 1932
Los Angeles
is gleaming with light,
a shiny modern city surrounded
by groves of lovely oranges,
and as you reach for the towel
a cloud of dust is rising
and I have been wondering,
which part of your body do you dry first?

After Lorca

Pink paper with blue lines
very nice

blue sky with big white clouds
very pretty

Face with big smile
very interesting

Why this smile?
Why are you smiling?

Blue paper with big white clouds
very nice

pink sky with blue lines
very pretty

Ode to Bohemians

1.

The stars at night
Are big and bright
The moon above
A pale blue dove

The trees bent out
By windy shout
Of West Wind god
And the soldiers bolted from their ranks

—Did they O did they?—

And spilled across the countryside,
ants escaping some ant doom,
the final trumpet from the god of ant death. . . .

while their wives were waiting in the kitchen doorway
in red aprons and yellow bandanas,
really beautiful little black ants. . . .

2.

Two eyes bulging out with red lines
and rolling upon the ground . . .
all the better to see you with,
microscopic weakling!
You rush below the microscopes of government,
the government of Russia, the government of the U.S.A.,
the horrible governments of Argentina and Brazil, the suspicious
governments of Greece, Venezuela, and Turkey,
the governments strong and weak, a few weird bigshots

making you eat dirt and like it, buddy.
For me, I say "Fuck it."
I have a glass of red wine
and a beret upon my head,
I am tipsy in Montmartre,
my smock smeared with paint
and the lipstick of script girls,
and I salute zees life I lead,
O happy vagabond! O stalwart bohemian,
defying the ordinary rules of society
to express your inner self,
to tell those callous motherfuckers
what it's like, to achieve
the highest glory of man
and then sink back in its clouds
never to be seen again, like strange celebrities
whose caricatures grow dim and fade
from the pages of memory. Thank you, anyway,
you colorful individuals.

Song

Little violet,
all alone,
stem curved,
quiet zone.

Little snowdrops,
clustered, white,
patchy ground,
frozen night.

Little hawkweed,
casual, fierce,
sunny friend,
I like you.

Little daisy,
meadow's edge,
loose wind,
the world a stage.

Black-eyed Susan,
Spanish lass,
drowsy gestures,
long eyelash.

Gentian yodel,
clear blue,
dignified,
gentle lake.

Wild rose,
"I don't care,"
you're nonchalant,
crimson flare.

Pink clover,
home for tea,
do come in,
be like me.

Goldenrod,
drift in breeze,
catch a nose,
make it sneeze.

Daffodil,
crazy duck,
trumpet searching,
nice colors.

Velvet pansy,
ruffled cheeks,
jets of jet,
lie down on me.

Clean geranium,
nurse's aid,
red and green,
bills are paid.

Buttercup!
of yellow butter,
chubby kid,
just like his mother.

Blue Bananas

First came Patchen,
then Ferlinghetti,
the giraffe has a long neck,
I live in a house.
It is warm in the rooms and cold out,
but they cannot utter a sound
and you have a big mouth!
I put on my bus driver's costume
and sputter around the apartment
as chateaux fall across the sea,
the First World War, you know,
with the champagne of Rheims
fizzing underground while *des obus*
sailed through a Beethoven dream
in which he is surrounded by
statues of Muddy Waters.

There should be hundreds of statues
of Muddy Waters in the front lawns
of every home in America, all wired
to belt out his various hits, such as
"Tiger in Your Tank," "Hoochie Coochie Man,"
and "Moonlight in Vermont." In Vermont
and "Moonlight in Vermont" people are stirring
large bowls of soup in which some trees
are reflected, green images on red steam.
Picasso placed some blue bananas
on the table—it was green—but hey,
they really were blue those bananas,
harvested in South America by bright blue insects
that wear glasses and are seen
through prisms when the electrical charges

of the brain generate enough magnetism
to pull the whole system into an ellipse.
I told you I had a big mouth.

Love Poem

We have plenty of matches in our house.
We keep them on hand always.
Currently our favorite brand is Ohio Blue Tip,
though we used to prefer Diamond brand.
That was before we discovered Ohio Blue Tip matches.
They are excellently packaged, sturdy
little boxes with dark and light blue and white labels
with words lettered in the shape of a megaphone,
as if to say even louder to the world,
"Here is the most beautiful match in the world,
its one-and-a-half-inch soft pine stem capped
by a grainy dark purple head, so sober and furious
and stubbornly ready to burst into flame,
lighting, perhaps, the cigarette of the woman you love,
for the first time, and it was never really the same
after that. All this will we give you."
That is what you gave me, I
become the cigarette and you the match, or I
the match and you the cigarette, blazing
with kisses that smoulder toward heaven.

Poem

It'd be so good
if the one you love
would get up early every morning
and call in for you,
"He won't be coming in this morning."
Navy blue
with dark red trim.

Lucky Strikes

Turn me every which way, three-cornered God,
and batter the corncobs with your fury,
that I might be everywhere I am
and those who do not understand this
fall into the fold of the paper they are written on,
others written on the wind, seraphic
creatures! tilted sideways
so as to enter your heart the easier
once you have opened it up to them,
and like metrical perfection that disappears
in its very perfectness,
your heart will be of wind,
your head up in the clouds,
where the hard candy of all nations
floats in colored wrappers the sun hits.

Unfortunately, most people
have alarm clocks that run down the road
as fast as they can, from sheer fright.
Eventually, over the blue hills, you'll
hear a distant ringing, a feeble, final ding
that causes all the bodhisattvas in heaven
to rise in their yellow robes
and cry Hurrah to the ever-expanding soda crackers,
next to the tomato soup
that steams tranquilly in the breakfast nook
where a rainbow woman, striped pretty colors,
radiates across the toy kitchen.
Yes, it was only a play house,
it was only a play
written for the toys that had come
all the way from Bethlehem,
camels and all.

Second Why

I have always found Mark Twain to be a rather depressing character, especially in movies about him, and I have always avoided his books like the plague, hated even the titles; but why? He's like me, with whom I have this love-hate relationship! The psychoanalyst rose from his desk and approached with his trim gray
beard. "Young man,"

he said gravely, "you have nothing
to fear. Float now, out the door,
on a river of electrical confidence,
and give off sparks, and be a sign,
and when you will have gone
they will say, Jesus! what a guy!"
Some clouds left the sky

and its blue was purer. It
was a lovely deep baby buggy
into which the universe had plunged,
happy and innocent as a baby
going goo-goo and its mother's
lovely legs crisscrossing in the afternoon,
with the light through the trees
the way it used to be in 1948,
so primitive but beautiful in a stark
sort of presentation, pine
trees clustered at the Cozy Pines Motel
where the dim pink neon is restful
and the prices are reasonable,
sane, civilized, benevolent.

Cherries

for Robert Herrick

Three cherries lie
on the mahogany
whose sheen deepens
deeper than the sky
inside the windows
light makes on cherries

•

I reach for one
but to return
my hand to where
it was before
and stare at them
until I am
here as long
as ever is

Arrive by Pullman

How admirable to feel clear! To perceive without distraction or vagueness. To be in direct rapport with something. With what? Could be lots of things. . . . And to sustain this clarity for more than a few seconds. Usually such moments are doomed to destruction

by a wicked bolt of lightning that came out of nowhere and hit the car as it sped along the highway. The leather seat covers were singed, the radio wiring melted and the horn knocked out, but the driver, a Mr. Samuel L. Goldwyn, helped build an empire with his Hollywood savvy. Many were the young guys and gals who flocked to Hollywood fresh out of the high school play, but few were they who were hand-picked by this kindly old Negro who of course no longer goes to the cotton fields at 6 each morning, works until noon, takes half an hour off and works until the sun goes down, which in the summer months is not until 8 and sometimes 9 o'clock. At the age of 72 he has "earned" the right to sit back and enjoy his last few cigarettes. You know those gauzy white tents we saw along the road yesterday? That was tobacco. I mean, there was tobacco growing under the tents. I guess if you liked smoking, it would be interesting to puff away while harvesting the tobacco leaves. Didn't the Indians give us tobacco? Who was it, Sir Walter Raleigh? There's a cigarette named after him. I think he caused a scandal by appearing on the surface of the water, as if they had originated from beneath the surface. Gradually, as they grow more numerous, and you hear them hitting the roof, you realize that it has begun to rain. What sort of trance were you in, that you didn't realize this? Now the surface of the pond is a speckled, flowing mass of gray rivets and popping circles that interchange positions with the soft applause among the trees, which stand perfectly still in the cookie jar, the cream one with red stripes around it, and the tea pot, the cream one with green and silver edges, and with the curved spout from which a little bit of steam is issuing.

Mrs.
Harrington laid her book aside and let her head drop back onto the

back of her
easy chair. With infinite weariness she closed her eyes and heaved

the coxswain

into the blue Charles. A great cheer went up among the assembled undergraduates, many of whom had no idea of what had just transpired; that is, the boys had done it again for dear old Harvard. Some of us knew, though. Our aching backs and arms and legs told us. The sweat on our brow told us. The pride in our hearts told us, too. Beyond us the city, wreathed now in the golden light of the setting sun, kept its granite face turned toward the sky which would soon arrive by Pullman.

Déjà Vu

I'm back in the saddle again,
splitting every situation into three equal parts
and hearing the voice of Aunt Jemima
emerge from the Delphic Oracle.
It's pancake time in Greece, huge
flapjacks draped over the countryside:
shadows of moving clouds
blotches of ideas projected down
from the great old Mr. Everything,
he who at this very moment checks his watch
and looks down at me.

Poem for El Lissitzky

—Bgawk!
There goes that Polly again!

The big storybook closed
and it was bedtime for real . . .
all little children go to bed now,
and sleep you well inside your pajamas,
and let your dreams rise softly
as the bubbles on the decal
over the headboard

by which you sleep
your wooden sleep,
little wooden children
with ragged edges that must be sanded.
Time is the sandpaper—
isn't that original?

"Time is the sandpaper,"
I said as the housewife
opened her door to me.
I was selling vacuum cleaners door-to-door.
Once they let me in
I sweet-talked them into the bedroom,
where once again I said,
"Time is the sandpaper."
This time they swooned.
Never did sell many vacuum cleaners, though.

Framed Picture

The baby Jesus
was born in the corner of a cardboard box,
the shoebox
my cowboy boots came in,
all sparkling with rhinestones
and echoing with the voices of German maidens
off in the hills behind the castle:
the red rose blooms in her cheek
and she smiles to the blue heavens.
It is 1819.
What am I doing here?
Tending the trellises, culling a few yellow roses from the vine,
carefully wiping the watercolor pigment off my hands,
heading back up toward the house.

THE BIG SOMETHING

American Cowslip

Nothing is
the way you think it is
going to be.
Take this little flower
from me, and let it go
into the way you think of it.
And so it grows
and is the face
of Daisy the cow speaking,
she my young grandma
growing and wearing
a pink slip and who fell
from the sky that was
clear blue and pure
all over the place
you called home
as it moved out
from under you
in the slow
rotation of the sphere
you call a star,
a flower, a mind.

First Drift

The writing of poems
and the living of life
seem to require
paying hard attention
to any and everything,
and experiencing
a kind of mental orgasm.
Yikes! Do I
mean that?
Unfortunately, I'm afraid
I did, dipped to scoop
an idea from the roadside,
the mental roadside that runs
alongside the mental highway
that leads to a mental hospital.
I have never been a patient
in a mental hospital, because
I think it would be an extremely bad place to be.
So I stay out.
And stay home.
And go down the street,
looking intently at everything.
Sometimes the people in the street
laugh and turn into sheet music
torn from the sky and left to flutter down
into the metaphor that hides behind the deity,
and will not show itself,
like a basement beneath the ocean,
with a tree that grew through a sheet of glass
on which your face was painted,
like a clown's, in the early morning
when it was just starting to rain

and the animals are moving, and the tents
are rippling in the breeze, and inside Glenda
the chimpanzee is completing a quadruple somersault
from shining bar to shining bar.

Greetings from Dalmatia

When I lie down in bed
I stand up in my head;
and when I start to snore
you come walking through the door
like a giant ear of corn
that is learning how to sing

And you sing:
"The world is flat, your head is flat, your beer is stale,
your turnips need glazing and highlights,
the chilly kiss of old Jack Frost,
mythical renegade grandfather of us all,
smiling imbeciles who gaze ominous and blissful at the fog,
translucent figurines in the dawn!"

And my language was changing.
I would not speak to my master.
I tore him off the page
whose blinding whiteness threw the ambiance
into an advanced brilliance,
pure moonlight on the hair
of the college boy in sharp 1935,
the knot in his bowtie a coordinate conjunction,
like the state line between the Carolinas:
there is a Carolina that hovers in our idea of both Carolinas,
neither one nor the other, nor both, really,
something nowhere
like the perfect Dalmatian that leaps out of the sky
and shakes your hand and says excitedly,
"Welcome to Dalmatia!"

2.

Here I am in Dalmatia.
I have tied my shoes to my feet, and now
I clomp clomp around the hotel room
studying its Dalmatian objects.
Outside in the hallway the so-called bellhop takes a nasty spill,
but dusts himself off and bursts
into radiant song, something about the blue sky
and silver stars, and how the magic of sunrise
gradually filled his heart with love,
and all he ever wanted to do was work at the factory
so as to see it better outlined against the dim pink
into which his forefathers had disappeared,
black and white shapes upon an attractive heaven.
Have you been there?
Was the white really quite that white, the black that deep?
I'll have to ask Fred Dupee.
He's on one of those totem poles over there.
I never understood the totem pole
until I went up in an elevator, and
then down again, and examined the pencils
in the display case. Only three more days until school!
Then two! And then that first,
so heavy with moment, pristine, so silly, and slightly irritating
with the parade of faces that come back to see you
just as you open my eyes.

The Little Past Midnight Snack

On the big oak table I lay out a fresh peach on a white dish, some provolone, a knife, a glass, and a bottle of white wine. As I turn to go back into the kitchen I glance sideways at these objects. It is a Fairfield Porter painting come to life, and a painting *of* Fairfield Porter come to life. Because for just that moment he was there. He was there in the casual arrangement of beautiful things in daily life, and in the impulse to say something direct about them.

When I looked at the bread in the kitchen it reminded me of French bread, such as the funny baguette, and of the year I spent in Paris, among the baguettes. I was always happy there, even when I was sad, and I'm always happy to be there. There must be unhappy people in Paris, but I don't understand them. It sounds crass, but it's like what John Havlicek said near the end of his athletic career: "I can honestly say that I have never been tired in my life." How could anyone not be happy in Paris?

How could anyone not love Fairfield Porter? Or the food on my table?

Dog

The New York streets look nude and stupid
With Ted and Edwin no longer here
To light them up with their particularity
Of loving them and with intelligence
In some large sense of the word:
New York's lost some of its rough charm
And there's just no getting around it
By pretending the rest of us can somehow make up for it
Or that future generations will. I hear
A dog barking in the street and it's drizzling
At 6 a.m. and there's nothing warm
Or lovable or necessary about it, it's just
Some dog barking in some street somewhere.
I hate that dog.

The Human Being and the Human Nothingness

The question in my mind was whether we had seen Sartre at La Coupole that night or whether we had been told, entering La Coupole, that he often sits at that table over there, alone or with friends, having dinner or drinks, a great intellectual in a big restaurant crowded with people sophisticated enough to pretend he's not there. Just let him have his dinner. The second question was whether I gave a casual passing glance at the philosopher whose two eyes stared off at separate walls—*Being and Nothingness*—or whether I had only imagined doing it, the moment I was being told that he often sits at that table. 1966.

In 1935 Rudolph Burckhardt, the photographer, visited Paris. One of the photographs he took there showed the rooftops of the buildings across the street from his window, and the rooftops beyond. The name "Hôtel Edgard-Quinet" on the façade across the street could still be read in 1981, in the same old *fin-de-siècle* script. I looked at it as I was being told that Sartre had lived in the building I was staying in, straight across from the Hôtel Edgard-Quinet. That it was the last building he had lived in. That for a renowned philosopher he had a curious calendar, the pin-up kind you saw in old gas stations and used car lot offices in America in the 1950s. Every year Sartre added new calendar pages to the same old pasteboard backing, with its full-color photo of a naked girl.

Her body begins with the head in the upper left-hand corner of the picture and stretches down to her ankles in the lower right-hand corner. The feet are cut off. Enclosed in a yellow rectangle, she leans a little on her right elbow, and her left arm is raised up so her hand can hold the top of her thrown-back head, which has a yellow scarf around it. Her right breast is tilted slightly toward the viewer, and her right leg is drawn up in an inverted V, knee at the top, to conceal her pubis. Behind her is a glassy light-blue area, probably a swimming pool, in which two parallel rectangles, a slightly darker blue, are reflected. They look something like the World Trade Center. For a moment I imagine this photograph being taken on a rooftop in lower Manhattan, and when I do I realize, with a shock, that the girl is the actress Natalie

Wood, who died so miserably, drunk and drowned off a yacht inside of which something unclear was happening; or at least bears a startling resemblance to her.

I look at the words above the picture. They say "The Center Store" in large type, and centered below them, in progressively smaller faces with italic variations, "Brian and Judy Shatney, Owners. Groceries. Beverages. Game Room. Route 14. Woodberry, Vermont 05681." I do remember staring down at the peppercorns on my steak that night at La Coupole, wondering with embarrassment how I could have assumed that *steak au poivre* would be the same thing as pepper steak.

Extra Star

I am under the impression
that I once wore a space helmet
upon my head, a gray
and very powerful space helmet
that said to me,
"You were born
to learn to keep your mouth shut,
and now that you've learned how to do that,
you can speak." I barked
like a human imitating a dog.
Barked and barked.
And now the midget world
is filled with little barking dogs,
but Mrs. Ferguson will not come
to the back door this evening,
in the great Forever where
she has been since this afternoon,
collapsed on the kitchen floor.
She was a nice old lady,
at least that was my impression.
Every impression has two sides:
the front is what you see. You,
though, are "under" the impression,
where all streams run free and
there's a funny kind of very attractive frost
on everything and a little less gravity and
a little more serenity, the even
flow that makes the great nervousness
that is your interior settle
back in the afternoon shade
and just take it all in,
one extra hour.

A Brief Correspondence Course

When I close a letter
with "Cordially," I
blush with shame.
It sounds insincere.
But when a letter
comes to me
with that same closing,
I glow with warmth.
I smile. I think
this person is cordial,
although until
a few moments ago
I had never heard
of him. In fact he is
a wild palooka in a half-
lit office, his
hair crazed with
enterprise, large
rubber mice
in the corridor.

Sincerely,
Ron Padgett

Snow

The light pink cone, the light green square, and
the light blue sphere, your baby eyes receiving their dancing,

and lords and ladies weaving patterns in the manor house
among the teacups and the straight lines of perspective
the Renaissance had imposed on the old crooked world,
    The Book of the Courtier replacing
    The Nature of the Gods, which wobbles around
in its various dubious and weird knobby arguments, elegant
yes
but was Cicero always like this? Castiglione
creates the motion of his thesis through its rhythmic,
stately, measured pace, I think . . .
    because a heavy coat of dust
has just buttoned itself around my memory
and the chocolate milkshake I had that afternoon
is clearer and more certain than the words in the book.
I was embarrassed to be an undergraduate at Columbia.

I could feel, though, the bite in the fall air and yearn
in some semi-magnetic way for the all-wool sweaters
of several beautiful undergraduates—but for what?
That we would stare tenderly into our light coffee
as pastel dawn spread along foggy Morningside Heights!

But now I think I know something,
that the pale cream trapezoid
has a laughter of pale blue little sticks inside it,
that the very big snowman
who invented the alphabet
has not yet melted,
that in dreams begin responsibilities,
that I am stark raving sane.

How to Be a Woodpecker

1.

I was once asleep, in Florida.
My mental state had been redesigned.
It was now quite pretty
with blue and white curtains and clouds.
I felt like what a new restaurant
looks like after a beautiful woman walks into it,
and I was asleep. I had dropped
off the deep edge of consciousness,
here depicted as a cliff in big Montana,
say. So tell me, O Virgil
& Virgil "Fire" Trucks, what I am
when I'm asleep, and my eyes are open.

2.

I would rather not participate in this society anymore, hello, but I must because I do not have the money to live outside it, *on my yacht.* This paragraph is a verbal checkerboard. It's your move. You jump around the board until my consciousness gradually disappears into yours. Now when *I* tell a joke you laugh your long gray wooden laugh, woodpeckers in its future, woodpeckers who have decided they definitely will not participate in their woodpecker society.

3.

Dagwood outlines with Blondie dishevelled
in floppy nightgown
curls over slippers under
and barks!

Bow wow.

Someone's coming
in out of the rain
which is falling
blood red
on the other side of the paper.

4.

Take *film noir.*
It didn't exist until the French
gave it the name.
It became
film noir,
but in English
it was neither
black film nor dark.
"Who art as black
as hell, and dark
as night." Make up
your mind. I have
mine. I'm "going
with" just *film noir*
because that's what
it is. I say "postal
scale" when I'm in
the warm post office
with snow on my stocking cap
and I spy through
the window a gray
postal scale, a gray
postal scale *noire.*

5.

There must be a place as funny
as the one I describe, somewhere,
perhaps an imaginary night club
that has plenty of "class"
in the attractive riffraff
who are its habitués, the accent mark
carried like a dagger in the brain.
Among the palm and banana leaves
printed in dark green on the wallpaper
dance wallpaper men and women
of the green Caribbean. They are having
a pretty good time just dancing all day.
I wish I were more like them, more
thoughtless silhouette than the vibrating
consciousness I think I am.
The funny place I describe
is the one found here, on this page.
I had to leave it for a while,
because I had stopped believing it.

Goethe

When Kenneth Koch
picked up a black camel
so neatly with his fingertips
and held it to the light—
yellow and red plaid,
and several dozen of those jackets, please—
the face of the earth
had shadowy clouds over it,
tall hay waving in the wind
and pleasant adjectives alongside the brook.
Some airplanes appeared
but they were only one inch long
and so far away you have to smile
because some yellow triangles
have entered the air,
sent by the goddess of Geometry,
and whose figures are transparent
like our souls, sort of existing
and not existing at the same time.

The Rue de Rennes

I have always had an irrational fear
of the city of Rennes, in France.
I have never been there, don't
really know exactly where it is.
I do know that it stretches out
and scares me. Do I associate it with
the rue de Rennes? A street
that seemed to begin and end
nowhere and always gray,
sometimes with a glaze of rain
over it, rainy day in Paris
at the turn of the century,
and a few years after when
Pierre Reverdy walked down it
toward the Imprimerie Birault
with a manuscript under his arm,
it is *La Lucarne ovale!* Which
I secretly liked to speculate
had something to do
with a crazy carnival, totally
unlike the severity of light
in Pierre Reverdy's world.
I saw him pause at the door
of the Imprimerie and go in.
How strange he must have felt
entrusting his modern poetry
to the hands of an old Parisian typesetter!
"This is my poetry," he begins
but the old man just nods and smiles
distantly as he takes the pages
into his hands. It is kind of wonderful.
Outside, buttoning his coat
in the November wind, Pierre heads

up the street and suddenly accelerates
into the far distance. I
am alone here on the rue de Rennes.

The Way of All Handwriting

As long as there is hair on the human head
And people wish to arrange it
There will be combs.

But I don't want to sign my autograph,
I want to follow a coil
Down into my desire
To fall face first
Into a blue-green swimming pool
The shape and size of my own body,
So the joke will fly away from my physiognomy
And the steel strings that hold it to my interior monologue
Fall into the ionosphere
Where even combs go when they die,
Perfected, like first crayons,
Bright basic colors.

Oklahoma Dawn

Everything is nice nowhere.
That red windmill is nice and nowhere.
My impulses are confused somewhere.
They wave up at me
like crazy wires
each with its own voice.
One says, "Go to the woods,
now." Another mutters
about scholarship, erudite
dust on the frown, cough,
hand me that lexicon, Wilmer.
A younger voice has a conscience,
and one still younger
sings to a tree,
as the big red sun sinks
over behind the refinery
last seen in 1959.
It was kind of depressing, actually,
with a sense that it was in fact a depressingly boring view,
but there you were in a white Chevrolet
and it was 4 o'clock in the morning,
with the strange agony of breakfast
ahead, in a neon diner, with trucks, big ones,
and guys who came in and laid their pistol on the table,
so it wouldn't go off in their pants
as they lunged toward the steak and eggs
and hash browns and plenty of good, hot coffee,
black, and a slice of peach pie to go.
Where did he go, with his hands,
the right one a massive nicotine stain museum,
and the smoke of a thousand Camels in his voice,
the roll of lucky seven in his eyes
as he pays the green check and saunters out,
a funny nobody, on his way in the Oklahoma dawn.

Poem

When I am dead and gone
they will say of me,
"We never could figure out
what he was talking about,
but it was clear that he
understood very well
that modernism is a branch
that was cut off decades ago."
Guess who said that.
Mutt and Jeff
who used to look so good
in the comics.
I especially liked their mustaches,
and the sense in it
that God is watching
from some untelevised height,
and sometimes
throws himself on the ground.
There is a tremendous impact,
for the molecules of God
are just tremendous.

Tom and Jerry Graduate from High School

It is an English countryside
though not in England.
Two Englishmen stroll in it,
small figures in the distance
and down among the willows.
It is a year
that existed
in the mind of the painter
who also existed.
My overalls are half on.

My hands reach toward the moon,
clutching a teddy bear in one arm
and a blanket in the other
—I have four arms—
and as I face the right sky
the stars in its eyes shoot out
the stars in your eyes,
when most men your age
are driving nails through someone's forehead,
who are driving nails through someone's dog,
which in turn lets out a small chuckle and rolls over.
His pattern in the dust
forms a question mark
and the litter bearers run into the jungle screaming.
The savage rhythms of life
pound in my idea of Wallace Stevens.
And each day is a sentence
in the novel your life is writing,
the way cream and the coffee and the cup
come together at the same time,
fingers, fingers, oh fingers that snap
with little lines of sound emanating,

sticks mysterious in the air,
and a bird is flying, bluebird,
onto the fence for me and my girlfriend
to observe. We are scientists,
young people who build for a better "tomorrow."
We have straight eyebrows
which equal about one cement block.
Get enough of those blocks together
and you could build a house around your personality,
the glass Indian that roamed the prairie.

Once he did. Now, forget it.
Too many smoke signals blown into the sky!
The sky being of course
just an idea, but one powerful enough
to have things blown into it
and disappear.
We have been blown backward through the empty sky,
like ha and ah reversed,
it was symmetry,
it was postmodern figurine oink,
it was Manager Alvin
roaming the aisles of the darkened theater
where modern life had shown its last film,
The Maltese Falcon,
directed by John Huston
and starring Humphrey Bogart
and a tingling Mary Astor
and a great jiggling weirdo menace played by Sydney Greenstreet
with a svelte and intensely funny Peter Lorre.

What a film!
"I'm sending you over, sweetheart."
What an amazing thing to say to anyone.
That is what I'd like to say to modern life in general,
which is not always a sweetheart, either.

A little like Mary Astor, though:
one minute you hate her,
the next you have this overwhelming desire
to rip off her dress and wad it up
as you approach her,
a Maltese cloud.
Yes, it has transported you, this scene,
a little too much. It is heady
like heaven, or Heidi in heaven,
that little by little you slip up into,
an ordinary man
in shoes that glow
a bright yellow.
And an orange lightning tieclasp.

Euphues

I dunno about this *Euphues.*
Lyly's language is gorgeous,
of course, occasionally irritating,
too, so you feel satisfied
to have the experience just
behind you. You get up and go outside
and have a hot dog in the sunlight and
think about the conjunctions,
those pinions
that allow our sentences to rotate in midcourse:
"The afternoon was mild, although not yet over,"
placing the dependent clause in direct opposition
to the main clause, like a woman who suddenly
turns to face you and it takes
your breath away—there is a moment
of silence and intensity—the boats
are frozen on the bay and no little doggie barks.
"I've been meaning to say something to you . . . ,"
she begins. And your heart
sinks: something massive
is about to happen,
you will be joined to this woman
with a tremendous force, something like gravity, in which
hats float down onto our heads and we smile.

We smile toward this Countess of Pembroke
with her delicate lips and translation
of *The Psalms* with her brother Sir Philip Sydney,
the great poet and of the great tradition of
fine comportment. His conjunctions
were in perfect order
and he exuded a harmony,
a tone actually heard in the air.

My Room

For many years I had wanted to have a room of my own in a house of my own making, and when the opportunity came I went ahead and did it. I built the room the way I wanted it: rough, clean, wooden. It surpassed my dream—it was a form of paradise. I came in and admired it. Then I went out. I put things in the room and then went out. I looked in from time to time, from the hall, as if to see if I had yet arrived in the room.

I began to wonder. Maybe this wasn't exactly what I had had in mind. I grew disgruntled. The room looked dark and mournful, as if someone had died in it.

Then I rushed in, rearranged the furniture, hung pictures on the walls, and tossed out all the junk. Suddenly the room was clarified: I could feel the electrical paths in the walls, and the nails holding like guardians against destruction and chaos. And a delicious sadness for the objects comes over me.

The desk lamp, for instance. My friend Ted Berrigan stole it from the dormitory room he was being lodged in at the University of Michigan, where he was giving a series of poetry readings, as was I. Shortly after his return to New York he received a letter from a dormitory official, taking him to task for stealing the lamp. Actually it was a letter I concocted using stationery I had taken from my dorm room. I got a good laugh out of this practical joke. Until Ted wrote to the school, apologizing for his behavior and saying many other things. Fearing the hoax had gone too far, I confessed. But Ted had the last laugh—he gave *me* the lamp for my birthday. How many years ago? The original event plunges deeper into the smokey past, but sometimes flashes forward into the present and the memory hits me and I look at the lamp and feel this mellowing sadness that seems to be sinking into, surprisingly, my arms and legs, which for some reason leads me to the idea that memories come from deep inside our spirits, flash past our brains, and dissipate into our extremities.

This is what happened to the Latin language. It flashed from our predecessors, through our high school students, and is now fizzling out on the edge of our culture. In two days my wife, son, and I will begin a private, family Latin class, with my old textbook *Using Latin* and its astounding opening sentence, "America est patria mea." Who the hell could care less! But it is a classic case, a strange hybrid of language study and propaganda. At least it fulfills the promise of the title: you can study Lesson One and walk out in the street and exclaim, "America est patria mea!" Sort of like giving yourself Roman citizenship when in fact you are a happily crazed Nubian they call Spook, and you cannot understand the color illustrations in the textbook: dragon teeth sowed in the earth immediately turning into armed warriors. At that dark moment the tree in the front yard was thrashing in the storm.

I can hear a brook from my window now, and I think of it running into the little spot we call Wayne Pond, named after my son, who was named after my father. All this confluence in a room I didn't feel comfortable in until a few minutes ago, a room that, broken like a mustang, becomes a friend to man, we who are so desperately in need of friends among the plants and animals of this earth, and yes, the humans too, and the rooms we build around ourselves.

Famous Flames

With all my faults
I do have one virtue:
I respect the idea of the noble book.
(No kidding!)
I take seriously the works of Aristotle,
although I do not usually like them.
I take seriously the *Tao Teh Ching*
and I always bark like a dog,
with the gray silhouette of a factory
against a deep red sky
and it is the France of Zola,
he whose high heels clicked
against a marble bust of Pallas.
These gentlemen are very interesting.
Take Montaigne. A peculiar guy, and
very interesting. Or Spinoza,
he of the face ugly
and geometry as divinity.
He looked in the mirror and said, "Ouch!"
and he looked into the ouch
and saw a perfect circle.
A leads to B and to C
and that explains the universe!
Unfortunately that face belonged to René Descartes!

Me, I bit into the cole slaw
and killed the dragon where he breathed
funny fumes on the pages of Literature.
"I am Everyman."
What a funny thing to say!
Would a tree say, "I am tree"?
I do not think so,
I do not think so just yet.

An ominous sensation steals over the back
as though a magnetic field
were searching, vaguely,
for another magnetic field.
Card players, in marathon games,
smoking Camels, have claimed
to have seen visions, one
in which the Virgin Mary came down
out of the sky and gave him the three of spades.
Others believe they can change the pips
by force of mind, as the card flies through the air,
and it's your open.
You sit at the present moment
with the future ready to welcome you,
until the bubble bursts
and the crowds begin to move again.
It is Christmas, 1944. The man
who invented the question mark
was laughing in heaven. Human beings
had turned into exclamation points
that threw skinny shadows across the earth
as it turned in space lit only by an old flashlight.
It was a pretty cheap production,
and when Tommy entered it in the science fair
Mr. Bushwhanger was embarrassed.
He ran and banged his head
against the wall of the faculty lounge
until his glasses fell on the floor,
burst into flame.

Popular Mechanics

"Hey, Wayne, come in here for a moment!" I called out to the doorway, down the hall, and into the room where Wayne presumably was. After a moment (and what sounded like a light groan) I heard his stockinged feet coming up the hall. I thought he took a long time, but to him it probably seemed even longer, something approaching a stretch in the penitentiary.

"Yeah?"

"Come take a look at these. They're really pretty amazing," I guaranteed, showing him the copies of *Popular Mechanics.*

He looked at one cover. On it is depicted a man working on the motor of a small orange race car, while his wife looks on admiringly. Behind him is the front half of their green family sedan. At the bottom, in slanted black letters, it says, "How to Build This Midget Racer —Page 201." It is July, 1951.

I opened another issue to an article by a Richard F. Dempewolff, entitled "Lightning Strikes Your Dinner," with lightning zigzagging through the title. The article tells us of a technological breakthrough in food preservation. A grapefruit is bombarded with three million volts of electrons and left for three months. Next to it is a grapefruit that has been refrigerated for an equal amount of time. The refrigerated grapefruit is a shrivelled, twisted piece of rope. The "electronized" grapefruit looks as fresh as the day it was bombarded. This is followed by comparison-test photographs of peas, corn, carrots, ham, and frankfurters, next to photographs of gigantic bombardment chambers and tiny men in white coats.

Wayne laughed. "What is this? Is this true?"

"Beats me. I never heard of it. But this is a great magazine. Even the ads. . . ."

I thumbed through the issues at random. The advertisements were a compendium of the kinds of gadgets an industrial society produces in its declining years. On a single page there was a moon in that deep-blue sky, and stars there, in the dark empyrean. You can learn how to start your own civilization, how to cut meat at home for fun and profit, and how to bend neon tubes. You can fill your Crosley Hotshot with the chinchillas you have raised, hose down its fender skirts and mud flaps, gaze into your amazing mystery fishbowl, wake up your scalp with the astounding Vitabrush, practice the art of deadly judo, and throw your voice while speeding along on your jet bicycle. What a grim and contorted view of life these ads would project had they not been designed in a most stylized and almost amateur commercial-art manner: cartoon faces, pale-orange backgrounds, and lines that just swish across the ad, apparently to create an illusion of dynamism. The sum effect is hypnotic, this quite incredible union of two wildly differing views of life. Cathedral music is heard.

"And look at this! 'Mystery of the Spinning Dust'! Huh. Look! There's the spinning dust!"

A grainy photograph of a wobbly ring of light: "Graphite particles, exposed to sunlight, make beautiful spiral patterns in vacuum." Why? How?

We do not know.

Some of them rotate on the same plane, others follow an elliptical orbit through various planes, some form coils rotating on their own axes while in a free-floating pattern. Professor Ehrenhaft has his own theory. He thinks they are controlled by a magnetic force that does not figure electrically in our universe, except for these particles in the vacuum. No one else seems very enthusiastic about this theory. They think maybe the professor had better go on vacation for a while.

"See this drawing!"

"Yeah."

"It's what you might call in the manner of Mighty Mouse."

"Oh, he was dumb."

"Mighty Mouse? Well, yes, he was, in a way. But that isn't the point. What was great about Mighty Mouse was the bright yellow of his costume—*Respectez, au moins, le costume que je porte!*—with its red trim and black boots and the very blue sky around him as he flew through it. He didn't *need* a good story."

"I still think he's dumb."

"Dumb to you, because you have different values, you were born in a different age, sort of. That's O.K. All I ask is that you realize that it's

O.K. for me to have values a little different from yours—in other words, to feel it's O.K. for me to love Mighty Mouse. It can't hurt anything, can it?"

"O.K."

"See what I mean?"

"Yes. O.K."

I wondered. It's hard to tell what your children are thinking, especially when they are very much like yourself.

"You want to go outside?"

"What for?"

"Well, we'll find *something.*"

"So let's go."

At Apollinaire's Tomb

The death of Guillaume Apollinaire still calls forth feelings of sorrow and loss, sorrow for his death at a relatively early age and loss for the extraordinary works he might have written. It is jolting to realize that if he had lived as long as, say, Eubie Blake did, I could go see him this very moment! Across the ocean, an aged but vital Gui. . . .

He *is* over there, of course. Six feet under. Describing the funeral cortege and gravesite, Blaise Cendrars claims that a few minutes after the burial no one knew which of two similar graves held the coffin of Lieutenant Apollinaire. Cendrars adds that when he looked down he was transfixed by a clump of turf that bore a perfect resemblance to Apollinaire: *avait exactement la forme d'Apollinaire.* Other writers, such as Allen Ginsberg and Michael Brownstein, have written about that grave. We are all drawn to that grave.

It was late in 1965. I went out to Père Lachaise for the first time. It is a magnificently odd cemetery that put me at ease by its surprising lightness and pleasantness. When I finally located the gravesite of Wilhelm de Kostrowitsky, I stood there facing it. That wonderful pearly gray French light streamed down over everything. I looked at the crudely hewn headstone that looked out of place, still modern. Then, slowly, a soft image appeared on it, the image of a cross. A little shiver went over me when the image appeared, so lightly it was cut in the stone, and when I looked back down at the ground I saw Apollinaire tilt up toward me straight as a board. He drifted right up through the ground. I felt my heart give a little jump, but I wasn't afraid.

I looked around. He was gone. Everything looked the same. Well, sort of.

M'sieur Tarzan

There comes a point at which you have to sit back and let things unroll according to their own sweet will. You can put on your best suit—a nice dark brown wool—crisp white shirt, and snappy tie, slick back your cowlick in the polished mirror, adjust your shoulder holster, align your cufflinks, and go lilting out the door toward a star-spangled evening, but if you're deep in the heart of the African jungle you're in for a surprise. Your house got towed away. You forgot to put money in the meter. As you drift deeper into the undergrowth, you hear, louder and louder, great numbers of trumpets, and it hits you right between the eyes: this is where all those Louis Armstrongs come from! Such a discovery would not have been possible had you insisted on champagne and the tawny slope of a shoulder that night.

Next slide. The shoulder had its own adventure, too. It dipped into a soft monkey fur that sank back into the plush leather backseat of a Rolls Royce that went in all four directions at once it was so fine an instrument of travel. Voyage I think they call it. "We voyaged across an ocean of currency and when we floated in to our destination the coastline spread its distances under a sky bathed in hues softer than anyone's dream of a cloud, but when we stepped ashore the trees turned jagged and great wild hair waved in the gathering darkness. I went straight to the hotel and had room service send up an urn of iced pearls. It was then I noticed that—how shall I put it—the other end of the room had been erased. I mean there was . . . just nothing there. And when I went toward it I got smaller, and when I went through it I got to be you." Next slide.

Not everyone can afford a mobile home. Or even a mobile dollhouse, in which the dolls wear goggles and bow down before images of Barney Oldfield. In one image Barney is seen squirting some oil from an oilcan onto the arm of an old lady who was later identified as his grandmother, a stately gentlewoman who claimed to have sewn the first flag ever to fly over the jungle just outside the dollhouse. Barney wants to examine the rooms, see what's there, and maybe wash up before dinner. The bathroom is wonderful, all gleaming white tile and pink and blue bars of light coming through the windows painted on the far wall. Pretty soon Barney's in the shower singing up a storm that sends down ripping bolts of lightning that execute the great race driver then and there: he is found dead in the tub. Sic transit authority. Next slide.

You are six years old. Let's see, that would be in 19–. That's my favorite year, 19–. It is like my favorite author, Anonymous. Anonymous was born in ___ and died in ___ and is still alive, like the other archetypes. They have it pretty easy, those archetypes. Big houses and cars and moonlight and things that money can't buy, like air and pain and Johnny Weismuller. But I have Johnny Weismuller, have him in my sights at this very moment, as he steps off a high ledge and sweeps like a maniac through the trailing vines, dressed in his best suit, a nice dark brown wool.

To Woody Woodpecker

I love you, Woody,
when you peck
on the head
of a bad person
and laugh and fly
away real fast,
speed lines
in the air
and clouds of invisible
dust dissipating,
I love the way
you last only seven minutes:
never boring!
The heart has seven minutes
with Woody Woodpecker,
seven minutes of pure bliss.

Who and Each

I got up early Sunday morning
because it occurred to me that the word
which
might have come from a combination of *who* and *each*
and reached for the *OED*
which for me
(I think of it not
as the Oxford English Dictionary
but as the *O Erat Demonstrandum*)
has the last word:
"Hwelc, huelc, hwaelc, huaelc, huoelc, hwaelc, wheche, weche,
whech, qwech, queche, qheche, qwel, quelk, hwilc, wile, hwilch,
wilch, while, whillc, whilk, whylke, whilke, whilk, wilke,
whylk, whilk, quilc, quilke, qwilk, quylk, quhylk, quilk, quhilk,
hwic, wic, hwich, wyche, wich, hwych, wiche, whiche, whyche,
wych, whych, which, quiche, quyche, quich, quych, qwiche,
qwych, qwych, quhich, hwylc, hwulch, hulch, wulc, whulc,
wulch, whulche": Teutonic belching.
    But in little tiny type: "For the compounds *gewilc,*
aeghwilc, see *Each.*"
Now, if you want to talk *belching*. . . .
It was raining outside
with the blue-gray hiss of tires
against the wet street
I would soon walk my dog in,
the street I drove an airplane up
earlier this morning in a dream
in which the Latin word *quisque* appeared to me,
as if it meant *each which*
in the sea of *eisdem, quicumque,* and *uterque.*
Thus I spend my days,
waiting for my friends to die.

Coors

When I laid out the slices of olive loaf next to the can of Coors, I was hit with an intense sensation of being around three or four years old, in Howard Donahue's welding shop in the afternoon, with my father and some guys standing around shooting the breeze. It was a very empty feeling, imbued with ignorance. The heavy shadows cast by cylinders of compressed gas echoed with pointlessness. Still, among the grease spots and dusty tools, there was a sense that life was going strong, no questions asked. These guys didn't have any idea why they were on the face of the earth, nor had it occurred to them to wonder why. Hell, they had things to do. Slick back their hair. Punch some son of a bitch in the nose. Laugh. Say "much obliged." Pop the clutch and roar off down the street on a wave of energy.

The warm summer breeze pours around my head and whips my hair around into my face when I turn it just a little. I am flying through the air, me and the air. The '49 Ford has disappeared. My daddy is happy behind the wheel. In the backseat are forty-two boxes of Tide. "Lifetime supply," he laughs.

Since then he has spent his life trying to obtain a lifetime supply of everything. All that time, he never put lettuce on his sandwiches. Just lunchmeat between two pieces of white bread.

Which is how I had mine tonight, with this Coors, a beer I didn't think they sold this far east, until I discovered it in a new supermarket today. And when I laid out the slices of olive loaf next to the can of Coors, I was hit with an intense sensation, the pang of loving someone I don't really know.

Light as Air

1.

It's calm today. I sit outside, or inside by the window, and look out, and for a moment I realize my left hand is holding up my head. I see the light on everything, trees, hills, and clouds, and I do not see the trees, hills, and clouds. I see the light, and it plays over my mind that it is any day, not today, just day.

2.

The wind is making the trees swoosh and the volume goes up and down. I have been sitting here for some time, at first looking out at the grass and trees and sky, and then, turning more and more into my mind and its noticing things, gradually looking at nothing of what was before my eyes. A great cutting slash arced across the last turn of the mental pathway I had wandered down and up, and was approaching me from the left. I cocked my head to that left. Slash, slash in the woods. My legs chilled. I will wait until I hear it once more, then I will get up and go inside.

Silence.

3.

In times of trouble and despondency I turn to sportswear. I have just added to my wardrobe three pairs of pastel-colored shorts and four light-gray T-shirts and a yellow cotton pullover so elegant and offhand it must have been designed in France. I put on my new clothes, lace up my new white shoes, and see people. They say, "You look nice. Are those shorts new?"

"Yes, they are," I answer.

Then I go back home and sit on the porch under the sky in my new shorts.

4.

I look at you sometimes when you're not aware of it. I look at you in those moments the way a stranger might so I can see you better than I usually do. And in fact you do always look fresh and new and similar to the person I think of as you. I love the way you look. And I feel happy just to be here looking at you, the way the dog sits at the feet of us, his great gods. I sit at the feet of the thing that is you. I look at your feet.

5.

I take off my clothes and am in the air, me flowing through it and it flowing around me. I look to the right. The first cottages of the little village, the first houses of the town, the first buildings of the city: bones, flesh, and clothing. Air around it all. Air I cannot breath, because I am also a structure I am moving past, a tomb, a monument, a big nothing.

6.

He is a man of many vectors, which assemble and reassemble, the way music comes first from the air, then from a piece of wood grown in air. Then the air is in a museum in a country you are not permitted to enter at this time because your vectors are not in order. You must go home and reassemble your rods and cones: night is falling, the soft gray mist of his breath.

7.

I dreamed I had become a tall hamburger piloting a plane going down in a remote jungle waving up at me with inexpensive green cardboard natives ecstatic at the arrival, at last, of their messiah. A radiant hamburger bun top opened above me as I floated softly into their gyrating angular green midst.

8.

I come to a mental clearing where I can speak only from the heart. Free of the baggage of who I happen to be, and of all the porters who must carry the baggage, and the exorbitant taxi ride into a fuller version of the same small personality, I take, for what seems to be the first time in a long time, a breath that goes deeper than the bottom of the lungs, and in the pause that comes at the end of that breath there appears a little mirror, light fog on it clearing quickly.

9.

The palm of my hand is in Sunday, groggy, sabbatical. The rest of me is in Wednesday, up there and to the left, in the sky. I see you need a light, though you have nothing to smoke. You left your smoking utensils in Thursday. Let me recall my hand and fetch them for you. There, now you are creating puffs. But they do not dissipate. They form shadow copies of my hand that is moving toward your face.

10.

It dawns on me that I'm repeating myself. Another day and there I am, calm outside in the air with my hand returning along its vectors. In this mental clearing the photons are jumping all around the savages. Suddenly the witch doctor brings his face to mine and shouts, "Mgwabi! Mgwabi!" pointing to my photons. I reach up and take the light from his face and fold it with the fingers on my hands and it dawns on me that I'm repeating myself.

11.

At the end of the light I raise my voice from down there to up here and you are not here. I could shout until the words change colors and it would make no difference. Your vectors are heading out away from the voice of my hand and toward what it is pointing to, that bright cloud over there, the one with the burning edges, handsome and lighter than air at last.

12.

A cold streak runs through the sky now the color of wet cement that forms the body of the man whose brain is at a height of more miles than can be found on earth. This emotional absolute zero is like a spine conducting thick fog and thin rain through him, and when the sun's vectors approach his surface they turn and move parallel to it. Who is this big cement man? And how do I know whether or not he is the same who came this morning and threw on the power that sent the electricity branching through my heart?

13.

It's dark today. I sit inside, my right hand touching my head. I look at the floor, the fabrics, the smoke from my mouth. It's as if there isn't any light, as if part of things being here is what light they have inseparable from themselves, not visible. The table doesn't stand for anything, although it remembers the tree. The table isn't immortal, though it hums a tune of going on forever. The table is in Friday, with me, both of us here in this dark, miserable day, and I have the feeling I'm smiling, though I'm not.

Indian Territory

My wife told me I should come in and write down what I just said, which was "That blue and white frying pan looks just like one that Gabby Hayes's beautiful young wife might have used in 1903, although I have no idea what his wife might have looked like, or even if he had one" and "If you took away his beard and age and the cantankerous, grizzled old coot he played, you'd probably find an exceedingly handsome young man."

She told me that I was probably the only person on the face of the earth to have ever had that idea, of Gabby Hayes as a handsome young man, and I agreed that such ideas are probably not legion these days, when fewer and fewer people know who Gabby Hayes was, or what he might have meant with all the "You dern tootin'"s he must have snorted out.

He was like an Olaf C. Seltzer image come to life, in black and white, with a genuine aura of what the Old West felt like—a vast landscape peopled with raving eccentrics who loved the open air and the call of the coyote, dusty panhandlers with their dense donkeys, lost galoots blown across the desert, escapees from human history.

And now the bacon and eggs are ready in this Manhattan apartment, which, years hence, might well suggest, to the sympathetic eye, a wide open space itself.

The Salt and Pepper Shakers

My wife and I have been meaning to buy a set of salt and pepper shakers for the past several years. We have one set, which we carry back and forth between kitchen and table. For some reason, we have never gotten around to buying the second set. Apparently it isn't quite important enough for us to do but is important enough to make us think we *ought* to buy them at some point. "Where's the salt and pepper?" I am heard frequently to ask.

"Oh, they're in the kitchen," my wife answers wearily.

At which point our son says, "O.K., I know," and goes to get the salt and pepper.

And so we do not remember to buy the second set. If someone were to come up to us on the street and offer to give us a set right there on the spot, we would exclaim, "It's exactly what we need, it's amazing!" But no one does. I went outside a few minutes ago to check. Instead the streets were occupied by very bland "people" with no interest in giving me some salt and pepper shakers.

Perhaps our *mañana* attitude is caused by the satisfying beauty of the ones we do have. They are of the plain old diner variety, glass in vertical facets, with aluminum caps—transparent identical twins, except one is labelled "moi" and the other "tu." We bought them for twenty-nine cents in Arkansas in 1967. They evoke home fries and coffee, and I have no doubt that there is someone who just by looking at them can describe the society that produced them, just as you can read this and know me.

Smoke

"I'm going out for a pack of cigarettes."

At one point in the history of our language—roughly from the 1920s into the early 1950s is my guess—those words meant simply "Good-bye forever," as the back screen door slams shut and he disappears across the darkness, never to be seen again, at least in Joplin.

Those were the days when men were men, guys who looked straight into the eyes of the little wife or the crew boss and said, "I'm going out for a pack of cigarettes." They left, and they looked, but they never did find that pack of cigarettes.

from
NEW & SELECTED POEMS

Getting Along

We stride briskly down the country lane, bluejay squabble overhead in the last wisps of fog, and the night's breath of the woods still around us. That's a poetic way of saying that we are two old farts out for a morning constitutional, like the gray-haired but trim couple in nice sports clothes who are walking, smiling and tanned, on the covers of magazines devoted to "the issues of health and aging." Those people, however, also have huge retirement funds, and will never have to "worry." On the one hand, I am a bit nonplussed at finding myself on a magazine cover, and on the other hand I like to think that, like these model people, as I age I will enjoy good health. I will not only walk down country lanes, but right up the sides of houses and over their tops. To leave the doctor's office after my annual checkup, I will simply crash through the walls. I will approach the condition of the scientist who not only died and came back to life, but was able to rearrange the molecular structure of sticks and leaves to form a cowboy hat. I will walk unafraid through a forest of cowboy hats.

Talking to Vladimir Mayakovsky

All right, I admit it:
It was just a dream I had last night.
I was trudging along a muddy path
in a column of downcast men
on the blackened outskirts of New York,
the twilight dingy and ruined,
the future without hope
as we marched along
in our soiled, proletarian rags.
To my left was Mayakovsky, head shaved,
and next to him his friend
with gray beard and dark cap.
"You've got to admit," Mayakovsky
was saying, "that this is a pretty good
way to write a poem."
"Yes," I said, "the momentum
is sustained by our walking forward,
the desolate landscape seeps into every word,
and you're free to say anything you want."
"That's because we're inside the poem,"
he said, "not outside." Puddles
of oily water gleamed dully beneath the low clouds.
"That's why my poems were so big:
there's more room *inside.*"
The hard line of his jaw flexed and
the men dispersed. I followed
his friend behind a wall
to hear the poem go on
in the lecture the friend was giving on history,
but no, the real poem had finished.
I went back to the spot
where the poem had finished.
Vladimir had left the poem.

Beaujolais Villages

We have to wait. It's not yet time? But the door is still locked. The *patronne* has not yet arrived this morning. She was indisposed last night. That is, she was heaving her guts out down by the river, where she had staggered, alive and drunk under the weight of her anxiety over the shelling of her native city, far away, while here the people go on as if nothing were happening. Except, of course, they know that they do not understand why the café door remains shut and locked. The sunlight is hitting it at a slant, as if to say, Let me in, it is time to open up and let me in. The wooden door is growing ever brighter and warmer to the touch of the major as he shoves it first with his palms, then leans into it with his full body weight and makes it sag a bit. All those kilos converging with the sunlight on the door, and Arlette the pomeranian going by leaping and barking at little Michel who is holding a doggy treat just out of the reach of her snapping jaws.

Yak and Yak

I am saying
that grammar is the direct result of how humans feel in the world;
or rather,
that grammar follows from what we experience viscerally
and punctuation keeps it that way;
that, for instance, people walking down the street
are forming various sentences with their bodies,
and as the schoolgirl turns the corner the meaning
changes, oh so natural. Just so the wind
that suddenly turns the corner has just blown your hair off!
You go indoors and write,
"The wind has blown my hair away,"
then shift your weight and add, "almost."
For in your mind your arms have stretched to catch your head,
in which Pig Latin is understood but Dog not.
"Omecay erehay, etlay emay elltay ouyay omethingsay atthay ouyay ughtoay otay owknay." In Hawaiian countries there was a battle over there,
anyhow, and when she heard the racket and the battle
of the fierce pineapples clashing under a warm moon,
she wrote across the sky, with her magic finger,
in glowing light, that she would not love her man anymore.
The palm trees stood like so many silent exclamation points
in the flowing beat of the night's heart.

More of This Light

This evening's clear light and light blue pink look like the Penguin edition of *Elective Affinities,* but something was missing there, my stomach is nervous, Goethe I should have said, and the deep green of the fields was glowing an inwardly deeper green the blacktop wound through and on which I sailed along, with just the first hint of feeling that I might someday accept not being here anymore, if only the light would stay this way.

My Coup

The bright light of what could be an electric angel hits my face head-on, a light into which I am asked, as it were, to step and speak. Actually I've just stepped into it, and I'm now speaking: my mouth is saying one thing and my brain is thinking another. The mouth is that of an imaginary head attached to a real body standing at a podium on those wide steps on Kreshchatik, the main street in Kiev. Behind and above me wave the bright red flags that sprang from the blood of Lenin. The crowd before me has turned their faces up to the sky to watch the angel flitting back and forth, like a leaf dancing in the wind, a leaf that should be at the top of a Christmas tree. Their ears hear only the vibrations from the angel's hospital gown as it flaps contrapuntually with the red flags. I give out a sigh of relief and step down from the podium. Now I can go back home to my window and wife, and gaze out at the little yellow bird that comes to the windowsill almost every morning.

Essay on Imagination

So I go to the baseball stadium. It is large, larger than I had thought it would be, and it is surprisingly fast, moving along at about forty miles per hour. At this rate we will be playing Saint Louis by morning! By a stroke of good fortune, I happen to be the only person on the promenade deck, a real treat. The smooth green expanse of field before me is, for this moment, all mine. Am I dreaming, I ask myself. The answer is no, you are not dreaming, you are having a fantasy that you are at a baseball stadium that is also an ocean liner. The answer makes me slump deeper into my personality, the part I sleep in, and so I get sleepy. If I go to sleep, I can dream about the ball field, and what might have happened there as we crossed the ocean, me and the blonde girl who has just arrived, wearing black shorts that are cut achingly high in the back and a black bandanna across her chest, and as she mounts the stairs with a drowsy rolling of her hips I realize that she is a composite of all the girls I've ever glimpsed in the street with that pang of fleeting lust that glows for a moment and fades away into me and then rolls back out, because the power of the imagination cannot be contained, no matter how hard we try.

Sleep Alarm

Just as some guy
is proposing to
Suzanne Pleshette in a cough
syrup commercial,
I realize
I've dozed back off and snap
to, crack my left
eye and see you,
dog formed
by shadows of art
books along the wall.

Prose Poem

The morning coffee. I'm not sure why I drink it. Maybe it's the ritual of the cup, the spoon, the hot water, the milk, and the little heap of brown grit, the way they come together to form a nail I can hang the day on. It's something to do between being asleep and being awake. Surely there's something better to do, though, than to drink a cup of instant coffee. Such as meditate? About what? About having a cup of coffee. A cup of coffee whose first drink is too hot and whose last drink is too cool, but whose many in-between drinks are, like Baby Bear's porridge, just right. Papa Bear looks disgruntled. He removes his spectacles and swivels his eyes onto the cup that sits before Baby Bear, and then, after a discrete cough, reaches over and picks it up. Baby Bear doesn't understand this disruption of the morning routine. Papa Bear brings the cup close to his face and peers at it intently. The cup shatters in his paw, explodes actually, sending fragments and brown liquid all over the room. In a way it's good that Mama Bear isn't there. Better that she rest in her grave beyond the garden, unaware of what has happened to the world.

The Fortune Cookie Man

Working for ten years now at the fortune cookie factory and I'm still not allowed to write any of the fortunes. I couldn't do any worse than they do, what with their You Will Find Success in the Entertainment Field mentality. I would like to tell someone that they will find a gorilla in their closet, brooding darkly over the shoes. And that that gorilla will roll his glassy, animal eyes as if to cry out to the heavens that are burning in bright orange and red and through which violent clouds are rolling, and open his beast's mouth and issue a whimper that will fall on the shoes like a buffing rag hot with friction. But they say no. So if you don't find success in the entertainment field, don't blame me. I just work here.

Blacktop

The newly blacktopped highway with the bright yellow stripe down the middle slides under and behind you like a deep carpet as you whiz toward home in the silent and starry night, but deep inside the motor the pistons are incredibly hot and intense, and the noise is terrible, and the sparkplugs are spitting little zaps of electricity like crazy—and all for you, moviegoers laughing on your way home.

Flower's Escape

What have we here, a little daisy alongside the footpath, hmm. But as I bend to pick it, I pause, I freeze, I am a statue, and the daisy expands to the height of a man and begins to move off down the footpath, barely skimming the ground, its petals flared back in the breeze. But I don't mind. Being immobile like this will give me time to contemplate the eternity that lies before me, and whose silent voice insists on reminding me, from time to time, "Ron, you are not." Sometimes this happens when I've gone to bed and am lying there suddenly aware of how dark it is in the room; sometimes it happens when I'm driving along a country road, a ghost in my pickup truck! And I think how funny it is that I, who am not, am also a man driving a red truck, and the flexibility of my body is enjoying itself as I wind up and take the curves in a gentle centrifugal arc and my body weighs a little more on that side for a moment, and Nat "King" Cole is telling me I'm unforgettable, which I appreciate, although I know full well that I will be forgotten, unless I stay like this, bent over a flower that has fled my touch.

Olivetti Lettera

Good-bye, little Lettera.
It was nice with you again.
I once loved a girl and oh
Well I once loved a girl.

You are so small, the way
what I remember is
packed into my human skull
and it's dark in there.

And it's singing in there,
this typewriter who is a
girl, then, an Italian girl,
undressing, slowly, in the dark.

Licked by Igor

As I lick the back of the head of a man named Igor Sikorsky and then push his face down with my thumb and give it a thump with the meat of my fist, I glance up to see Connie the postmistress extending her hand with my four cents change in it. Our eyes meet, and for a moment neither of us is certain what to say. We are so used to joking with one another, but something about this Igor Sikorsky has made us sad.

Clunk Poem

I pick up the pieces
and stick them together.
They remain far apart,
so far apart I can't
even take them apart again,
so I add them to other
such clusters, and then
I have an idea: I will
go down and make myself
a peanut butter, blueberry,
and banana effigy of Hitler.
That'll show the bastards.

Stork

As I write I keep looking back
over my shoulder to the spot
where the road comes out of the trees
and stops in our yard, as if I'm
expecting a stork
with an actual baby suspended
in a diaper from its long beak,
the way they used to. When I had
a birds-and-the-bees man-to-man chat
with my son (age four or five) and told him
in the nicest, neatest, healthiest
way how babies are made, he thought
for a moment and said, "Nawww."
If a stork were to alight this very
moment where the shade cuts the light,
I'd look back and think, "Nawww."
I wish it'd happen.

Medieval Yawn

Who really sees anything when he yawns? The boy bent over his algebra textbook is starting to yawn, and then two or three other yawns blossom around the room. But none of the students has seen the others, the contagion has been silent and invisible. Down in the boiler room, old Mr. Harris has just plunked down in the tattered easy chair next to the fuel line, but now a blank look surfaces in his face as he remembers that he left his magazine in the tool room. Maybe he doesn't really feel like reading today, anyway, though the pictures would be nice to look at: in the distance a snow-topped mountain, with dark forests somewhat lower, almost down to the level plain, across which an army of medieval warriors is sweeping toward you. They are coming to demand the return of young Gretchen, the blonde girl who got carried off by Sigismund, he whose black hair flashes blue in the forest light. That's where his head is now, in the forest, along with the rest of his body, which is only partially clothed, alongside the body of Gretchen, whose body is also partially clothed, and around which the light is exploding silently, as the advancing army starts to dematerialize, as if erased, like a problem with two unknowns that turns out not to be a problem at all simply because the bell has rung and everyone is moving quickly toward the door on this Friday afternoon, 3:30.

Alphonse Goes to the Pharmacy

"For the third time, Alphonse, no, I will not go to the pharmacy with you tonight. You must obtain your powders and elixirs on your own, just as you must affix your peruke to your head each day on your own. I will neither go to the pharmacy with you nor affix your peruke. Not now, not ever."

Alphonse the miniature chihuahua did not suffer rejection easily. His big dark eyes expressed the full measure of the despondency he felt as he pushed his head into the little sombrero and turned for one last look at his mistress, then wended his way out the door.

Untitled

On the album cover of my ten-inch *Kindertotenlieder*
are two squares floating in a cloudy sky:
in the left-hand square is the face of Kathleen Ferrier,
that of Bruno Walter in the right. I feel sorrier
for her being dead than him, because she was a woman
and closer in age to a *Kind.* I almost never play
this record: it is too beautiful, and too sad.

The Benefit of Doubt

When I was at the age when one's intellectual training seems to happen by itself, I became quite sure about the value of doubting one's own convictions, on the grounds that it prompted one to reevaluate opinions that might be outdated or stale. Years later I saw that doubt allows us to dispense with the *missigosh* of being right or wrong, conditions virtually useless in making art, which is what I like to do. I also like to look at things.

Outside the window at this moment, for instance, is a visual field of green and brown, flecked with yellow, all of it shifting and swaying, then wobbling, then suddenly stopping and stretching—wait, that's a deer. And it brings a message from the King. I am to come to the royal court, as swiftly as this deer can fly. Up on his back I leap, and we're off, over hill and dale, down village lanes, past men with thick spectacles and nightcaps that drag the ground behind them, the village street cleaners!

At last the castle looms in the distance, with golden beams radiating from it up into the sky, projecting a song that would have us believe that inside the castle walls there are thousands of people working and singing joyously. I come to you as summoned, O King, although you are not there, and never were.

Oswaldo's Song

Be glad that, as the world is in various forms of turmoil, you don't have to worry about anything, for a moment. You lean back in your chair and let your head fall back, and you notice a spot on the ceiling. What is it? It looks like a miniature South America. It wasn't there before. The tingling in your feet was there, but you didn't notice until you had stopped thinking about South America, how romantic it might have been under certain circumstances. It is 1948 and you are standing on the veranda of a large manor house perched on the side of a cliff above which the moon has parked, and off in the distance an old man is gently strumming a guitar and singing about the day he met his young bride in their village. She was seven, he was barely eight. They ran through the village until they got larger and larger, so large their shoes didn't fit, and when they went to their respective homes that night, they dreamed of some day coming to America, North America. "That's enough, Oswaldo," says a man standing in the shadows, and the singing stops. A light breeze rustles the banana palms.

YOU NEVER KNOW

Morning

Who is here with me?
My mother and an Indian man.
(I am writing this in the past.)
The Indian man is not a man,
but a wooden statue just outside
the limits of wood. My mother
is made of mother. She touches
the wood with her eyes and the eyes
of the statue turn to hers, that is,
become hers. (I am not dreaming.
I haven't even been born yet.)
There is a cloud in the sky.
My father is inside the cloud,
asleep. When he wakes up, he
will want coffee and a smoke.
My mother will set fire
to the Indian and from deep inside
her body I will tell her
to start the coffee, for even now
I hear my father's breathing change.

Glow

When I wake up earlier than you and you
are turned to face me, face
on the pillow and hair spread around,
I take a chance and stare at you,
amazed in love and afraid
that you might open your eyes and have
the daylights scared out of you.
But maybe with the daylights gone
you'd see how much my chest and head
implode for you, their voices trapped
inside like unborn children fearing
they will never see the light of day.
The opening in the wall now dimly glows
its rainy blue and gray. I tie my shoes
and go downstairs to put the coffee on.

To Myself

And another thing.
This same window
I looked out of
how many years ago
and heard my future
in the form of car tires
hissing against pavement
and now read of it
in a poem written that night
I had on an old bathrobe
black and gray and white
thick heavy cotton
out of a thirties movie
and at the bottom
of which my legs stuck out
with wool socks on feet
that shuffled me over
to the window
that had raindrops
all over it and shuffled me
back to my desk to write
that poem, feeling moved
by the height of the quiet waiting,
an animal in the dark
wanting to sing in English.

Advice to Young Writers

One of the things I've repeated to writing
students is that they should write when they don't
feel like writing, just sit down and start,
and when it doesn't go very well, to press on then,
to get to that one thing you'd otherwise
never find. What I forgot to mention was
that this is just a writing technique, that
you could also be out mowing the lawn, where,
if you bring your mind to it, you'll also eventually
come to something unexpected ("The robin he
hunts and pecks"), or watching the *Farm News*
on which a large man is referring to the "Greater
Massachusetts area." It's alright, students, not
to write. Do whatever you want. As long as you find
that unexpected something, or even if you don't.

The Missing Lips

In the flower garden behind the cottage whose foundation rests in the gentle hills of Sussex, England, ca. 1920, a small black-and-white terrier is writhing around on the lawn and snorting in joy, snorting because he's had the urge to writhe and snort under the blue sunny sky, then trot off into the shade and plunk down on crossed paws and wait for Marian to come home from school, little Marian who feeds him treats and kisses him on what would be his lips if he had any!

Not Particularly

Out of the quarrel with life
we are a whirlwind
of invisible whirs that
go around a statue by Giacometti.
Or,
if putting new experiences
in a basket and taking them
on a picnic is the best way
to heal a wound, then
all of life is a way of forgetting
whatever it was.
There was something else besides a tree
at the end of the road, a train
waiting like a series of rulers
placed end to end, or like
the sensation of falling without information
and it is white,
or fairly white
and not particularly funny.

Fairy Tale

The little elf is dressed in a floppy cap
and he has a big rosy nose and flaring white eyebrows
with short legs and a jaunty step, though sometimes
he glides across an invisible pond with a bonfire glow on his cheeks:
it is northern Europe in the nineteenth century and people
are strolling around Copenhagen in the late afternoon,
mostly townspeople on their way somewhere,
perhaps to an early collation of smoked fish, rye bread, and cheese,
washed down with a dark beer: ha ha, I have eaten this excellent
meal
and now I will smoke a little bit and sit back and stare down
at the golden gleam of my watch fob against the coarse dark wool of
my vest,
and I will smile with a hideous contentment, because I am an evil
man,
and tonight I will do something evil in this city!

Jay

The blue jay's cry goes up on stilts and takes
a few brisk strides through the mixed deciduous trees,
some of which rustle. It's not their answer.
They reach out and catch
him as he lands on branch and branch,
then flutters and stops: this
is his domain, and he is king.
He wears a little crown and in
his heart there is murder,
i.e., breakfast. The stilts rise again
in him and he cries out.

Sudden Flashes

hit the sky hot
as javelins vibrating in a baobab
that became a mast with chevrons
aflutter, and the ghost ship
floats into an icy abyss,
and the abyss heaves forth
a mighty guffaw shot through
with jagged rays of yellow light:
the curtain rises and before you
is a desert decorated with a solitary
snack bar owned and operated
by you! So get to work, you lout!
Serve up those corn dogs and *zut alors!*
the telephone. Another takeout order!

J & J

O.K., here we go, running down the hill, the three of us, Jack and Jill and you, the wind up, the clouds blowing left to right, and Jill's hair bounding adorably, Jack's legs a little too short for the rest of him, especially his head, big blond block head and the deep chortle that issues from his red lips as he sees Jill's sandal catch on a rock and her look of surprise as she pitches forward into the haystack that you, the great artist, were able to draw for her just in time.

For a Moment

It's funny how
if you just let go
of things they

will come to
you. That is to say
sometimes. So what

good is such a
generalization?
Ah, it makes you

feel good to say
such things from
time to time,

as if you actually
and really and truly
knew something!

Fixation

It's not that hard to climb up
on a cross and have nails driven
into your hands and feet.
Of course it would hurt, but
if your mind were strong enough
you wouldn't notice. You
would notice how much farther
you can see up here, how
there's even a breeze
that cools your leaking blood.
The hills with olive groves fold in
to other hills with roads and huts,
flocks of sheep on a distant rise.

My Son the Greek

I rather like the idea of having an adult
be my son,
        on top of a mountain turned
on its side and chained
to a flatbed truck
heading down a steep grade toward a cloud
called sleep.
All the little shepherds are snoozing, safe
and secure in the knowledge
that their sheep are facing forward
and not inside out. Yes,
it is good to bed down for the night
and the day and the intermission
in which you realize that you are alone
at the opera and the stage is empty
because the singing, the beautiful singing
and the very loud and beautiful singing is going
on inside your head that is now glued on
top of the neck of the boy whose birth made you cry out
to the hillsides on which the sheep were humming
as the stars listed to one side and went out.

Small Pond

As a child
I wanted to have a boat
and row
around a room
filled with money
the way
Scrooge McDuck
did, but I didn't
want to be
stingy or light
a cigar with
a twenty. I
just wanted to
see the coins
and bills fly
sparkling up
as oar and oar
went dipping
and churning.

Amsterdam

The sky has been scrubbed
by the sails in the harbor.
In the gutters of de Hooch
the rivulets are sparkling
because they are Dutch and
very clean. Even the bricks
are happy to be there, with
splashes of soapy water
on their faces every morning
and Benedict Spinoza inside
the house creating his book
theorem by theorem. Outside
the window a man says something
and a girl laughs and says, "No, Willem,
that is not the real reason."
Everything freezes.

What to Do

"Show, don't tell," they say, and I agree:
so here, take a look at my naked body, of which
I will tell you nothing, and here is my naked soul,
into which I will jump with both feet clad
only in socks, bright red ones from which
sparks are flying as I whiz into its depths.

Rectangle Obligation

I have a rectangle that I must fill. Overhead it resembles a rectangle, but seen from the side it is invisible, because it is an idea. I twang its sides and they vibrate, but so does everything else. A concert is coming up the road, and a whole sheet of laughter is ripping away from the surface and flying up the way this rectangle would if it had any energy. But it doesn't, until my head turns into wood and gets warm inside. Then the rectangle starts to glow and hum. Suddenly "hilarity bubbles" spread throughout the entire system and the four sides of the rectangle let go of each other and float off in different directions, rotating and tumbling slowly through the dark. I am very glad to be rid of it.

Embraceable You

I don't mind Walt Whitman's saying
"I contain multitudes," in fact I like it,
but all I can imagine myself saying is
"I contain a sandwich and some coffee and a throb."
Maybe I should throw my arms out and sing,
"Oh, grab hold of everything and hug tight!
Then clouds, books, barometer, eyes wider
and wider, come crashing through
and leave me shattered on the floor,
a mess of jolly jumping molecules!"

Obit Backlash

Today I read
in the *New York*
Times that
author James
Baldwin had
died of
cancer, in
France, at
his home,
and
I remembered
sitting in
an apartment
rental office
twenty-seven
years ago
and watching
the agent
ask an
applicant
if he was
a "friend"
of James
Baldwin, or
did he just
know him,
or had he
heard of
the apartment
through him
or any of
his friends,
and the guy

hesitated
and said
Well
yes sort of,
and the agent
said Get
out of this
office right
now! and turned
to me and said
Jesus Christ!
How may I
help you?

The Happy Whistler

When I was a child, the phrase "whistle while you work" came to mind easily not only because it was the title of a song made famous by the film *Snow White,* but also because people whistled. They whistled melodies while they worked, while they walked down the street, while they shaved. Men gave a wolf whistle when an attractive woman walked by, and they gave a loud whistle to get someone's attention, such as a taxi driver or fellow worker in the distance. Their mouths and tongues went into whistle positions, the breath was exhaled or inhaled, the eyes took on a casual inwardness, and the tones emerged into the air, sometimes pure and simple, sometimes with elaborate flourishes. When did widespread whistling begin to die out?

I taught myself to whistle, by trial and error, eventually becoming a passable whistler. In recent years, I have found myself walking down the street and whistling some tune or other that has been going through my head. Passersby glance at me and then look away. But I am immured inside the world of whistling. The mouth and tongue form various configurations, each one corresponding to a particular note, a note that my brain has miraculously chosen, but I don't know how I do it. My legs alternate in moving forward, thrilled with blood and sensation, but I don't understand how I control them. My heart is beating, my lungs are going up and down, my head turns to look left and right: I am like an aircraft carrier moving across the water with systems fully operational. A little man comes out and blows a whistle. Permission to come aboard?

The Austrian Maiden

I wish I had blonde hair
and was a maiden, on a farm, in Austria,

in the nineteenth century, on a sunny day,
with rosy cheeks and blue eyes, just

like those Nazi images of healthy farmgirls.
But are my great-grandchildren going

to be monsters? Then I will have none.
I will milk the cow and tell Hans

and the others to keep their mitts off me.
I will fill my evening hours with the sad music

of Schubert and the sad poetry of Heine.
It will be so beautiful.

Mountains Are a Feeling

Said Byron. I sat up
with a revision
of who he was because
of how he said that:
so straight out, and he
so windy and full
of commas. Mountains
are a feeling: the mountains
get inside him and he
in them, and then
he's free of Byron's body
and the rush to death.
I can see that, or thought
I could, as his four words
swept into me and I stayed
up until some other words
began to fly around inside
my head and out, and he
was gone again.

The County Fair

The Holstein looks at us with big eyes but with no expression in them. What images are flashing in its brain? The white goat walks over as if to ask a question, but it has no question to ask: there is no question mark in the goat world. The rabbit's pink eyes dilate when a hand draws near, but it does not move, and like a houseshoe, it says nothing. The two holes in the top of the goose's beak are in search of something to get huffy about: the poor goose is angry and without real nostrils. The black-and-white feathers exploding from the head of the rooster show that he is ready for war against the Infidel. The piglet walks and trots around with white eyebrows. He *likes* the Infidel.

The Abyss

We skid to a stop at the edge of what we realize is a cliff and our breath goes out over it and falls slowly into the abyss. The abyss is so hungry that it will accept even breath—it sends back a deep, hollow "Thank you"—the abyss so empty of everything but sorrow. We put the car in neutral, get out, and shove it over the cliff. This time the abyss burps back its satisfaction. We empty our pockets, take off our clothes, and hurl everything over the edge. But we will not hurl ourselves. We will never do that, because nothing that falls into the abyss ever hits bottom.

The Saint Lurches

The trick is to have a feel
for which is the best way
to find the way to heaven
without using any idea of heaven
or any idea of anything: I
have an idea: the saint
says So What, My Child,
and sits down on a rock.
It is dry and empty
in the desert and it is
very dry and full inside
the rock that automatically
becomes the saint's heart,
thumping and banging. But
no one can hear them, this
sacred thumping and banging,
this silent lurching here
and there where no one is.

Voice and Fur

I touch my dog and she wags.
I straighten up the atmosphere
by viewing the fog and rain
through the screen door and she
takes a look too: dog eyes
that go flat gold and turn
to orbs. Her vocal mechanism
won't let her give out
the soft bursts of "papa" or
even the bubbles of baby talk.
So I talk to her so my voice can be
to her ear what her fur is
to my hand, drizzle across the clouds
that are now starting to separate.

Poem in a Manner Not My Own

to you, Max Jacob

It's Sunday, the day of rest. Should you lie back on a pink satin cushion and doze the afternoon away? But of course! This is, after all, 1889, and the boating party will not return for hours, and then you will hear the concertina from far away. You will have plenty of time to adjust your clothing and slick back your bushy eyebrows.

But wait, the boat has come back early, with no music! Skirts uplifted, the ladies are coming down the . . . you know, the slanting walkway down from the side of a ship that has docked, it has rope handrails, there is fog, and the foghorn gives out a foghorn blast, like the deep grunt of a whale that has eaten one of the ladies! The one with the concertina!

The Sweeper

I like to sweep the floor
with a cornstraw broom
and watch the dust mass up
and move along
each time I swing the broom.
I like the swoosh and scratch
along the boards
that brighten up as I go by.
And when I have a pile
that's big enough, I nudge it
in the dustpan, this way
and that, until it's all aboard,
except a thin line of dust
that can't be smaller.
Tough little dust! I raise
the broom up high and bring
it down and past the line
to make a gust and then
the tiny dust is gone. I love
my pan of big new dust.

Listening to Joe Read

I'm reminded that what made him great
was not that he was a great reader (he wasn't)
but that he was Joe: "History.
What with history piling up so fast,
almost every day is the anniversary
of something awful." Was Ted
in the audience at the Ear Inn
in 1983? I think I hear his chortle.
Joe's voice in my ear and his ashes
up in the meadow now dark, it's night.
I have plenty of time to say all this,
as long as Joe has time on this tape to read
as many times as I want to play it,
as if he's here, as of course he is,
inside this little brain,
its wheels turning round and round.

Bluebird

You can't expect
the milk to be delivered
to your house
by a bluebird
from the picture book
you looked at
at the age of four:
he's much older
now, can't carry those
bottles 'neath his wing,
can hardly even carry a tune
with his faded beak
that opens some nights
to leak out a cry
to the horrible god
that created him.

Don't think I'm
the bluebird, or that
you are. Let him get
old on his own and
die like a real bluebird
that sat on a branch
in a book, turned his head
toward you, and radiated.

Hug

The older I get, the more I like hugging. When I was little, the people hugging me were much larger. In their grasp I was a rag doll. In adolescence, my body was too tense to relax for a hug. Later, after the loss of virginity—which was anything but a loss—the extreme proximity of the other person, the smell of hair, the warmth of the skin, the sound of breathing in the dark—these were mysterious and delectable. This hug had two primary components: the anticipation of sex and the pleasure of intimacy, which itself is a combination of trust and affection. It was this latter combination that came to characterize the hugging I have experienced only in recent years, a hugging that knows no distinctions of gender or age. When this kind of hug is mutual, for a moment the world is perfect the way it is, and the tears we shed for it are perfect too. I guess it is an embrace.

Bobbie and Me on Bicycles

Reading Hazlitt's essay "On Going a Journey" tonight, I had the fleeting recollection of approaching a corner, in Holland. I was riding a bicycle down a quiet two-lane road, looking for the sign that would tell me where to turn right, onto the road to the museum. It was one of those days that seem pleasant in the memory because one can remember being neither hot nor cold. There must have been a sign, because I am making a right turn, and as I do I look back over my shoulder and see the face of my companion, which is smiling and sparkling, and which seems to be growing larger and larger as it detaches from her neck and floats up, tilted a little, like a balloon wafted by a breeze, and in the space around her head are pink and white ovals, slowly rotating and tumbling. By now we are pedaling straight down the road and her head has returned to normal, and the ovals have vanished. She is laughing a little, girlish and free, happy to be gliding along on a bicycle past the big trees on both sides of the road that is taking us to the museum.

And Oil

If a certain society of the past thought of you as a smelly, hairy beast who would eat tin cans, they might designate you as a scapegoat. But would a real goat care all that much? Surely the tin is brighter on the other side, the applause louder, because don't tin hands make more noise? The tin people are waiting for you with open arms.

Poem

Though we're all deep
it isn't that easy to be profound
and get away with it. Aeschylus
and Jimmy Schuyler do, though.
Jimmy's flowers plunge into a more resonant
version of themselves while staying
exactly the same. How do they do that?
The surface of this table
is a smooth white that starts to suggest
something else and then doesn't. It's
just a tabletop. When I run my fingers
over it, it makes a cool swoosh.
I do it again. Cool swoosh.

The Drummer Boy

Oh what a sleepy night! The eyelids are drooping, the shoulders are slumped, the nostrils are wheezing, and Tommy the miniature drummer boy statue is yawning on the haystack where he landed last night when the farmboy hurled him into the dark sky. And now above the new-mown fields the stars burst into the drummer boy's brain and rain silver fear into his nervous system. He will have to get used to the fact that—oh, it makes me tired just to think of it—the fact that there are so many miles between him and the stars that are so immense but look so small and may not even be there anymore, just as he is not there anymore for the farmboy, the boy who himself will soon be leaving home.

Medieval Salad Dive

I don't see why I can't dive into that salad bowl
and rough up the lettuce, shaking my blubbery jowls
and uttering great guttural growls, Grrr, I'm
a medieval German and I'm feeling frisky and
in need of salad dressing! So bring on the fine lady
who wails perpetually, "O Wotan, strike me dead
if I'm to face another day!" Strike the tambour
and stomp your cruddy feet, men of my tribe,
for tonight I dive into the salad bowl!

The Drink

I am always interested in the people in films who have just had a drink thrown in their faces. Sometimes they react with uncontrollable rage, but sometimes—my favorites—they do not change their expressions at all. Instead they raise a handkerchief or napkin and calmly dab at the offending liquid, as the hurler jumps to her feet and storms away. The other people at the table are understandably uncomfortable. A woman leans over and places her hand on the sleeve of the man's jacket and says, "David, you know she didn't mean it." David answers, "Yes," but in an ambiguous tone—the perfect adult response. But now the orchestra has resumed its amiable and lively dance music, and the room is set in motion as before. Out in the parking lot, however, Elizabeth is setting fire to David's car. Yes, this is a contemporary film.

You Never Know

1) What might happen.
2) How people will behave.
3) Oh anything.

Three rules that live
in the house next door.

Along comes the big bad philosopher,
and at their door
he hurls the mighty bolts
of lightning
from his brain.

The door is unimpressed.
Behind it the rules
are chuckling.

I witness this scene
through the kitchen curtains
as I rinse the dishes.

A Prescription for a Happy Sort of Melancholy

A small gray-brown bird sat on the power line and chirped a few times, flipping its tail up and down. Then it flew a few feet over to a branch, where it sat, jerking its head this way and that. Then it flew off into the heavier woods, but a moment later returned, landing on a higher branch, then flapped up to an even higher one. After looking around and chirping a few more times, it fell silent, flicking its tail. It seems contented, perhaps because it is plump and alert, prosperous and chipper. The branches cannot complain about the bird's landing on them: they are deeply involved in branchness, so deeply they do not even "know" the bird is there. The bird doesn't know I'm watching. What is watching me? I am watching me.

Metaphor of the Morning

The morning is as clean and bright
as a freshly shaved cheek splashed with water
and rubbed with a new white towel.
Ah, the joys of metaphor!

But what if the morning were as dirty as
an old hag with a wen for a head
that is licking its chops and drooling on you?
Ah, the joys of metaphor!

But what if a blank metaphor descended from the sky
and landed lightly in your living room,
a cloudy, shifting swirl of gray tones and smoke?
It would be a Greek god! It would scare you!

Toybox

Let's say that we have only one number, one shape, and one color: six, square, and dun. No, let's not say that. Let's have two numbers, one shape, and three colors: two and two, a triangle, red, white, and green. Wait, isn't two and two just one number? No. You are a man with two triangular heads. Your face is green, with red eyes and teeth and white hair and nostrils. Your nostrils are sneeze exits. Achoo! Achoo! Two and two triangles of sneeze zoom out and fade, like fireworks in the night sky, glittering and falling to the *oooh*s and *aaah*s of your red lips, your wooden lips that we must now put back in the box, which we close and slide back under the bed.

To Anne Porter

I never wrote back to you about
the poem you sent at Christmas
because I did not know how to, exactly.
The shouting voices in the dark
hills a few days A.D.
brought out a scary memory in my head
of actually being there, one of those
shepherds, the one who felt suddenly tender
and filled with exploding ladders of light
whose sparks fell among the sleepy animals.
I wanted to come back swiftly
to tell you I'm still there
for you, though not for me myself.
The me myself floats up the evening street from work
a wisp of muscled doubt
invisible in the snow falling among traffic lights.

The Future of Your Name

Put the word *Marvin*
in front of any other word
and you'll see it's funny.
But if you put it
after any word, it isn't.
If you say only the first
syllable, pause, and say
the second, it will lose
all meaning, just as some day
your name will lose all meaning.
Its phonemes will dash about
in search of meaning, but
the future won't have any meaning
left for it. It will be all used up.

A Rude Mechanical

Whisk the curtain away and reveal
the new scene, hurrah!
it's the little village
again, with its little villagers
and the light coming
from everywhere
on this day without sun.
Their blue faces fly
around in the air
and red and green stripes
crisscross the atmosphere,
for today is a holiday
and the cows are folded up
and placed inside of envelopes
in the cool barns. But now
I must think of something
to say in my speech. "My dear
fellow villagers. . . ." Yes,
that's the stuff!

Poet as Immortal Bird

A second ago my heart thump went
and I thought, "This would be a bad time
to have a heart attack and die, in the
middle of a poem," then took comfort
in the idea that no one I have ever heard
of has ever died in the middle of writing
a poem, just as birds never die in midflight.
I think.

The Idea of Rotterdam

This idea
has an undertow like a philosopher
staring at breakfast in a room
whose dim light comes in through one small window
and his wife is clanging pots and pans
as in a comic strip, and all of Rotterdam goes
out and hits the windowsills with hot
soapy water like those big puffy clouds
tinged with gray and pushed across the sky
above the lowing cattle whose shepherd boy
now turns to look at you
and then away, his hat flapping
in the wind this
way and that.

Exceptions to the Rule

I take exception to the rule
that says I may not love you forever
because that's too long a time
for mortal man: we get forever
minus a big chunk.
More than a bug gets.
Such as the one I just killed.
A watched pot never boils
unless you watch it after it boils,
and then all the water is gone,
up in smoke, like spirit,
for the spirit is thoroughly exceptional,
subject to its own regulations:
everything is one-time only,
like the glass electric gun of Alessandro Volta,
like the formation of these words in their ink drying,
subject to smudge. I lean
to kiss you: we are smudged
by each other's softness
and a little of it rubs off on us,
like the smile as it first entered
the environment several hundred thousand years ago
via the exceptional head of homo sapiens
who still unrolls a red carpet
in your idea of yourself: out there
a fresh breeze is rising about the faces
of young girls still so pretty and free,
the way I want to be
the originator of a chain reaction
that sends a jagged love throughout the world and on.

Crossing the Alps

Are you really going to try? That's a pretty steep drop. I wouldn't even get close to the edge if I were you. It has a grassy fringe that looks friendly, but remember, this is a drawing in a style that is meant to look friendly. Even that stone on the left looks as though it had been put there just to say howdy. But don't be deceived: because the line of the cliff extends no further than the bottom of the paper, you have no way of knowing how far down it goes. And the echo you hear is simply the memory of the sound of a word you thought of saying, but didn't. So if you want to get to the other side, I wouldn't just run and leap. I'd get another piece of paper and draw a nice, sturdy bridge, over which some clouds are floating. This one drawing is not enough.

Think and Do

I always have to be doing something, accomplishing something, fixing something, going somewhere, feeling purposeful, useful, competent—even coughing, as I just did, gives me the satisfaction of having "just cleared something up." The phone bill arrives and minutes later I've written the check. The world starts to go to war and I shout, "Hey, wait a second, let's think about this!" and they lay down their arms and ruminate. Now they are frozen in postures of thought, like Rodin's statue, the one outside Philosophy Hall at Columbia. His accomplishments are muscular. How could a guy with such big muscles be thinking so much? It gives you the idea that he's worked all his life to get those muscles, and now he has no use for them. It makes him pensive, sober, even depressed sometimes, and because his range of motion is nil, he cannot leap down from the pedestal and attend classes in Philosophy Hall. I am so lucky to be elastic! I am so happy to be able to think of the word *elastic,* and have it snap me back to underwear, which reminds me: I have to do the laundry soon.

My Trip to Italy

And the white silk blossomed and bloomed and blew over the white bed out into the room in the hill town that flew each night over all of Italy to see that all was well and it was,
And it was wonderful, actually, in place, straight up and down, with curves, and ideas, such as where is my old friend now, my old friend who now is never aging here or there, as in *ecco mi qua,* and out I go into the sunlight, as a star goes out into space and becomes a stove, *bing! tac!*
And those rays of light you see everywhere, those traveling stigmata that set fire to a little patch of forehead, oh! ouch! hey! I don't want to be a saint, get off my forehead,
Because I have a red fire engine and a red fire of my own, two yellow dogs go woof, one in each of my ears as I enter and the walls slide to and fro a little, I get scared, I'll never take an airplane again!
Except I do, one whose curtains are decorated with a cherry motif and a border of little blue ducks because this is a children's airplane drifting o'er the clouds besmashed with radiant gold streaks across the stratosphere and, ah, the service, the in-flight rumba and the rum punch, knocked silly, sideways, big tears in your eyes.

Haiku

That was fast.
I mean life.

The Periscope

"I"
is the way to see things as if
through a periscope
through which fear arrives
or the satisfaction of the captain
and the crew when the enemy explodes.
And then we dive, dive
and hide deep down, go
inside ourselves like animals
whose memories have lost the things
they've killed as well as who they are,
a great gift and greater terror
when animal and angel unite behind a star
the skinny "I" floats past in the dark.

Little Ode to Suzanne Farrell

No ode is big
                    or fast enough to have
    the very all of you inside it
            so I will have to be like you
  and climb inside myself and fly
                into the outline that the pattern
        of my moving self has left behind

the outline of the possible you impossibly beautiful in everyone

like a little girl suddenly seeing the angles in
a light blue protractor and therefore being them

Where was I and who?

You for whom
we get dressed up
and go uptown and up
the elevator shaft as
    the curtain goes up and when
          you glide in on your diagonal
we fall into the elevation of the dream
  that has a hummingbird and Saint Teresa of Avila in it

                          and you

who hover in the air like a disembodied heart
shocked into eternity for the split second the music
turns to face you and you find your face up there
in the dark where we are and a smile on it

There is space here and air and breath, clarity
    of perfect tears that beauty makes us cry so automatically

        as you wrap the world around
    your finger, then wrap yourself
                        around the world

Bob Creeley Breakthrough

This is going well today
I mean the fingers typing
and the face smiling
and the breath going in and out

like a nice girl on a date
who for the first time removes
her blouse, but your heart

is pounding so hard you
can't actually
see anything
except a mental
image
of Robert
Creeley

—Bob, go away
so I can see this girl and do
whatever it is I'm supposed to
do. Your line breaks
are making it
impossible!

How to Become a Tree in Sweden

I look up ahead and see
the trees of Sweden waving at me

Gently they wave their bending heads
The light goes dim above the land

And down below the lights come on
And Swedish people one by one

Come out to shop and say hello
as crisply as a Swedish cracker that

fresh out of the package goes snap.
And soon the air is full of snaps

And schnapps and weimaraners and
me, my various selves united,

for a moment Swedish, a tree myself,
waving and lost among the others.

Aquamarine Fantasy

Me? I am presently falling off the front end of a great battleship, to honor the god of the sea, Frank O'Hara. We are little figurines in a bottle you can see through and can't figure out how we got in there. Heigh ho! Wooden waves advance against our noses, but to no avail, for Frank and I, with the wind in our spirits, sail bravely on. Heigh ho! Our bottle rolls away. Heigh ho! The highballs are jiggling their ice cubes and the tropical images are swirling amidst the frosted panes, the fish are hanging in midair outside. They form a pattern that continues onto the seashore and the hills, onto the department store and your pajamas, onto the aria and the idea. Drink hearty, lads, for tonight we're falling off the front end of a great battleship, the *Frank O'Hara.*

Frisky

The black-and-white terrier
flexed his body
in midair, turned
and yelped

It was his birthday
and he was two

Elegy

It's a little too dark and deep the ocean
for me. It's a little too "offset press."
And if gorilla, striped rubber ball, and baby
disappear, there's always the way they
disappeared, to think about, and find inside,
and take it outside, and place it on the ground,
and sing the light up out of it, whoosh, into
the clouds, to make you happy, and not fall down,
and dinner is on time and where it should be,
on the table, this evening, again!

Feathers

fly up and pow apart
from the bird they were.

Now we will shoot the post
and kill the fence. It is

good to knock things down
and destroy them. We are

like a good storm or an
earthquake and some lava.

Life will come back by itself.
And we will come back too.

We are not bad people.
We are happy monsters.

Flash Photo

Once again I am having the fantasy of seeing my father on the front porch at night as he watches the rain come down through the trees, but this time, instead of standing behind him, I am hurled around and I see his face, his actual face with light on it, and his eyes open, and it is so real and frozen in time that I cannot bear to look. I jump up from my chair and walk around.

Old Song

What kind of fool am I?
An older fool!
The bells on my costume
gleam dully
in the flickering firelight.
A moth flutters
around my cap.
The massive King snores massively
in his massive chair.
Dare I wake him?
Or tiptoe down the hall?
An ember crumbles.
Would that I,
like the humble bee,
were flying back to paradise!

The Poet's Breakfast

What does a writer do? A writer sits and goes through hell. I'm not exactly going through hell, but then, I'm not driven by the belief that the world is waiting for my next bit of hard-earned genius. No, I would rather be raking and piling the grass, wrapping the two weeping birches for the winter, or patching the hole in the woodstove. I seem to feel that since I can do nothing to save souls, it is my job to slow the material world's inevitable slide into rack and ruin. I like the material world. I think objects should be respected, the same as people and ideas. I even respect art, especially when we consume it and it becomes us. Juan Gris's 1914 painting *Breakfast* became part me in 1962, when I first saw it. I had never seen anything that was beautiful in the way that it was beautiful. I should add that I was looking at it with Joe Brainard, who knew how truly beautiful it was, and I was seeing it through his eyes and wanting to leap into the paint and be refracted through and along its various angles and disappearances. And now, as Joe and I drive to town, I'm struck by how bizarre it is that in a few years he will be gone and by how brave he is to keep enjoying the details of everyday life. I am forty-nine years old and surrounded by death. Does writing help? Probably not.

I Guess

I had forgotten that
when Ted Berrigan sent
Conrad Aiken his *Sonnets*
Aiken rebuked him, and
the letter was published
in *The Collected Letters*
of Conrad Aiken—one
of his last, actually—
so that when I
read about it yesterday
in an interview Ted
gave, I was surprised:
the blue fox jumped
over the black log
and ran like hell.

Lullaby

Another little poem
before I go to bed
and there to sleep,
a little poem to bid
the world goodnight
and lay me down to sleep
inside the warmth
of being fast asleep,
then slow and slower,
down into the deep
warm way we have
of sinking to the far away
inside our body's self,
inside our pillow head,
inside our sleeping bed.

The Song of Grandpa

Let's take the squeak of a chair.
Not creak. Creak is for wood. This
is a squeaking spring, a sound effect
for when Grandpa stands up: *squeak,*
Oh no, it's his stiff back! Grandpa puts
a hand back there and groans a little.
He does this every time, even when
his back has been removed by thought,
such as the one that has him in Egypt
with a scepter and tall hat, and the light
is flickering across his face as he breaks out
in eerie, holy song and the Pharaoh himself
kneels down and weeps. The high priest
wails out his melody, and Egypt weeps.

Music

He was listening to the lariat as its loop swept round and round above his head and he stood perfectly still, hat and chaps unmoving, eyes fixed on the ground, which had only some dust and the marks to show where his feet should go at various points in the performance. It looked like a diagram for the tango, only it was in full color and tilted slightly toward him, as if to make it easier to read. But nothing could be made easier for the cowboy whose tears were ready to burst forth, nothing could be made easier for him.

Wisconsin

It's hard to find that little room again,
the one you like to find yourself in
but not have to find. A certain plateau of tranquility
spreads evenly over the face of the coming night
and there is large smiling in the cracked darkness.
The puzzle holds, though, even when your little sister
tips the table over with a silent crash
against the loud floor. And now there is some
two-colored radiation from the carolers
who have upper bodies and lower stilts
that vault their voices into a Renaissance
whose inside is entirely covered with a floral pattern
and cisterns placed every twenty steps along
the long hallway that leads to the little room
with its fireplace and burning logs
and terrible buildup of soot on the stone legs
of the Fireplace Giant, who seems born
for this terrible destiny, always to have
darkened legs and flaring eyebrows
that rise as if lifted by invisible threads
into the evening above his stocking cap,
a blue dome that holds in his massive idea
that thunders in the distance and wants out.

Literature

Bang! goes the gun. Big bang! goes the shotgun.
Bong! says the shogun.
The sound waves of his bong emanate out into the clear night
that is taking place in what
the French call *le Japon, avec son soir japonais.*
Pan! dit the fusil. *Pain!* dit le shogun, *pain*
pour tout le monde. Il prend son fusil et tire
sur les baguettes qui volent dans le soir japonais.
And all the rest is literature.

The Lips of the Dairymen

It's midnight, and the thirteen dairymen are working at fever pitch, in a desperate effort to save their company, the little creamery in the hills. And they are singing a song from the old country, a plaintive song about being slaughtered by Cossacks, but rather than depressing them it seems to feed an inner glow that radiates out through their dark blue lips. Along the rounded sides of the silver vats, the reflections of their lips curve, glint, and slide away.

Morning Poem

Open the side window and let
the morning air in and the light
that has erased the fog
so chirping comes in
as if to say "It's alright, Ron,
we're here just as
we've always been,
the same blue jay on Fourth Street
in 1952 as now," the robin
redbreast, the wrens and sparrows
and all those others inside my chest
when they call out to say
"This is my place, my cage."

Album

The mental pictures I have of my parents and grandparents and my childhood are beginning to break up into small fragments and get blown away from me into empty space, and the same wind is sucking me toward it ever so gently, so gently as not even to raise a hair on my head (though the truth is that there are very few of them to be raised). I'm starting to take the idea of death as the end of life somewhat harder than before. I used to wonder why people seemed to think that life is tragic or sad. Isn't it also comic and funny? And beyond all that, isn't it amazing and marvelous? Yes, but only if you have it. And I am starting not to have it. The pictures are disintegrating, as if their molecules were saying, "I've had enough," ready to go somewhere else and form a new configuration. They betray us, those molecules, we who have loved them. They treat us like dirt.

The Love Cook

Let me cook you some dinner.
Sit down and take off your shoes
and socks and in fact the rest
of your clothes, have a daquiri,
turn on some music and dance
around the house, inside and out,
it's night and the neighbors
are sleeping, those dolts, and
the stars are shining bright,
and I've got the burners lit
for you, you hungry thing.

Nuts

I read *Fear and Trembling*
expecting to be scared
but instead I found a nut
had written it in Denmark,
a man obsessed with thoughts
about the story of Abraham and Isaac
and what it meant. I didn't see
what it had to do with fear *or*
trembling, but the more I read
the more I liked the title and
its being on that book. I guess
I am a nut too.

When George Calls

I'm looking forward to the moment when George calls me from Italy to say that he's just gotten a phone installed. It is always a pleasure to talk to George when he's across the ocean, but it will be an even greater pleasure that he will be using his own phone to call me at my own phone. We will be two grown-up men talking on our own phones from our own homes. Why does that thought give me such pleasure?

And Was It Leeds?

for Trevor Winkfield

At an early age I should have started writing books for children. Well, I did, but they weren't suitable for children. And they weren't really books. They were whiffs of books. A few adults liked the whiffs, but I could see that these adults were strange. That is, they were artists, tiny artists only a foot or so tall, barely able to lift the books they read, hearts going thump thump thump.

People with Heads

I am unafraid of the guillotine
because they would never chop off the head
of a stick figure, the shape
I assume when I travel back
into the past far enough
that you never can tell what the locals
might do to you. I stand
in the Place de la Concorde and watch
the rising, heavy blade and I gleam.
These poor fools! They
chop and chop, head after head,
but no matter how fast they chop,
there are always more and more
people with heads.

Pensée juste

Gustave Flaubert—how did his breath
smell as he roared out each phrase
alone in his room, night after night?
Bad, I bet, the drooping mustache hairs
blown out by the booming wind,
Mom's cutlery rattling in the sideboard,
the dog trembling beneath the cupboard, and
Mom herself turning down the gaslight
and slipping into bed with the thought,
"He's perfectly normal."

Ape Man

Why is it that I seem to want to write so often about writing? I'm not a theoretician of language. I do seem to feel, though, that there is something about writing that no one has ever quite described or explained, something about the way words are like a food chain that goes down simultaneously to the smallest creature and to the pit of our stomachs. But that doesn't come near to the mystery. Perhaps it can't be put into words, because words can't be used to describe themselves, just as an eye can't see itself. It can see only a reflection of itself, a glimpse at the fascination of being, like the pre-human creature that got split in half by the shimmering water he was about to drink. He bent down and drank from his own lips. I bend down and suck my own words up off the page.

The Woodpecker Today

The wings of the redheaded woodpecker flashed white as he landed on the deck rail, well fed and magisterial, and rattled off a quick succession of pecks. Then he hopped and drilled again, paused and drilled, then raised his head and turned his neck to the left, as if to receive a message from the sky. Then he sprang into the air and flew around the side of the house. There were two brief bursts of drilling, then silence.

While he was drilling the rail, I recalled an article that explained why woodpeckers don't get headaches. Apparently their skulls are lined with a spongy material that cushions the shock, a structure that resembles that of a football helmet. In fact, the article stated, modern football helmet design owes something to the woodpecker. As these thoughts ran through my head, for a moment I saw a small helmet materialize on the woodpecker's head—a silver Detroit Lions helmet. I hope he comes back. I would like to get the entire uniform on him.

Little Elegy

Blaise Cendrars in his final days, old
and ill, wrote down his final words:
This morning on the windowsill a bird.
I find that so beautiful and moving
I can barely stand it, though
it makes me see the aged poet, head
turned toward the window and a small bird
perched there, staring in, angling its head
at the bulbous nose and squinty eyes:
I have come to visit you, old man.
But now I'll lift my wings and they will beat,
for flying is my great thrill,
and where the wings sprout out
is calling me to leap and fly.
Good-bye.
Morning, windowsill, and bird
all flown away. Good-bye, good-bye.

Sacred Heart

Last night I dreamed that my sister-in-law and I were snugly bedded in a dark cocoon, talking softly, safe and alone. With that part of me that once was in love with her, I said, "I missed you when you were gone."

"Oh," she said, "you missed me because I speak English."

"No, I really just missed *you.*"

It was deeply satisfying to open my heart this way.

My father had torn off his oxygen mask, flung his gown onto the floor, and now, stark naked and peeing into the air, was clambering, tubes and all, over the bed railing, giving loud grunts.

I sprang up, grabbed him by the shoulders, and slowly talked him back down onto his pillow, where he drifted off again. After mopping the floor, I went back to my cot.

It was still dark out.

I lay down and thought about my dream, the dream that was filled with the same rush of sweetness that had come over me the day before, when I had looked out the hospital window, at early light, and far below saw a person walking down the street alone, and felt the words *thank you* bursting from my chest.

Amy,

it's interesting that
no matter how one starts
a poem, the poem can lead
to something else.
I left home
to grow into
the poet I thought
I'd like to be, the one
whose work would
show the way he found
to live at peace with
his mortality. So
far I've only found the way
to go upstairs
and bang against the wall
of silence, the one that moves
from room to room,
and laugh. It's fun
to stand there
puzzled for a wink,
then go back down
and ping! remember
what I went up for
and go back up
for it. And there
it is: this poem for you.

from
POEMS I GUESS I WROTE

Nunc

I have two hours to
kill. With nothing to kill them
with. If this were the end
of my life and I were offered
two more hours, I'd rasp out
"Yes, give me two hours more!"
Now that I think about it, who
knows what I'd do, or why I'd
think that two more hours would make
a difference.
The time inside this room now feels rosier,
pregnant and sorrowful, the painting
of the china elephant, the smell
of wet weather, the *Complete*
Do-It-Yourself Manual, and now
an hour and forty-five minutes left.

Poem to John Berryman

I got that little *frisson*
you mentioned, and I'm from
Oklahoma, like you, went
to Columbia, like you, walked
over the bridge in
Minneapolis, the one
you waved good-bye from,
to me, I thought! I liked
your book on Stephen Crane,
saw you drunk in the Guggenheim,
left your reading at halftime:
you didn't make it: flames
bursting against the ice,
and you went right down
into the ground, where you
are now. And here
in the mountains, at
night, my little boy says,
My fingers shiver when I'm scared.
Not my feet, though.
They're braver than my hands.

Postcards

1. FROM CHARLES BAUDELAIRE

Hello, dainty monster
This place is in my brain
The weather is some grim nocturnal feast
The folks are the Swan
I'm feeling caresses upon your body
I spend my time like the dumb brutes
I need a loathsome bill
I'll see you upon the finite ocean
Give my regards to the finite ocean

2. FROM GÉRARD DE NERVAL

Hello, widower
This place is "Why did I come?"
The weather is by the abolished tower
The folks are in a carriage, having just woken
I'm feeling all Rossini, all Mozart, all Weber
I spend my time in another life
I need a boa constrictor
I'll see you on fire
Give my regards to El Desdichado

3. FROM STÉPHANE MALLARMÉ

Hello, calm block
This place is Edgar Poe's tomb
The weather is good-bye
The folks are these nymphs
I'm feeling my nose in front of the blue

I spend my time over there
I need to open my mouth
I'll see you transparent
Give my regards to the Chinaman

4. FROM MAX JACOB

Hello, people of Saumur!
This place is in scarlet automatic machines which we shall own
The weather is for sale
The folks are sixty years old
I'm feeling less hard
I spend my time in front of the hostile armor
I need its boat shape
I'll see you with my chisel
Give my regards to Mr. Chocarneau, 18, boulevard Carnot

5. FROM GUILLAUME APOLLINAIRE

Hello, lovely lightning flash that keeps going on
This place is the future
The weather is just between you and me
The folks are sweet and noble
I'm feeling you
I spend my time wounded in the head
I need several languages
I'll see you under chloroform
Give my regards to these flames that promenade

6. FROM TRISTAN TZARA

Hello, b-b-b-b-b-b-b-b-b-b-b-bird
This place is in helicopters
The weather is on the tips of the black branches
The folks are a new invention
I'm feeling honest
I spend my time in the evening of the 10th of June 1921
I need to put the child in the vase
I'll see you and you go by
Give my regards to 10054

Prose Poem

Where the street crossed the ravine it was dark in the rest of the town, and walking there at dusk was like crossing two square feet, with an assortment of thirty marvelously detailed attacking Indians and defending soldiers, for milk inside seems to disappear: sit it upright and it's full again.

Horatio Street

is way over in the West Village
N.Y.C.

in a one-room basement apartment
I'd wake up
Morning? look
out the window
Shoes

The light a sort of pleasant untorn gray
a life made simple
by the absence of weather
which made reading a breeze

symbols of transformation

my desk a discard
from a dentist bent
on going modern
and a toaster with faulty wiring which mysteriously got better
and is still my toaster

and James Baldwin who had lived upstairs
until a few weeks ago now a ghost

For local color the local yokel
The White Horse was some drunk people's White House

Gelatinous water slapdash against the West Side piers
and those refrigerated diesel meat trucks
pink in the dawn light
rolling up Horatio at 4 or 5
4 or 5 inches from my interested ear

and late-night rain against the all-nite diner where
giant Men came in in white smocks
smeared with blood dried brown

and the drunken stranger in suit and tie
who chased me down the street
tears streaming down his face
crying "Peter! Peter!"

It was a nice street
not spectacular or pretty
pleasantly remote
pleasantly near
1961–62

I figured the space between me and Nero

was infinity

on the balcony
overlooking the cemetery

I had an idea

of what it would be like to be a tornado of speech driving away the celery

The next day

I returned to the tomb

Gilgamesh Gets Confused

I am a nothing, a nothing.
I hail from a village in Fear
and I waver as I approach the market
with my little basket of russets.
It is September in Omsk
and it is July in Martinique
and it is no month on the moon
because the moon *is* the month.
The face of the man in the moon
is larger than usual tonight
as he sings his happy aria about being
over several oceans at the same time.
We walk upright through trees,
toward the moon that keeps inching
its way off the scale and onto our insides
with a soft nudge. Bump. Now it's
inside me and I am as big as an ancient
Near Eastern religion and can explode
pottery all over the region
just by getting mad in my mind—
I want that red thing! Give me your red love
right now!—explode and break
your china closet glass objects and make
the dogs howl like Moctezuma's revenge
as it roars through your insides
that thought they'd gone to sleep already.
Wake up, world, and walk upright
through trees before they fall
in little packages to the earth
that is spinning in one
direction only, that is, no direction.

Second Cummings

see
here i am
me
big bam

here i am
sky blue
big bam
so you

sky blue
hey what
so you
think not

hey what
is that
think not
big hat

is that
your face
big hat
human race

your face
up there
human race
in air

up there
ee
in air
see

A Cloud in Diapers

Humans seem to be the only animals
that enjoy clouds. You never see a worm
rapt before a sunset, nor
a weimaraner. Maybe a chimpanzee
can find aesthetic pleasure
in those crimson indigo streaks:
look, he's clapping his hands and
leaping all around the promontory
above which the clouds keep drifting
and rolling, solemn, majestic, oddly huge,
in profile, free of charge, really oddly huge.

Solidus

Why am I making myself
do and be things that I don't really want to?
Because I have an idea of what I *should* be doing and/or
I don't have an idea of what I really want to be and/or do.
And/or both. I seem to be very and/or,
with an urge to flex everything until it loses
what I secretly feel to be its false polarity.
E.g., there is such a thing as good and
such a thing as evil, it's just
that they aren't opposites.
Am I a good person? Yes, after
a certain point, and no, after another.
Deep down I'm just down there, a kind of gurgling
black Jell-O that doesn't have any idea
of what's going on up here. Up here
I have on a baseball cap and have
a vague desire to fix the closet door.

Matins

I come in and sit down
with no faith in what
I'm about to do, that is
keep these words from flying
off the whoosh there goes one
and whoosh another, little paper
airplanes that take off on
their own, one to the first
blue jay of the day,
the other to the pulsing
inside of my entire body.
And it's quiet outside,
rain on the way.

9/16/5746

Monday I get up and go to work,
air's fresh there's a bunch of it

Shadow of a boom across the phone
company's face in sunny light

Atoms look O.K. arranged the way they are
I'm not thrilled but Jews, say, are or see

Same street different buzz and rush
My face Nordic in elevator goes up

I had until today
Forgotten all about it
How when you're standing there
Still pretty excited
In the late afternoon
The gray comes falling through the air
  The gray comes falling through the air

September 1970

Uh huh

Slanted

The year before, Chuck and I were in a downstairs room with Nelson Demarest and Ham Hamilton, a very small man with a very big talent. Ham animated the key "personality" scenes in our cartoons, and they always received enthusiastic applause from the staff when previewed at the studio. Ham could do amazing things with his diminutive fingers. He would often catch a jarful of flies, then make dozens of tiny paper airplanes, onto each of which he would glue a fly, feet down. Occasionally visitors entering our room would, much to their amazement, see a whole fleet of paper airplanes flying overhead.

Angel

Pretty little angel eyes
on a dark background
follow you into the foreground
and then close the moment

you feel they are
about to tell you something.
Do you wish to continue yes
or no, please indicate.

The angel eyes reopen,
this time with tears in them
and welling with even more tears
but this time it's your eyes

that close and inside
there's the song you sang
when you weren't afraid
anymore and a dog is barking

at a dark building in the dark,
parts of a collage without glue
whose pieces can be moved
around inside your head

that has neither ceiling nor floor,
for the house flew away
with the angel that keeps
coming back to look at you and cry.

The Control Tower Has Babel in It

and a couplet and a pig and a dog or mother
who flies and doesn't get embarrassed by

the whole social shift around her who is from
another world an old one a hick one a non-

contemporary one one with an accent that says
she's a hill girl she's from a movie she's my mammy

HOW TO BE PERFECT

Mortal Combat

You can't tell yourself not to think
of the English muffin because that's what
you just did, and now the idea
of the English muffin has moved
to your salivary glands and caused
a ruckus. But I am more powerful
than you, salivary glands, stronger
than you, idea, and able to leap
over you, thoughts that keep coming
like an invading army trying to pull
me away from who I am. I am
a squinty old fool stooped over
his keyboard having an anxiety attack
over an English muffin! And
that's the way I like it.

Rinso

The slight agitation
of pots and pans
and a few dishes
in sudsy water
into which hands
plunge and fingers
operate like in
a magic act in which
bubbles burst
into flowers presented
to the blonde girl
who rotates on
a wheel that flies
up through the
ceiling and
disappears.
The dishes
are sparkling.

Tops

When I was little I had a top
that spun on its point.
A lot of kids had tops,
I guess they spun them.
The tops went round and
around—but?
(The mystery
of centrifugal force?)
My top slowed down and
went crazy-wobble, and I
got up and spun
and staggered dizzy,
flopped and threw
the spin into the floor.

The Swiss Family Robinson

I never quite understood who
the Swiss Family Robinson were.
The inversion of their name
confused me at an early age,
just as the name of Mary Baker Eddy
sounded as though she started out
as a woman and turned into
a guy named Eddy. At Walt
Disney World there is an attraction
called Swiss Family Robinson that
involves a tree house, so I assume
they lived in a tree. Why they did
I don't know. It sounds rather
stressful to me, the fear
of falling out. I could look up
the Swiss Family Robinson
in a reference book, but
it's interesting not to know
something that everyone else knows.
However, I *would* like to know if there
are many people named Robinson
in Switzerland. If there are,
I would know something that
most people don't know.

Blizzard Cube

I'm going out to see the blizzard
that is approaching in the form of a cube.

I am in a children's book
where a blizzard won't hurt me.

After I have experienced the blizzard
to the fullest, to the very core of my being,

I will return to the house,
my head wrapped with the bandages

I put there to keep my brain inside my skull.
Later I will take them off, revealing

my mouth enough to tell you what
it was like inside the blizzard cube,

assuming, of course, that you will still
be there and interested.

Rialto

When my mother said Let's go down to the Rialto
it never occurred to me that the name Rialto

was odd or from anywhere else or meant anything
other than Rialto the theater in my hometown

like the Orpheum, whose name was only a phoneme
with no trace of the god of Poetry, though

later I would learn about him and about the bridge
and realize that gods and bridges can fly invisibly

across the ocean and change their shapes and land
in one's hometown and go on living there

until it's time to fly again and start all over
as a perfectly clean phoneme in the heads

of the innocent and the open
on their way to the Ritz.

Everybody and His Uncle

I was waiting to happen.
At a stoplight
the buildings curved up from my ears,
office buildings
with offices in them and people
doing office things, pencils
and paper clips, telephone rings—
Where is that report?
At Echo Lake the vacationers
have made the city only slightly
emptier, how did they get there?
By station wagon and dogsled
in the "old" days. The forest ranger
was Bob. He said we could spell his name
backwards if we wanted, then
our laughter vanished into his tallness.
I thought maybe he was not a forest ranger,
just a guy named Bob, but
it turned out he was part of the echo
of everything around there, which radiated
out a few short miles before the farmland set in.
The farmland had waited to happen
and then it did, just as it knew it would.
A farmhouse appeared and a front porch
and on it sat my Uncle Roy. He was very farmer.
"Get on this horse," he said.
But the horse said, "Don't."
"I would prefer to play baseball," I said.
Later we took Rena Faye to the hospital.
"Darn that horse," Roy said, "when his ears
laid back I saw trouble." The light changed,
my shoes went across the street
while I rose straight up into the high part of the air

so as to form a right angle
with the dotted line that lit up behind my shoes
as they turned into pots of gold
receding into that smaller and smaller thing
we call distance. But I was already there
in the distance, I had been waiting my whole life
to be wherever I should be at any given moment,
a ring around not anything. "Wake up, Rena Faye,"
said Roy, "we need to take you to the hospital."
She gave us the most beautiful smile
but it bounced off our faces and we forgot
to pick it up and put it somewhere safe.
It's probably still lying there on the road
in front of the house. Come to think
of it, I did pick mine up
as I looked out the back window of the car,
and as we skirted Echo Lake
everything got twice as big and then three times,
like laughter and hiccoughs flying among children
whose immortality has turned them
into temporary rubber statues of curvature in confusion
that slides into the appeasement of early evening.
That is, Rena Faye felt better, at least she was able
to know there was a bump on her head, and inside
the bump a small red devil running furiously in place.
"Rena Faye is going to be okay," said Roy,
but I wasn't so sure, there was a doctor involved
and a hospital with a lot of white in it.
The house hadn't changed, but the barn
was gone and the land stretched out flat
to far away. The horse was still waiting, for what
who knows? I was waiting at the light, and when it changed
I went on across the street
to where another part of town was waiting,
it was Europe and I was in or on it,
I had Europe touching my foot, the train

was pointing its big nose toward the Gare Saint-Lazare,
where you wake up even if you aren't asleep.
Rena Faye opened her eyes and said, "I don't think . . ."
and then a funny look
came across the street toward me, the one big horrible face
of surging forward, but I was like whatever bends
but doesn't break because I didn't give a whit about any of it,
I was in the forest and my name was almost Bob and the trees
didn't care about any of it either because tallness can't care.
Roy wasn't really my uncle, we just called him that.
When the sun rose his new picture window could be seen through
to the lone mimosa tree, its pink blossoms smiling frizzily,
and a car went by, not a Chevrolet or a Ford,
not a green or blue car,
just a car, with a person driving it. My notebook
and its pencils were ready to go and I
moved toward them as if music had replaced the sludge
we call air. I.e., Swiss cheese had become Gruyère.
The car started, then rolled back and stopped.
We got out and looked, then kicked ourselves. Moon,
is that what that is, that sliver? I was thinking,
the car was not thinking, my pencils were almost thinking,
all three of them, but they took too long and so
time went on ahead without them.
Then an angel from the side touched my head inside
and my head outside surrounded less and less.
His wristwatch is a street, green, yellow, blue, and open
as a meadow in which your parents are grazing
because the fodder and forage are stored away
in the kitchen cabinet too high for them to reach
with their muzzles. And lo the other parents are mooing
plaintively, tethered to an idea they like to dislike:
The fox is free. Silly old cows, the fox is never free,
he is just running, and with good reason, and with good legs,
from the ooga-ooga. Brrrrring!
Waterfall of afternoon!

And I left.
I went east three miles and then
fifteen hundred more, and then
three thousand five hundred more,
and then I turned around
and came back five thousand and no hundred.
My mother was still in the kitchen
standing on the yellow tiles
as dinner rose up out of the pots and pans
and hung in the air while she adjusted it.
Soon Dad came home and we dined
but he didn't and neither did Mother
and neither did I. We put the food
in our mouths and chewed and swallowed—
it tasted good—and we drank liquids
that also tasted good although
they were across the room and on the wall.
The phone rang. It was meaningless
like a proton, but Mother laughed
and said words that were exactly the words
she would have said, total illusion
and total reality at the same time, just as
Dad coughed fifty years later, it was me coughing,
which is why I left, heading east, and stopped
after fifteen hundred miles, and coughed again.
So this is Echo Lake? Sure looks nice.
Ice had once gone by.
High overhead was an iceberg just checking on things,
wings folded and in flames.
The soul materializes in the form of an echo and says
"I've been following you."
"But you are a shadow and only a shadow!"
"Only in the dark am I a shadow," the soul replies.
"In the light I am a very good lightbulb!"
"You are a big nothing something," the soul says.
The light changes and I start across.

Toothbrush

As the whisk broom
is the child of the ordinary broom,
which is cousin to the janitor's broom,
I am a toothbrush
when it comes to bristling,
insufficiently angry
or maybe too angry
to keep my bristles intact
since I know the debris
of the world is too great
for me to handle.
If I could save the world
by being crucified
I certainly would.
But who would nail
a toothbrush to a cross?

There Was a Man of Thessaly

There was a man of Thessaly
who jumped into a bush

and why, may I ask?
Because he was afraid of something?

Because he saw a bush and told himself
"I will jump into that bush"?

Maybe the fact that he had the idea
of jumping into the bush frightened him.

From great heights I have looked down
and thought, "What if I went crazy for a moment

and found myself plummeting?" and stepped
back to remember who I am. I am

a man of Tulsa who jumps into his car
and by a miracle ends up somewhere else,

then jumps into the miracle and ends up
what?

History Lesson

I think that Geoffrey Chaucer did not move
the way a modern person moves.
He moved only an inch at a time, in what
we call stop action. Everyone in his day moved
like that, so they could be shot into a tapestry,
but also because time moved in short lurches
and was slightly jagged and had fewer colors
for them to be in. But that was good. Humanity
has to take it one step at a time.

The Question Bus

What about your friend? Will he shoot flames from his nostrils as he hurls you across the lawn? Or will he fall on his knees and adopt you as his one and only god? Somewhere in between.

Somewhere in between a rock and a click, where the abstractions roam about in their ghostly attire. They are haunting our thoughts, we who wear human attire. When they ask you to dance, you should refuse.

You should also refuse to pay the check when having dinner with sunlight: it's evening, and he should be in bed! He might not even be sunlight!

He might not even be a ghost. He may be the one you have grown weary of waiting for, the last one off the bus at the end of the line. He may be the bus itself, belching flames as all four tires explode. Is he really your friend?

The Nail

Just sitting here,
relaxing,
stretched out,
dead as
a nail
bent over
and smashed
into the grain
of a door
carted off to
the dump
some years
ago, you
get sleepier
and sleepier at
the thought
of that nail,
buried in wood,
with no lips
to tell the tale.

Mir

—There is no synonym for synonym

In the shtetl,
only the crowing
of two cocks
that sound alike.

I bang into the water pail,
blue in the morning light,
though to tell the truth
I am blue in any light,

a powdery royal blue.
Our village does not fly
through the air—it is
nailed to the ground

and we hold on for dear life—
to each other, to the trees,
the cottage doors, whatever,
and we sing our local ditty:

O the cats and the wellsprings!
O the dogs and the birdbath!
O! O! O!

Why I Would Like to Have Been a Twelfth-Century Christian

I see
in my mind's eye
the crush of the faithful,
shoving jammed
into the Basilica
of St. Denis
so tightly
they were
according to Suger
immobile
"as marble statues,"
some of them
screaming
while others
burst into riot,
and the priests
jumped
through a window
and ran away
with the holy relics.

For Morris Golde

It might have been when
I was standing in front of
Kierkegaard's grave thinking
that his name means
churchyard that Morris
Golde was breathing his
last in St. Vincent's, where
Jimmy died too, and what
was I doing then—and
what am I doing now?
Death throws everything
into high relief, itself
the highest—its uppermost
crag is where we sigh,
relax, and stretch out as
far as the mind can go.
I'm part-way there is
a "deep" thought I can do
without, though I just
had it. I wish it would
get lighter faster. If it
were two weeks ago it
would be bright outside
instead of blue-gray.
Morris, you old thing.

Now at the Sahara

Where are those books I ordered and what
were they, oh yes, the *Divine Comedy* in three volumes
which I keep telling myself I am going to read
in toto, although I wonder about the "divine" part
that Dante himself didn't even have in his title
and to us "comedy" sounds like Shecky Greene
at the Sahara, Shecky who was funny and actually
kind of sad though not tragic. What is tragic is
that I started out thinking about Dante and
ended up thinking about Shecky Greene!

How to Be Perfect

> *Everything is perfect, dear friend.*
> —KEROUAC

Get some sleep.

Don't give advice.

Take care of your teeth and gums.

Don't be afraid of anything beyond your control. Don't be afraid, for instance, that the building will collapse as you sleep, or that someone you love will suddenly drop dead.

Eat an orange every morning.

Be friendly. It will help make you happy.

Raise your pulse rate to 120 beats per minute for 20 straight minutes four or five times a week doing anything you enjoy.

Hope for everything. Expect nothing.

Take care of things close to home first. Straighten up your room before you save the world. Then save the world.

Know that the desire to be perfect is probably the veiled expression of another desire—to be loved, perhaps, or not to die.

Make eye contact with a tree.

Be skeptical about all opinions, but try to see some value in each of them.

Dress in a way that pleases both you and those around you.

Do not speak quickly.

Learn something every day. (*Dzien dobre!)*

Be nice to people before they have a chance to behave badly.

Don't stay angry about anything for more than a week, but don't forget what made you angry. Hold your anger out at arm's length and look at it, as if it were a glass ball. Then add it to your glass ball collection.

Be loyal.

Wear comfortable shoes.

Design your activities so that they show a pleasing balance and variety.

Be kind to old people, even when they are obnoxious. When you become old, be kind to young people. Do not throw your cane at them when they call you Grandpa. They are your grandchildren!

Live with an animal.

Do not spend too much time with large groups of people.

If you need help, ask for it.

Cultivate good posture until it becomes natural.

If someone murders your child, get a shotgun and blow his head off.

Plan your day so you never have to rush.

Show your appreciation to people who do things for you, even if you have paid them, even if they do favors you don't want.

Do not waste money you could be giving to those who need it.

Expect society to be defective. Then weep when you find that it is far more defective than you imagined.

When you borrow something, return it in an even better condition.

As much as possible, use wooden objects instead of plastic or metal ones.

Look at that bird over there.

After dinner, wash the dishes.

Calm down.

Visit foreign countries, except those whose inhabitants have expressed a desire to kill you.

Don't expect your children to love you, so they can, if they want to.

Meditate on the spiritual. Then go a little further, if you feel like it. What is out (in) there?

Sing, every once in a while.

Be on time, but if you are late do not give a detailed and lengthy excuse.

Don't be too self-critical or too self-congratulatory.

Don't think that progress exists. It doesn't.

Walk upstairs.

Do not practice cannibalism.

Imagine what you would like to see happen, and then don't do anything to make it impossible.

Take your phone off the hook at least twice a week.

Keep your windows clean.

Extirpate all traces of personal ambitiousness.

Don't use the word *extirpate* too often.

Forgive your country every once in a while. If that is not possible, go to another one.

If you feel tired, rest.

Grow something.

Do not wander through train stations muttering, "We're all going to die!"

Count among your true friends people of various stations of life.

Appreciate simple pleasures, such as the pleasure of chewing, the pleasure of warm water running down your back, the pleasure of a cool breeze, the pleasure of falling asleep.

Do not exclaim, "Isn't technology wonderful!"

Learn how to stretch your muscles. Stretch them every day.

Don't be depressed about growing older. It will make you feel even older. Which is depressing.

Do one thing at a time.

If you burn your finger, put it in cold water immediately. If you bang your finger with a hammer, hold your hand in the air for twenty minutes. You will be surprised by the curative powers of coldness and gravity.

Learn how to whistle at earsplitting volume.

Be calm in a crisis. The more critical the situation, the calmer you should be.

Enjoy sex, but don't become obsessed with it. Except for brief periods in your adolescence, youth, middle age, and old age.

Contemplate everything's opposite.

If you're struck with the fear that you've swum out too far in the ocean, turn around and go back to the lifeboat.

Keep your childish self alive.

Answer letters promptly. Use attractive stamps, like the one with a tornado on it.

Cry every once in a while, but only when alone. Then appreciate how much better you feel. Don't be embarrassed about feeling better.

Do not inhale smoke.

Take a deep breath.

Do not smart off to a policeman.

Do not step off the curb until you can walk all the way across the street. From the curb you can study the pedestrians who are trapped in the middle of the crazed and roaring traffic.

Be good.

Walk down different streets.

Backwards.

Remember beauty, which exists, and truth, which does not. Notice that the idea of truth is just as powerful as the idea of beauty.

Stay out of jail.

In later life, become a mystic.

Use Colgate toothpaste in the new Tartar Control formula.

Visit friends and acquaintances in the hospital. When you feel it is time to leave, do so.

Be honest with yourself, diplomatic with others.

Do not go crazy a lot. It's a waste of time.

Read and reread great books.

Dig a hole with a shovel.

In winter, before you go to bed, humidify your bedroom.

Know that the only perfect things are a 300 game in bowling and a 27-batter, 27-out game in baseball.

Drink plenty of water. When asked what you would like to drink, say, "Water, please."

Ask "Where is the loo?" but not "Where can I urinate?"

Be kind to physical objects.

Beginning at age forty, get a complete "physical" every few years from a doctor you trust and feel comfortable with.

Don't read the newspaper more than once a year.

Learn how to say "hello," "thank you," and "chopsticks" in Mandarin.

Belch and fart, but quietly.

Be especially cordial to foreigners.

See shadow puppet plays and imagine that you are one of the characters. Or all of them.

Take out the trash.

Love life.

Use exact change.

When there's shooting in the street, don't go near the window.

Sea Chantey

Hello, sailor.
I hear you are sailing
on a craft across
the water, crossing
the big blue liquid
that is green and gray
and sometimes boiling
with lobsters and
other seafood that
roaring-with-laughter
King Neptune sends
swirling up through
vertical currents in
his ocean domain, at
the bottom of which
he sits on a seashell
throne, holding a small
goat on his face most
unpleasantly! So when
you go floating across
the briny deep, never
visit the bottom,
even if you have bubbles
and rubber tubes and plenty
of life inside your body.
Remember that goat.

Downstairs

In Edwardian England the women's knickers
were slit all the way up the inside of the thigh

for convenience in the loo, given the corset
and layers of other bindings that held

the body in place, but also for easy access
when a randy fellow would no longer be able

to control the bulge inside his trousers
and you were alone with him in the pantry

while the male servants were asleep, or
so you thought, for some could hear the clatter

of pots and pans as he pushed you against the wall
and the glaze in his eyes shot you a delicious panic.

Nails

How did people trim their toenails in ancient times?
The Virgin Mary's toenails look fine
in the paintings of the Italian Renaissance,
and it's a good thing too, for it would be hard
to worship a figure with very long toenails.
Perugino scoffed at a religion aimed
toward God but whose real attention
was on Mary, but he gave her nice toenails.
I've never looked at Jesus' toenails, even
though they're near the holes
in his feet, where the other nails were.
Cruelty is so graphic and hard to understand,
whereas beauty, even the beauty of a toe,
makes perfect sense. To me, anyway.

It Is Almost Unbearable

that people are so different from us
whenever we lift the veil

on which lilacs are shifting
and their eyes are still there

among the gyrations and flattened
slantings of their spirits, as if

spiraling upward through time
until they hit us and our cups

runneth over, though clear
is the liquid and bitter its taste

to our narrow tongues. And
we rejoice for only a moment

and joke for the eternity in which
we know we will never dart about

happily, for the veil we lift is
our own skin, a tarp in wind.

Country Room

You are in a room
in the country
in a country
that has plenty of room

to walk around
in.
You walk to one
end of the room,

turn and walk
out the door
into the room next
to the door

that leads out
to the country
side and to
everywhere

so you turn
around and go
back in to
where you were.

But now the room
has advanced
in time ahead
of you and you

will have to hurry
up or else
the room will leave
you far behind.

Jeopardy

Sometimes when I phoned
my mother back in Tulsa, she would
say, "Hold on a minute, Ron, let me
turn this thing down," the thing
her TV, and she would look
around for the remote and then fumble
with its little buttons as an irritation
mounted in me and an impatience
and I felt like blurting out "You watch TV
too much and it's too loud and why
don't you go outside" because I was
unable to face my dread of her aging
and my heart made cold toward her
by loving her though not wanting to give up
my life and live near her so she
could see me every day and not
just hear me, which is why she
turned the TV down and said,
"Okay, that's better," then sometimes
launched into a detailed account
of whatever awful show she was watching.

Sitting Down Somewhere Else

I look out the window and the first thing I see
is a large, immobile god (a tree).

The house is surrounded by such gods
whose heads, like mine, are in the clouds

that have come far down to drift and be vague
the way they were that first night in The Hague

when I sat alone in a Chinese restaurant
whose waiter didn't ask What would you like

and I heard the owners a few tables away
repeat the words the language records had them say:

Hello! How are you? I am fine.
Is this a good place for me to dine?

The emptiness of the room was worse
than the emptiness of the universe

and I had nowhere else to go but here,
which is where I think I am, or was, or there.

The Art of the Sonnet

Last night I said hello
to the little muse
the smaller than usual muse

She was floating toward me
a plaster figurine
on a cloud

but her plaster lips
could not return my greeting.
That's the first part

and in Japan.
Now the figurine
drifts past and turns

a smile erasing
her face

The Alpinist

I have a body without a head
and a head without a body
If only I could get them affixed
to one another
but the head cannot walk
and the body cannot know
that the head exists
so I must hover between the two
like whatever it is
that links the two parts of a simile

The simile, however, is unhappy
lying there all by itself, it wants
to be part of a sentence, preferably one
without other similes crowding in
like sheep

Next to the sheep is a river
you never noticed, for you saw
the one that was there yesterday
and the one the day before that
which was also never

I am climbing I think it's a ladder
but I don't have to hold on
I don't even have to climb
I just do
Or it's something akin to climbing
on something akin to a ladder

From up here I can see both my head
and my body and the river between

and when the river stops flowing
I will find myself next to a hut in the Alps
with cows and flowers but without words

But that's for later

Gothic Red

That is a very beautiful growl you have,
Great-Grandpa, but it is scaring me a little.
If you would please ask Great-Grandma
to growl a little too, it would help.
You could even harmonize your growls
so they could hang from your faces
in complementary colors and not just
black and white, and your eyes, glazed
with what we used to think of as age,
could close slowly and then stay that way,
for a while, anyway, for the wind
is coming up the lane and into the window
to enlarge you to sky size not
for the sake of your so-called immortality
but so you can growl even louder
in the sleep that has become both yours and ours.

Charlie Chan Wins Again

Now honorable leg broken.
The fog drifts over the docks.
It is a terrible movie
I can't watch, but I do.
Charlie goes into the next room
and removes his hat: ladies.
They fuss and fret, but Charlie
shows them his broken leg
and receives honorable sympathy.
His son dashes in: Dad,
come quick! Charlie tells ladies:
Do not leave room please.
Their fluttering flustered looks
bounce off the walls, which
change from medium gray
to pulsating red. Charlie peeps
in door, says, Red good luck.

Thinking about the Moon

As a child I thought the moon
existed only at night:

there it was
in the dark sky.

When I saw it in daytime
I knew it was the moon

but it wasn't the real one.
It was that other one.

The real moon had moonlight,
silver and blue

And the full moon was so big
it seemed close, but

to what? (I didn't know
I was on Earth.)

This for That

What will I have for breakfast?
I wish I had some plums
like the ones in Williams's poem.
He apologized to his wife
for eating them
but what he did not
do was apologize to those
who would read his poem
and also not be able to eat them.
That is why I like his poem
when I am not hungry.
Right now I do not like him
or his poem. This is just
to say that.

Nelly

Nelly was a girl I once knew in Brooklyn.
She was a nice girl, a bit on the heavy side,
but generous and with an easy laugh
when you tried to kiss her, which was pretty much
every minute you were with her, though
it was all in fun, there was no question
of the thing actually getting "serious,"
though when you lay in bed sweating
through the summer nights, you turned
your head toward the window and thought
about maybe she was the girl for you.

Very Post-Impressionism

The trouble with listening to this music
is that it turns you into a lily pad
on a small pond on a rural property
not far from Paris, and sitting on you
is a large frog named Claude Monet.
You want to strangle him, not
for his paintings, but for the fact that
he doesn't know you're there.
He thinks you are only a lily pad,
and you know that when the music stops
you will be a person again, but
by then he will be dead and gone,
beyond the reach of your fingers.

The Absolutely Huge and Incredible Injustice in the World

What makes us so mean?
We are meaner than gorillas,
the ones we like to blame our genetic aggression on.
It is in our nature to hide behind what Darwin said about survival,
as if survival were the most important thing on earth.
It isn't.
You know—surely it has occurred to you—
that there is no way that humankind will survive
another million years. We'll be lucky to be around
another five hundred. Why?
Because we are so mean
that we would rather kill everyone and everything on earth
than let anybody get the better of us:
"Give me liberty or give me death!"
Why didn't he just say "Grrr, let's kill each other!"?

A nosegay of pansies leans toward us in a glass of water
on a white tablecloth bright in the sunlight
at the ocean where children are frolicking,
then looking around and wondering—
about what we cannot say, for we are imagining
how we would kill the disgusting man and woman
at the next table. Tonight we could throw an electrical storm
into their bed. No more would they spit on the veranda!
Actually they aren't that bad, it's just
that I am talking mean in order to be more
like my fellow humans—it's lonely feeling like a saint,
which I do one second every five weeks,
but that one second is so intense I can't stand up
and then I figure out that it's ersatz, I can't be a saint,
I am not even a religious person, I am hardly a person at all
except when I look at you and think
that this life with you must go on forever

because it is so perfect, with all its imperfections,
like your waistline that exists a little too much,
like my hairline that doesn't exist at all!
Which means that my bald head feels good
on your soft round belly that feels good too.
If only everyone were us!

But sometimes we are everyone, we get mad
at the world and mean as all get-out,
which means we want to tell the world to get out
of this, our world. Who are all these awful people?
Why, it's your own grandma, who was so nice to you—
you mistook her for someone else. She actually was
someone else, but you had no way of knowing that,
just as you had no way of knowing that the taxi driver
saves his pennies all year
to go to Paris for Racine at the Comédie Française.
Now he is reciting a long speech in French from *Andromache*
and you arrive at the corner of This and That
and though Andromache's noble husband Hector has been killed
and his corpse has been dragged around the walls of Troy by an
 unusually mean Achilles,
although she is forced into slavery and a marriage
to save the life of her son, and then people around her
get killed, commit suicide, and go crazy, the driver is in paradise,
he has taken you back to his very mean teacher
in the unhappy school in Port-au-Prince and then
to Paris and back to the French language of the seventeenth century
and then to ancient Greece and then to the corner of This and That.
Only a mean world would have this man driving around in a city
where for no reason someone is going to fire a bullet into the back of
 his head!

It was an act of kindness
on the part of the person who placed both numbers and letters
on the dial of the phone so we could call WAverly,

ATwater, CAnareggio, BLenheim, and MAdison,
DUnbar and OCean, little worlds in themselves
we drift into as we dial, and an act of cruelty
to change everything into numbers only, not just phone numbers
that get longer and longer, but statistical analysis,
cost averaging, collateral damage, death by peanut,
inflation rates, personal identification numbers, access codes,
and the whole raving Raft of the Medusa
that drives out any thought of pleasantness
until you dial 1-800-MATTRES and in no time get a mattress
that is complete and comfy and almost under you,
even though you didn't need one! The men
come in and say Here's the mattress where's
the bedroom? And the bedroom realizes it can't run away.
You can't say that the people who invented the bedroom were mean,
only a bedroom could say that, if it could say anything.
It's a good thing that bedrooms can't talk!
They might keep you up all night telling you things
you don't want to know. "Many years ago,
in this very room. . . ." Eeek, shut up! I mean,
please don't tell me anything, I'm sorry I shouted at you.
And the walls subside into their somewhat foreverness.
The wrecking ball will mash its grimace into the plaster and oof,
down they will come, lathe and layers of personal history,
but the ball is not mean, nor is the man who pulls the handle
that directs the ball on its pendulous course, but another man
—and now a woman strides into his office and slaps his face hard—
the man whose bottom line is changing its color
wants to change it back. So good-bye, building
where we made love, laughed, wept, ate, and watched TV
all at the same time! Where our dog waited by the door,
eyes fixed on the knob, where a runaway stream came whooshing
down the hallway, where I once expanded to fill the whole room
and then deflated, just to see what it would feel like,
where on Saturday mornings my infant son stood by the bedside
and sang, quietly, "Wa-a-a-ke up" to his snoozing parents.

I can never leave all the kindness I have felt in this apartment,
but if a big black iron wrecking ball comes flying toward me,
zoop, out I go! For there must be
kindness somewhere else in the world,
maybe even out of it, though I'm not crazy
about the emptiness of outer space. I have to live
here, with finite life and inner space and with
the horrible desire to love everything and be disappointed
the way my mother was until that moment
when she rolled her eyes toward me as best she could
and squeezed my hand when I asked, "Do you know who I am?"
then let go of life.

The other question was, Did I know who I was?

It is hard not to be appalled by existence.
The pointlessness of matter turns us into cornered animals
that otherwise are placid or indifferent,
we hiss and bare our fangs and attack.
But how many people have felt the terror of existence?
Was Genghis Khan horrified that he and everything else existed?
Was Hitler or Pol Pot?
Or any of the other charming figures of history?
Je m'en doute.
It was something else made them mean.
Something else made Napoleon think it glorious
to cover the frozen earth with a hundred thousand bloody corpses.
Something else made . . . oh, name your monster
and his penchant for destruction,
name your own period in history when a darkness swept over us
and made not existing seem like the better choice,
as if the solution to hunger were to hurl oneself
into a vat of boiling radioactive carrots!

Life is so awful!
I hope that lion tears me to pieces!

It is good that those men wearing black hoods
are going to strip off my skin and force me
to gape at my own intestines spilling down onto the floor!
Please drive spikes through not only my hands and feet
but through my eyes as well!
For this world is to be fled as soon as possible
via the purification of martyrdom.
This from the God of Christian Love.
Cupid hovers overhead, perplexed.
Long ago Zeus said he was tired
and went to bed: if you're not going to exist
it's best to be asleep.
The Christian God is like a cranky two-thousand-year-old baby
whose fatigue delivers him into an endless tantrum.
He will never grow up
because you can't grow up unless people listen to you,
and they can't listen because they are too busy being mean
or fearing the meanness of others.
How can I blame them?
I too am afraid. I can be jolted by an extremely violent movie,
but what is really scary is that someone *wanted* to make the film!
He is only a step away from the father
who took his eight-year-old daughter and her friend to the park
and beat and stabbed them to death. Uh-oh.
"He seemed like a normal guy," said his neighbor, Thelma,
who refused to divulge her last name to reporters.
She seemed like a normal gal, just as the reporters seemed like
    normal vampires.
In some cultures it is normal to eat bugs or people
or to smear placenta on your face at night, to buy
a car whose price would feed a village for thirty years,
to waste your life and, while you're at it, waste everyone
    else's too!
Hello, America. It is dawn,
wake up and smell yourselves.
You smell normal.

My father was not normal,
he was a criminal, a scuffler, a tough guy,
and though he did bad things
he was never mean.
He didn't like mean people, either.
Sometimes he would beat them up
or chop up their shoes!
I have never beaten anyone up,
but it might be fun to chop up some shoes.
Would you please hand me that cleaver, Thelma?

But Thelma is insulted by my request,
even though I said *please,* because she has the face of a cleaver
that flies through the air toward me and lodges
in my forehead. "Get it yourself,
lughead!" she spits, then twenty years later
she changes *lughead* to *fuckhead.*
I change my name to Jughead
and go into the poetry protection program
so my poems can go out and live under assumed names
in Utah and Muskogee.

Anna Chukhno looks up and sees me
through her violet Ukrainian eyes
and says Good morning most pleasantly inflected. Oh
to ride in a horse-drawn carriage with her at midnight
down the wide avenues of Kiev and erase
the ditch at Babi Yar from human history!
She looks up and asks How would you like that?
I say In twenties and she counts them out
as if the air around her were not shattered by her beauty
and my body thus divided into zones:
hands the place of metaphysics, shins the area of moo,
bones the cost of living, and so on.
Is it cruel that I cannot cover her with kisses?
No, it is beautiful that I cannot cover her with kisses,

it is better that I walk out into the sunlight
with the blessing of having spoken with an actual goddess
who gave me four hundred dollars!
And I am reassembled
as my car goes forward
into the oncoming rays of aggression
that bounce off my glasses and then
start penetrating, and soon my eyes
turn into abandoned coal mines
whose canaries explode into an evil song
that echoes exactly nowhere.

At least I am not in Rwanda in 1994 or the Sudan in '05
or Guantanamo or Rikers, or in a ditch outside Rio,
clubbed to death and mutilated. No Cossack
bears down on me with sword raised and gleaming
at my Jewish neck and no time for me
to cry out "It is only my neck that is Jewish!
The rest is Russian Orthodox!" No smiling man tips back
his hat and says to his buddies, "Let's teach
this nigguh a lesson." I don't need a lesson, sir,
I am Ethiopian, this is my first time in your country!
But you gentlemen are joking. . . .

Prepare my cave and then kindly forget where it was.
A crust of bread will suffice and a stream nearby,
the chill of evening filtering in with the blind god
who *is* the chill of evening and who touches us
though we can't raise our hands to stroke his misty beard
    in which
two hundred million stars have wink and glimmer needles.

I had better go back to the bank, we have
only three hundred and eighty-five dollars left.
Those fifteen units of beauty went fast.

As does everything.
But meanness comes back right away
while kindness takes its own sweet time
and compassion is busy shimmering always a little above us and
    behind,
swooping down and transfusing us only when we don't expect it
and then only for a moment.
How can I trap it?
Allow it in and then
turn my body into steel? No.
The exit holes will still be there and besides
compassion doesn't need an exit it *is* an exit—
from the prison that each moment is,
and just as each moment replaces the one before it
each jolt of meanness replaces the one before it
and pretty soon you get to like those jolts,
you and millions of other dolts who like to be electrocuted
by their own feelings. The hippopotamus
sits on you with no sense of pleasure, he doesn't
even know you are there, any more than he takes notice
of the little white bird atop his head, and when
he sees you flattened against the ground
he doesn't even think Uh-oh he just trots away
with the bird still up there looking around.
Saint Augustine stole the pears from his neighbor's tree
and didn't apologize for thirty years, by which time
his neighbor was probably dead and in no mood
for apologies. Augustine's mother became a saint
and then a city in California—Santa Monica,
where everything exists so it can be driven past,
except the hippopotamus that stands on the freeway
in the early dawn and yawns into your high beams.
"Hello," he seems to grunt, "I can't be your friend
and I can't be your enemy, I am like compassion,
I go on just beyond you, no matter how many times
you crash into me and die because you never learned

to crash and live." Then he ambles away.
Could Saint Augustine have put on that much weight?
I thought compassion makes you light
or at least have light, the way it has light around it
in paintings, like the one of the screwdriver
that appeared just when the screw was coming loose
from the wing of the airplane in which Santa Monica was riding into
heaven,
smiling as if she had just imagined how to smile
the first smile of any saint, a promise toward the perfection
of everything that is and isn't.

Afternoon

Who is here with me?
My mother who is an Indian.
(I am not an Indian.)
She is sweeping the teepee
with a broom of sticks
as if to cover her tracks.
(She has no tracks she
is so light.)
I have come through
the air as a drawing
on a piece of paper
to tell her that she
is not an Indian,
but the sound
of the sweeping drowns
out my crinkling voice
and an updraft lifts
me up and out
over the village
that seems to sail away.
(It is so light.)

All in White

All in white my love went riding—
is that a misquotation? and if so
of whom? It's the kind of line
that Ted loved back in 1960
because of its lilt and in his mind
a kind of Irishness. Kenneth
Patchen? What did I see in him
that I don't now and still want to?
A dark lilt and a slide through pain,
both of which I wanted and didn't have
—I had a light lilt and moderate pain.
Ted had a dark and light lilt and
was fleeing from pain. I said
"I don't have any pain." Ted said
"Yes you do ha ha!" The springtime
was lovely and out there all
in white my love went riding.

Dead or Alive in Belgium

Somebody you think is dead is alive
and somebody you think is alive is dead

Sometimes it comes as a happy surprise
and sometimes you wonder

She was given a few days, hours perhaps
Now she looks stronger and even prettier

His chances of surviving were so-so
Now he's going to Belgium

which takes strength, just the thought
—Why do I say such things?

Because there's a Frenchman inside me
who jumps out every once in a while

Bonjour! Voilà, un bon café bien chaud!
Then he forgets to jump out

Or I jump out in front of him
I am much bigger than he is

He does not want to go to Belgium
or even say anything nice about Belgium
I don't want to go to Belgium
though I would like to go to Bruges

Ghent Antwerp and Brussels
and go inside the paintings there

and stand next to the Virgin
her forehead so large and pure

and be there alive with her again
oil on board in Belgium

Whiz and Bang

You hammer away on
the hills and braes of
bonny Scotland, where
oh the thrill of the thought
of it the heather
runs up like a girl all fresh
and windblown to shake
her head and wag a
finger at your naughty
naughty thoughts,
about her, of
course, and you
hammer those hills and braes
with all your might.

Standoff with Frosty

Every time I sit down to do some serious work
my stomach tells me it's time to go downstairs
and see what's in the fridge, but when
I reach in there an icy hand
grabs my wrist and thrusts me away
from the territory of the snowman.
Yes, Frosty himself.
He lives in there with a banjo and a carrot.
He plays the banjo and thinks about the carrot,
but it is a dull existence, and he is disgruntled.
How can I make him happy? There is no way,
for he can neither hear nor understand my words.
I cannot reason with him, describe the arctic nights
that gave him "life," nor lure his melancholy world
away from him. He is stuck and so am I.

A Train for Kenneth

One train may hide another
or it might hide the mountain
into which it disappears and
hides itself. You step
into that tunnel, stop,
the tracks gleaming at your feet
but no light further on.

(This is not a metaphor.)
(So what is it?)

It's a stanza, in which
the train is hiding. You
can't see it because
the letters are so dark—
the light around them
makes them even darker.

But now the train comes
out the other end and smoke
is trailing from its stack, for
this happened in olden days,
when chugging existed.

In Memoriam K.

So what will you do tomorrow
now that he has died today?
Why, you'll get dressed and
fix your breakfast as you always do,
then make some coffee for your wife
and bring it to her bed, where she will say
Thank you—the nicest moment of the day,
for me, anyway. And then the sunlight
on the lawn, song in feathers
high in a tree and hidden,
as if their notes were sung
inside my head which is
come to think of it where
I hear them, as I hear him,
he who made me so much
who I am and now must be alone
with him now he is gone.

The Goldberg Variations

When I heard Glenn Gould talking
on the radio today—his voice from long ago—
I knew no matter how eccentric how
difficult how crabby he might have been
I knew I'd trust whatever he had to say
and I did, so well-structured his sentences
were, and precise his words,
and for a moment
I felt regret I never knew him though
I don't think I could have talked all night
on the phone with him but then
maybe I would have especially when
I was young enough to kill myself for art.

Mad Scientist

Up goes the mad scientist to the room in his tower
where his instruments gleam in the half-light
while his thoughts are surrounded by the half-dark
that filters out from his heart, but when he goes in
and looks around, all he can see is the chair
covered with a bright red and green serape
and sparks are fizzing in the thought balloon
above his head, for yes, he is a cartoon scientist,
just as everything I think about is a cartoon something
because anything cartoon is immortal
in its own funny little way.

Hound Dog

"You ain't nothin' but a hound dog"
sounds like an insult and if it were directed
to a person yes I would say it is an insult
but if it were directed to a dog I would say
that it is not an insult, it is simply a statement
of fact, like telling a rock that it is a rock,
though of course since a rock cannot hear the words
it would make less sense to speak to it, whereas
a hound dog could not only hear but in its own
dog way understand the feeling of the statement
via its tone and some other method dogs have
of knowing things. For instance the hound dog
would know that if you said such a thing you
would be either a rather daffy ontologist or a shit,
but either way you would fall over sideways if
the dog were to answer back, "You ain't nothin'
but an ontologist" or "a shit." Fortunately for you
the hound dog says nothing. It rolls its supposedly sad
eyes up to yours and just looks at you, and whether
you are an ontologist or a shit it makes no difference.
You ain't nothin'.

Fantasy Block

I would like to have a sexual fantasy
about the young girl I see in the gym,
the one who undulates up and down
on an aerobic machine revealing
the smooth skin of her lower back
as it swells out toward her hips,
her hair pulled up in back
with a tortoiseshell clasp
and a misty blush spreading
from her high cheekbones back
to her ears in each of which
a small silver ring is glittering,
but I can't think of anything.

Words from the Front

We don't look as young
as we used to
except in dim light
especially in
the soft warmth of candlelight
when we say
in all sincerity
You're so cute
and
You're my cutie.
Imagine
two old people
behaving like this.
It's enough
to make you happy.

I hold the door open for a frail, elderly woman.

•

She looks surprised.

•

I will never recover from having a mental flash of Jimmy Durante the moment I learned that Dante's real name was Durante.

•

The more our public officials talk about integrity, the deeper burns their hypocrisy. (Thinking up such a truism makes me feel contaminated.)

•

The French have a reputation for verbal exactitude, so why do they call a tuxedo a "smoking"?

•

When I first looked in the mirror, I had always been there.

•

Waiting for the streetlight to change, a nice-looking young man in his twenties unwraps a candy bar and drops the wrapper a few feet from the trash basket.

•

The American economic system—if anything so out of control can be called a system—requires ever more production and consumption, resulting in greater and greater destruction of the natural world and increasingly invasive attacks on the nervous system. This juggernaut knows how to go in one direction only. I am part of this system, being invested in it, mostly, I tell myself, to protect my wife from a future of penury. My first duty is to her, despite my mounting shame and disgust at the ruin that we, especially in the West, are wreaking upon the world. It's strange that these monumentally important—if obvious—ideas sometimes strike me as tedious, as if they were a minor annoyance.

•

She walks in and asks, "What are you doing?" when she means something else.

•

I have to call Ted Greenwald.

•

For a writer it's good to be angry all the time because then more people can like your work.

•

On the last day of a stay in a distant city, I try to remain interested and busy, although I know I am just marking time until the hour of departure: I stand in the Luxembourg Garden but I am not fully there. Now I notice that I have begun to do something similar in my life in general. On the verge of sixty, I have started to mark time. Hey!

•

Fiddlesticks.

•

(A secret homage.)

•

We refer to the decades of a century as the twenties, thirties, forties, etc.—even the teens—but why do I not know the name of the first decade of a century? Is it a blind spot particular to me?

•

Fantasy and Fugue in A Minor.

•

"Morning ablutions" used to sound like something that people did in the nineteenth century. Now *I* do them.

•

Differences of race, national origin, religion, social level, wealth, gender, age, political ideology, philosophy—all can be barriers to compassion. But what about intelligence? How many people of noticeably lower intelligence do you count among your true friends?

•

It's almost midnight. No wonder it's late.

•

I'm not sure what it means that when I learned to tie my own shoes, at the late age of six, I did so by myself, inventing a curious series of loops and moves that I still use, fifty-five years later.

•

When the footsteps in the hallway stop, a long shadow flows under the door. Then he moves on.

•

In movies about Indians there is never any evidence—in the teepees or elsewhere in the village—of a bathroom. So where did they . . . ?

•

Shop name in upper Manhattan: "Explosions 2000—Men, Women, & Children."

•

The miracle of existing and being able to say so and have drapes.

•

Farrago.

•

The day I was born, German saboteurs came ashore on the coast of Florida.

•

Title: "Whatever May Happen to Your Hair in a Song."

•

"By convention sweet, by convention bitter, by convention hot, by convention cold, by convention color: but in reality atoms and void." (Democritus, quoted by Sextus)

•

"One day, looking at a painting by Matisse, I lost my back." (Bernard Noël)

•

The origin of the word *turmoil* is unknown.

•

How many people, alone in the privacy of their own homes, have ever sung the national anthem? Probably very few. Maybe none! Solitude is not patriotic.

•

The fly
on the countertop
is not there

•

Buenos Aires, Argentina. At least 60,000 people attended an outdoor Roman Catholic mass Monday to mourn the theft of former President Juan Perón's hands.

•

"As a result of this luxation of our intellects the shameful misconception of Marxism could be put about and even believed, that economic forces and material interests determine the course of the world. This grotesque over-estimation of the economic factor was conditioned by our worship of technological progress, which was itself the fruit of rationalism and utilitarianism after they had killed the mysteries and acquitted man of guilt and sin. But they had forgotten to free him of folly and myopia, and he seemed only fit to mould the world after the pattern of his own banality." (Jan Huizinga, *Homo Ludens)*

•

For the past thirty-five years I have been meaning to find and read *The Heart of the Continent* by Fitz Hugh Ludlow, 1870, wondering if it might be one of those "lost" classics, which I seem to find more alluring than "found" ones.

•

"He has bought a Madonna by Andrea del Sarto for six hundred sequins." (Goethe, *Italian Journey,* translated by Mayer and Auden)

•

According to Oscar Wilde, women are sphinxes without secrets. Does he mean that they are simply colossal statues? If so, he is right.

•

(Just kidding.)

•

"No man who is in a hurry is quite civilized." (Will Durant) Is this one way that technology is taking us to new forms of savagery?

•

Some things everyone should know:

1) How to swim
2) How to administer cardio-pulmonary resuscitation and the Heimlich maneuver

3) How to whistle loudly
4) How to treat kitchen burns and banged parts of the body by immediately applying cold water

•

I must go back to the Louvre to see an intensely erotic and silly painting called *Aurora and Cephalus.*

•

It's irritating to be almost old without having grown up.

•

A sudden whim to drive 300 miles to Vermont and get new tires.

•

Hearing that Wittgenstein came from the wealthiest family in Austria has made me—for the moment, at least—less excited about his ideas. What does that say about me?

•

You are dying for lunch, so you heat up the soup. But now it is too hot to eat.

•

My guilt at not wanting to be buried in Tulsa—as if I were abandoning my mother for eternity.

•

Looking up *Pyrrhic victory* in the dictionary isn't worth the trouble.

•

What to do while a democracy votes itself out of existence?

•

When asked what he wanted done with his body after his death, Philip Whalen said, "Have them lay me out on a bed of frozen raspberries."

•

A sound enters the room like a cardboard box the size of the room entering the room.

•

An hour ago I was going to write, "My life hasn't been what it might have been, because I haven't saved the world from unhappiness, rapacity, destruction, fear, and hate," but the phone rang, and when I finally returned to the blank page, I stared at it with no idea of why it was there waiting for me. Then: "Ah, evil!"

•

On some level, things don't get better or worse, they just *get*. That I don't know what this means is an example.

•

Whether civilization wants to admit it or not, at this very moment all over the world little girls are masturbating.

•

This notebook, I think I bought it in Kiev. I had gone swimming in the Dnieper, mainly because I liked the idea that one day I would be able to tell myself that I had once swam in a river whose name begins with *D-n*—forgetting that the recent and nearby nuclear power plant disaster at Chernobyl might have rendered the water highly radioactive!

•

Courtesy is more efficient than the lack of it.

•

If I get a fatal disease, I am going to be very mad at it. I will blame it for my death.

•

"The worth of that is that which it contains / And that is this, and this . . . ." (Shakespeare, almost Gertrude Stein, *Sonnet 74*)

•

Does Euclidean geometry say that the angle of reflection is equal to the angle of incidence? If so, it can't be true. The angle of incidence must come first. But if we turn it around, the same problem arises. (Only by focusing on such ideas can I avoid raging at the way "things" are.)

•

Fyodor = Theodore. Therefore, Ted Dostoyevsky.

•

And, as the bombs fall in Baghdad tonight, how charming the melodrama of thunder outside my window.

•

Is it snobbery or nostalgia that makes me sad when I think of how it has been decades since I heard the two words that echoed throughout my adolescence: *intellectual curiosity*. And although one still hears the word *conformity*, it is no longer a pejorative term; now we are *on the same page, getting with the program, team players*.

•

If you live long enough and look hard enough, you will eventually—to your great relief and your great sorrow—find your humanity.

•

A French friend wrote to me, "C'est la fin des carottes" (It's the end of the carrots), but I don't know what it means. Maybe "That's all she wrote"? (I sent your saddle home.)

•

How could I have bought this notebook in Kiev when the word on its cover, *Pikakirjoitusvihko,* is, it turns out, Finnish?

To the Russian Poets

If I write poetry thirty minutes a decade,
that's enough! if I write very quickly

filling hundreds of pages with *If* and *Oops*
but with other, nobler words as well,

like *Poland* and *mustache, no job now,*
fall by the wayside, bone, and *finger, wisp,*

so that I emerge an Iron Curtain Country
Iron Man, poet whose jaw is stronger

than Mayakovsky's, whose imagery
is quicker than Pasternak's, heart

more broken than Akhmatova's and
whose shoes are whizzing more

than Khlebnikov's with their waving yellow laces.
Slavic poets of the great undertow,

you can smile now, it's snowing and cold
and empty and you're hungry again, almost starving.

Construction

He was as stiff as a board
and as hard as nails

are not really similes,
they are clichés,

which means we hear them
as single units whose meaning

we already know, unless
we have never heard them before.

If we add
He was as big as a house

there appears the image of the man
using his own body and spirit

as building materials,
adding story upon story

until the architecture of the house
and the architecture of language

both collapse
like a ton of bricks.

Why God Did What He Did

God hates you
which is why he created the world
and put you in it
and gave you the power to realize
that you're here
for a while
and then poof

and while you're here
you come to see
that the world too will be destroyed
by a fiery bowling ball,
ten thousand times the size of the earth,
hurtling through space
at this very moment

so that nothing absolutely nothing
means anything
because that's what God wants
and he wants you to know it
because he really hates you
and he wants you to know that too

The Idea of Being Hurled at Key West

What if she, in her magnificence,
picked you up and held you high aloft
in a glittering instant, then, with
a grunt, threw you down the beach
two hundred yards, to where
the stars are now both in the sky
and circling round your head as she
comes loping down the long decline
to pick you up and hurl you once again?

Judy Holliday

Don't think of saying a word about it I
will kill you positively and I'm not kidding,
mmm mmm mmm. The Romans
did not brook interference. They
liked water and plenty of it, it was all
around them, they had toys too,
so why not? Why not what? Why not
anything? I mean if you like water that much
you may as well like everything and
lots more and they did, up to a point, then
they were a dud. The barbarians
made them be a dud. But up
they arose in handmade robes and sang
and curls appeared, on rocks and air,
and before you knew it, boom,
they were back in business.

Method

Sometimes Kenneth Koch's method I guess you'd call it
was to have a general notion of the whole poem
before he started
such as the history of jazz or the boiling point of water
or talking to things that can't talk back
(as he put it) that is apostrophes
whereas my method I guess I'd call it
is to start and go
wherever the poem seems to lead

Sometimes it doesn't lead anywhere
other than to a dead end, and when I turn around
the street has disappeared and I find myself
sitting in a room.
Sometimes it leads somewhere
I have no interest in being
or the way I get there is contrived or silly

I have a face
that stays mostly on the front of my head
while inside my head wheels
are turning with a sound like music heard across water
over which a breeze rises and falls
cooling my face.
I should be nicer to my face
send it on vacation or just let it go relax
over there under that shady maple
Instead I let it carry all kinds of packages
back and forth from my brain to the world
though of course my brain is a part of the world
I should send my brain on vacation too
though it tells me now that I should consider the possibility that it
has always been on vacation

Tricky brain! in which
the personality skates around
and the moral character rises and sits, rises and sits
and whose doorway at the bottom has a sign
that says . . . there's not enough light to read it.
I wish there were.

Kenneth said Write a poem in which each line begins with
"I wish. . . ."
I wish gorilla
I wish squish
I wish *deux tiers*
I wish onrushing cloudburst
and the hundred thousand one-second-old wishes came
    pouring forth
and still are pouring forth
like babies in trees and all over the place
in French postcards after World War I
like water streaming down Zeus
like the concept of optimism when it entered human history
like the simile when it said Do not end your poem with me
I am not like The End I am like a doorway
that leads from one thing

to Cincinnati, and who
am I to argue with a simile
I am a man of constant similes
that buzz and jumble as I walk
then shift and ramble as I buzz and jumble
At any moment the similes can line up
to form the log cabin Lincoln
is said to have built with his own similes
I am like a president
I am like a stove
I am President Stove I will chop down
the cherry tree over there on that page

But someone else is already chopping it down
a boy with a mad grin on his face
a glint of impish fire atop his head
Those cherries were too red!
So much for history
History that rolls above us like an onrushing storm cloud
while we below knit booties and adjust our earmuffs

Young Bentley bent over his microscope
and clicked the shutter of his box camera
thus taking the first photographic portrait of a snowflake
which is how he became known as "Snowflake" Bentley
Outside the blizzard came in sideways
like a wall of arrows
That is all you need to know about Snowflake Bentley

Who else would you like to know about?
Whom! Whom! not Who!
There actually was a great Chinese actor named Wang Whom
who immigrated to the United States in the mid–nineteenth century
and found fame and fortune in the theaters of San Francisco
due mainly to his ability to allow his head to detach
from his body and float up and disappear into the dark
The curtain would close to great applause
and when it opened his head was back
but his body was in two halves split right down the middle
Wang Whom never revealed his magic secrets
even to the beautiful young women who lined up toward him
like iron filings toward a magnet
powerful enough to lift President Stove out of his chair
and give him life again as a mountain
struck repeatedly by lightning
That is all you need to know about Wang Whom

Now for some commentary on things that are always horizontal
The earth is always lying down on itself

and whirling
It is totally relaxed and happy to let everything happen to it
as if it were the wisest person who ever lived
the one who never got up from bed
because the bed flew around everywhere anyone would want to go
and had arms and hands and legs and feet
that were those of the wise horizontal bed-person

Lines indicating very fast movement are horizontal
because the horizon is so fast it is just an idea:
Now you see it now you are it
and then 99 percent of every beautiful thing you ever knew
escaped and went back out into the world
where you vaguely remembered it: your mother's smile
in the glint of sunlight on the chrome of a passing car,
her tears in a gust of wind, her apron in the evening air

as if she were a milkmaid standing in Holland
while those silver and gray clouds billowing across the sky
over to scarlet and burning violet tinged with gold
were just for her and that one moment.

You are next in line, which is exciting,
which is why life is exciting: every moment is another line
you're next in. Or maybe not, for what about when
you don't know what "line" is and "next"? A goat
comes up close and stares at your sleeping face.
The instant you wake up it turns into a statue
that starts out a goat and ends up a banjo,
something you can neither milk nor play.
But it doesn't matter because you started out a man
and ended up a pile of leaves in a different story.
In the library the other piles are saying Shush, they know
it is late autumn, they can tell by the ruddier cheeks
of the girls who come in and, when they see their books
    are overdue,

stamp their feet in a fit of pique.
They are so cute
that some of the leaf piles shamble across the floor toward their
dresses,
but the girls laugh and throw their hair around and dash away.
If only you weren't a pile of leaves, you would run after them and
throw yourself on them
like a miracle!

That's what it used to be like to be fourteen and surrounded
by miracles that never happened.
At fifteen the miracles started to crackle and at sixteen
they were positively scary—Look, a miracle on the ceiling!
By seventeen a miracle was a car you could ride in
and then one year later drive beyond the limits of consciousness.
The tapioca pudding was there.
You ate it.
The tapioca pudding was gone
but there too.
May I have some more anything?
Why, my fine young man, you can have anything
you want. Here, have this mountain!
Oof, it's too heavy! Do you have a smaller one?
No, only a larger one.
Then no mountain will I have today
and as for the future I cannot say
because I have no idea where I would ever put a mountain.
But, young man, you will become President Stove!
I will? But I don't want to be a president or a stove,
I want to glue a president *to* a stove.
Then go right ahead. Here is the glue.
Now go find a president and a stove.

Bed

There's a saying
"You can't make the bed you're lying in."
Actually you can,
though it takes a bit of practice,
and when you've finished
it is nice to lie there
as part of the bed. But soon
you have the urge to move
that surges up against the urge
to keep the bed as is and you
become a battleground.
Before this point it's best
to slip out 'twixt the sheets
and go about your day,
the figure from a Japanese screen
who was there only a moment.

The Breakfast Nook

If I had a cup of coffee
as strong as a hammer
I would drink it so fast
that nails would fly
out of my face and
into the wall of
your silence onto
which we could hang
a picture of the cup,
the hammer, and
the nails, and we
could then have a
cup of hammers and
a nail of coffee
and a lion would
come in and roar
so loud that it
would scare you
until you saw
that it was really
a board of sugar
and a saw of cream.
Would you tell me
your secret then?

The Stapler

When my mother died
she left very little: old clothes,
modest furniture, dishes, some
change, and that was about it.
Except for the stapler. I found it
in a drawer stuffed with old bills
and bank statements. Right off
I noticed how easily it penetrated
stacks of paper, leaving no bruise
on the heel of my hand.
It worked so well I brought it home,
along with a box of staples, from
which only a few of the original 5,000
were missing. The trick is remembering
how to load it—it takes me several minutes
to figure it out each time, but I persist until
Oh yes, that's it! Somewhere in all this
my mother is spread out and floating
like a mist so fine it can't be seen,
an idea of wafting, the opposite of stapler.

Different Kinds of Ink

Inchiostro is a long way to go
for *ink,* but when you get there
it is darker and more liquid and glistening
than anything you could have imagined,
you with your fables and epics, flourishing
signatures and official documents,
and drawings of beasts of the sea.
Only the squid can eject such darkness
when he hastens to flee your liquid writing,
for he squirts at his deepest level: he
is a *calamaro* and he knows you will try
to eat him, which he does not agree to,
for he must go make more *inchiostro,*
which is how he writes: all inside himself.
You have your dark and human tales
but you will never have his.

Sketch

I wonder what Clive van den Berg
is doing right now. I'll bet he's surmising
as he peers perceptively at his new drawings
though in the back of his head there
is a drawing of lunch outdoors in the shade
at a table spread with the finest little things
all tasty and symmetrical, so he adds
some shading and pepper and the outlines
of Zoë and Ingrid as a breeze rises
and falls like the edge of the tablecloth
that suggests heaven and then settles
back down into tableclothness, which is heaven
for the tablecloth and those of us who are us.

Aubade

New as a baby who has an idea for the first time
while rolling down a hill in a land no one
has ever set foot on, and as bright as the eyes
of a man who found himself mysteriously shot
up into the air where he hovered before chirping,
and as absolutely confident as the patient
that the crazed dentist will not hurt her, despite
the roaring chainsaw thirsty to rip and tear—
is how I am each day for a split second before
I remember what a lowly worm I am,
lifting the front of my long body to poke softly
at the air that is still fresh with dew and night.

Do You Like It?

We now take the next
step into the forest of
the imagination that William
Shakespeare walked
into when he wrote plays such
as *As You Like It,* so dark green
were those woods and filled
with fairies and enchantment
that, like sounds offstage,
are hovering near, hovering near
the hut where you have taken refuge
and the deer stand stock still because
they might have heard something
that could harm them, then look down
and go on grazing. You stop for a moment
to think of how scared you would be
if you were being introduced
to the actual William Shakespeare.
His dark eyes penetrate your head.
You look down. His shoes
make you feel like screaming.

Drive

When the cowboys sang
Get along, little dogie,

I knew they were addressing
small cows, I mean calves,

but in the back of my mind
I saw small dogs, I mean puppies,

loping alongside the herd
that mooed especially hard

when the music came up
and painted the Old West

in all its wide marvelous expansive
day and night affirmation of

sheer existence, in which even
a little dogie had a part to play,

doggy too.

The split infinitive was discovered and named in the nineteenth century. Nineteenth-century writers seem to have made greater use of this construction than earlier writers; the frequency of occurrence attracted the disapproving attention of grammarians, many of whom thought it to be a modern corruption (one commentator blamed it on Byron). In fact *to* was originally limited to use with the gerund and not until the twelfth century did it become attached to the infinitive. By the fourteenth century writers were occasionally separating *to* and the verb with an adverb; the practice went unnoticed until the nineteenth century.

—*Webster's Ninth New Collegiate Dictionary*

It's a big beautiful omelet made of children.

—Fragonard, referring to his painting *The Swarm of Love*

Before, behind, between, above, below.

—John Donne, "Elegy XIX: To His Mistress Going to Bed"

Using an attribute to illustrate the point that attributes are not attributes in and of themselves is not so good as using a nonattribute to illustrate the point. Using a horse to illustrate the point that a (white) horse is not a horse (as such) is not so good as using nonhorses to illustrate the point. Actually the universe is but an attribute; all things are but a horse.

—Chuang Tzu, in *Sources of Chinese Tradition*

Mum

—Word spelled out in flowers on a grave near an abandoned village on Achill Island, Ireland

History vomited up George W. Bush so he could defecate on the human spirit.

—Wall graffito, New York City

Seán Ó Neachtain . . . in *Stair Éamuinn Uí Chléire (The Story of Eamon O'Clery)* . . . evolved a strange lingo which, two centuries before Joyce, trembled on the brink of *Finnegans Wake:* "and 'tis name to him, old hog son foal, and he is in the house of your ear handsome seldom hundred. sick . . ."

—Declan Kiberd in *The Oxford History of Ireland*

To my surprise the heaven in my heart leaped into your eyes.

—From the song "Remember When," words by Buck Ram

The day will come when your life will seem to have lasted an instant.

—Unknown source

The acquisition of voluntary muscle movement, i.e., the fact that the ego discovers . . . that its conscious will can control the body, may well be the basic experience at the root of all magic.

—Erich Neumann, *The Origins and History of Consciousness*

Abraham Lincoln was born in a log cabin that he built with his own hands.

—Unidentified schoolchild

We've gone to a lot of trouble to be humanity. It seems odd to throw it away.

—Something Kenneth Koch could have said

Blink

I don't mean that there's a way to reach that high
and say anything to or for you, it's
that an impulse is darting around
in search of something that can happen
or might if we were to happen to float
through some bright rectangle standing up
into cool rooms whose surfaces are
radiant with the way you used to be,
girl giggling atop my shoulders with
sweet mischief in your glinting
and it rises again, this hand, as if
in blessing, to draw a misty figure in the air
and disappear when we most wanted it
which is forever.

Don't we know better?
Why do we await this momentary wafting that
flares up the petals of a tulip when
that voice is leaning toward
the larger outline things slip through
on their way to lightness in the light
that grows when the angel doesn't look lost
and doesn't even walk on the air it's in
in perfect symmetry that lasts for an instant
because you blinked and now it's paint so blink again.

Bird's Eye

You can use words
to clear the space where words
clutter up your view, and there's

the cottage with thatched roof
and a wisp of smoke that shows
the roof has just caught fire,

with peasants in the fields
on this, a harvest day,
their ruddy cheeks and snaggle teeth.

They scythe and bind and call
across the field, "Olaf, you nut,
come sit in the shade

and have your supper," but he
scythes on and on, for he is angry
at the gods today and in

a mood for cutting, unaware
the sky has sent a spark
to visit his abode.

But now I'll clutter up the view
again, and close your ears
to the sound of distant peasant laughter.

Now You See It

What you don't see
helps you see what
you do see: the keyhole
sharpens the thrill
in your brain,
even if there is
no one
in the room,
shadows
wafting across
the white sheets
as a song drifts in
the window,
her voice so pure
you can see
the face it rises from,
for what you see
helps you see what
you don't see.

Hercules

stood on the hillock
and roared just
because he was
Hercules. The waves
below crashed below
the churning sky.
It would have
been Christmas
but it was too
early in history,
therefore no
gifts for him.
But he didn't
need a gift:
he was Hercules!
An outline was
always around him—
in case he went
away there would
be a drawing left.
That's what we
see now. If you
want to hear him
roar, listen.

Bible Study

And they entered the ark
two by two

except for the studs
which were two by four

The hammers and nails
got on board too

Everything that existed
got on board

to go to a new place
and build an exact replica

of the old place
after the flood subsided.

And subside it did
so that later

a new one could rise
again, like the old flood.

The new flood would say
Ha ha! and

The new Noah would say
Ho ho!

Elegy for No One

Time passes slowly when you're lost in paradise,
then gradually slows down to a disappearance

but only for a moment, as if inside a footstep
that pauses on the stair to wait for its shadow

to catch up, for it had not yet vanished as
the other had, and you have the idea you

wanted to have had when
the candlelight took away the distance,

leaving only the residue of dimness and fading
falling to one side and off. Time goes past or you

go past time, the outcome is the same if you think
of it that way, but if you don't think at all

the footstep will have existed on the stair
without you, as it always has, and perfectly so.

C Note

Hokusai, or
as they used to spell it,
Ho-Ku-Sai
painted 100
views of Fuji,
then stopped.
No 101
for him!
And I say
Bully!
because
I've written
99 poems
this summer,
not counting
this one.

Bastille Day

The first time I saw Paris
I went to see where the Bastille
had been, and though
I saw the column there
I was too aware that
the Bastille was not there:
I did not know how
to see the emptiness.
People go to see
the missing Twin Towers
and seem to like feeling
the lack of something.
I do not like knowing
that my mother no longer
exists, or the feeling
of knowing. Excuse me
for comparing my mother
to large buildings. Also
for talking about absence.
The red and gray sky
above the rooftops
is darkening and the inhabitants
are hastening home for dinner.
I hope to see you later.

HOW LONG

Scotch Tape Body

I never thought,
forty years ago,
taping my poems into a notebook,
that one day the tape
would turn yellow, grow brittle, and fall off
and that I'd find myself on hands and knees
groaning as I picked the pieces up
off the floor
one by one

Of course no one thinks ahead like that
If I had
I would have used archival paste
or better yet
not have written those poems at all

But then I wouldn't have had
the pleasure of reading them again,
the pleasure of wincing
and then forgiving myself,
of catching glimpses of who I was
and who I thought I was,
the pleasure—is that the word?—of seeing
that that kid really did exist.

The Death Deal

Ever since that moment
when it first occurred
to me that I would die
(like everyone on earth!)
I struggled against
this eventuality, but
never thought of
how I'd die, exactly,
until around thirty
I made a mental list:
hit by car, shot
in head by random ricochet,
crushed beneath boulder,
victim of gas explosion,
head banged hard
in fall from ladder,
vaporized in plane crash,
dwindling away with cancer,
and so on. I tried to think
of which I'd take
if given the choice,
and came up time
and again with He died
in his sleep.
Now that I'm officially old,
though deep inside not
old officially or otherwise,
I'm oddly almost cheered
by the thought
that I might find out
in the not too distant future.
Now for lunch.

Grasshopper

It's funny when the mind thinks about the psyche,
as if a grasshopper could ponder a helicopter.

It's a bad idea to fall asleep
while flying a helicopter:

when you wake up, the helicopter is gone
and you are too, left behind in a dream,

and there is no way to catch up,
for catching up doesn't figure

in the scheme of things. You are
who you are, right now,

and the mind is so scared it closes its eyes
and then forgets it has eyes

and the grasshopper, the one that thinks
you're a helicopter, leaps onto your back!

He is a brave little grasshopper
and he never sleeps

for the poem he writes is the act
of always being awake, better than anything

you could ever write or do.
Then he springs away.

Kit

Tamburlaine crashed through
around 1375. Marlowe
had written his play by 1587.
The intervening years bled
into history, the fourteenth
a very bloody century.
Good that Marlowe waited
to be born sufficiently later,
thus avoiding the real
Tamburlaine, who might have
torn his head off.
But he died young anyway,
did Marlowe, not even thirty.
The "high astounding terms"
he promised he delivered.
Still it makes me mad
that he got stabbed to death,
though I have to admit
it's part of his appeal.

The Curvature of Royalty

One of the surprising things about modern life
is that quite a few countries still have kings and queens
and palaces for them to live in
as well as great wealth to use or even have!
These kings and queens accept the idea
that they should be kings and queens,
just as many people born to money
accept their wealth as natural
and most poor people assume
that poverty is their destiny
no matter what they say to the contrary.
Everything points toward Fate:
the rocks are as they are, the clouds too, the giraffe
and the cantaloupe are all lined up
facing an imaginary point of origin
like lines in a diagram of perspective,
and though the lines bend slightly through time
everyone bends with them, so the dung beetle
remains a figure of comedy.
Further along the chain of evolution
he becomes the court jester
juggling words and jumping around
in the debris of falling syntax.
The King laughs mightily, the Queen quietly,
for though they have become playing cards
they still can be amused,
and at any moment they can roll off the cards
and onto the floor of their palace
where they can laugh all they want
and the servants will keep looking straight ahead.

Urn Burial

Sir Thomas Browne said
that it is useless to erect monuments
in the hope of being remembered
by generations far into the future
since the future itself
will cease to exist. That is,
the world would be destroyed soon,
hence "'Tis too late to be ambitious."
Apparently this belief was widely held
by English people in the seventeenth century.
My grandmother, in the twentieth century,
took a curious pleasure in pursing her lips and stating
"The Bible says the world will last
one thousand years but not two," which meant that I
could not live past the age of 58
and might be there for The End of the World.
Fortunately I did not believe her
and unfortunately it made me think
she was a little bit crazy and certainly thoughtless
in saying such a thing to her young grandson.
The Bible also says that Methuselah
lived to the age of 969. They should have chosen
a more credible number, for, as Joe Brainard asked,
"If a hundred-year-old man can barely stand up,
can you imagine what it would be like to be five hundred?"
I can barely imagine what it is like to be *any* age,
though I can imagine what it is like to be dead
because I have woken up after a deep sleep
with no memory of it.
So you don't have to imagine anything
to know what being dead is like.
One less thing to worry about!
Unless, of course, I'm wrong about the afterlife,

and fiery demons prod you with red-hot tridents
into the writhing maw of an inferno of glistening snakes.
Fortunately this happens only to Christians—
fortunately for me, that is.
Sir Thomas Browne was a Christian
but I hope he believed he'd go to Paradise,
for it seems too bad such a wise and learnèd man
should think that he would go to Hell.
Browne lived to 77, to the day.
I'm not sure the exactitude means anything here,
but for his time he was quite old,
and possibly surprised to wake up and find himself
892 years younger than Methuselah, or wake up
and find himself at all, in bed, and still on earth!
Then he died.
"I didn't plan on living this long,"
said my other grandmother, at 96,
"but I just keep on breathing."

We Three Kings

We three kings of Orient
are

disoriented.

We came all this way
only to get lost?

"Get lost!" is what
they said

when we said
"Are we here?"

Now we are really lost
and disillusioned too.

It's true
our cigars were loaded

on the backs of imaginary camels

but we thought the world
could use a good laugh.

I guess we were wrong.

Death

Let's change the subject.
In the hills an occasional noise—
shotgun here, bloodcurdling shriek there, hey
nonny nonny, and two boys,
lost, weird, homeless, starving, about to be
eaten by a big black bear! O muse avert thine eyes!
(I will look *for* you.)
                                        The bear shambles forth
on his hind legs, so shaggy they are
and smelly, and waves his forepaws in the air as if
he were erasing the blackboard on which
our fate is written, and the boys have hair
standing up on their heads and the trees lean back
as far as trees can lean and not fall down, they
hate that hair! I do too! (Muse, don't look yet.)

But then a man comes through the woods
with comb and scissors—it's barber Tom, come
to give those boys a haircut and the bear one too,
if it wants, and it does, and all three share
in this tonsorial moment, hair
falling softly on the forest floor.

Walking with Walt

When everyday objects and tasks
seem to crowd into the history you live in
you can't breathe so easily you can hardly breathe at all
the space is so used up,
when yesterday there was nothing but.
Ah, expansive America! you
must have existed. Otherwise
no Whitman.

It's funny that America did not explode
when Whitman published *Leaves of Grass,*
explode with amazement and pride, but
America was busy being other
than what he thought it was and I grew up
thinking along his lines and of course now
oh well

though actually at this very moment
the trees are acting exactly the way they did
when he walked through and among them,
one of the roughs, as he put it,
though how rough I don't know I think
he was just carried away

as we all are, if we're lucky
enough to have just walking
buoy us up a little off the earth
to be more on it

Inaction of Shoes

There are many things to be done today
and it's a lovely day to do them in

Each thing a joy to do
and a joy to have done

I can tell because of the calm I feel
when I think about doing them

I can almost hear them say to me
Thank you for doing us

And when evening comes
I'll remove my shoes and place them on the floor

And think how good they look
sitting? . . . standing? . . . there

Not doing anything

The Center of Gravity

The military Jeep was said
to have had a high center
of gravity, therefore
subject to tipping:
if you took a curve too fast
you might turn over.
A person with very short legs
has a low center of gravity
and will not tip over easily.
The ottoman likewise.
When a person is lying flat
he or she has the lowest center
of gravity possible, as does
a sheet of paper on a table.
People floating around
in outer space have little
or no center of gravity
because there's not enough gravity
to have a center.
Gravidanza is the Italian word
for pregnancy, which sounds
more serious than the English word
and may remind us of sentences such as
"The situation is very grave."
Every situation has gravity,
it's a question of how much.
People too have gravity—
of manner, of morals, and of body.
It is good to have gravity
but not too much of it:
like a bag of cement,
you might not be able to move
around or make ethical distinctions.

But with too little of it
you are flighty, your feet
hardly touch the ground.
Though cement and flightiness
have their charms,
it's better to find
your center of gravity
and have it be the place
you radiate out from.

Once I lay in bed ill, unable to move,
but in my head
I was flying and bouncing around.
But illness has no charm
and when it becomes very grave
your gravity edges toward
the most perfect center of gravity ever.

Earl Grey

That cup of Earl Grey
didn't perk me up.
What time is dinner?
It is approaching at the rate
of time, that is, one second per second.
I hear kitchen clangs and thumps.
What a joy to sit here and think
of oven mitts!
But what about Earl Grey, he
of the beautiful name?
What if Earl was not his name,
but a title, like *Baron* Munchausen
or *Count* Dracula?
The aristocracy is hard to understand,
its ranks and privileges and its nuances,
just as military ranks don't mean much
unless you're a Rear Vice-Admiral:
you know exactly who and what you are.
And here I am, a drowsy, happy bum.

Material World

Letting it stream in the light and air
and wanting it to and having it in the room next to you
as if a person made of light and air
could materialize here

I and everyone else
have materialized

Karl Marx
based his ideas
on materialism

and if you look at his face and beard
you cannot see a single ray of light
and you cannot imagine that he breathed air

Karl Marx
Ar ar

The pine tree, the fir, the larch
high in the cool morning

It is hard to say how far more important
trees are than Karl Marx

At the age of three Marx did not say
I wish I were a tree
and of course the tree is always saying
No comment

even though you are dancing with that tree
while overhead a small Greek deity
is circling on a glissando we call wings
on the verge of materialization
and here we are

What Are You On?

If you asked an Elizabethan
What are you on?
he or she would have answered
The earth, this terrestrial globe
whereas today it means
What medication
are you taking?
(Are you taking has less energy
than *What medication* it is an anticlimax
without a climax)
And today *What are you on about?*
would have sounded like
What are you of thereabouts in?
and will
So what medications *are*
you on?
I am taking italics it pokes
a hole in whatever is going to be
so I can slip through
and not have arms and legs all the time
You've lost me and I'm not even an Elizabethan
That's O.K. neither am I though both
of us bestride this terrestrial globe
and fain would lie down
for the earth is a medication a giant pill
we ride on
like the aspirin in the poem I wrote in 1966
and didn't understand until last night or was it this morning
A.M. and P.M. are medications
I take one in the morning and one in the evening

Some day people will look back
at the twentieth century and think

How backward they were
the way some look back now
at tribal societies and say
But primitive life was so dirty how
could you keep things clean?
not knowing that tribal people
lived in the Garden of Eden
comparatively speaking
That is they had more humanity
than later people
who traded theirs for technology
so that those people who look back at Earth
some day from a distant galaxy
will not be people at all
comparatively speaking
they will be cue balls

But this morning I am not in a billiard situation the sun
is shining onto my house and the trees
are feeling like their tops because they are still in the Garden of Eden
that is the gentle endless hush
of an endless mother to her endless newborn child
Things are there
covered with sparkles
that have nothing to do with sunlight
the way one night I got out of bed and found
that I was covered with sparkles very small ones
I wondered if I would be covered with sparkles the rest of my life
and if other people had them
But these are not the same sparkles that things have on them
except the ocean sometimes at night

By day the ocean moves away from where it was
but a mountain does not
Somewhere in between lies Hidden Valley
where Grandpa comes out of his cabin

and staggers around the dooryard
then goes back inside
where Grandma is holding a baking tin
of fresh hot biscuits
but she will give him none
Give me some biscuits he cries
but she smiles and shakes her head
They are all for me she exults
and then laughs she is only joking
Grandpa sits down at the table
and pretends to be dead
revived only by the muffled thud of the biscuit tin
Where's mah coffee he roars
even though he sees it in the cup before him
and Grandma says We're plumb out
That's how the day begins in Hidden Valley

But where are the grandchildren
They are scattered about the world in jagged pieces
that move like birds in spring
with colors and speedometers on them
Someday they will return to Hidden Valley
and form another mountain
to make Hidden Valley even more hidden
when the waterfall closes over it

You think I don't know where it is

or is that just a ploy to get me to tell you?
You are like the guy who looked all over
for his hat and later learned it was on his head
but it didn't mean anything until he realized he had a head
and that the hat was both on and inside it
and when he did
it was not a rabbit that he pulled out
but a rectangle in which the rabbit was imprisoned

You don't want to be that guy, do you?
You would rather be the rabbit
when all along you could have been the waterfall

We move ahead in our story to five years later
then we move five years back
because there is no story
only a collection of events with no beginning,
no end, and therefore no middle, it is all
one big beginning, middle, and end every second
and though you are in it you are also to the side
like an actor waiting in the wings for the cue
that will cause the stage to light up and expand
though it is also the cue for the audience to rise
and head for the exits, because *they* are the real players
and you, it turns out, are part of the scenery
propped up against a wall, gathering dust along your top ridge,
for soon you will be transported to Hidden Valley
and placed among the other mountains

One of these mountains is the Earl of Essex
covered with the crud
of having galloped all the way across Wales and England nonstop
Essex who dashed up the palace stairs and barged
into Elizabeth's private chamber unannounced
—where no man had ever set foot—
midst the gasps and cries of her ladies-in-waiting
and there it is
his face
on the front of his head
and her face coming off her head
and starting toward him
because she knew right then his head
would be severed from his body
but what she did not know

is that he too would end up in Hidden Valley
raining down his sparkles upon the house of Grandma and Grandpa

Are you enjoying your vacation
Yes I am
in fact so much that I don't even think of it as a vacation or as
anything else
and come to think of it I don't even think of it
it's just the way things are
How about you
Yes I too am enjoying my vacation
Well good

Silence

What you just said about your vacation I'm not sure I understand
what you mean
I didn't mean much of anything I guess
The mountains around here have a way of making me not think very
much
maybe because they aren't thinking at all who knows
and I tend to become like whatever I'm around

But you're always around air do you turn into air
Yes I'm always air
What about Grandma and Grandpa are you turning into them
No I can't turn into them I already *am* them

Well that is very interesting
but I have to scoot along now

And a fine day to you as well

Ireland rose up on the horizon
backlit by history
but Hidden Valley was too powerful it made Ireland sink back down

though the voices of Ireland could be heard in the distance
some singing others laughing and some wailing and scolding
and then they too faded when Grandpa brandished his lips at them

for he wished to sing himself
and all alone on the veranda of his own personality
the one built partly by him and partly by the celestial carpenters
who found his scratchy gurgling caterwauling arias to be as
astonishing
as he found them to be beautiful and moving—
arias that caused tears to gush forth from the sky
you could see when you looked up into his eyes
not long after you were born
the sky at night

and professional wrestling was on TV
Antonino Rocca bounded around the ring
evading horrible huge guys who fought dirty
the kind you would find only in New York City
when it was in black and white
little Antonino who looked like a short-order cook in a diner
but who dodged and slid and leaped so fast
the horrible big guys couldn't catch him
but when they did, Ow! Get away, Antonino!
and he came back to life and slithered free
and hurled the big guys down and one-two-three boom
they were pinned
and once more he smiled
at people like us out in the middle of nowhere
prompting Grandpa to clear his throat and say
It's time for bed it's way past time
and it was
but we were hidden outside of time
and no one would know
because they were visible inside of time

I was happy in Hidden Valley happy enough
and I'm happy I once lived there
Maybe I'll find myself there again someday
even though the mountains will be gone
and the rest changed beyond all recognition

The Hatchet Man

God
give me the strength
to raise this hatchet
over my head
and strike
with all my force
the cubic foot of air
that I imagine
to be in front of me
one foot off the floor
and to strike it so
as to cleave it right in half
and watch the two halves fall
to the left and to the right
still one foot
above the floor

But God did not
answer my prayer
and I remain here
with the hatchet

The cube
is not here

It went away
and took God
with it
and he doesn't have
a hatchet

What a funny life he leads!

Spots

And so once again
Father Time said to Mother Nature,
"Mother, put a few more of those brown spots
on him, please," and so she did,
dutifully and without malice she placed them
here and there
among the others she had left before
as gentle reminders, though if
you've ever looked in the mirror
and noticed several that weren't there
the night before . . . I lose
my train of thought, it was on Herrengracht
the cobblestones were irregular
for pedestrian feet such as mine
so I kept looking down when I most wanted
to look straight ahead and around.
"The Earth is a cobblestone,"
said Father Time to Mother Nature,
but she made no reply
for she did not like fancy allusions
to her cousin Mother Earth.
The kitchen became edgy
for a moment and then it passed,
the edginess, that is,
along with the moment: both
were moved along to the area
of Past Experiences and from there
shunted into The Forgotten.

But I remembered it was my birthday
and my mother is large with me
and her mind is full of ironing
like music you can't stop hearing in your head,

the music of ironing, and so
me, first a spot, then a boy
with a dog named Spot,
and now a man on whom more spots
are arriving in the night,
when Mother Nature makes her rounds
and Father Time keeps the watch.

Happy Birthday to Us

for Marcello Padgett

Seeing as it
is my birthday
I thought
I'd say something
cheerful
and true:
first thing
this morning
my grandson,
age now
90 days,
gave me smile
after smile
and I gave him one
for every one
he gave me.
That it's the ninth
straight day
of rain
doesn't matter
one whit
because
I've always felt
that June 17
is a special day,
a sunny,
blessèd day
I was lucky
to be born
on. And here
I am, a lucky

dog whose bark
means he's glad
you've come.
It's your birthday
too, Marcello,
because I give it
to you. Now
you have two.
I don't
really need
one anymore.

On Decency

Practicing decency
is easier when you are surrounded
by cannibals who are nice to you,
nice because they are line drawings of cannibals
and you are a cannibal also
though a real one.
But when you are not a cannibal
and you are among sheep and clothespins,
no, not clothespins, those are the fingers
of those who are pinching the sheep
to keep them awake in midair,
then it is much harder
and at times seemingly pointless,
like a cement philosophy
that dead-ends on both ends.

Thus we took leave of the city
where our five senses had been compressed
into a shiny black ball rolling always just ahead of us
along with the pink ball of our mortality
and the white ball of our idea of ourselves,
as if we were moving along on the baize
of a huge billiard table.

In 1942
I took leave of my senses
and became a person
and a stone and an oaf,
but deep in my little human heart
I wanted decency,
for the tree, for all of you, and for part of me
(the oaf).
I pulled myself up through time

against the undertow of my oafishness,
as if I were holding my breath
until the day when decency would be everywhere
the way everywhere already was,
but each time I opened my eyes
the decency fled—
I saw its coattails rounding a corner
just like that.

Mother, you had decency, certainly, and father,
you did too, though sometimes it was hidden
among the smoking fragments that fly up
into heaven behind Zeus as he ascends,
and you, Grandma and Grandpa, and Grandma,
you all had decency, you always had it,
fresh off the land that has no malice in it.
I had no land, but I had you.

Irish Song by an English Man

O there's a listening in the air
There's a hovering nearby
I know because I'm there
And it is I

O there's a mountain in the stream
All to ribbons torn
Almost a dream
The moment you are born

O my mother came to me
Without a reason why
I wanted to be free
Of her and die

I loved her like a harp
Whose strings have gone away
To ripple in the dark
No songs anyway

Except O the one I hear
And no one hears but I
A listening in the air
A hovering nearby

I'll Get Back to You

What was I thinking about
a few minutes ago when
another thought
swept me away?
Can't I have (pepper)
several thoughts at the same time
(carnival midway) or go back and forth
between (hyphen) them?
I guess so!
But since people (ooga) don't
like that kind of thinking (factory)
we don't do it (doghouse) much.
I never wanted to live (tree)
in a doghouse.
Now to get back (folding
map) to that earlier thought.
(President is guarding it.)
(No sense in asking *him* for it.)
It had something to do
with numbers (flying up
all over the place) and how
(smoke) sequence has properties
that (gleaming faucets) induce
certain thoughts and feelings,
such as reassurance.
I guess that's a good argument
for linearity. Don't you prefer
linearity in the long run?
(Low clouds over the winter field.)

Thinking about a Cloud

There's not a lot of time to think
when one is assailed by activities and obligations
and even less time to do it
when one is free of them
because then one spends one's time thinking
about how little time there is.

That's what it's like to be in America
early in the twenty-first century:
there are fewer spaces left
between things, and it is in these spaces
that thought comes forth
and walks around and lies down
sometimes all at the same time
it is so elastic and like an altocumulus cloud
with a sense of humor.
Hello, cloud. It's nice to see you again.
It says, "A cloud does not reply, it *is* a reply."
"But you just answered me."
"No, that was you answering yourself."
"But you enabled me to do so, didn't you?"
"Yes, but only because you believed it possible."
"Are you implying that anything I believe possible will happen?"
"No, I never imply anything. In fact I never say anything."
"Oh, I forgot. It's just that
it's hard for me to talk with you, knowing you don't talk."
"What makes you think that it matters?"
"I don't know. Perhaps my belief
that we may as well think that it matters,
for otherwise we would sit down and turn into a puddle."
"You are the first person ever to use the word *puddle* in a poem," said
the cloud. "Please don't do it again."
"I was thinking of you, how high up you are,

and yet sometimes even you become a puddle."
"I never become anything. You forget: I am not a cloud."
"I forgot because I thought you might go away
before I had a chance to talk with you."
"Well, you've had your chance, and perhaps you will have others later,
but for now, even as I speak, you feel me slipping away."
"Yes, I do, it's like knowing something terrible, little by little."
"Don't use the word *little* so much, either. You're a grown-up now."
"Are there grown-up clouds too? You sound like one."
"I sound like one because I am almost gone.
And when I am gone, you will hear
only the sound of your own personality
as it rises in you and pushes me away.
Don't you hear it now?"

Crush

Or heck
why not just, just
go over and tell her
how you feel,
you have a temperature
of 98.6 degrees F.
and a pulse rate of
175 and blood
pressure at whoosh
whoosh whoosh oh way
too high the cuff
is going to explode!
—or get up and go
home and cry your
heart out and be
a hopeless wimp
for all I care.

I Remember Lost Things

I remember getting letters addressed to me with my name and street address, followed on the next line by the word *City*. Which meant the same city in which they had been mailed. Could life have been that simple?

I remember the first time I heard Joe read from his *I Remember*. The shock of pleasure was quickly replaced by envy and the question, Why didn't I think of that? Aesthetic pleasure comes in many forms and degrees, but envy comes only when you wholeheartedly admire someone else's new work. Envying the talent of a person you love is particularly beautiful and envigorating. And you don't even have to answer the question.

I remember feeling miffed at García Lorca because he made me feel like crying about something that may never have happened. There is a 1929 photograph of him standing next to a large sphere on a granite pedestal that also bears a sundial, on the Columbia University campus. Passing by the sundial this morning, I suddenly realized that Lorca had stood on that very spot 70 years ago, a few years before he was shot to death. It was as if he had been there just moments ago. Such a brutal, stupid death! Tears came to my eyes. But on second thought, I found it hard to believe that someone would put such a large sphere on this spot: it would have come between the light and the sundial, no? Later, when I examined the photo again, I saw that it *was* taken there. But that sphere? I like it because it keeps distracting me from the idea of his death.

I remember the mill, a piece of currency that was used for a few years near the end of World War II and just after. A thick paper (and later a lightweight metal) coin with a round hole in the center, the mill was worth one-tenth of a cent. It was fun to press it hard enough between thumb and forefinger to create temporary bumps on those fingers. On price tags, it was written as if it were an exponent; for example, ten cents and four mills was written 10^4. I don't know if mills were used anywhere other than in my hometown, and since they went out of use I have heard references to them only once or twice. They have faded away, even more forgotten than the black pennies of the same period. But if you mention the mill to people old enough to remember them, their faces will take on a rising glow of recognition that turns into a deeper pleasure in your company.

I am trying to remember what it felt like to have never even heard of television, to be six years old with your toys and maybe a dog. You roll the wooden truck along the carpet and make a truck sound that turns into a honking horn as you approach the outstretched paw of the dog that jumps to her feet, just in case, and you say, "Aw, I wouldn't have hit you." Wagging her tail, she comes up to lick your face, which is fun at first, before the doggy breath becomes too strong. Then you wipe your face with your sleeve, turn back to the truck, and start up its engine again. The sound of dishes from the kitchen.

I remember when some cars, older ones, had running boards, and the fun of standing on one and gripping the window post as the car accelerated down the block to the corner, the wind in my ears. Gradually there were fewer and fewer of them, and then none. At least the new cars still had hood ornaments, the most memorable being the shiny chrome head of an Indian man, his profile knifing into the wind, headdress feathers blown back. And then he was gone too.

The Apples in Chandler's Valley

The apples are red again in Chandler's Valley
—KENNETH PATCHEN

I figured that Chandler's Valley was a real place
but I didn't need to know where,
it was just some place with apple trees,
in America, of course,
but when it went on
"redder for what happened there"
a chill went up my spine
well maybe not a chill
but a heartbeat pause:
who dunnit?
because blood must be involved
to make those apples redder.
Then ducks and a rock
that didn't get redder. . . .
You don't know what I'm talking about
unless you know this poem by Kenneth Patchen.
When I looked at it again not too far back
it didn't have the power
it had when I first read it
at seventeen
or heard him read it, rather,
on a record, but it's enough
that once it did have power,
and I am redder for what happened there.

How Long

in memory of Lorenzo Thomas

How long do you want to go on being the person you think you are?
How Long, a city in China

The nouns come toward you
"Knee how," they say
To the cluster of synonyms also approaching
          . . . has that evening train been gone?
How long, how long, baby, how long?

Let me know
if you ever change your mind
about leaving, leaving me behind
or at least tell yourself
before you find yourself on that train
winding its way through the mountains of How Much Province

The ten thousand yellow leaves of the ginkgo tree
kerplumfed onto the sidewalk on East 12th Street,
a deep-pile carpet of them on the roof of the parked car
proving that Nature does have a sense of humor,
though if a sense of humor falls in the woods
and there is no one there to hear it. . . .

for everyone has clustered alongside the railroad track
for the arrival of night and its shooting stars with trails like pigtails
I am among them and I know this track is mine
though it does not belong to me

Nothing belongs to me

for at this moment the boxes are being stacked
to make way for you to move through them,

reading their labels: family photos, Pick-Up Stix, miscellaneous

and the song of the porcelain, the celadon, and Delft itself
vibrating How long, how long
will this baby take to depart?

But I don't want to think about the past
I want to *be* the past,
with everything I've ever known and done
spread out on a two-dimensional plane
erected vertically and moving through the space I occupy on Earth

There is a lot more room left in me
though everyone I've ever known who's died is there
My mother my father say hello
to Ted and Joe and laugh with them
though Joe knows they are crying too
and that Ted is crying
and it sounds like laughter

They do this to console me
and I let them do it, to console them

What? I didn't hear you
or rather I heard you
but I couldn't make out what you said

The phone lay in its cradle
pretending to be asleep
and the blinking light made you think
that it was dreaming and that
there was someone you were supposed to call—
or were they supposed to call you?

Supposed. What does that mean.

It means no more than the contours of the landscape
that is as beautiful as the contours in John Ashbery's poetry
but it doesn't mean anything
unless you turn your mind on its side
and let it lie there
inert, and from this inertia
will arise a wing, the white wing
of a bird that has no anything else,
only this one wing
that folds and unfolds itself
like the magnetic field it rises above
in wave after wave after wave.

Then it's back to basics:
If you bone or debone a chicken
it comes out the same,
if you dust a cake with sugar
you add something
but if you dust your house you take away.
Oh to be a rock or a stone or even a pebble!
Momentarily,
for there is much that is unattractive about being a rock.
For one thing, I wouldn't be able
to finish this poem, I would sit here petrified
until they carted me away
to a park to serve as ornamental sculpture,
if I were lucky.

Now that you are convinced of something
that you already believed, the wallpaper becomes a fact
in the home of Anne and Fairfield Porter,
in the upstairs hallway and the bedroom
where Jimmy stayed, the wallpaper that here and there
was curling off the wall so Joe could tear it off
and glue it to a big white sheet of paper.
There is no other wallpaper

I would ever want.
Now the wallpaper goes away,
back on the wall in 1969
where I stood and gazed at it for a long time
and then went downstairs
to add coal to Fairfield's stove,
the big Aga he had shipped all the way from Sweden
because he was very determined to have it.
All day its warmth rose up to the second floor
and caressed the wallpaper.

Do you mind my going on like this?
You want something else, right?
Perhaps you want what you think poetry should give you,
but poetry doesn't give anyone anything,
it simply puts the syllables on the table
and lets you rearrange them in your head,
which you can do unless your head is a square
the size of the tabletop.
So why don't you lift your head off the table
and go lie down somewhere
more comfortable
and not worry about anything,
including the list of things to worry about
that you keep revising in your head,
for there is a slot through which that list
can slip and float down like a baby in a rocking crib,
down to a comfy dreamland
and be transformed into a list of gods whose jokes are wonderful.

But when the alarm goes off
the jokes don't seem funny
now that something is missing from them—
but what? (You weren't even asleep.)
It's not something you feel you're going to remember,
it's not as if you can go down the alphabet

until you get to a letter that has a special hum
because it's the first letter of the name
you can't quite recall,
it's not as if you can look just to the side of where
you think a dim star is and thereby have it magically appear.
The glow is gone,
and knowing it comes back sometimes
is little consolation.
But I'll take it
and go not to a deserted island
but to the factory where they make the bottles
that are washed ashore with a message inside,
and though the message has been blurred by water stains
it's a message, like the poetry in Valéry's saying
that poetry is something written by someone other than the poet
to someone other than the reader.
To you, Paul Valéry, *chapeau,*
though in some of your works no *chapeau,*
for in them it is not a bottle but a test tube
one finds one's finger stuck in.

•

What do you want to do with your life?
is a question asked of a young person
but slightly modified for an older one:
What do you want to do with the *rest* of your life?
Having control is an illusion we like to be fooled by:
the pinball machine of experience has bounced us
off one thing and onto another bing bing bing!
Life might be like a pinball machine
but it isn't one, and the trouble is
that you might be like a person
and you *are* one, as if in reverie,
but then it all seems crambe.

And so Sir Thomas Browne walks in
with an insane look on his face, he is searching
for examples of the number 5, do you
have any new ones for him? If not
please step aside, and out he goes
into the garden, eyes locked
onto the vegetation, the afternoon light
on the back of his coat.

You're relieved he didn't stay long.

For God's sake
here he comes again.
Lock the door!
But he performs osmosis
and becomes the door and then
the room and then you!
And you go about the house
looking for examples of the number 5
and you don't know why or where
it will all lead to.

But I do.
Who said that?
I did.
Why did you say that?
I didn't.
You didn't what? I heard you!
You mean you hurt me.
No, I . . . I see
there's no point in talking to *you*.

And there wasn't
for there was no one there,
only the residue of an idea
that lasted a few moments,

like the history of Bulgaria
or the rattling of bamboo trees in the wind
or the Millennium Hotel in Minneapolis.

The water lilies float on the surface of the water
unaware that they are being depicted
by brushstrokes

"I love to be beside your side
beside the sea, beside the seaside
by the beautiful sea!"
we sang
underwater glub glub
as the propeller turned to face us
and we fled
because Hitler was the propeller

and he was unsanitary

So Père Noël took a bath
whose bubbles rose up around his beard
and tickled his fancy
enough to keep him ho-ho-hoing throughout the holiday season,
for he was in denial
about his powerlessness
in the face of Hitler

Hitler kept a special area on his face
for the powerlessness of Santa Claus,
he wore it like a merit badge
among the many others that covered his face
so that no one could see what he really looked like,
the way Santa Claus used his beard to hide
the deep sadness he felt for all humanity,
for if he arrived on their rooftops weeping and wailing
it would not do,

it would not do to bring the children
model replicas of Auschwitz
or dolls in the form of the Butcher of Buchenwald
or even of himself with downcast eye and ashen brow.
The doctor comes in and says, "What seems to be the trouble?"
for the twenty-fifth time today
but you are only once today
so you say, "There's a pain in my chest it's been there for three days it
started on Sunday night right after dinner,"
but the doctor is thinking about the dinner he is having tonight with
an incredibly attractive woman
He is more worried about her than he is about your symptom
In fact he isn't worried about you at all
though he might be worried about being sued by you
if he tells you to go home and take an aspirin and when you do you die
But maybe you were going to die anyway
no matter what he said or did
and the lawyer who eagerly took the case on behalf of your family
was hit by a car as he crossed the street toward the courthouse steps
and your entire family was killed in a plane crash
on their way to a Grief Management Center in Arizona
But none of this happens because the pain
was due to a strained muscle in your chest
and now you do remember that right after dinner
you tried to stop in midsneeze
Two hundred dollars for half a sneeze
is the going rate these days

The cost of living sticks a hose into your wallet
and vacuums out the money in a trice
and you are so grateful you aren't having heart surgery
that you don't even notice
until cold air drifts across the floor
like fog in a horror film,
the one you decided not to be in,
and now it pursues you

in the form of frozen air,
the evil brother of cool air
that filtered down out of the early summer evening
and told you that the world is kind,
that atoms rearrange themselves to make you feel better,
that the sun is departing only because it felt
you wanted to be alone for a while

It didn't say, "I will never rise again,
I will go far away and be a pinprick in the sky
among the billions of others, and you
will never know which I am
and I will never tell you."

And you will never answer back, "Sun,
I do not think you have that power:
only I do, and I will go away and be the sky."

Is that what is meant by "aesthetic distance"?

Say what?

It's as if the Panama Canal had been given aesthetic distance
by becoming a passageway in your brain
and you floated down it and came out
on the end that you started at!

Hunh?

I keep a ball of laughter inside that *Hunh.*

The Joke

When Jesus found himself
nailed to the cross,
crushed with despair,
crying out
"Why hast thou forsaken me?"
he enacted the story
of every person who suddenly realizes
not that he or she has been foresaken
but that there never was
a foresaker,
for the idea of immortality
that is the birthright of every human being
gradually vanishes
until it is gone
and we cry out.

Anniversary Waltz

I wake up on my forty-fifth wedding anniversary alone,
sky overcast, floor fan whirring quietly,
and I feel pretty good, considering.
Forty-five is hard to pin down, it doesn't
have the solid force of forty or fifty
though it does have the feeling of being
a nice round number that isn't round,
technically speaking. But who could be technical
on a day such as this? My wife
in New York is not technical ever.
I love her. What does that mean?
It means something that you, if you're young,
might be lucky enough to feel someday
though you, like me, won't know
what it is. You'll wake up and think
Now I know what he meant
by not knowing, and you'll feel good.

An Air for Sir John Suckling

The sun just went behind a cloud
and/or a cloud just went in front
It's a dance they do and the moon
joins in with the stars sometimes

That's up in the empyrean
where no one goes anymore
nor to sylvan dells
where sprightly maidens dwell

I used to think that life
with such a lissome maid
would be heaven and
it is! here in this sylvan dell
I look up from and see
a car of fire streak 'cross
the blue and dark green light
bathed in its own embrace

The Best Thing I Did

The best thing I did
for my mother
was to outlive her

for which I deserve
no credit

though it makes me glad
that she didn't have
to see me die

Like most people
(I suppose)
I feel I should
have done more
for her

Like what?
I wasn't such a bad son

I would have wanted
to have loved her as much
as she loved me
but I couldn't
I had a life a son of my own
a wife and my youth that kept going on
maybe too long

And now I love her more
and more

so that perhaps
when I die
our love will be the same

though I seriously doubt
my heart can ever be
as big as hers

Statue Man

Could I have the strength
to lift my stone fingers to wave at you,
cloud,
in the dark of night
when I know you are there
above my roof
as I lie in bed
looking at the ceiling?
Could I have the strength
of character to salute you
whom we think of
almost as a person,
though it's a wasted gesture,
a whimsy that serves no purpose
but its own?
Why yes, I could,
if I wanted, but a man
with fingers made of stone
can't want to do that
or anything else,
for the only desire he has
is the one sent to him
on invisible waves
that shake his insides
so hard he wants to laugh.

Snake Oil Song

Let me walk right up to you
in this square on a fine September morning
and tell you of this fine elixir
known only to the old grandees of Spain
and the great pashas of Turkey

The shadow of the Flatiron Building
falls across us like a slab in a cemetery
but this elixir is as powerful as a sledgehammer
and as potent as a potentate,
it'll grow a mustache on a turnip

No of course not sir I did not mean
to say that you are in any way a turnip
or even incapable of growing a mustache,
I was speaking hypothetically
even about the cemetery and the shadow

For lo though I walk through the valley
of the shadow of the Flatiron Building
I will fear no turnip nor will I flinch
before the onrush of each day's horror,
for I have in hand this fine elixir
known only to the old grandees of Spain

and of course the great pashas of Turkey.
But you are thinking I am trying to sell
a bottle here and there—to you, perhaps.
But no, the answer is no, never,
I'll not give up this fine elixir,

though you outstretch your hand and beg
I'll take a step away and then one more,

and as you start toward me I'll step two more
then run, and you will chase me down the street
that leads away from the Flatiron Building,

you will chase me night and day,
though my image fade and disappear,
for the bottle never disappears and the elixir
flashes brighter, as if made of laughter.

From Dante

for George Schneeman

I

Guido, I want you and Giorgio and me
To dig a ditch just by singing
And mess around in a boat, which at every wind
Goes flying o'er the sea to your wish and mine.
Bad Luck, laughing all the while,
Cannot throw big rocks at my feet, but
Ouch! it hurts always living by your talent,
To stand always inside a crescendo!
And the moonlight hits two mountains
Like the number 50 coming in for a landing
And shining with our great songs,
For I have a reason to love you always,
Each one in his ditch contented,
As I think we all soon will be.

II

From that lady I see a gentle shiver
Go through all the passing saints
And our almost springlike snow
Falls like daytime on a broad lake.
From her eyes a light shines out
Like a little squint of flames
And I grow red hot like a cherry
And look—now I'm an angel.
On the day you say hello
With a piano in your kind attitude
You'll stab us to the heart with virtue

And the sky'll open up like a soprano
And your gaze will come across the earth
With the closeness of wind.

III

One day Melancholy came back to me
And said, "I want to stay with you a while."
And it seemed she had brought along
Grief and Rage as company.
And I said, "Go away!"
And she fell upon me like a Greek
And raged in my great head,
Made me look at Love arriving
Dressed again in that black curtain
And on her head a little chapel
And certainly pure glass tears
That made me cry, "I too have one bad thought
That, sweet brother, kills our love and makes us die."

Snowman

I don't know what I thought
when I looked out the window
at age eighteen in my dorm room
the snow whirling around above 114th Street
in a hard, fast, and sometimes cruel New York
or later in Paris age what was it
twenty-three on the Passage Rauch
which felt wonderfully like nowhere
to be so hidden in Paris and in layers and layers
in the drafty old atelier
and then looking down at that big white-topped thing
what is it it's an Alp!
though at seven I do recall waking up
and seeing the snow outside and thinking
snowman snowball sled
which my dad tied to the rear bumper of the car
and pulled me down the snow-quiet street it
was the kind of thing we did in those days
the car went slowly and my dad said
If I stop, just roll off you'll be alright

I'm still alright or alright enough sixty years later
as I stand in my apartment and watch
the snow fall out of the cold-colored sky
and down between the buildings that line East 13th Street
Nothing can hurt me today I'm warm
and I don't have to go to a job or anywhere else
I can fix a pot of jasmine tea
and have half a prune danish,
take the other half on a tray to my wife
in the bedroom where she's taking it easy
with telly and a cup of tea for her too
and suddenly I cry for you I wish you

were looking out your window on St. Mark's Place
so I could call you and say *Sono io*
and hear you laugh at our inside joke
and say *Ronnie!*

I just heard you say it through your ashes

The Japanese Garden

In 1958 or '59 when I was sixteen
I came up with the idea
of replacing my parents' backyard
with a Japanese garden—
this in a middle-class neighborhood
of Tulsa, Oklahoma.
I even showed a design to my mother,
who tried to imagine her smooth green lawn
replaced by rocks, gravel,
and, somehow, a stream.
Even before she said diplomatically
I'll show this to your daddy
I saw that the whole idea was unrealistic,
and I put out my hand for the drawing,
relieved to be denied.

But what if my parents had gone on
not only to put in the garden
but also to demolish our house
and replace it with a Japanese one,
donned kimonos and learned Japanese,
my dad strutting among the pines like a samurai,
mother on bended knees, head bowed?

The house stayed the same, the grass grew
and got mowed, I went away to college,
my parents divorced.

Now someone else lives there,
happy among the cherry blossoms that never fall.

The Song of René Descartes

René Descartes is seated
at his table. He writes
with a pen on a piece
of paper that is exactly
the same size as that
of the table. The candle
is melting. Descartes begins
to melt, but he stops:
he must stay human a little longer.
Now he puts down the pen.
He is tired. Being Descartes
is very tiring
in an evening of yes
or no or yes and no.

Drat

The waitress
at lunch today
could have been
in a 1940s movie,
an innocent,
cheerful, and open
young woman—ah,
girl!—with a smile
that brings back
a time
that probably
never existed.
Did people
really say *Drat*?
Or just characters
in films
and comic strips
who now
are as real
as real people.

The Hole in the Wall

Through the wall to my right,
behind the bookcase with some books
that I first read as an adolescent,
my grandson is sleeping—his afternoon nap,
the kind you take when you're two years old
and which I'd have taken myself
had I not had a cup of dark English tea.
Some day I hope that he will sit where I am now
and have a cup of tea and be thrilled
to think his grandpa built this room, this house,
and this poem—the poem for him,
and though I didn't know it then
the room and house as well.

And when he's old enough to do that
I won't know what he's become
unless I live to a ripe old age
(which maybe I will, who knows?)
and have my wits about me,
at least enough of them to see
what kind of man he is.
I hope he's good and kind
and nobody's fool
except a fool like me,
a fool for him.

The Red Pool

Oh dear here we are again in a pool of blood
below a heavenly board in a sky of thought,
not the way Andrew Marvell thought
but more the way that history leaned, i.e., sideways

I am bending over backwards
to dodge the ideas that graze my face
before I tuck and roll and hit
the surface in (not of) a cannonball

and the red explodes concussing up
and out in a fine spray, leaving a hole
in Andrew Marvell's conversation.
What was all the talk about?

Hull, perhaps, the casks of wine delivered there,
unloaded on the docks at eventide.

The Brick of Bach

Come ye joyful nations, rise
Join the triumph of the skies

Register upon register
of nations and nations of angels
seraphim cherubs all the gradations
of heavenly spirits dappled pink
that fade out into pure white light
and singing not through their mouths
but through their being there
clavier upon clavier stacked
and fanned up and out amidst
the architecture of heaven

Who would not want to be a brick
in this city made of music or a note
like the one that becomes two when *rise*
becomes *ri-ise* and *skies* become *ski-ies*?
Can a brick sing yes
if it is invisible
and they are winning, those bricks

So come ye joyful nations, rise
Join the bricks up in the skies
and have brickness so much

that you too are an angel
a visible one
though the other you
is a little above
invisible and singing
the exact same note as you

Flame Name

I saw my name in boldface type
lying on the ground among the orange and yellow leaves
I had placed there to simulate autumn,
but someone else had placed my name there
and set fire to its edges.
The effect was lovely.
This was not, by the way,
a dream. It was also not
something that really happened.
I made it up, so I could
set my name on fire
for a moment.

The Coat Hanger

Starting from the left but seen from the right I am
an open parenthesis just like a doctor
told me I would be if I didn't start standing up straight
and I didn't. Almost fifty years ago
we heard a recording of Lord Buckley doing his Naz routine
in which Jesus of Nazareth encounters a poor hunched-over man
and asks him why he's like that and the man replies
"Mah *frame's* bent, Naz!" and we curled up
in spasms of laughter, and later Ted
put it in his poems as if he too were hunched over
though he wasn't except at the typewriter
and he was sometimes bent out of shape
psychically. He developed, as we say, a "bent" for it,
the way Whitman developed a bent for standing up straight
in his poems and proclaiming openness and Mallarmé
opened up his way of saying things in "A Throw of the Dice"
and Pound opened up the page to bursts of history literature economics
and general whatever you want, Olson declaring that
the poem is a field of energy you can put anything in and Frank O'Hara
putting himself in that field that turned out to be his heart,
—"you can't plan on the heart, but
the better part of it, my poetry, is open"—and Kenneth in later life
writing in a private journal that he had decided not to think about death
but about "things that keep opening up," and Joe too
always wanting to be as open as possible.
It's hard to do because everything rushes toward you
and demands that you close up a little here, a little there,
so you can have for instance breakfast instead of floating off over a star
ringed with glory and an immortality that goes on for an instant.
That's why or partly why (because everything is "partly") I
when seen from the right am an open parenthesis,
though at this very moment I am closing slightly
because I came to and found myself alone in a room:

the open part of me had disappeared
and been replaced by a strategy. But I am smarter
than any strategy when I remember that I am,
that majesty can build from its own underground
and exultation rises like a train station in the mind of a boy,
a station built of straight lines and sunlight-dappled water,
though you are dragging your great trunk along the ground
trying to figure out if you are legless or an elephant
and the dust rises about you like a chorus of angels
come not to sing thee to thy rest but to giggle like curlicues
in the air around the head of a headless person,
for though the body is dead the head is alive inside itself,
even more alive than when it was connected to the body.
I don't care what it will say to me
if I allow its lips to move for I
am feeling somewhat bent this morning and in no mood
for ghoulishness or foolishness: the water in the stream
flows onto this page and now onto you.
What did Whitman say? "This is no book;
Who touches this touches a man." With him that was very
almost true. Me I am at an angle,
but when I stand up straight as the lines in that station,
I see, before the fog rolls in, the tracks that take us all across ourselves,
metaphorical fog thicker than real fog,
just as barking is thicker than a dog,
though the dog is clearing up too, like a sky
whose translucence is arriving as the metaphors depart
and I start the day as a man for the first time again.

The Great Wall of China

This morning I am striding among the Chinese
on their way to work or school I'm on my way to breakfast
They don't seem unhappy the streets are clean
and they're in black more than I am in New York City black
Everything is OK the way it is

The rain on the Great Wall today makes it look sad
not because rain is sad
but because it makes the Wall seem even more useless
The Wall that was built to keep people out
now brings people in
I was thinking this this morning in bed
happy to be imagining the Wall and my being there later today
a place I've wanted to be ever since the moment I learned it existed
But now Anne Waldman walks up and says *Ni hao*
bowing slightly at the waist with a smile
How does she go on being Anne Waldman?
The same way the Great Wall goes on going on
—the great bonus of life—
but look out I am becoming too grand not great
and I haven't even seen the Wall yet I have hit
a wall the wall of seeing my old friend in the street
so I walk along the top of her head the view
on one side is New York on the other is the thing
the incredibly big and old thing the thing
that is secretly smiling it is what we call China
a large vase that shatters and reassembles itself time and again
like a clock that goes tick and then tock

Chinese air in my lungs I am lighter than usual
and the wall even the little part of it I am standing on at Badaling
is suddenly heavier than it was because it is connected to my feet
those of a millipede rolling its 4,000-mile-long body

into the past and back, I am thrilled at Badaling I am thrilled
by the very sound of the word *Badaling* and what
is useless in my life has taken wing into the aether that protects the
    human race

Am I great yet? No I am smaller and smaller
and happier to be so, soon I will be only one chopstick tall
and though they say that the journey of a thousand li
begins with a single step what they don't say is
that the single step is a thousand li long and it is joyous
because you don't know what a li is and you don't care
for there are li everywhere and they're fine where they are

The Wall of course has nothing to say
It used to groan and growl but now it's like a very old man
you think is grumpy but no he's not
Perhaps at a certain age holiness slips in automatically
and says Just sit there and don't say anything it's alright
But what did I hear was it the holiness of the Wall veering into the
    distance?
Then I come back standing there atop it
and above me the clouds on their way to New York
one of them shaped like the Wall and I am on it too

Children's Story

Ronnie did not want to take a nap.
Why take a nap?
He wasn't sleepy.
It was the middle of the day!

The teacher said it was time to take a nap.
Look at the other boys and girls.
They are lying down to take their naps.

That's fine for them, thought Ronnie,
and he said, I ain't gonna take no goddamned nap.

The teacher looked funny.
He thought she was like a babysitter
but she was different.

With the palm of her hand
she gave him a little whack on his behind.
Now don't you talk like that, she said.
You behave and take your nap.

Ronnie began to cry
as he got down on the pallet
where little cowboys and Indians were playing.
He laid his head on the pallet and cried.
Then after a while he stopped crying
because he had fallen asleep.

Later he and the other children woke up.
They rolled up their pallets
and started to play a game with the teacher.
Then it was time for his mother to come
with the other mothers.

And there she was.
The teacher told her that Ronnie had said *Goddamn.*
He did? said his mother. Well.
You can't say that at school, she told him.
And they went home together.

POEM AND OTHER POEMS: UNCOLLECTED

Joe's Walk

Joe's walk

(with all his troubles
and tired legs)

light
and
breezy

like
a nice guy.

8 Ball

Edwin Denby is depressed!
That such an agile personality
is down in the dumps is enough
to send me there too,
to The Dumps, not far
from the foul rag-and-bone shop of the heart,
though Yeats and I, thank God,
are far apart.
But when Joe Brainard and Ted Berrigan
and I are far apart too, then
it's the year of parrot fever,
it's a bad year, everyone says so,
it's been a fairly horrible year.
And now it's going to be a horrible Christmas too,
I can feel it coming,
because part of my attitude about Christmas
or any holiday
is horrible already,
I can't seem to "swing" on a national level.
Instead I go skittering across the road of my own emotions
into a cornfield.

Everyone is calling me Scrooge,
all for various reasons, all wrong,
none based on the deep, complicated facts,
all too personal, petty, and unpleasant to relate here.
When I leave, they say,
"Scrooge was just here."
Dogs in the street nip at my heels
and I never have enough money
to satisfy my increasingly expensive tastes.
Kenneth Koch
said, last summer,

"The older you get the more money you need because you develop
more expensive tastes,"
and the other night at a party
he looked sideways at me, as I was chatting with
The Academy of American Poets,
as if to say, "It's rough, isn't it?"
And smiling he was, brightly.
And almost all the new people I meet
are terribly square, and I have this bump on my wrist,
and my mother arrived in Texas with her "companion,"
my step-father,
who three months ago left her on the highway alone
at two a.m. in Idaho,
and what's worse now is that I hate his stinking guts,
I wouldn't puke on his grave.
Almost a year ago today
I took a snapshot of my now-dead grandfather
holding my still-alive son,
and the robbers have broken into Dick's
apartment four times now with no sign of letting up,
and they've stolen almost everything that's anything,
including a TV that belonged to me and a typewriter,
and what about Dick? Anyone in this room know about old Asian Flu?
And as it turns out I'll never play Bobby Fisher
and though Patty's learned to play chess
this has easily been the worst year of our marriage.

The nicest people I've met this year
unless I'm wrong
are Alex and Ada
and I think George
is having a good year
but Katie isn't really,
though Sandy might be,
and it's nice to have both Toms in New York,
along with the unbelievably cute and sexy Joan Inglis!

I do know that Ted and Joe and I are
all riding this one to a close,
to the edge of the woods
where we'll dismount
and, shooing our mounts away,
turn and start walking back
on January first.

Holiday Inn Satori

I sit in the Holiday Inn ha ha
    snow & driving rain outside
            & whizzing vehicles
 lounge music inside
                insane outside ludicrous inside

& terribly
      not exciting

but I am extraordinarily beautiful

& sane. It's true

I am.

To the Chinese Acrobats

1.

If gravity were from up
we would float down.

When two words run
head-on in the dictionary

they change polarity.
A silver needle penetrates an immense ball

2.

There are forty-nine thousand
characters in Chinese.

Four hundred and fifty
million people write them daily.

When each of these people
writes all of the characters
the silver needle is exciting!

Honeymoon

This funny picture postcard has a drawing
called *Escalera de la cárcel.*
On the other side is the message,
address, stamp, and wavy black lines
across the face of Abraham Lincoln.
Wavy gray lines rise from the campfire
out on the windswept prairie,
but this is a sheltered spot with pine trees,
and the stars slide across the dark blue sky,
with a crescent moon near at hand.
Forever,
all you've ever really wanted,
so near to hand,
Monterrey, Mexico, 1947.

Thirteen Ways of Looking at a Haiku

Three pairs of big red shoes
in the closet
with yellow laces

The broom leaning in the kitchen
late afternoon
door wide open

The old woman snatching at the vines
tearing away dead leaves
sputtering and cursing

On the cookie sheet
a gingerbread man
reading a book

Wooden clothespins on the grass
at the picnic
for the factory workers

In the air
a glass face
about to materialize

Fog on the gardener's cottage
she snuggles closer
he opens one eye

A mosquito hovers
over the stile
to the apple orchard

If you look hard enough into the air
you will see something there
even if you are a hammer

An old man dressed like a mass of soap bubbles
walks in the woods
singing happily

From left to right
the sweet, meticulous script
in the old notebook

Red cherries on the cotton dress
on her body
as she opens the curtains

A man is a damn fool
unless he talks through his hat
as it gets blown down the street

Jerry Lewis Nightmare

Year after year
you pick up your fork
and aim it at a tiny bright green pea
that slides off the edge
of your head
onto your other head
high above the Pyrenees.
O Jerry, Jerry

Poem with P. B. Shelley in It

Sitting here in Limbo,
which has been abolished,
isn't so hard as you might think:
I don't know where life will lead me
and I don't care, really,
just don't give a flying fuck, ha ha,
ha ha ha ha!

He or I was carted
down the hall in the laundry hamper
with the *Complete Works* of Schopenhauer,
that's Edna Schopenhauer,
a book painted as black as a ship midocean,
the one I am on now
watching my friend set fire to my heart.

Windows

On January 6th
(Twelfth Night)
I read *Twelfth Night,*
wove my way through
Viola and Olivia's
confusions of identities,
ever on the alert
for a mention of
Twelfth Night, which
never occurs. How funny
that red carnation is,
blooming in the window
over there, small enough
for a boutonniere
gone out of style,
not yet back in.

Giovanni's Bunny

A little rabbit stole his nose from a greeting card
and popped out
and bit the leg of the man
who had designed him—
so began the opera
Giovanni's Bunny
with cardboard stars and Saturn
suspended where past and future
intersect and the music of the spheres was floating
past the music of the triangles
that once belonged, briefly, to Spinoza
as he once, briefly, belonged to you,
when you were still a bunny
freshly sprung from the stiff card.

The Long and the Short of It

I'm all dressed up with no place to go
so I wander around the streets for a couple of hours
looking at the periods at the ends of sentences.
I feel like a man who bears a startling resemblance to Herschel Bernardi.
A long face on a long day.
I felt like smoking, almost.
The rain came down across the French poetry of the nineteenth century.
I was in Paris
in a café
operating the telephone.
A lady tells me my wife is pregnant.
I tell my wife.
We have a grand crème,
then a big laugh.
Our child will be Made in France.

He had nothing to do with my long face,
in fact he considerably shortened it
by adding a comma here and there
and striking out across great fields of parenthetical expressions,
until his sidereal gait
was synchronized with the stars
that fled before him.
No, he had nothing to do with the long face.

But it was stuck on the front of my head,
and so consciousness stepped forward and blew a bugle,
and soon the ideas were jitterbugging
in and out of each other, creating
abstraction, just as the various woes
of my friends blend to make me feel abstract,
like a Gorky, maybe, or the feeling you get

when you aren't suffering enough
and *il n'y a pas de Popeye aujourd'hui*
and my friends accelerate up the chimney like sparks.

Birthnight

It's getting late
turning
thirty-nine.
My hope is
that I will live
long enough to say,
"Most of them
are dead now."

Actually there's
more to it.
I have a rendezvous
with my own tears
and a slow submission
to the grinding
juggernaut
of the everyday,
and with having
that grinding enter me.

Bats for You

What you see of me
is what you see here; the rest
you must surmise,
such as me riding a bucking cactus
over the wild pink prairie,
which I once did, in 1962, sort of.

I sort of got off the cactus and ran
into the present tense,
crashing
through the words
you are reading now,
and now you hear me
saying Hi and laughing
and hearing you think Hi back.

To Charles Reznikoff

On the subway today
a guy tried to pick my pocket,
managing only to slip a piece of paper half
way out.
It said, "Lex Ave IRT
to Nevins." I think maybe
he was Haitian, about five nine,
fingers of concrete.
I should have slipped
him a few bucks.

Pumpkin

My little pumpkin,
I like to think about other girls sometimes,
but the truth is
if you ever left me
I'd tear my heart out
and never put it back.
There'll never be anyone like you.
How embarrassing.

Translating Catullus

I get down to the final phrase again
and it's still "off" and as usual
it's three o'clock in the morning
on the watch face my two eyes roll around,
but it's quiet outside
with only the click of dog claws
on cool lineoleum in the kitchen
as she rolls over and stretches back
into her doggy sleep where everything is okay.
Catullus, you won't quite get across
town to your lady love tonight.

Mexico

I call my home and hear
my own voice in my ear
telling me I'm not there.

I take a comb and comb
my hair straight up like flames
surrounding lurid dames.

It's a decal, that's all,
on the window of a car
that went too far and hit

the spit and image of itself.
It sits now on a shelf
in the museum of Who You Are.

The Eccentric Center

On the cover of the Penguin
edition of Pascal's *Pensées* is
his face, a portrait superimposed
on a death mask.
The eyes stare off
over my right shoulder
in their own milky light.
His dictum
"God is a football team
whose center is everyone"
fills my heart with dismay
as I hike these lines
into themselves.

Thumbtacked

Human history is an accident
proceeding nicely through space. Don't
drink that. The artist
paints the portrait of the human race
while his feet get lost at the foot
of his chair. Prepositional phrases
are more like toys than adjectives
are. I take a breath. That's the moon.
This orange juice is orange and green.
(An imp put in more green.)
The lights are going out all over
Tulsa. What did you expect?
My thumb does a lot more than I thought.
The street name changes.
There is a tremendous amount
of rumination going on in New Hampshire.
Bells send the color red behind the dark evening.
No one wants to sit on a tack.
Algebra is filled with them, their points
glistering in a gloomy antechamber.
Tomorrow is almost
on a stamp. My dog is sniffing
my shoes. I was there.

Visit with the Fulgent Avatar

He sits there like a cheap statue
flashing off and on in his dark niche,
and he looks back at you
like the son of a bitch

he is.
You'd like to roll a bowling ball
with its heavy whiz
and crashing waterfall

and hit him bam
just as his light goes on
and his soul's light says, "I am
the river flowing on

and on inside your veins,
and I own a used car lot
and I have a serious lot of brains
for knowing what you know not.

So wind your bowling ball back up
and into time back then,
come sit and flash and have a cup
of mud with me, my friend."

And so it was.

I put away my bowling shoes
and sat down by his side.
The loud, persistent moos
that came from his inside

soon drove me like a herd of beef
back up a path that led
past the human misery and grief
that turns into our own heads,

on past the summit and the sky
to a perfectly composite place
that held everywhere you and I
and the rest of the human race

have ever been. "That sound,"
I said, "is much too strong.
It makes the very ground
rise up like some great wrong

to offend the part of me that's
nice. Why do you, avatar,
want to drive us bats?"
"Bats is what you are"

was his reply. I went away.
His spirit wasn't deep.
Awakened by the light of day,
the light of day went back to sleep.

Dark Fragment

Again tonight I'll take that giant step into the ground
of the air and have it not be there, where
neither rhyme nor reason makes sense
to the humans with their little blue faces turned up
to the big blue face of their own understanding
that if there is one thing we know about God
is that he's not named Mel.
   Some part of me is deeply tired tonight and another
deeply happy to be aware of it and both
on vacation in a country where I am not,
because ideas bouncing all over the place create
a great racket of isms that lurk and clang
in our various mental casbahs encircled by smoke
in the shape of a bullseye into which the real world
is being sucked like the missing parts of this poem,
parts I do not miss at all.

Notebook of a Visit to Someone Else's Native Land

The first word the pen wrote was *blue,* the color of its ink.

I like it when people unlike me like me.

That tin shack is moving to the left and the sky is moving in all directions away from the shack.

French men have legs and hair.

Every once in a while I have to take a vacation from the possessions I can't bear to part with.

She told me what style the building is in: every style.

As a child I took a silent vow, in a movie theater, never to go to Devil's Island.

A black boy in short red pants carries a tray of orange and yellow iced drinks.

I have never been able to get over having two eyes, one of which sees things a little differently from the other.

Sex in foreign hotels.

Those palm trees are whizzing.

Most people's legs are too short.

A sunset peach, guava, and baby blue.

I can say anything I want, but I can't say anything else.

Beavers vs. the Surrealists

Instead of an inflated theoretical hooey expert
with cobwebs covering my visual apparatus,
I'd rather be a beaver with an overbite
to mow right through the trees
toward your love at the end of the day
and kiss you till dawn comes up like the face
of a big scary melting Surrealist
who had a bad night and now
is staggering back to his crypt
with an ordinary headache.
But we in our little beaver bedroom
are snug and safe. You whap
your tail against the bed and fall
into a deep and satisfying sleep
in which you fling your ideas off
and scamper through their fading outlines in the air.

It Turns Out

I haven't turned out
to be the person
I hoped I would,
but that's just
too damned bad.

Night Poem

The lights go on,
heart
pitter-pat-clunk-bop.
I go out
in the dark,
stars up
behind a tree
past which the wind
is shifting and flows
along the back of
my neck, where
childhood is.

Shift to Stay Put

I guess I *am* a hick
who prefers to "grapple with shifting formal problems"
that come up in any situation that
changes from word to word
—though *problems* isn't the right word—
but I like to shift back and forth
so as to give the other side of myself
a chance to feel half human again,
though atoms are swirling in everything
and jumping around, so tiny down there
and at the basis of everything
material. Add spirit
and voilà it's Wednesday night
and the stars pierce the sky
in your heart and you say so,
hick or no.

Today

I heard the click
click click of a moth's wings
and got scared
by the possibility that it
was a mechanical moth,
for what lunatic would build
a mechanical moth?

Then some clouds
took Nathaniel Hawthorne's
story with them to the edge
of the page and left it there,

and I got up and tiptoed
into my reflection
in the pond.
I had no metal parts
and was as quiet as the moon
that would come out later.

Whatever It Is

Much poetry is depressing
because it is about things
that have happened
and then been brought
into the poem to die,

whereas

the real poem lives in its own
little house that moves along
the landscape that moves
along the mind of the reader,
and no one has ever seen it.

Versatile Tarzan

Tarzan sinks
through the whizzing vines into the arms
of a gorgeous little gorilla (a symbol
of death but also of transfiguration and going
on without end though being dead and
sort of alive if you know what I mean).

And then in walked a truly spiritual monkey,
radiant with lack of willpower and filled
with the kind of food that gets cooked
only in the mind of a great chef,
and it meant absolutely nothing.

Shadows fall over
and die.
            Although the wind drifts through the woods,
it sounds about half-bad. I will go
into the next room and stop
splitting in half. I'm tired of being versatile.

Coat Hanger

This is entirely
too much, this is
pure coat hanger across the
room, this
is getting to be
too many coats on
that hanger, and this
is it: it
gets up there in
the air and hangs
in the brightness
of any time of
coat and hanger,
any weather,
extreme coat hanger.

Lost and Found

Man has lost his gods.
If he loses his dignity,
it's all over.

I said that.

What did I mean?
First, that the belief
in divinity has almost
disappeared.

By *dignity*
I meant mutual
self-respect, the sense
that we have some right
to be here and that
there is value in it.
(Values are where
the gods went
when they died.)

My dog Susie doesn't seem
to have any values, but she does
have Pat and me, gods
she gets to play with and bark at.

Flying Down to Up There

A thought in a brain and uno,
there, whale, here, whaleness:
footprints across the top of the world
where it levels out into what
we call space,
                                        several spaces
and later I genuflect to the phone
and say hello to South America,

I think it is going to blow up!
like a saint who flies not
to make a point and an appointment
with the arriving rays that turn
you into a burning bird whose song
freezes even firemen in their aureoles,
arms and wings of pomp and flame
whiplashed into place.

Driveway

Again I slid up over the horizon
and the lights of Tulsa spread flat out before me.
"Ah, there you are," I said,
"like a porch light left on
for almost thirty years."
                                        "Don't get carried away,
Ron. Yes, the lights are on for you and anyone
else who wants to rush toward me in a stream of light,"
the awakened city said, "but I knew
it was you. Who else would talk to me like this?"
I said, "There always was this special thing between us,
no?"
      "Between you and me,
not between me and you. You're like all the rest,
you think you're the only one to come along, that
I was made for you."
                                    "I know, Tulsa, but
remember, I was an only child."
                                                    "I know, Ron, but
you're not a child now, so why act like one?
Why don't you settle back and take a deep, long look
at things the way they are? Why not just let go
of your love-hate thing with me? Do you really need
this longing and regret and so much useless anger?"
"But what'll I have of the me who was a little boy?"
"Whatever you already have, no more, no less,"
the voice said evenly.
                                        Suddenly I cried
into the dark, "Where's your mouth?"

"You don't know? It's all around you—"
    I was pulling
into the driveway where I used to live
        "—it's your skin"
and opened my eyes and was
here, in New York, typing these lines.

A Newsstand in Central America

Sometimes I fear I live
too much to the side of things,
uncommitted to a cause or party,
and yet, as I walk
down the street and glance
into the bodega or feel again
the wind at the corner
of Second Avenue and Tenth,
I can't help but swing up
onto the stairway
with an X-ray look
into the future of me
selling pale green newspapers
in some dusty *zócalo* in Central America
with the rain just starting to fall
in large drops that thump the dust
as the air grows cooler and large orange
individuals are approaching me,
one of them saying
"My friend, come walk with me,
to that table over there in the shade,
and have a lemonade, and talk awhile
of pleasant things. And then the others."
Your vision rakes the surrounding hills
for the sight of your brothers who will come
to liberate you from this great angelic jailer,
but you will never be free
of the various yous arising through the silky coil of time
and spiraling away with all their might.

Les Choses

The supple act of existing is miraculous enough
and anything on top of that
means you are detached from "you."

Thus
I hate it when the mail comes too late
and I have to go to work
with a desperate desire to read my mail.
Then there isn't any!
You are in Detroit!
It is night (you think)!
Your name is Mabel,
that's all you remember,
you can't explain
why you are wearing something called "Switzerland."
There are bright lights
and dark sticks emanating from the portrait
of Pierre Reverdy on the far wall
and he is looking deep into your conscience
and there is nothing you can do about it.
Oh those French!

Poem Begun in 1961

Spring air,
students crossing
the quadrangle
in pink
evening light,

and over there
up
in that huge stone
edifice, locked
in a climate-
controlled room,
on a shelf,
in a dark,
acid-free box,
the journals
of Ted Berrigan.

Edge

At first it's good to feel that your body has a crisp outline, slicing its way through the natural world like a new can opener going through the lid of a can of peas, like a glowing red maple leaf blown flat against a dark green fir, where it hangs, for a moment, like the moon at the edge of a cloud that now is covering the moon that glows through it, then darkens completely, like the face of the young man who lost his mind when it slipped out of him like a piece of paper coming out of a xerox machine, then another piece, and another, his mind in multiple copies one on top of the other, 8 1/2 x 11.

Polish Star

In the city of Lodz
a young girl is reading
The Idiot in Russian
by candlelight.
The flame flickers
as her eyelids close,
the book slowly slipping
from her hands.

Autumn Almanac

Today there's supposed to be a break
in the weather. I sound as if I care
when I sort of don't.
Like weather in diaries—it always sounds
more important than it was: "Low
clouds today. Cold and wet." Or
"No rain again. Six days in a row."
If these were from the journal of, say,
Herman Melville, you'd say, "Hmm,
six days in a row. Herman sounds grim,"
and then you'd feel like him.
And in a poem that starts "A break
in the weather" you sense significance
because it's in a poem, where words
have more significance, ho ho.

Poem

A movie star fades in
above the rooftops
of a country village,
a pink light is rising
and her blonde hair
sheds its shimmering
that birds take wing from,
they bank and swoop,
flying healthy blue birds,
her soft warm shoulder tilted now
against a light blue sky
with her distant smile's dark red message
beaming over the cottages
of farmers who rise and yawn
to stretch their faces into day,
put on socks and boots,
approach the bowl where a pat
of butter is melting
along crevices of gruel.

On

It was afternoon.
A mustache was on my face
and we were waiting at the bottom of God,
in the toe area.

A tree stood in the yard,
there was not another tree for six hundred miles.
It swayed gently, like a beautician.

And then Victor Hugo came over
and invited us to dinner,
hamburgers *en pleine air*

beneath a big yellow triangle in the sky,
just about nine p.m. I'd say:
You heard it in the distance
and then it was all around you.

Red Jemima Polka

There's a big fat red and green woman
down in New Orleans, city of a thousand
woes, with Venice, Italy, "written
all over it" in large bold letters
the way Gertrude Stein the woman
and Gertrude Stein the legend
were "one in the same." But
one in the same what?
She's a big fat woman
down in New Orleans, wears a
cloak on the back of her personality
and shatters the detective in his reverie.
He peers through the smoke from his brain,
grits his three teeth together,
and curses the day he ever laid eyes on you.
He's a big fat woman
down in New Orleans who
breaks the streetcar door down
and demands a seat, but it was a bus
and she was real, then
she was an illusion and the bus got lost.

How about the stairs?
The ones depicted in this photograph.
Bend closer.
There you see the maid
standing by the bushes. Over here
is Mrs. Covington. That's her dog
Maxwell. No, that's her husband, Shorty.
Over here next to the shed
is this gigantic . . . what do you call it?
Irises nod
in the evening breeze,

with a spritz of dew on them,
though,
and a haze of moonlight.
It is the most romantic evening of your young life,
and at the window you see, loping across the hills,
your boyfriend, now a wolf man,
real long hair all over him,
and it is as if your feet are encased
in blocks of cement and you
are falling from a great height,
a big fat woman
down in New Orleans.

Angel of the Pots and Pans

When you see someone anew (you
may go back to the nineteenth century)
you say hello
or some variation thereof (you
may go back into the house)
and so I say to you (you
may go back into the kitchen)
Hello, pots and pans,
you may go onto the stove
for a rendezvous with cuisine—
the exalted pan, clarified butter,
and exquisitely transformed face
of the woman who bends over you
like a terrifying angel who
kisses you, once, slowly,
and many times slowly, drawing you
higher into her face until
you have gone past it
into a big nothing (you
may go back into yourself now).

Right and Wrong and a Third

What is the point of learning to read
if you read all the wrong books?
(Strictly speaking, of course there are
no such things as "right" or "wrong" books.)
What is the point of learning to paint
if your heart is in the wrong place?
(Strictly speaking, of course the heart
does not "beat," it speaks.)

I went down the road to think on these things.
I thought about them, under them, and through them,
until the sparkle of intellectual diamonds filled my being with light

and the ceiling blew away
the way it does in Venice
at the Accademia
where Fairfield told me to go.
When I got back
I gave Fairfield the ceiling

and our reunion threw the switch
on a circle of energy
that whirled away like a refrigerator light.
This must mean something lovely,
something suggested by the union
of two other meanings.
But strictly speaking,
there is no such thing as strictly speaking.

Au Flammarion

In the shadows
of an office in Paris
the eyelet is glinting
on a shoe
worn by a boy
who disappears
when the light
is switched off
because the day got tired of waxing
and the varnish
on the black walkingstick of night
began to flash
back to the storks of the century
you are in
every time you close your eyes.

Clap Trap

When at fifteen or so I first read
the Zen koan about the sound
of one hand clapping, I saw a hand
clapping the empty air in silence.
Thirty-four years later I said
"But the idea of clapping predicates
two objects," but it was too late:
to the joy of one hand clapping is
now added the joy of being tricked into
thinking that one hand *could* clap.
And the other hand?
What other hand?

Life Savers

If ever I walked through a giant roll
of multicolored Life Savers
behind which light was glowing,
it was for a moment, a moment
ago, when the scene glimmered
in my head. The imagination's alright,
but it's 9:30. I have work to do.

The Rule of Three

In 1492 Columbus discovered America.
In 1942 I was born.
In 1492 Sandro Botticelli drew in silverpoint and ink his
Ascent to the Primum Mobile.
Christopher came over,
I came forth,
and they went up.
Like a comic strip character that comes to real life,
you enter from the left,
step into a new scene—
here's one that has you in a hammock
for your little siesta—
and in the final box a punch line.
Then the newspaper is folded
and dropped beside the armchair
as Dad rises into the evening air
with the evening news and the evening chair
all suddenly sort of Chinese.

Another Crevice

This time he returned
with no dark cone
in the board house.
You, darkened rider
on the curving sweetness
of the old north, save
our Existentialism. It's a grain
echo, immortal as fainting,
dissevered memory of 1902.
I was two.

Animals and Art

I was saying that sometimes I feel sorry for wild animals, out there in the dark, looking for something to eat while in fear of being eaten. And they have no ballet companies or art museums. Animals of course are not aware of their lack of cultural activities, and therefore do not regret their absence. I was saying this to my wife as we walked along a path in the woods. Every once in a while she would go Unh-huh or Hmmm, but I suspected that she was wondering why I was saying such things. I was saying them in order to see how they would feel when spoken without any hint of irony. Then I quoted the remark about human life as nasty, brutish, and short, but neither she nor I could recall who had said that, though I offered a guess. In fact I had seen the quotation ascribed to someone recently, but I did not mention this to her, for fear of appearing senile. But the truth is that I do not bother to try to remember information that I can look up in a reference book, thinking, I suppose, that I would prefer to fill my mind with the impressions and sensations and spontaneous ideas and mental images that fly past so quickly. Would such a person as I make a good animal? The news today is that scientists have finished the genetic mapping of the human being, and it turns out that we are 99 percent chimpanzee. I don't feel 99 percent chimpanzee. It makes me wonder about the enormity of the remaining one percent, the sliver that causes me to take the subway up to the Met and look at pictures and sculptures and other beautiful and interesting objects, then go to the museum cafeteria and have a cup of tea and a bun, all without the fear that some creature is going to eat me. But back of all of it is a spreading sorrow for those that hide and tremble in the dark.

The Flag of Finland

Ever since I was little I've had a secret attraction to the flag of Finland, secret only because there never seemed to be the right moment to go up to someone and say, "Excuse me, I've always loved the flag of Finland." I loved it the first time I saw it, in a dictionary with a colorplate showing Flags of All Nations.

Finland's was special. It was free of the symbolism that makes some flags so fussy and editorial. The flag of Finland looked like cool, clean air in a blue sky, the essence of a zero that had just disappeared.

And so I always imagined that being a Finn would be very simple. You would be free of the daily gravity that weighs down so many other nationalities. You would be living six feet off the ground, approximately where your head is. You would, in fact, be in a kind of imaginary Lapland, where no one could hurt you: in your white parka, white leggings, white skis, and white eyes, you would simply flash away into the snow. No one could catch you, not even an adult, not even a truant officer, not even a government. You would glide through the air like Ariel, a cerulean vibration, an invisible paradigm of spirituality. That's what I learned from the flag of Finland.

Cold Front

Layers of meaning stack up into the sky
and move laterally away from the onset of winter,
the season that hits you a little too hard
like a friend punching you in the shoulder, and you
get steamed up and your head squirts open and you
see your friend standing at the lip
of a volcano and you are bearing down on him on a
bright yellow bulldozer going clank, clank as you stand up
at the controls wearing a chef's costume and holding a silver
tray on which a map of Polynesia lies folded into the shape of
a long, pointy airplane from which a plume of smoke is rising.

Poke

Perhaps Cendrars's poetry disappeared
into his life is one explanation
why he stopped writing poetry
and it strikes me as a good one because
I think some of the poetry I might
have written over the past ten years
disappeared into my everyday way
of doing things, just under
the surface it was flowing and all
I had to do was poke a hole in the paper

The Real You

When you feel tired it is easy to become more and more aware of how tired you feel. Soon you create a character who is tired, with you in that role: your feet ache, your back is weak, your eyes are dry, you can barely hold your head up! But deep inside, the real you has been taking a nap, so that by the time the character falls asleep you will be wide awake, skipping along the darkened rooftops.

Homage to Bobby Czyz

Hmmm seems to be without a vowel. It's as if one of them had tried to squeeze in between the *h* and the first *m,* but the space was not large enough to allow it for *him* or *hum* or *ham* or *hem*. The ensuing *m*'s are like a hillbilly family that will shoot anyone who sets foot on their land. *Hmmm* will remain a sound, never to develop into a full-fledged word unless we accept it the way it is, and say, for once, that an English word need not have a vowel. *Hmmm* could enter the arena of daily life the way Bobby Czyz enters the ring, his hands raised over his head, the head his opponent will batter and pummel for twelve rounds and still emerge the loser. Nobody can beat Bobby Czyz.

Solesmes

The brothers opened their mouths, and though no chant came out, they continued to "sing," looking straight ahead, changing their faces to suit the "music," hands folded inside white robes. A grainy light filtered down and stopped in midair. Slowly the sound came on, the sound of a tree arriving from deep inside the piece of wood that was nailed to the wall inside each and every one of them.

War Correspondent

A little fear goes a long way. With only the slightest impetus, it goes several miles—deep into your "gut." That is to say, into the nexus that makes your heart start bucking. It's the signal for the footsoldiers to clamber out of their trenches and rush forward shouting, little figures that soon rise into the air and float there in what for us would be uncomfortable positions. Two other soldiers float amongst them, one brandishing a tripod and the other a camera. You mean Jean and Maurice? Yes, how did you know?

Bird Watch

Absolutely normal in the cool morning
is the bird that hops on stick legs
from branch to branch and does not say "Argh."

The steam from my coffee forms a veil
through which I see him hop and sit
and hop some more, then fly away.

But there he is and hops to branch up
and hops down, then stops. Then he and I
get bored and away he goes. I'm glad

he's gone. Now I can drink
my coffee and get to work. Argh.

Son of Søren Sonnet

I see the bright orange face of Abraham
as he raises the knife
high over his son.
Kierkegaard went nuts

in *Fear and Trembling*
obsessing on this moment
in the horrible story
of a dolt who'd obey a god

who said to stab his own
innocent son. Søren relayed
this seriously disturbing wave
that vibrates my head and how

about later when *your* son
got pierced and pierced and pierced?

In Elbasan

The live music hard-driving in loudspeaker blare

over little white plastic tables and chairs
where Albanian men in short-sleeve shirts

sit drinking and smoking in the early evening as
elbows leap at fluttering clarinets

and hands fly up and down electric keys
—four skinny guys inhaling

the Ottoman Empire and swirling
it back out in the modern air

my head bending into the whirl
and feet turning at the corner that

cuts down the sound down the street to where
a wife and two daughters are fixing

dinner that starts with a candy bar.

Pastoral

The boy and girl are in medieval times, but they aren't unhappy on the hill, with the music of the trees and birds around them. No, they are dancing, the way that only people who haven't experienced the Renaissance can dance, with the great joy of a wooden door whose grain is exploding with energy and delight at being in the world. Up, up! shout the things around them, your blood is full of vitamins and vigor, and the dawn itself has come to kiss your cheeks and spread its radiance around your heads, you blessèd youths with graceful arms and garlands woven among your thoughts that now turn quizzical as an old shepherd appears at the top of the rise, with his aura of goat and sheep, the animals he dances among when night is falling because he has an impulse to dance, to lend delight and be delighted, to spin and hum among his fleecy charges as the moon rises and turns its laughing face away, for it must dance too and let its stars go wild and free to dance among the gods that send down their invisible hands to dance around the boy and girl who sway like gods inside doors among trees.

Southwest Serenade

In a dusty gulch
viewed by a burro
depicted on a patch sewn
onto the shirt of the boy
who has formed his own club,
the Friends of Cactus,
a skeleton is tipping his hat
to you, amigo.

A Small Glass of Orange Juice

on a white tablecloth
with light blue legs below
in a hotel restaurant
in a small town in Poland
in 1936
is being contemplated
by a man
whose homburg
is tilted
at an angle
parallel to that
of the picture
on the wall
behind him,
a mountain scene
with forest below
in which a lone deer
has turned to look at us.

Amsterdam Again

The sky has been scrubbed
by the sails in the harbor.
In the gutters of de Hooch
the rivulets are sparkling
because they are Dutch and
clean. The bricks are happy
to have soapy water splashed
on their faces every morning
and Benedict Spinoza inside
the house creating his book
theorem by theorem.
Even his theorems are happy
to be placed side by side.
Outside the window
a man says something and a girl
laughs and says, “No, Willem,
that is not the real reason.”
The real reason she will not kiss him
has nothing to do with his mustache.
But her ideas bounce off his exterior.
His own ideas barely get out of his interior.
“May I place my lips on yours?”
will never achieve the desired result,
nor will “My mustache will I mow.”
And then she kisses him and darts away.

Apartment 6

My landlord tells me that for the past thirty years I may have been ingesting lead from the paint on the walls of my apartment, and that it may cause brain damage. Good. Hair will grow crooked all over my body. I will shuffle around the apartment at night in the light of a single bulb, followed by my pet fly. The neighbors will glance up at my window and then hurry on. Music will rise and the screen credits will roll as the camera comes to rest on a close-up of my bedroom wall, which I will crash through, filled with a strange joy, for the lead has transmuted me into an enormously strong giant with glittering metal teeth. I have put my landlord in a headlock and used him as a battering ram. He is sputtering and coughing plaster dust.

Palm Tree

Make me feel better, palm tree
imagined in the distance and around which
I allow some blue and green to fade in and
a breeze to blow along the sound of the word *sarong*.
Wave a little, as if to me, to say
"I am your friend, a tree who knows
you let me have that blue and green and she
who floats among my fronds, though she is but
an idea curving with the wind."

You can go now, tree. I feel
a little better. Downstairs
my son gives out a mirthful laugh.

Dîner en ville

I would like the buffalo served in a catcher's mitt
and topped with race cars, followed

by a pack of reporters shouting questions and
thrusting swords into the air.

If the service and ambiance match the promise of the menu,
then I shall recommend this place to my friends.

Do you see that wall of water over there?
Would you care for a glass of wave?

O time between ideas!
You have to wait.

And then it arrives, the limousine,
and you depart, an occupant

with credit cards and wishing
the buffalo had been a little angrier.

Hello, Central

I attended a high school whose name was colorless and odorless: Central High School. It was called that because it was built in the middle of town, so that students could converge on it equidistantly. Then the city added other high schools, all named after illustrious men. The students there could associate their schools with these figures, but we at Central could no longer even associate our school with centrality, since by then the city had expanded and become lopsided. The name Central had become totally abstract. After sixty years the structure was deemed inadequate, and a new Central was built—in the northwest corner of town—disconnecting the school's name from its last vestige of meaning.

In the many times I have returned to my hometown I have never once driven out to see the new Central. Instead I cruise past the renovated old structure that now is used as an office building. In my mind's eye I dash up the steps and into the hallways crowded with students who only an hour ago were lost in sleep. I enter room 212 and take my seat at the back of the center row and feel the day click into place when the bell rings and Miss Quesenbery looks at her roll book, brushes back an errant strand of hair, and starts down the alphabet. A rush of anticipation rises in me as she approaches my name, and when she says it, I answer "Here" in a voice that makes me feel useful, like a brick.

Boxing Day

Everything starts as a box
inside of which is you
don't know what. And
every time you open it, it
is something else. Today
an island, tomorrow a toy island.
But those palm trees are unsatisfactory.
Take them back to the factory!
I open the box to release the men
who will bring me a new island.
But that's tomorrow. So I'm grumpy.
I'm in a grumpy box. Is there
anyone out there who
will take me out? No. Because
they don't know I'm in here,
and I won't tell them. I don't
want them to take *me* back to the factory.

Take This Hammer

in memory of Ralph Weeks

The Estwing, with "Unbreakable Handle
in Normal Use," made in USA,
is the most beautiful hammer
I have ever seen, a shaft
of burnished steel with handle wrapped
in leather strips mysteriously bonded,
the weight a distribution of perfection,
head through handle.
It took me eighteen years to figure out
that all I had to do was go into a hardware store
and buy one,
one of the most beautiful objects in the world,
$24.95!

The Story of Monarchy

The King speaks to the Queen:
"Darling, my slippers are gone missing."
To which the Queen replies,
"I shall search for them."
And so she does.

All over the palace she wanders
and across the countryside.
Months later she returns.
"I have brought your slippers,"
she says, proffering two frogs.

And then
the royal bugle blares: it is
the call to war. There has been an uprising
of frogs in the north. Even now
they hop toward the palace.

A Good Example

in memory of Virginia Quesenbery

The clang of sword
on halberd in light blue
wash over black lines,

the walls of Carcasonne
in the paper and the ink,
where decades later

Je suis touriste.
Eh bien,
bonjour

M. Blanc,
Mme. Blanc,
et tous les petits Blancs.

Who

Who is that knocking at my chamber door?
Who is that whose foot is standing on the floor?

It is me mum, come to say one word:
"Ron" in a tone no one can understand

for it is not a name, it is an engine that
drove her life up to a point and then

off. The boy at 58 who held her hand
and felt that final squeeze, so strong

for one so near to death, now sits
and puts his Ron foot on the floor.

Lynn McClaskey

She
and you,
age 13,
moved
around in
shoes to
music.

Mattone

Scrivo questa poesia
per il mio amico Giorgio,
amico di molti anni,
e mi ricordo il muratore
in un film di Fellini,
chi dice,
"Mio bisnonno è stato muratore.
Mio nonno è stato muratore.
Mio babbo è stato muratore.
Anch' me, io sono muratore.
Ma la casa mia, dov'è?"
Per te, Giorgio,
in questo momento
la casa è questa poesia,
piccola ma vera.

RJG BD

Richard John Gallup, wake up,
it's your birthday, or maybe you're
already awake and the spotlight
of the day is following you around
the stage and you can't get away,
you are shining and special all
this very day you came sliding out
and your mother said Oy vey
though she was not Jewish
and in fact had never even heard
that expression before you taught it to her,
but let me explain that she said it
because having a child can hurt
and plenty, and being a child can hurt too,
which is why we never grow up or if we do
we're awful, so it's great that you never did
and I never did and probably won't,
for even though we might totter and drool
we can always say Oy vey!

Down and Up

A metaphor knocks on the door.

Metaphor, there's no one here
but us chickens who cluck
in English, but you understand
any language because you are
in the way any language is.
If I go back to just before you knocked,
you are in my going back, as I
am in my going back, or
the going back is me—

and the metaphor breaks away
as I break up through the
water wow it's
cold along the edge of Sweden!

Now You Don't

I open my eyes: you are no longer there.
I close my eyes: you are no longer there.
I open and close my eyes and you
are there, darkness, my companion.
Of course you're nice and there is no moon
because my mother took the moon away
with her, she wasn't going to leave such
a beautiful thing behind. And I gave her
my left hand to carry it with. I wish
I hadn't done that, for now the left side
of my chest has shooting pains like
small silver spears flashing
when I think of her, how real she was
though mostly imaginary.

In Fact

A lot of bugs on the windshield tonight—
let's make a right up there and go down
that dirt road into the pasture
and turn off the lights and the motor
and roll down the windows: hello,
crickets and air, such air! so sweet
and mild and soft coming into the car
with us and into the moment we know
we can't stay in forever.
It's tempting to make something
out of this, something more than it is,
but nothing is more than a fact.

The Mediterranean

I don't really want to do any
of the things I'm supposed to do,
I want to be standing
in a white room and looking
out the doorway at the blue
Mediterranean below as the sun pours in
with the soft and distant crashing,
the breeze along my face
and then. . . .

"He's 36."
"He's going on 37."
"Everyone is going on something."
At every moment every creature on earth
is about to do something. I am
about to write one thing and
I almost do, but then I turn
my head and write something else.
I could have shot a hole in this page
but that is too extreme for me
and noisy, and what would I have?
A hole in my desk. No, I mean what
if we all turned just slightly and did
the other thing that is always there.
Instead of "Thank you" "Thank you, Henrietta,"
or instead of Indianapolis Fiji.
The Ron Padgett I have become
is not the only Ron Padgett.
I could be Ronald now,
he who stands up only when asked
to fill out a form. And though little Ronnie
still runs around inside me, I think

I'll leave him in there. As for Padgett,
ouf! It's like cutting down the family tree
with a blade of grass. So

let's get back to the Mediterranean,
where I have just shaved and have
my face again. Or is this Nantucket,
where my face has never been?
William Carlos Williams keeps asking
if he can get into this poem, he wants
to read us his poem about the white bed
in the sunny room. He reads it dryly,
in that doctor deadpan way of his, tough
and everything right in front of you.
It is unusual for a dead person to arrive
in someone else's poem, and now he's gone
since something else was next for him,
we know not what. The dead are busy
moving energy around
and making our hearts flutter and not being.

Though it's easier to forgive their sins,
the dead are still not any nicer than the living
and we miss them and their sins
that were more interesting than ours
and their virtues stronger, since we
cannot ever believe that we equal our parents
in their humanity. Or so we think.
My parents never saw the Mediterranean
or had the fantasy of standing in a room
that overlooks it. I wish they had.

I want them to have been more like me
so I won't feel lonely without them, I
in my little self, to whom I say,
"Bald little orphan,
cast off your cloak and walking stick
and fly away to the blue Mediterranean,"
and he replies, without moving his lips,
"Father, I could have saved you.
Mother, I could have saved you."

Several Unresolved Questions

One was
how Ted and I had a running discussion
as to whether you get warm faster,
after coming in out of the cold,
by removing your coat
or by leaving it on.
Another involved getting wet.
Let's say you are one hundred yards
from the house and it starts to rain.
Do you stay drier by running
to the house or do you simply
get hit by the same amount,
only faster? A third question
was whether hot water or soap
is more important in dish washing.
We spent hours
examining the variables and propounding
our points of view, only to come back
to these same questions
weeks and even months later and have
basically the same discussions.
Our level of agon was low,
but sometimes I think about these three questions
and wonder which position I held.

Mr. Statue Head

As if finding the head of a statue
and putting it back on backwards

by accident, because the statue
had turned around to look

at the sunset, as it has done
for thousands of years, you

have an idea of what to do
with the rest of the day that

just turned around to face
you who are walking away.

Poem

Phone rings
but I'm not ans—

Hello? Yes.
No, I'm up.

Small voice
inside phone ear

has voice
rhythm. Delphic

oracle makes
no sense.

Vertical snakes
spin midair.

The Luminous Parentheses of Verse

And then I woke up.)
Much verse is somber,
Come down from a height.
But the maker said otherwise:
Let there be light.
(And then I woke up.

Trip Away

I must brush my teeth alive
and get into the car and drive
to the train station today,
the little station of Umbertide,
and let descend with my tears
my little bride of forty years,
who used to be slightly taller,
so she can go get even smaller
by going away and then
get bigger again, and when
she does I'll be waiting there
with brilliant teeth and not much hair,
a sort of slumpy skeleton
happy to have found the station.

Performance Anxiety

In 34 minutes I have to drive
into town, so composing a lyric poem
is going to be hard
because 1) I'm not Frank O'Hara
and 2) having a time limit is tough.
Frank dashed off a poem
("Quick, another poem before
I go off my rocker!")
but with a time limit?
I don't think I'll ever go
off my rocker, though I will get older
and sadder and if bad things happen
deeply depressed. It took
three minutes to write that,
only three minutes to depress myself!
Now three minutes
to write myself out of it,
for who wants to drive depressed,
especially in a pleasant little car
along a country highway
with green hills and dairy cows?
Not I, said the little white poet.
Actually I'm not so little.
I'm a good height, six one
and change. Thinking of it
I feel better already,
almost okay!

Baton

That is your baton.
That baton is yours.
Your devoted servant,
Yours very truly.

Yours what?
Why the *s*?

That is her baton.
It's hers.

Hers very truly.

Our baton. Give it back.
It is ours. Right now.
Yours truly,
yours *nel mezzo del cammin di nostra vita.*

It is our lives we lead
but we need the baton
and the baton twirler
no matter how silly he,

she, or it looks or is.
Truly and very truly
and even extremely truly
though sometimes

sort of truly,
for there is no *s*
in baton
until it is twirled.
Very twirled.

Stairway to the Stars

"And then there were three
whereas before there had been four
or two

And then there were four or two."
Thus spake the King.
No one dared ask what it meant.

He seemed satisfied by the beauty
of the logic that had arrived,
the royal hall now lightly radiant

as he arose from his throne
and the world fell away,
courtiers, battlements, and clouds,

and he rose like a piece of paper
on which his effigy had been traced
in dotted lines whose dots came loose

and flew away to a place in history
where nothing mattered.
And then there was one.

And?

That is, is it like what you thought it would be,
when with an assumed calmness you said
to yourself I will become a wonderful old man
basically the same as I am now except,
well, a little different. Now I'm a little different
and beyond that a little more different
and so on. Yes, and so, on
toward the person you thought you wanted to be
but who has turned out to be the one next to him.
And what about that other one, off to the side?

ALONE AND NOT ALONE

What Poem

What poem
were you thinking of,
my dear,
as you breezed out the door
in your long coat fur-tipped
at the top?
What animal
once wore that fur
and licked it
with a long, raspy tongue
that lolled to one side
in the afternoon shade?
If only you too
could lope across
the Serengeti Plain
and grab something
in your powerful jaws,
instead of pausing
at the door and saying,
as if in afterthought,
"Write a poem
while I'm out."

The Roman Numerals

It must have been hard
for the Romans to multiply
—I don't mean reproduce,
but to do that computation.

Step inside a roman numeral
for a moment, a long one
such as MDCCLIX. Look
at the columns and pediments
and architraves: you cannot move them,
but how beautiful they are
and august! However, try to multiply
MDCCCLXIV by MCCLVIII.

How did they do it?

I asked this question some years ago
and never found an answer
because I never looked for one,
but it is pleasant,
living with this question.

Perhaps the Romans weren't good at math,
unlike the Arabs, who arrived
with baskets of numerals, plenty
for everyone. We still have
more than we need today.

I have a 6 and a 7 that,
when put side by side, form my age.

Come to think of it,
I'd rather be LXVII.

Butterfly

Chaung Tzu wrote about the man
who dreamed he was a butterfly
and when he woke up
wondered if he weren't now
a butterfly dreaming he was a man.

I love this idea
though I doubt that Chaung Tzu
really thought that a man would think
he is a butterfly,

for it's one thing to wake up
from a dream in the night
and another to spend your whole life
dreaming you are a man.

I have spent my whole life
thinking I was a boy, then a man,
also a person and an American
and a physical entity and a spirit
and maybe a little bit butterfly.
Maybe I should be more butterfly,

that is, lurch into a room
with bulging eyes and big flapping wings
that throw a choking powder
onto people who scream and fall dead,

almost. For I would rescue them
with the celestial music of my beauty
and my utter harmlessness,
my ætherial disregard of what they are.

Reality

Reality has a transparent veneer
that looks exactly like the reality beneath it.
If you look at anything,
your hands, for instance, and wait,
you will see it. Then
it will flicker and vanish,
though it is still there.
You must wait a day or two
before attempting to see it again,
for each attempt uses up
your current allotment of reality viewing.
Meanwhile there is a coffee shop
where you can sit and drink coffee,
and where you will be tempted
to look down at the cup and see
the transparent veneer again,
but that is only because you are overstimulated.
Do not order another cup. Or do.
It will have no effect on the veneer.

Sometimes the veneer becomes detached
and moves slightly away from reality,
as when you look up and see a refrigerator
in refrigerator heaven, cold and quiet.
But then the veneer snaps back
to its former position and vanishes.
This is a normal occurrence—
do not be alarmed by it.

Instead, drive to the store
and buy something
that looks like milk, return
home and place it in the refrigerator.

Days go by, years go by, people
grow older and die, surrounded,
if they are lucky, by younger people
who do not know what to do
with feelings whose veneers
have slipped to the side, far
to the side, and are staying there
too long. But eventually they will grow hungry
and tired, and an image of dinner and bed
will float in like a leaf
that fell from who knows where, and sleep.

The Chinese Girl

When I order a coffee that is half-real, half-decaf, with half-and-half, the women behind the counter invariably give me a blank look and wait for something to come clear in their heads, and when it doesn't I repeat, slowly, my order, gesturing with my fingers to demonstrate the half-real, then the half-decaf part. When it finally registers on them and they fill the cup, I point to the carton of half-and-half. Then one of the two—they work in pairs—asks, "Shu gah?"

However, the youngest of the morning crew of five understands better than the other four, so I always hope to have her wait on me, not only because of her better English but because she is the cutest. Of course not all Chinese girls look the same, but descriptions of them tend to sound the same, so I'm not sure that it would help to say that she has straight black hair, parted in the front and held in place by the bakery uniform's light-green kerchief, a slightly flattened nose, and dark eyes, with a small mole on the right above her top lip. Her modest demeanor lends her an air of innocence. She is what, around eighteen?

I always look forward to seeing her on my weekly visit to the bakery. This morning when I walked slowly along the display case of dazzling muffins, buns, rolls, danishes, and other pastries, trying to decide among them, I heard her voice on the other side, asking, "Can I help you?" Never before had one of the crew left the cash register area to do this.

Concealing my surprise, I asked her, "Are the croissants ready yet?"

"I will see."

When she came back from the kitchen she said, "Five minutes."

"Then I'll have one of these danishes."

"You want small coffee, no? Half-regular, half-decaf, with half-and-half?"

Astonished, I said, "Yes, that's right. You have a good memory."

"I remember *you*," she said, causing my heart to flutter. But my composure returned when she asked, "Shu gah?"

At the register she handed me the change from a five. I took a single and, pointedly ignoring the tip jar, handed it to her, saying "This is for you. *Sheh sheh*."

"Thank you," she said, lowering her eyes and almost imperceptibly drawing back.

I got the signal, so I headed toward an empty table, where I removed the plastic lid from the paper cup and took a bite out of the danish. A band of steam rose from the coffee, like a curtain on a miniature stage. The Chinese girl and I are living in a remote part of China. Our past lives have been erased. She is unspeakably devoted to me and I adore her. We say little, passing our days in a state of calm I could never have imagined.

Smudges

Smattering of gray puffs   rocks are they
large ones but   if you pick them up   light
too light   but fun to lift   and marvel at
they don't make "sense"   they
aren't broken   they are what   you
have laughing in you   almost out
smudges come out   of the rock
you breathe in   and out   the same gray rock
each time as if looped in a cartoon
of a sleeping man   from whom z's
emanate

Smattering of gray puffs   a man is one of them
a cloud   a smudge   a powder of stone
from which a city arises   with people in it
and ideas   that flow toward you and through you
it's too late   it's already happened   to the next you
and the gray smudge   that is your face   turning
into your next face   the one you forget
as soon as it happens   as you fall away
among other smudges that are falling away
smudges and puffs falling away

It Takes Two

My replacement in the universe
is the little tyke who'll soon arrive
and let me be superfluous if
and when I feel like being so.

I don't really mean that.
It's just the openness
of what will or might be,
when what matters most
is the right now of now,
which,
when I draw back and look reveals
an old fool in the foggy bliss
of whatever this morning is.

Straighten up, old thing!
You aren't *that* old and he or she
will reach right up and grasp
some years and break them off
your psyche—what is it? like stardust?
glittering on those tiny tiny fingers.

The First Time

The first time Marcello went outside
the sun and moon were at his side
(his happy mom and happy dad)
(also the happiness known as granddad).
The first time Marcello breathed the outside air
he seemed to like it there.
The first time he got in a car
it zoomed him fast and far
(for such a little guy)
to Brooklyn: "Hi,
Brooklyn!" he didn't shout:
his words were too little to get out.
But clearly in his sleeping face
he felt comfy in the human race.

Circles

Marcello sees
    the sun is yellow.
But then at night
    it's white.
No, that's the moon
    or a white balloon
above his bed—
    wait, it's his head!
Colored circles rise and fall.
    Marcello seems to like them all.

Grandpa Brushed His Teeth

This morning Grandpa brushed his teeth
so hard it knocked Marcello down
but he got back up to watch
Grandpa brush those teeth

Ah Grandpa brushing up and down
with joy he sang almost Glug glug!
The toothpaste tasted excellent
and the brush it zigged and zagged

It's a good thing he has teeth to brush
and that he likes the brushing of them
The only missing ones are Wisdom
and Marcello does not need them

And Grandpa doesn't either
Good-bye to Wisdom teeth and Wisdom
Buon giorno to Marcello
Little toothbrush fellow

Coffee Man

She might be hearing the burbling song of the bird outside, but it is impossible to tell, since she has rolled over and I think gone back to sleep. If I were to say quietly, "Good morning, dear, here is your coffee," she would open her eyes and manage a groggy "Thank you." But when she realizes that I am standing there without coffee, I would forget which tense I'm waiting to lift from the jar with the red lid in the kitchen.

Where Is My Head?

It makes you nervous to think not about death
but about dying and being dead yourself
but when you don't think about it
it doesn't exist,
at least in your universe.
And since that's the universe you happen to be in
you want to stay there:
you have to fix the world
and then save it,
you have to do that one thing
you can't remember what it is
but you know it's there somewhere
like the death you forgot for a moment.

I should have spent my life
meditating so deeply that the thought of death
would be relaxing like a breeze or a feather
but instead I have spent it promising myself
that someday I would go to that special place
in my psyche where the spirit enters and leaves
and make my peace with the beast I call myself.

I hate myself for dying, how
could I have done this!
But all I did was nothing
other than believe that I was actually important!
Everything my mother did proved it.
But when she died she just glided away—

she didn't mind at all.
She didn't think she was important
and she had a farmgirl's view of dying:
chickens do it all the time,
they run around the yard with blood
gushing from where their heads used to be.

I wish I could do that!

In Paris the heads that dropped into the basket
—were they still thinking about the executioner?

Today I am my own executioner.

Survivor Guilt

It's very easy to get.
Just keep living and you'll find yourself
getting more and more of it.
You can keep it or pass it on,
but it's a good idea to keep a small portion
for those nights when you're feeling so good
you forget you're human. Then drudge it up
and float down from the ceiling
that is covered with stars that glow in the dark
for the sole purpose of being beautiful for you,
and as you sink their beauty dims and goes out—
I mean it flies out the nearest door or window,
its whoosh raising the hair on your forearms.
If only your arms were green, you could have two small lawns!
But your arms are just there and you are kaput.
It's all your fault, anyway, and it always has been—
the kind word you thought of saying but didn't,
the appalling decline of human decency, global warming,
thermonuclear nightmares, your own small cowardice,
your stupid idea that you would live forever—
all *tua culpa*. John Phillip Sousa
invented the sousaphone, which is also your fault.
Its notes resound like monstrous ricochets.

But when you wake up, your body
seems to fit fairly well, like a tailored suit,
and you don't look too bad in the mirror.
Hi there, feller!

Old feller, young feller, who cares?
Whoever it was who felt guilty last night,
to hell with him. That was then.

The Young Cougar

The doors swing open and in walks a young cougar wearing white shoes and light-blue socks, come to help his father. "Where do we put this in the registry?" one servant asks another. Or *they* were wearing the shoes and socks.

Radio in the Distance

for Yvonne Jacquette

Beneath the earth covered with men
with snow atop their heads, down
to where it is dark and deep, to where
the big black vibrating blob of wobble
is humming its one and only note, I lie,
orange hair not in the idea of diagonal,
a Betty not composed of vertical fish
or dog with grid-mark cancellations,
but easy as an orchestra of toy atoms
lazy with buzz and fizzle in their drift
as if above this late and lost Manhattan
spread out like a diagram of what we want
from heaven, wherever it is when we think
we know what it is and even when it really is.

Face Value

From a face comes a body an entire body
and from a body everything

but I can't face you
fully
not yet
maybe never

and even if I did or thought I did
how would I know

How would I know
what face value is

From a face comes face value
and from face value a lot of baling wire
 —the face scribbled over with dark coils of it

I was born in Kentucky almost
There were no faces there
so I was born elsewhere
from inside a fencepost
to which barbed wire had been affixed
by Frederic Remington

The air was cool, the night calm
and each star had a face
like a movie star's or someone in the family

They too had star quality I thought

but they had statue quality
and then turned sideways
like music blending into fabric and little curtains
along the kitchen windows

attractive kitchen windows

Now you can sit down at this table
and look me square in the eye
and tell me what you've been wanting to
or you can stand up like a photograph on a piano
and sing to me
a song that has no words or music

Which is it? —But

a heavy magnetic force pulls you to the wall
and holds you there

As soon as you get used to it
it lets you go

for a while

and then *your* heavy magnetic force pulls the wall to *you*
and you walk around with a wall stuck to your side
The Wall of Forgetting
it's called

but it's not a wall it's a mirror
that picks your face up off the floor
and whirls it onto a head
that has gone on without you

The Plank and the Screw

There *is* one thing.

In a fishing village on the coast of Norway
an idea came forth and spread
over the country and from there
to the rest of the world, namely
that floating inside the sun was its power source:
a plank and a screw
that had come loose from it,
and as long as they floated around,
never far one from the other,
the sun would continue to burn.

Let's try to imagine how hot it is
one inch from the sun.

Now that we have found it
impossible to imagine
we can go on
to the next thing we do not understand.

Meanwhile, the plank and the screw
continue to float—
the plank is roughly an eight-foot
one-by-ten, the screw a three-inch flathead—
but since there is nothing around them
except burning gas
they are both highly visible.

Many years passed.
Gradually the idea that had come from Norway
became so assimilated into the everyday lives
of people that they never thought of it—
it changed from an idea into people,
so they forgot
and for all practical purposes
the idea ceased to exist.

But everyone has inside them
a plank and a screw
floating around.
Everyone is warm enough
to be alive.

102 Today

If Wystan Auden were alive today
he'd be a small tangle of black lines
on a rumpled white bedsheet,
his little eyes looking up at you.
What did you bring?
Some yellow daffodils and green stems.
Or did they bring you?

Auden once said,
"Where the hell is Bobby?"
and we looked around,
but there was no Bobby there.
Ah, Auden, no Bobby for you.
Just these daffodils in a clean white vase.

The Pounding Rabbit

After a clock designed by Neya Churyoku (1897–1987)

If you know the Japanese folktale
about the rabbit that ended up
on the moon, you will not be puzzled
by a table clock depicting a rabbit
pounding rice cakes on the moon,
but if you do not know this story
you will look at the clock and pound
your own head in disbelief,
as if to knock from it the spirit
you wish to offer to the gods
who munch the rice cakes
and never turn to say thank you
except by sending down a genius
to create such a clock, such a rabbit.

Mountains and Songs

Mountains of song
exert their force up through the earth
and rise above it

Peasants and villagers
cling to it as it rises
and they sing

and then they don't
for this is a pause
in the history of the world

and its mountains and songs

I saw them rising
and I knew it was weeping
this rising

for the mountains were going away
the villagers and peasants too
folded away in cupboards

in mountains and songs

It All Depends

Que reste-t-il de nos amours?
—CHARLES TRENET

Et nos amours, faut-il qu'il m'en souvienne?
—APOLLINAIRE

But it is not love that I would speak of
for as you see, I am of
the nineteenth century, when love was
. . . well, it all depends,
and I can't get out of it,
whatever this love is.
I will die in it and I hope
of it, it is the preamble
to walking in and sitting
down and saying "Hi"
before anything else has a chance
to happen. And then
of course nothing does,
which is why you keep saying it—
you can't get out
of saying it. So you may as well
take off your hat and stay a while,
which is what you always planned on anyway.

The nineteenth century,
what a tremendous thing
to be in love in!
Cottages go by
and music piles up

like excited dead people.
They stop but don't,
like sleeping people who are alive,
but it's not that easy,
the century is more complicated
than one had expected
now that everyone has a pot and a pan
but not a love of the pot and the pan.
Still, look at those sailing ships
on the wide main and the stairways
that spiral into heaven
and that bird with a long red beard
sticking straight up!
It's our chance to separate ourselves
into numerous pieces and have them
go in different directions,
reassembling what time had dispersed
in the form of granules and mist.
Or was it even really there?
A nightingale warbled
the tune it was supposed to
so the world would calm down.

There's nothing wrong with resting
alongside this shady rill and taking medications
as if they were piles of stones placed at intervals
by people who must have had a meaning
in mind but with no thought of telling you
what it was, for they didn't know that you
would exist. Therefore, lie down and rest.
The afternoon is mild and your love
is not driving you crazy, temporarily.

A rest might give you the strength
to look love straight in the eye
and not fade into granules and mist.

Reverdy said
"One must try to live"—
the statement of a man
who didn't love
or wasn't loved
enough. A small rectangle
of light lay on his floor
and his shoe
flashed as it went by.
His wife was hidden
in the kitchen, his girlfriend
hidden in celebrity,
his God just hidden.
Pierre opened the kitchen door,
the trap door of fame,
and the side of the cathedral,
but there was nothing there,
and when he opened his heart
he found only a rectangle
of sunlight on the floor.
But it was enough.

Perhaps his wife was hiding
her love in the kitchen,
the dark kitchen in Solesmes,
where I saw her walking
briskly down the street

at the age of 97 or 98,
the same street
a few years later
she would move slowly up
and down the way
to lie down in the tomb
next to Pierre, her Pierre.

By then the girlfriend
had twirled into Eternity,
and God had hidden so deeply
in Pierre's poems
Pierre didn't know
He was there—
He had gone back and disappeared
beneath the period
that ended Pierre's first book,
like a dark glint.
But God too was trying to live.

He hasn't been around lately,
which is perhaps why
the landscape is so cheerful—
it gets to be just itself,
brutally wonderfully so, and birds
veer and chirp and lift
their wings to see what's there.
It's air.
And so singing.

"But that's what *I* did,"
says Pierre
out of nowhere.
"And you can't tell
if the singing made the air
or the other way around—
or both, which is most likely."
And then, like a Frenchman,
he left, before I had a chance
to throw him around the room,

but with respect,
affection, and mountains,
the kind they had in the century
he was born in, mountains as black
as his tomb, which I am unable
to throw around now
that his wife's in there too.

Henriette: her name.
(Henri: his real first name.)
(Her name a little feminine version of his.)
(But we all get smaller and smaller.)
(Hoping to fit
inside a rectangle of sunlight.)
(And not be a shoe!)
(Though have the calmness of a shoe.)
(Beneath the bed at night.)

I will tell you this tonight.

The Elevation of Ideals

To construct a set of ideals, a toy tool kit suffices, provided that the handles of the hammer, saw, and screwdriver are of wood and painted light blue. However, a full set of adult tools enables the builder to work more rapidly and with greater precision. Of equal importance are the raw materials, though it is possible to use various bits and pieces that one finds along the way. Remember, though, never to use metaphors in the construction, for over time they will shift, and the entire construction will sag and perhaps collapse. (Of course these rules apply only if you live on dry land; another set covers undersea construction.)

(If you end one ideal in parentheses, you must begin the next also in parentheses. Otherwise, the joint will not bond.) To construct a solid set of ideals, do not begin too early, for all too often the ideals do not turn out to be ideals at all: they are ideas, and, like bubbles, they tend to float away and pop. In doing so they can be beautiful, but æsthetic beauty is not of great importance here, unless it happens to be the same as moral beauty, which happens very rarely in modern societies. So allow your ideals to evolve through the decades. If you cherish them and don't think about them too much, they will change themselves by rotating on their axes while flashing on and off, to show you that all is well. When you turn fifty, they stop flashing, and for a while you think they have vanished, but it is you who have vanished, so thoroughly that even you do not know you are there. But you are.

You are, the way your mother is there, and your father, too. At this point you can obtain a set of tools and start thinking about the construction, how to begin it and where. These choices will be up to you: some choose the head, some the heart, and others even elect to build it outside themselves. The choice of location might bedevil you, but I will tell you now that the location doesn't really matter, except to you.

Deciding on the design of the construction can prove extremely difficult. This is normal, so don't fret about it. Just pick up the first ideal and see how it feels in your hand, then pick up a tool in the other hand. You will know immediately if they match. If they don't, try others. If nothing seems to work, you are not really fifty, and it is best to put the tools away and try later.

But do not postpone the resumption too long, for you might have grown so old that you no longer remember your project, or you may not be physically strong enough to make difficult moral decisions. Assuming, however, that you do resume, aim to build a perfect structure, no matter how small, for if the one you do complete is good enough it will float up of its own accord and stop in midair, where you can sing to it any time you want. If a door or window falls off, do not be concerned. Another door or window will appear in its place. And anyway, you will be inside, looking out.

Birgitte Hohlenberg

for Bill Berkson

I do not know who Birgitte Hohlenberg was
or why C. A. Jensen painted her portrait, in 1826,
but I'm glad he did, because then I could see it
in the Statens Museum for Kunst in Copenhagen
and buy a postcard of it and send it to my wife:
"Isn't she beautiful?" She being
Birgitte Hohlenberg *and* the painting of her.
I don't know which of them I love more.
Both are bright, calm, and sweet—
she had a way with beauty. You see it
in the brown satin dress with fluffy sleeves
and big white collar edged in lace, the hat
a light white puff around her head
and neatly tied beneath the chin,
her curly chestnut hair an echo
of the ribbon curling around the brim
and returning over the shoulders
to a loose knot at the collarbone,
her slender neck rising to a face whose high color elevates
how interested she is to be sitting there
looking straight at you without the slightest hint of carnality.
Just being in her presence would be enough
for me, now, at my age.
When did I send this card? August 15,
2001. That long ago. Before the Towers came down—
before a lot of things came down. But she

has stayed up, on my wife's dresser. How
she died I don't know, or at what age.
C. A. Jensen lived to 78, a long life
back then. Good for him.
I hope he was as happy
as he makes me every time I see his picture.
I hope you see it too.

Pep Talk

Dinner is a damned nice thing
as are breakfast and lunch
when they're good and with
the one you love.
That's a kind of dancing
sitting down and not moving
but what dances exactly
we do not know nor
need to know,
it is dancing us around
and nothing is moving
in the miracle of dinner
breakfast and lunch
and all the in-betweens
that give us pep.

Preface to Philosophy

> *An ugly day it must have been, when the first man stood face to face with the idea of the worthlessness and absurdity of life.*
>
> —W. MACNEILE DIXON

But it wasn't such an ugly day when I read Dixon's remark, at the age of fifteen, because I had already been *charmed* by the idea of the worthlessness and absurdity of life, which seemed far more sophisticated than the idea that life is meaningful and wonderful.

Now as I read it again for the first time in fifty-four years, what strikes me is not the truth of his statement, but the image of an early man's finding himself "face to face" with an idea; that is, with a ghostly being three times his size, wavering before him and communicating without speaking. Of course this is not what Dixon meant to convey; he was using "face to face" metaphorically, as an expressive device. But now I am face to face with his metaphor.

However, I can escape it by trying to picture the room in which I first read his remark, my bedroom, with its front window and side window. Sitting at my desk, I could have gazed out the front window and across the street to the window of my friend, from whom I had bought the book in which Dixon's writing appears, but if I was propped up in bed I could not have seen out the window directly behind me, whose curtain I usually kept drawn so that anyone stepping onto our porch would not glance in and see the back of my head. I did not want anyone to look at the back of my head.

As for its having been an ugly day, who knows? That is, "ugly" meaning what? Stormy? Dark? Probably the latter. Again he is speaking metaphorically, referring here to the psychological weather of the human nearly struck down by an idea, as I am struck, though not down, by the idea of a dark cloud in a protohuman shape fifteen feet high that descended and stood before the man and emanated the idea of the worthlessness and absurdity of life.

What made the man believe it? And then go on, as I have gone on?

You Know What

Every once in a while
it occurs to me
that I am a vibration
as hard as a living creature
and that that creature is me.
It occurs when I look out of my eyes
at it and it skulks away
into the dark area.

But you know what?
Take your philosophy
and put it in a paper bag
and carry it to a destination
and open it and see
if it looks back at you
and if it does
then you are occurring
because it is occurring too.

I learned that in my childhood
and I did have a childhood it was better than most
but I got nervous
when my mother got nervous
and my father was always quietly nervous.
We were a bundle of secret nerves sometimes
and at others we had quite a good time
especially my mother and me.
We would sing duets in the car

in harmony.
Sometimes she'd take the alto sometimes I would.
It was oddly satisfying
to come to a stop sign
and stop.

Lithuania
wasn't something I had heard of
and Stalin was I thought a cartoon character
because he had only one name and a mustache.
No one in America had a mustache
because Hitler had had one and he
wasn't funny he was shouting
and shaking his face around a tight nervous fit.
Our family was a little nervous but not like that.
He had a real problem we had a slight one.

One day someone told me to relax.
I didn't know what they meant,
I thought we were just the way we were.
We had names and identities and we knew
who each other was and what to say.
So what is "relaxing"? It is turning
into someone else in your own body
which is what is happening every moment anyway
but so slowly we can't see it—
in effect it isn't occurring
though really it is.

A Bit about Bishop Berkeley

Bishop Berkeley
is fond of saying,
in the middle of making a point,
"This is obvious
to anyone who takes a moment
to examine it with an attentive mind."
Then he says
"Abstract ideas do not exist,"
which sounds odd
until you see what he means
by *abstract*
and remember that he says
that language makes everything unclear,
though we need it
to get what we want.
He convinced investors
to give him a tidy sum
to open a school for colonial
and Native American children,
but the final funding fell through
so he bought Rhode Island
or a chunk of it
and went back to England
and told his investors,
"Abstract ideas do not exist."
This is obvious.
And oh, his name was George.

The Step Theory

An idea went by like a bird
and a bird went by like a cloud
and a cloud went by like a moment:
this is the Step Theory of Reality
and its by-product the Ziggurat Configuration.
Then a bird went by like an idea—
the idea of the Step Theory itself,
for no one thinks of it anymore,
because its pieces lock together seamlessly,
the way a play on words
is just words and not just words
at the same time, for a moment.
It can't come back
because it never went anywhere,
unlike a cloud that can't come back
because it went everywhere.
And so we jump around and sputter,
to the great amusement
of our higher selves,
the ones we can't find,
their laughter echoing forever
in the few moments we have.

That's step 1.
Now sweep idea, bird, and cloud
into a little pile and put them in a box.
(They will come in handy later.)

For step 2 you must forget
who you aren't, that is,
everyone else, even though you
are part everyone else.
This in itself is not difficult:
you do it all the time
when you're not looking.
What *is* difficult is what follows:
you must make yourself
as flat as a pancake
and try to avoid having syrup
poured onto you.
Most people will not
pour syrup onto a human pancake,
but there are a few who would.
Once you are flat, just lie there
for a while. Look at those clouds
and the bird that flew into the idea of them.

Eventually the Ziggurat Configuration
comes into play. The weather is hot and humid
but the ziggurat keeps climbing itself
until it gets to the top, then
it comes back down, only to climb back up,
and so on. I once had an aunt like this
—there was no stopping her—
her face in profile formed a ziggurat.
We children put glasses of water
on the steps, thus representing the soul
without knowing that it takes a while
to learn that we have one, but

by that time the soul had vanished
into the process of being itself,
like the idea, the bird, and the cloud:
song, song, and song.

Step 3 is for later,
but I can tell you now
that it involves rolling green pastureland
you step into but not onto
and follow your nose,
no cloud, no bird, no idea.

My '75 Chevy

Out in the yard
sits my 1975 Chevy pickup truck,
repainted red with a white roof,
body smooth, carburetor rebuilt, new tires,
new dashboard, black leather seat covers,
new floorboards, and two new side mirrors.
In a timeless yard—
it creates its own time zone. 1975.
I can't drive simultaneously in 1975 and 2012,
but I do
because when the truck goes forward
I enter the sliding zone known
as Miles Per Hour
and I'm just someone in something red.

For A.

The little blue heron's back again
Was he here when
Joe was here too
with Bill and me and you
when we were all just fifty?
If the three of us add twenty
we'll get something unreal
unlike what we are and feel
which is what Joe
couldn't imagine and ever know:
how my grandma said now and then
"I'm in good shape for the shape I'm in."

Art Lessons

Narrative Painting

The Madonna never walks.

The Portrait

Bronzino did for the portrait what the portrait did for the sitter.

Still Life

The best still lifes have emptiness.

The Self-Portrait

The self-portrait did for the self what the self did for the portrait.

Landscape

Landscape is a window through which you see what you thought.

Sculpture

Don't move.

A Few Ideas about Rabbits

It's hard to understand what
a rabbit is

It lifts a paw
and hesitates

For a moment its nose
and mouth are all cat

and those eyes, so worried
so harmless

but it might scratch you
accidentally

and that camel back
and tiger crouch

ears of lemur
perked up

Mouse-kangaroo

The rabbit runs around
eating and doing arithmetic

There is the story of the grateful king
who offered his subject anything

he wanted, and the subject said
Take this chessboard and put

a coin on the first square
then double that amount for the second

and so on, to which the king
readily consented

and when they counted
it turned out to be

a billion trillion coins
(or something like that)

more than the richest king
could afford

Imagine if the man had asked
for rabbits

Well that's what Nature asked for.
In Australia I think

there's an area that has
ten rabbits per square yard

Ah, we must shoot them
cry certain Australians

and others say No
ship them to a place

that has no rabbits
But there's a reason

there are no rabbits there
like at the North Pole

or in the Gobi Desert
or on Park Avenue

Anyway I do not trust a rabbit
because I have no idea

what it is thinking
I trust a worm because it isn't thinking

If rabbits could say
"I will hop into this garden

and eat the lettuce"
I would like them more

The Value of Discipline

I am very disappointed in you, Myron.
You are a very smart boy,
and we had high hopes for you.
But now this.
I don't know.
Go to your room.

Myron heads toward his room,
but does his head hang low?
No way!
He is looking straight ahead
and feeling a hot black liquid
trickle through his heart.

Great galleons
bound through the rough seas
and on them bearded men
are shouting sailor things
as if to the wind.

Back in his room
the objects look older.
What joy to make them
walk the plank!
Avast! Avaunt! Splash! Garrrr!

Pea Jacket

Years ago I had an old pea jacket
Slightly scruffy but not unclean
was my overall look and I lacked
the easy assurance that comes with money
because I had very little

It was okay, not having money
I wasn't starving or lacking anything I needed
though by contemporary standards
I should have been envious or angry
I wasn't
All I cared about was my wife and friends and family
Books writing perception great art and gigantic metaphysical
    questions floating in on good humor
Society could take care of itself more or less
(It turned out less)
and I was happy enough and eager
I think what I mean is I was young
so that no matter what anyone might think of my jacket
I liked it it fit well and was warm in the New York winter
collar turned up and hands snug in pockets

It came from a secondhand clothing store
at the corner of Bowery and Bleecker maybe it
had belonged to a drunken sailor
What do you do with a drunken sailor early in the morning?
Put him in bed with the captain's daughter!

There was a label inside with his name and serial number scrawled on it
It felt odd wearing his name I snipped it out

I don't have anything monumental or metaphoric to say about my jacket
It's just a pleasure to remember it and how good it felt on me
Then one day I started wearing something else
and a few years later I gave the jacket to someone I liked I don't recall who

The Ukrainian Museum

Just walking into the new and beautifully designed Ukrainian Museum was a pleasure: varnished hardwood floors, white walls, clean lines, understated lighting, and the luxury of newness. An older Ukrainian Museum had been located in a second-floor apartment in a tenement building on Second Avenue, without even a sign outside, several rooms of dismal paintings in drab light; the one time I ventured in, there was not a single soul in the place, not even a guard. Twenty years later the museum moved a few blocks up the street to a space protected by two security checkpoints. I was greeted, if that is the word, by a woman who coldly asked me what I wanted. The two exhibition rooms were slightly larger than closets. Now, walking into this third incarnation made me feel so light and carefree that I had to be reminded to buy a ticket.

The Alexander Archipenko exhibition was the largest I had ever seen of his work, and as I moved from sculpture to sculpture I felt grateful just to be there. But I wasn't really "there," I was in a wholesale meat market. The smell of raw flesh and gore oozes out the ramshackle front doors where trucks have backed up to disgorge sides of beef and pork. Just inside are butchers in threadbare aprons streaked with blood. One of them waddles his mammoth girth toward me, a cigarette dangling from his pudgy lips, a strange leer on his face. He is the one who lewdly propositioned a friend of mine who lives a few doors away. Nineteen sixty-one.

Now, in 2005, I am walking through this museum on the very spot where those butchers slashed and chopped up carcasses. The fat one is no doubt dead, like my friend and Archipenko. The exhibition is fine, but I can't focus on it, so I simply pause before each piece.

Finally I can't restrain myself from approaching someone, who happened to be a guard, an Indian or Pakistani woman, to whom I say, "Many years ago, when I first came to New York, I had a friend who lived a few doors down the street. Do you know what this place was then? It was a wholesale meat business." She looks at me and says, "Yes, it's amazing the way they change things so fast," and looks away.

The 1870s

Homage to Michel Butor

1870 Work on Brooklyn Bridge begun. Charles Dickens dies. Jules Verne writes 20,000 *Leagues under the Sea*. Rockefeller founds Standard Oil. Robert E. Lee dies.

1871 British Columbia joins Canada. Marcel Proust born. Rasputin born. Pneumatic rock drill invented. Stanley meets Livingstone. Whistler paints *The Artist's Mother*. The Great Fire of Chicago. P. T. Barnum opens "The Greatest Show on Earth."

1872 Jesuits expelled from Germany. Grant reelected President. Bertrand Russell born. First operation on the esophagus. Piet Mondrian born.

1873 New York financial panic. Germans evacuate France. First color photograph. Zanzibar abolishes slave trade. E. Remington & Sons, gunsmiths, produce typewriters. Tolstoy writes *Anna Karenina*. Buda and Pest unite.

1874 Winston Churchill born. Gertrude Stein born. First roller-skating rink. First Impressionist exhibition. Pressure cooking invented. Thomas Hardy writes *Far from the Madding Crowd*. First ice cream soda.

1875 Carl Jung born. Thomas Mann born. Rainer Maria Rilke born. Maurice Ravel born. Madam Blavatsky founds Theosophical Society. Camille Corot dies. Georges Bizet dies. Hans Christian Andersen dies. First swim across the English Channel.

1876 Korea becomes a nation. Brahms composes Symphony no. 1. Turks massacre Bulgarians. Pablo Casals born. George Sand dies. Bruno Walter born. Carpet sweeper invented. Degas paints *The Glass of Absinthe.*

1877 Edison invents the phonograph. Gustave Courbet dies. Queen Victoria becomes Empress of India. First contact lenses. Canals on Mars observed. First public telephones in the U.S.

1878 Greece declares war on Turkey. Hughes invents the microphone. Mannlicher invents the repeater rifle. W. A. Burpee does something with Burpee seeds.

1879 British/Zulu War. Joseph Stalin born. Albert Einstein born. Discovery of saccharin. First public telephones in London. Paul Cézanne paints *Self-Portrait.* Edison has an idea and invents the light bulb.

One Thing Led to Another

If it wasn't one thing
it was another.
You can't believe
how charged everything is
with meaning
because it is meaningless.
Joy in the curtains,
the farmer in the dell,
a fellow named
whatever it was—Floyd?
And then you had arms and legs
and it wasn't funny.
It was a freshly baked pie.
I could care
more or less.
Like a machine
in the heavens, shooting,
or an exclamation point
in the motion picture industry.
Cut.
It's always something.
"Tuck in your shirt"
is not said to a dog.
What's the use of whining?
No one really enjoys it.

The Rabbi with a Puzzle Voice

Wait a minute
I forgot something
The rabbi with a puzzle voice
Pieces flying around in the air
Texas Lithuania and now another one
A rectangle
He is singing them

I always knew he was
And the song is oh
I don't really know what
Very old like a doughnut
And a look through its hole
But he is singing
And that's the main thing, no?

The other main thing
Is that you're on that rectangle
Floating to the ground
As it loses its oomph
And other shapes are flying out above you
And you are on them too!
How can this be?

It is part of the jigsaw puzzle
And the sad voice that created it
Why did you have to be anyone
Whoever you are

Is what the rabbi sings
Whoever he is
Maybe he's not a rabbi at all

There was a reason I had forgotten him
And a reason I remember him
And his puzzle voice
But where are his edges going
As now he too breaks into pieces
Pieces pieces
That arc out in his song

Syntactical Structures

It was as if
while I was driving down a one-lane dirt road
with tall pines on both sides
the landscape had a syntax
similar to that of our language
and as I moved along
a long sentence was being spoken
on the right and another on the left
and I thought
Maybe the landscape
can understand what I say too.
Ahead was a farmhouse
with children playing near the road
so I slowed down
and waved to them.
They were young enough
to smile and wave back.

The World of Us

Who was the first person to say
"I think the world of you"
and how did he or she come up with it?
It's the kind of thing
one ascribes to a god
or a great philosopher
or a lunatic
on a good day. Now
it's a cliché
because we can't think it,
we can only hear ourselves saying it.

There are a lot of things we can't think
or don't want to. It's hard
for example
to think of skin as an organ
—an organ is a kidney or a musical instrument
or even a publication—
but ask any doctor
and the doctor will say
"Yes, the skin is an organ."
Imagine having that organ removed
(being skinned alive)
or rather don't
at least not too vividly.
It's better to keep a barrier
between oneself and things
that can be horrendous
like life.

Don't go around all day
thinking about life—
doing so will raise a barrier
between you and its instants.
You need those instants
so you can be in them,
and I need you to be in them with me
for I think the world of us
and the mysterious barricades
that make it possible.

But you say
"First you say to raise a barrier
and then not to."
Yes, because these
are two different barriers,
one a barrier against life,
the other a barrier against being alive.
Being alive is good, life is bad.

"So, what about being dead?
Is that bad?
And what about heaven?"
I don't know about being dead
because I can't remember what it was like,
but I do know
that it is awful and amusing to be part heaven
and not know which part of you it is.
Unless you don't think about it,
in which case
you find yourself looking up and saying

"That is *the* best cornbread I've ever eaten."
Along with it comes a yawn at the end of a long and satisfying day,
everything quiet and thrilling
inside a consciousness surrounded by a night
in which exclamation marks are flying toward a single point.

Curtain

Standing in the bathroom peeing
I look up at the curtain in front of me
red cotton with little yellow flowers
from Liberty Fabrics (London) 1970
and I feel I am flying up into the heavens
until I remember that soon
I will turn 70 and at any moment
I could feel a sudden paroxysmal pain
in my head and with the curtain
dropping away fall over dead—
this could happen right now!
But it doesn't, the curtain stays put
and I'm standing there
and the curtain still looks good.

Homage to Meister Eckhart

I promised myself
I would explore my void
the space I occupy
and won't
but I'm still waiting

waiting

waiting in a room
for the room to change into an idea a flower might have

The sun shines down on the flower
in the idea the flower does have at all times

and at all times you hear its thudding
and in between the thuds
is a silence in which a thud almost is

The first time I heard the word *void*
it was from the Bible: "And the earth
was without form and void."
I was a child. I thought it meant
the earth was without void.
Which meant nothing to me
because I did not know the meaning of *void*.
And I didn't know there was a comma
that changes everything:

"was without form, and void."
The cosmos changed by a comma!

Years later a big face with no features
came out of the trees in the night
and said, brutally, "Void"
as if handing me a gift

I opened my eyes and there it was
in the mirror it was I or something else
I wasn't sure
but I was happy to be in between
My soul was growing up
It had learned how to put quotation marks
around everything

which destroyed everything
to make two of everything
one for each eye and one for each ear

but the eyes get further and further apart
from what they see
as the ears get closer and closer
to what they hear
like the dot terribly far away
and big in front of your face
at the same time and loud

So move
the mirror
the Void

into another mirror
or Void
and just let go

But the eyes eventually alight
on words like SPONGEBOB SQUAREPANTS
printed on the side
of everyone's head
the way CLEM KADIDDLEHOPPER used to be
and MEISTER ECKHART and MAX JACOB
all appearing nightly
in a revue set in the void of heaven,
the void that allowed God to be there
as the sole spectator
until your void and his void were almost the same
as the void of Spongebob and Max, Clem too,
but not quite, for, as Eckhart says,
"The nothingness of God fills all things
while his somethingness is nowhere"
and so "The very best thing you can do
is to remain still for as long as possible"
and wait for the nothingness of God.

The Incoherent Behavior of Most Lawn Furniture

Suddenly the lawn furniture moves to different spots and stops, overturned or sideways on the ground or hovering in the air, then the pieces jerk, flip, or fly into new spots, in no pattern or rhythm. But the wooden fold-up lawn chair, with its wide strip of canvas forming a gentle sling from top to bottom, remains still. Its striped pattern ripples in the breeze, and though its wooden frame eventually turns gray it never rots or breaks, no matter how inclement the weather. Over the years, however, this lawn chair slowly grows less and less visible, so slowly that no one notices, until it disappears. It remains there, unseen and lost to memory, until one day someone remembers its green and orange stripes, its welcoming curve, its simplicity, there in the sunlight.

This Schoolhouse Look

is rather cute, no? This
is how I always wanted to have my writing look

It has the charm
of the desire for perfection
that I had
when I had the charm
of not knowing better

if you can call it charm

I wanted to do better
without knowing anything

I still do

The Street

The last time I came back to New York I didn't know
that it would be the last time you'd be here
though you *are* still here in the form of you
who a block away walk toward me until it *isn't* you,
it's someone with a fine head and silver hair and blue eyes
and the suggestion of not being like anyone else
and it's you I'm waiting for as I walk past Little Poland
or come out of New York Central Art Supply or stop to look
at the poppy seed cake in the window of Baczynsky's on Second Avenue,
the cake I brought up to your place sometimes
when we were working together and you'd say "Tea?"
as if it were spelled with only the one letter.

Knowing you were there made me be more here too,
made New York be New York,
fueled my anger at the new buildings that ruined the old ones
and at the new people with their coarseness and self-involvement
you avoided by going out to buy the *Times* at 5 a.m.,
then came back and made yourself a pot of espresso
and read the paper as if you were in Tuscany
which is where you soon will be
in that niche in the wall all ten pounds of you
and I'll leave the city that's slipped a little further away no a lot.

Paris Again

I'm afraid of the thrill of touching you again
and seeing you appear before my eyes
because you are beautiful the way things used to be.

One day I sat down in a café and ordered an *accent aigu*
and a *citron pressé* and looked at Paris.
I said to myself This is Paris and you
are in it so you are Paris too. *Garçon,*
encore un accent aigu s'il vous plaît
but he didn't look pleased he was Parisian.
Maybe I too could learn how to be grumpy
and snooty and Cartesian and quick all at the same time.

The Nord-Sud metro line ran all the way
from the tips of my toes to the top of my head
where it paused and went down again
and every time it went past Odéon I thought
of Reverdy and how grumpy
and suddenly fiery he could be and figured
he would have no patience with a guy like me
who had a touch of Max Jacob ready
to leap up and turn an angel into a sad witticism
about the God Pierre was wrestling with as if
they were both made of granite. But they weren't.
And neither was I, like those who love and have loved
and are still afraid of the thrill of the beauty of everything that is gone.

London, 1815

We go clippety-clop
because we are horseshoes
on cobblestones. O
to be a houseshoe
in a house
and resting comfortably
alongside another houseshoe!
But the horse clops on,
our echos echoing
down a dark alley
behind a dark house.

Of Copse and Coppice

When asked
if I knew the meaning
of the word *copse* c-o-p-s-e
I said "Of course, it means . . .
I think it means a field
or meadow." One
of the first poems
I ever wrote said
"Where is the copse
with verdant green?"
because at age thirteen
I wanted to use
words new to me.
Now *copse* is new again
because I'm now not sure
just what it means.
A *coppice* is a thicket,
no?

Oh you're such
an American! out
of touch
with the natural world
and English English
and your own adolescence
all at the same time!
Alas, I've wandered
lonely as a crowd

of words
blown down the street
this way and that,
vagabond lexicon
dressed as a citizen.

Maybe a wood or a grove?
I've always liked
my grandfather's name Grover
and one of the most beautiful girls
of my adolescence was named
Madeleine Grove
and back then
my favorite publisher was Grove.
Shady Grove, my true love
the song goes. Them
I remember. *Copse*
and *coppice* are phonemes
from literature. I preferred
cops and robbers.

But it got better.
I nabbed the robbers
and shot a few Indians
clean out of their saddles
but they didn't have saddles
and weren't even Indians
and it didn't matter:
you had to go
and in a few minutes
I did too,

due as I was
in this verdant copse
splashed with shadows
that shift and wave like plaid
in the wind from off the brae.

Manifestation and Mustache

I love living here
away from a lot of things
that annoy me
and close to a lot
of things I love
like air like trees
and emptiness.
But the thing
I love best
goes where I go
and will go with me
when I am gone
from where I am
and into
where love
doesn't figure,
which I have done
a few times
in my life,
if memory serves.
Then
the mustache
comes in
and says,
"You can't be right
and wrong
at the same time,"
but I don't believe it.

Shipwreck in General

Is there no end to anything ever

I release the question mark
From its tether and it floats
Like a life jacket
In search of the shipwreck
That every question is

But today it finds no victim
No flotsam no captain's cap
For today is shipwreck-free it is
The end of shipwreck in general
And the curl and the dot below
Can go their separate ways
And be whatever they like

French Art in the 1950s

Ronnie is finding out about art in the 1950s. He is learning that it had a palette and brushes and colors, and the palette had a hole, in which the brushes were inserted and where they seemed debonnaire and ready to do something but also happy not to. There is an artist in the room. He wears a smock and a beret, and he has a pencil mustache. His name is Pierre, for he is French. Art comes from France. Pierre is going to bring some more of it to us. But at the moment he is thinking about what he is going to paint today. A pear? A young woman who is wearing no clothing? Or perhaps just a lot of colors flying around on the canvas, to represent his feelings?

But wait, it is time for lunch. Later in the afternoon he will execute his picture. For now he must go to the café and greet his admirers, who, on seeing him, call out "Pierre!" and "Over here, Pierre!" and, cleverly, "There he is, the rascal!" But everyone knows that Pierre is not a rascal. He is a French artist. You can tell by the smock he has forgotten to remove. Later, when it has paint smears and spots on it, even an imbecile will be able to see that he is an artist. Ronnie already knows.

I Felt

For a moment
as if I were talking to you
and you were listening
and taking me seriously
the way a grandfather does
when he's open and kind,
you knew what
was troubling me
and you knew
that the best thing to do
was to listen
and say nothing,
allowing a calm to settle
into the grandfather
that turns out to be me.

The Door to the River

You walked through it before
you even knew it was there

The river came up to the door
and asked to come in

Then the river came through the door
and the door floated away

I once threw away a river
because it looked old enough

And I bought a new one
and a door along with it

Except it never was a door
It was a doorway

Like Norway
with windows

Zot

In de Kooning's painting, the word *zot.*
I thought *sot?*
Then learned that *zot*
is Dutch for *foolish.* So
foolish and *drunk* swirled around
and separated out
into the Dutch *foolish* and the English *drunk.*
He wasn't such a big drinker
when he did that painting,
but maybe he felt like a fool sometimes
—of course he did.
He was *zot* and he knew it
and he told you so, you
being almost nobody,
so almost nobody you were
even more *zot* than he!
Zot is vat I tink.

Alone and Not Alone

Out of the water
came the one
who reached back
into the water
and pulled out the zero.

The time is now.

The time is now 8:15 p.m.
Eastern Standard Time.

In Beijing Lan Lan
is getting up
tomorrow.
I see her pretty, smiling face
as she curls back the covers.

Tonight I
will get under the covers
and think of her face
not because I
am in love with her
but because I
like her face
though I
do not want it
on my head.

Out of the water
came my head,
head first, whoosh!
A person's head
does not belong
underwater.

Look at fish!
Who wants to be one?

I would
for a moment
or two. Then
back to me.

It would be terrible
to alternate
being fish
and person
every few seconds.

We inhale
then exhale
every few seconds.

Lan Lan's
two daughters
are inhaling and exhaling,
still asleep—
it is Sunday
in Beijing.

Lan Lan's husband
is sitting at a table
in the kitchen
thinking
about the poetry
of Alexander Blok.

Alexander Blok
is pouring hot water
into the teapot.
Out of the water
came the tea
and out of the tea
came the scent of jasmine.

And then Alexander Blok
was not there.
He had to go away
and die again.

He exhaled and then
exhaled, and then
was like a dead fish,
wrapped in a newspaper
whose headline says
BLOK DEAD.
He reached back
and pulled himself
out of life
and into those two words.

Lan Lan's husband
looks up confused—
his mind is in Russian
but everything else
is in Chinese
when she comes in
and the jasmine is deeper
and more of you now.

It is 8:33.
What happened?

You were not alone
in thinking you were alone.

BIG CABIN

Big Cabin

I like it here in this cabin.
I like looking out the window
at the pond and the trees beyond
and with quiet inside.
Sixty years ago I was a boy
with a baseball glove in Oklahoma,
looking down at it and knowing
I would give it away
and not buy a new one.

The Up Side

The pines are
stately

still

reflecting
upon themselves

without knowing it

in eternity

upside down.

And Truly

We use italics
to put electricity into words.
Then we plug lamps
into the words.
That's how we light our homes.
Really.

Chickadee

The chickadees went away
a few months ago
delightful little things

Now they're back
chattering away

Wait for me
I'm the biggest chickadee
in the world

Glump glump

Clocked

I'm going to look at my watch
though I don't really care what time it is.
Just slightly curious.
It's funny when you see
it's much earlier or later
than you thought,
but even funnier when it's *exactly*
the time you thought.

But at my back etc.
Etc. being
"Desarts of vast Eternity."

I give up.
It's eleven eleven.

What ever happens
at eleven eleven?
Vast eternity!

Thin

My skin has grown
thinner, as thin
as the paper
on which I write.
Sometimes
I accidentally cut myself
and don't even know it:
a thin line of blood is there.
It's hard to talk to.

People

People are so
fucking nutty
it's amazing
that we get through
the day
without one of them
undoing the parts
of his body
and then putting them
back together
in the wrong places
right in front of us.

Sandwich

I'm in a cabin
about 300 yards
from my house
in the woods
on a cold, damp day,
sky overcast bright gray.
At home
in the fridge
is sliced ham
I will put
between two slices of bread
with mustard
and raise the ensemble
to my mouth
and go chomp,
a chomp
300 yards away.

Hope

Is there any hope for you
or anyone else?
Sure there is,
but hope for what?

Hope isn't *for* anything.
It's just a big bunch of feeling.

Harold Clough

In 1895 or thereabouts
Harold Clough was born
in East Calais, Vermont.
I knew him for the last oh
twenty-five years of his life,
and deep into that time
I thought to talk with him
with a tape recorder running.

I never did.
You'll never hear his voice
saying anything.
What a dope I am.

When he started driving a car
there was no such thing
as a driver's license.

He was under five feet tall,
with huge hands and feet,
and his hair stuck out
from beneath his dirty baseball cap
like quills on a porcupine.

It didn't bother him
to hold live wires
and he could find water
with a stick or coat hanger,
it didn't matter which.

The skin on his hands was so tough
he could just reach in
and take a pie out of the oven.

He showed me how to hold a nail
and at the same time
to drive it with a hammer—
using only one hand.

Around eighty he discovered *Playboy,*
amazed that he could see those girls
all totally naked and glowing, right there.

He once mailed a donut to my dog.

He knew how to lift a barn
all by himself.

One day I got a call from a friend
who said, "Old Harold just died.
In the hospital. Heart attack."

An hour later
the friend called back:
"Harold ain't dead.
He come back to life."
Not only that, when the nurse returned
he was sitting up and smiling.

A few years later he really did die,
of a fire, in the house
he was born in.

I once asked him for his mailing address.
“You can put Harold Clough,
East Calais, Vermont.
Or Harold Clough, Adamant.
Or North Montpelier.
Woodbury. Or Calais.
Don’t matter none. It’ll get to me.”

In the Winter of 1969–70

In the winter of 1969–70
I went out to an old shed
behind Fairfield Porter's house
and fired up the coal stove,
cleared a spot on a workbench,
sat down and started translating
the poetry of Blaise Cendrars.
Sometimes the room got so hot
I'd open the door wide open
and outside snow was falling.
It was one of the happiest times of my life.

Life without You

I leap from the title to this first line as if over a stream
and find myself on the other side, safe
but for how long there is no way of knowing.
The wind dances the trees lightly
and the leaves rustle as if they are happy to be moving
instead of just hanging there all day.
I think I will like it here, but I will
have to forget about a great many things,
in fact almost everything, including you
and thus myself. A piano note
appears in the air.

It has leaped as if over nothingness
to be here with you, and soon
other notes appear, lined up and going up
and down in one long wave that says hello
to no one in particular, except you
are particular, a dust mote,
an idea one almost has.

What's the matter with matter?
Something has to be wrong with it, no?
Or is something wrong with you? Oh
plenty. The mole, the squirrel, the flying fish
didn't ask to be matter, they don't ask anything:
who would answer them? Not I,
said the little red dot. And thus the dress
your mother wore in 1948.

The year 1948 leaps out of itself
and lands on your doorstep,
a writhing mass of strings and bubbles,

and when you open the door and peer out
there is only a drawing of the street where you currently live
in black and white. Across the ocean
the colors are vibrating,
as if preparing to come your way,
and there is no way of stopping them,
for they want to wrap their mysticism
around you and carry you off in their traveling circus.
They need a clown.

Paul Éluard

Paul Éluard said,
"There is another world
but it's in this one"
or something to that effect.
I would say,
"Everything is odd enough
as it is"
or something to that effect.
My handwriting, for example,
and my hand writing.
Hand, say hello to Paul Éluard.

Lunch Jr.

Saved again by lunch!
At school at work at home
millions of people
are saved by lunch!
I put the words
right into my mouth.

It’s Good

It’s good to have a heater
you can hold your hands in front of
to get them warm enough to hold a pen
to write “It’s good to have a heater,”
and to feel the warmth
spreading into your knees
and down your shins
though you can’t do much with them
in a sitting position.
They’re just down there
being shins.

Ticking and Tocking

When people say
"Time is running out"
I see an alarm clock
with a bell on top
and with arms and legs
dashing out the door
of a room in which
time has stopped
reminding the human race
that *we* are running out.

I carry this idea
to a corner of the room
and set it down
gently.
I don't want
to wake it up.
Then I tiptoe away.

Sweeping Away

What I want to do
is to forget everything
I ever knew about poetry
and sweep the pine needles
off the cabin roof
and watch them fly away
into this October afternoon.

The pen is mightier than the sword
but today the broom
is mightier than the pen.

Poem

You're here—
and if you relax
for a moment
your back
and other parts
will arrive
and you can be
together,
with yourself,
a little happiness.

On Fire

The afternoon light across the pond
is doing a good job today, the sky
a gray smudge with a trace of puffery
but the trees stand out in perfect clarity
and here I am, and if I weren't
I wouldn't know the difference,
just as, say, Shelley wouldn't.
"O sky and song entwinèd in a wild embrace
and hid asleep inside the human race,"
he might have said.
It's good to think of Shelley
as a person and not
the great Romantic poet
who died at thirty tragically,
Percy a young man gifted and serious
with a big heart and an open mind
who wrote some mediocre poems
and a few truly great ones.
Every night I read a few and try
to see him writing them, but
all I get is a dim view of the back
of a man at a table in a chilly room in Italy,
his arm moving slightly,
and in the flickering candlelight a woman
with a sleeping baby in her arms.
From time to time the baby says "Umph"
and another sheet of paper flutters down
with flowing, glistening words in black.
Shelley is on fire tonight.

The Hook

All it takes is a hook
even a small one
of any color
and you're in. Today
it's gray that grabs you
and won't let go
and you don't want it to.
It's a tree.

The Porcupine

If you've ever come face-to-face
with a porcupine
you know how beast-like they look,
but to the porcupine
you are of very little interest,
like a stone on the ground,
though unlike a stone you wave
your arms and shout "Hey!"
The porcupine swivels his head
and waddles a few feet away.
He isn't very funny.

Songs of the Skeleton

1.
How interesting it would be
if one could suddenly dart ahead
of one's body and turn around
and see it standing there, dumbfounded!
But to leave it there like that
would be sad.

2.
I've known people who thought
they were someone else
and then came back
to being themselves,
though sometimes they seemed
uncertain, as if that other person
were about to sneak up behind them
and go *Boo!*

3.
When I was a child
I knew skeletons
were *supposed* to be scary.

4.
When you see a real skeleton
you know that one day
those bones were walking around
inside someone who was whistling
and feeling good about being alive
and not thinking
about some day becoming a skeleton.

5.
Most skeletons would be lying
if they said,
"I am the skeleton of Shakespeare."

6.
Jesus was almost a skeleton,
which is one reason he came for dinner—
or, as they called it, The Last Supper.
It's better than coming for The Last Lunch,
though if you're really hungry
you just eat anytime, and your body
loves you for it,
and you're in a kind of heaven.

Plume

A path wends its way
through the woods
to a whitewashed cottage
with thatched roof, a plume
of smoke on top.
Is the cottage on fire?
No, it is not.
I won't let it be.
I will open its door
and find you there again,
my plume, my smoke.

Wristwatch

I've just written six
or seven short poems
in about half an hour,
in a cabin
on a pond
with raindrops.
Maybe I should
just sit here
for a while, let
some time pass
so my wife will think
I've been working hard.

See that?
Some time just went past
but so quietly
you might have missed it.
It morphed
into the sky.
Look, another one!
It came out
of my wristwatch
and morphed away.

I Give Up

I give up
for today
but I'll be back
tomorrow
with my pen
and paper and identity
that keeps an eye on things.

Completion

I am writing this in a school notebook whose puzzling name, printed on the front cover in large type, is *Completion,* with a sort of subtitle: "Take your fun where you can find it." The notebook was made in Japan, which perhaps offers some explanation of why this peculiar title and subtitle have been joined in such an unlikely place.

I am in a place that is neither likely nor unlikely: a cabin on a pond in rural Vermont. I have come here to write in this notebook—for reasons that are even more mysterious than the notebook's title. I can say with certainty, though, that I am sitting at a small, cheaply made table with fold-down aluminum legs, which an artist friend of mine bought thirty-five years ago, and if I part the curtains in front of me I will see the same view as I did around forty-five years ago when I sat in this very cabin writing poetry, two poems in particular ("Radio" and "Arrive by Pullman"). The pond made an appearance in the latter when rain started to fall. It rained earlier this morning as well, but now the sky is just an overcast gray. But weather is not what I had in mind when I thought of coming here to write in this notebook. I was thinking about . . . or rather I had an *impulse* to write about aloneness.

That word struck me as just right, but odd. Shouldn't one say *solitude*? No, solitude is something else. In solitude you have no one around you. With aloneness you can have others around you or not. Solitude is usually good. Aloneness is usually not, at least in the way I'm thinking of it.

To be honest, my thoughts on the subject are vague. The one thing I do understand clearly is that being an only child has had such an all-encompassing effect on me that for most of my life I was unable to perceive that effect. Growing up, all I knew was that I was glad I didn't have to share a room with anyone. My friends and classmates had brothers and sisters who were mostly annoying, to hear them tell of it. But as I have grown older, the impact of being an only child has revealed itself more deeply, and what I thought of as a privileged status has begun to feel like a deprivation.

Fortunately, I have a wife, a son, a daughter-in-law, two grandchildren, and a sister-in-law, as well as a number of friends, some for more than half a century. This takes the edge off my aloneness—the soothing effect of being with people I would give my life for. This deep bonding (let's call it that, for want of a better word) . . .

I forgot what I was going to say! I *do* know that I was preparing myself to leap into the image of a man holding his head in his hands, not from fatigue or dismay or grief, but simply as a way of having the physical sensation of encircling his inner self, of locating it in the material world, for I believe, simplistically perhaps, that my self is centered in my head, or at least spends the great majority of its time there. By *self* I mean the conscious self, the one you can talk with, the one whose thoughts are in the words you think and are aware of thinking, and even in the semiconscious self, the one of half-sleep and intuition, of unexpected conceptual jumps and seemingly bizarre associations. It's the self that appears on waking and fades out in sleep. In short, it's the person you have to live with all day. You might like this person or you might not—which of course is very important for your everyday life—but either way you are stuck with being who you think you are, and though the identity of that person can evolve over time, the fact of its being there does not change, until you die. And after that . . .

■ ■ ■

I have drawn aside the curtains and taken a glance at the pond. Its surface is absolutely still. In fact everything outside is immobile—trees, sky, air. The only things moving are my arm, hand, and pen, though from time to time I shift in my chair and take a swig from a small bottle of water.

What if suddenly I had no wife, no family at all? Such things have happened to people—I'm thinking of the Holocaust—and continue to happen—the Middle East. Or Middle America. Suddenly they're gone. How do you manage to go on living? Clearly you could not be your "old" self anymore. But where do survivors find the strength to endure such violent revisions of reality? I can't imagine being able to. I do not have the physical stamina, nor do I have the emotional strength, the strong self as an independent entity capable of not only surviving but also of taking some pleasure in life. I depend on those close to me, more than they know. Yes, yes, I'm a writer who is convinced that he is a writer, that it matters, and that the time I devote to it and not to my family is justifiable, but when I peel away my identity as a writer, a husband, a father, and so on, right down to the isolated creature that I fundamentally am, I turn away from that creature, unable to look into its sad, bewildered eyes that seem to be asking—aha!—the same eternal questions that arise in a sensitive adolescent: Why am I cursed with consciousness? Am I the result of a freak accident in the universe? Is the universe itself a freak accident? And why do I have a consciousness that presses these questions on me? Why can't I be more like an ant, dutifully shuttling to and fro as part of a society in which the idea of anxiety does not exist? In fact no idea exists! Surely the universe would go on without ideas in it.

In my first year of college I read *The Origins and History of Consciousness* by Erich Neumann. As I recall, he offered a psychological interpretation of the story of the Garden of Eden: the expulsion of Adam and Eve symbolized the birth of higher consciousness, when humans separated themselves out from animals. Thus the triumph, however tenuous, of the conscious over the unconscious entailed a loss as well, the loss of innocence, that is, the loss of being an animal unaware of its own mortality, but also the loss of the bond with the other animals of the earth. Humanity had taken the first step toward isolating itself, and it would seem that we have taken many more steps in that direction, to the point that now we are isolating ourselves from one another. The final step would be to isolate ourselves from ourselves, in effect erasing our humanity. If you want to see that in a positive light, imagine it as a return to the Garden of Eden. Except that the Garden itself would be gone, too.

■ ■ ■

Give a man pen and paper and he will obliterate the Garden of Eden!

I look out the window. Small ripples on the pond, fog in the treetops—was it there before? The day is ahead of me: things to do, things to think about doing, and whatever happens to come up. I will be normal, the way the person I am known to be is normal. I am by no means saying that this is a bad thing. After all, one cannot live entirely in an existential quandary. We need breakfast, too. And in the end who is to say that breakfast is less important than quandariness, or even that the two aren't fundamentally the same thing in different forms? That is, you do what you do.

■ ■ ■

Aside from a bit of amateur psychology, I have never been able to understand other people. That is, to grasp what drives them. Perhaps no one does, but what surprised me was how long it took me to realize that my knowledge of other people, even those I called my best friends, was superficial. Perhaps this is one of the reasons I have gotten along with them so well, another reason being our deep affinities, despite our differences. Little did I suspect that as they died, one by one, they would take a little part of me with them, just as I kept part of them. Or so I believe. Perhaps this is simply a way of making their absence less . . . I was about to say *painful,* but *empty* is a better word for it. Outside the window the pond is only a few feet away, and I can't help but see Joe on it again, floating around in the afternoon sun, his eyes closed as he goes into a deeper relaxation, the little floatation mattress under him slowly rotating and drifting. And suddenly they come back—Anne Kepler, Ted, and George, my mother and father, my grandparents—and I feel as if it is my fate to represent them, which I do, automatically, by being alive.

■ ■ ■

And so we have the voice in our head, the one we think of as ours, the one we have listened to and even replied to since early childhood, when words became things and not just meaningless sounds. ("I can pick up that word and move it over there!") And so, the dialogue that lasts a lifetime, the dialogue that sustains us no matter how tedious or repetitious it becomes.

Can you have a thought that is *completely* unlike any you've ever had? I don't think I can. The words for it seem to be locked out of my head, where my consciousness is dashing around looking for something it can't find—and doesn't even know what it is. The day goes by, and late in the evening the mind assumes it has done its best and turns part of itself off for a while, leaving the other part to do whatever it does. I used to put great stock in that other part—the dream life—and I suppose I still do, but now the paradigm of conscious versus unconscious seems utterly simplistic. There is something beyond my concept of my own mind, beyond my sense of my self, but I do not know what it is.

A dragonfly hovered over the water's surface for a moment, then sped on, as if with an absolute sense of purpose.

The new pine boards in this cabin smell good.

■ ■ ■

If I sit and wait long enough, something will come to me. That's a little like saying that if you stand long enough on a mountaintop during an electrical storm you will eventually be struck by lightning. And the light bulb above your head will explode!

■ ■ ■

My penchant for comic book imagery comes partly from having immersed myself in comic books as a child, alone in my room but not really alone, since I was with my friends Daffy Duck, Little Lulu, Plastic Man, Sad Sack, and a host of others, all of whom lived in a world in which order prevailed and the colors were bright. Most other children were unpredictable, their eating habits strange, their clothes unmatched. Actually, all my friends were boys.

Girls were objects of attraction, glowing with vague, romantic auras. Aside from a tomboy cousin, I didn't have a girl as a friend until I was in high school, and even she had been an object of attraction. Finally accepting that she was not going to return my full affection, I made a big adjustment that allowed her to be my friend, while all the time trying to figure out who she really was and what she wanted from life (and from me). I never succeeded in doing that, and when she died, at the age of twenty-three . . . I still see her as she was and for a moment I yearn to go inside her mind, and then I tell myself to stop wanting the impossible. Still, the urge does not go away, the urge to understand my dead friends and to go back and rescue them from the fate that took their lives. A classic case of regret, survivor guilt, or something worse! I should know better, and I do, but I don't. Why do I subject myself to such yearning? Why can't I be contented with looking out this window at the inverted reflection of tall pines and spruces, quavering on the water, the light blue-gray sky below them?

When written down, such a "poetic" image is at first pleasing, then mainly distracting, which makes me dislike it, though I like it out there on the pond, the "real" pond.

■ ■ ■

Over the past several years I have been compiling a list of expressions that were common in my childhood but are very rarely heard these days, if at all. This morning I remembered another one, though not a particularly good example: *Bats in the belfry.* As a child I knew what it meant even before I learned what a belfry was.

It turns out that what I really miss are not the expressions themselves, but the contexts in which I heard them. I miss words like *buckager,* but what I miss even more is hearing my grandmother say it, and the living room in her home, with my grandpa tilted back a little in his recliner on a Saturday afternoon, stockinged feet elevated, and grandma in the doorway to the adjoining dining room, through which she came from the kitchen to join momentarily in the conversation, with Ernest Tubb or Bob Wills on the big brown console radio across the room, near the front door.

I still listen to the radio and I still like old-time country music, and sometimes when I pass by a mirror I catch a fleeting aspect of my grandfather's face, so that in a sense all these things have not utterly vanished. But I am crazy (or juvenile) enough to want my real grandpa to still be there in his recliner, everything exactly the same for all eternity. In fact I want every moment of my life to still be there, the same, for eternity.

Perhaps an unconscious dependency on this yearning has kept me from making a greater effort to understand the people I have felt close to. What did my grandfather think about when he was alone? How did he feel about himself? Men of his time and class left very few records of such things. Even the diaries of rural and working-class people, kept, I think, mostly by women, often are made up of short, factual notations, such as "Cold and cloudy today. Helen visited."

What's that big ripple in the pond? Aha! The brown head of a beaver, cruising around, looking for what? Maybe it's a muskrat—I don't have my distance glasses. I look back up from the page. The head has disappeared. No, now it's back, and I can see more of the body, a length of twelve to eighteen inches along the spine. It seems to be holding something white in its teeth, unless the white *is* its teeth. Now another critter comes gliding across the pond—a small duck that goes over to some water lilies and seems to be feeding on something there. Seeing animals like this always strikes me as a privilege—a reaction that rural people would find amusing, the way I stifled a laugh when a working-class rural friend of mine in his late seventies, visiting New York City for the first time and looking down from the top of the Empire State Building at the streets below, kept exclaiming, "Look at all those yellow taxicabs!"

■ ■ ■

Who was it that used to say, "I got tired of hearing myself think"? (There must be people who would say the opposite: "I am very pleased to hear myself think.") Being unable to get a song out of one's head is aggravating, an extreme version of hearing oneself think in the same way too often. Maybe that's part of my problem. Do you remember when someone would say to another person who was repeating himself or herself, "Hey, the needle's stuck"? If you don't know what a record player is, with the needle in its tone arm, then that expression will mean nothing to you. But then you probably use expressions that mean nothing to me. That's the way the world is. However, we *can* make an effort to understand each other, even though we hardly understand ourselves. It is not given to us to understand everything, being swept along in the flow of life in which a million things are happening in and around us at every moment, and now sunlight falls across this page, as if making a cryptic comment on what I just wrote, like the fly that landed in the words of the poem "À la Santé" that Apollinaire was writing in jail. A few years later he was shuddering in the horrendous trenches in Champagne, bullets and artillery shells whizzing and exploding, poison gas drifting toward him, rotting corpses left and right. And here I sit, in a little cabin on a placid four-acre pond surrounded by pine trees, sunlight slanting through the window to my right, the only sound that of my pen scribbling away. What right do I have to bemoan my fate? The right that a spoiled only child assumes all too easily, virtually as a birthright.

■ ■ ■

I took a peek at an earlier part of this writing: "To be honest, my thoughts on the subject are vague." That sounds exactly like something I wrote fifty-seven years ago, at the age of fourteen. Perhaps I should get up from this chair and dust the windowsills. Or accept the fact that a fourteen-year-old boy occupies too large a space in my psyche.

He desperately wanted to be loved by a girl, a girl he was in love with, but it was not to be. A year or so later there was another girl, only this time I was not perplexed by her, I was fascinated by what I saw as the impenetrable depths of her soul. Again, my love was unrequited, but she did give me her companionship, and she said something that jolted me: "Why do you go by the name of Ronnie? You're not a kid anymore.

Ron sounds much more mature." From that moment on I was Ron. Years later I considered using my legal name, Ronald, but it sounded too formal for the person I am, and I'm still not happy that I was named after the film star who went on to become president. For a moment just now I tried to imagine what it was like to be Ronald Reagan, but the vision of it was so disturbing that I stopped myself.

I've never wanted to be anyone else, but being satisfied with one's own identity leads easily to a complacency about it, and though by my age it's better to accept than to reject oneself, that doesn't mean one should not be open to change. Staying open isn't easy, but it seems like an optimistic thing to do, and optimism is something we could all use more of.

■ ■ ■

I should be open to the idea that it is not a tragedy that writing in this notebook has brought me no closer to discovering what it was I might have been looking for, particularly since there is no way of knowing what it might have been. I came here not to find a pond, but in an odd way I *did* find one, one that I am happier than ever to be with. I found the new-sawn pine smell of the cabin walls. I found quiet. And I found a kind of release, however temporary, from the urge to understand. Perhaps now I can dust these windowsills without feeling that it's an evasion from doing something more meaningful. Perhaps I can now let the raindrops, which have started to fall into the pond, just be raindrops.

Rock around the Table

When I walked across the floor
the table wobbled a little
and the pen on it wobbled too,
making a rock-rock-rock sound
as if telling me
to either stop walking
or start writing.
I've done both—this
poem proves it.
Actually this poem proves nothing.
Fortunately I don't *have* to prove anything.
I can move around in the world
and just . . . move around.
Until a pen goes rock-rock-rock.

The Wanderer

I forgot to bring my watch.
Bright gray morning sky, no hint
of the sun.
I left the house around 9
and I've been here for . . .
an hour? Less,
I think.
          I have
a pond, a forest, a gray sky,
and a mind that wanders
from moment to moment.

Almost Statue

Am I going to end up liking myself?
It could go either way.
But is it important,
liking oneself? It helps

but it involves a lot of *self.*
What would I be
without my self?
Maybe a statue.
But what's the point of being a statue?

Maybe I could be *part* me, part statue.
Is that possible?
Yes, for a psycho or a saint.

Timex Blur

I was going to complain
about how irritating it is
to have to change one's clock
twice a year and not
understand why, but sunlight
just came down and hit
the pond and my brain
at the same time.

Things to Do

Today: collect
trash, put
in truck, take
to dump, sweep
out truck bed,
feel love
for truck,
then do other things
I'm supposed to do
but can't, fortunately,
remember now.
What I remember now
is from a moment ago,
seeing my father appear
in my mind's eye,
then not.

Down Under

People are wont to repeat the old advice
"Live every day
as if it were the last day of your life."
The last day of my life? What?
I'd be frantic, jumping
around like a kangaroo
in boxing gloves
and punching the air,
trying to fight off
whatever.
What people mean is
"Be fully engaged with life."
Like a kangaroo without boxing gloves.

Shanghai Cutout

Charlie Chaplin is on the wall
up near the ceiling,
a paper cutout of him
about ten inches tall
and hinged at the joints,
in his Little Tramp costume,
held up there by a nail
through a hole in his hat.

I stayed at the Astor House hotel
in Shanghai
as he once did,
though of course
it was a different Shanghai,
and I was a different cutout.

Haiku

First, calm down.
Next, stay that way
for the rest of your life.

Sideways Guy

I happened to catch
a glimpse of myself
in an old mirror,
cruddy and mottled
(the mirror, not me):
late medieval old guy
turned slightly and stopped,
black stocking cap sticking up
and eyes not exactly dead
but lacking the quickness of youth,
fixed on you as if
on someone you don’t care about
one way or the other.

Infusion

It feels cold in this room
until I go outside.
Is that a metaphor
waiting for its meaning?
Probably.
Isn't everything waiting for its meaning?
Go ahead,
infuse everything with meaning.
See how far it'll get you.

People vs. Leaves

Clever and powerful people
have taken control over my life
but for some reason
I don't care,
for I have that pile of leaves
over there.
Those people are wasting their lives
day after day.

For a moment I feel sorry for them
but then I look at the leaves
and don't care
what happens to humanity.

But if humanity disappears
who will read this poem?
Fuck.

Inside Happiness

Let's get inside a song
and live there,
happy in its refrain,
happy to be in it
again and again,
always the same.

It's Quite Something

It's quite something
how those ducks
out there on the pond
with fog drifting over them
don't seem to be cold
in the icy water—
my fingers cold
as the pen slides along
and veers around a metaphor.
Where'd the ducks go?

More about Whitehead

Was it Whitehead
who said that
there is no distinct line
between one's body
and the air around it,
that along the boundary
atoms are constantly
being exchanged?
I knew one of his students,
Anne Porter.
Maybe some of his atoms
stuck to her
and decades later
got transferred to me.
What a charming thought!
(And idiotic.)

Auditorium

No telephone, no computer,
no people, no cars, no TV
or radio, not even a refrigerator
to shudder and clunk off,
just the sound of water
flat with a few ripples—
that is, no sound of water.
For a moment
I hear its no-soundness
and then
a slow wave of chuckling,
an auditorium of children
all hearing the same joke
in their heads. Ah!
A happy pond!

A New Leaf

It all stems
from the fact
that I am a gay blade
who wants to turn over
a new leaf
because the grass
is always greener
on the other side
of everything.
Ah! there's
a new leaf
created out
of nothing,
hanging in the air
in front of my face
that suddenly turns
inside out
with joy.

OK

I'll bet that not one
in ten thousand people
knows where the expression OK
came from
and yet all over the world
even people who don't speak English
say it every day.
That's how it works,
"it" being life.
We don't understand much of anything
but it's OK!
(I guess.)

Any Future

Like a creature from the future,
glowing orange and rising
from a pond but
then frozen in place above it,
the reflection in the windowpane
of the elements of the electric heater
seem to be on the verge
of telling me something
I could never have imagined,
such as "I am all
that's left of you."
Who would want to be a heating element
in the future? Who really
wants the future?

My Eye

To disagree with someone
we used to say
"My eye!"
How did I
as a child
know that this
had nothing to do
with an eye?

"My eye!"
was a sharp stick
I could wave defiantly—
at nobody, really,
because at heart
I was a nice kid.

Long Distance

Drops of water drop
from the pine branch
over the pond
and for each drop a widening ring
is overlapping other rings
in the sky,
rings and rings and rings
up there in total silence.

To Yu Jian

Though we speak different languages
we seem to understand each other.
All it takes is a look in the eye,
a slight smile,
a gesture, and
we know.
We know how to get along well
because we respect each other
and we assume a lot.
Someday I'd like to talk with you
for hours and hours,
to see what would happen.
You are a completely interesting person.

The 19s

The sun rises and there's more.
I can say I've lived
until Tuesday, October 27,
in the year 2015,
a number that still sounds odd.
How can a year be
2015?
I prefer the numbers of the twentieth century.
They all sound good.

Topknot and All

Reeds at the pond's edge
bending and waving in the wind,
a long running row of them
like in a black-and-white Japanese film,
and here comes a sword
and two fierce eyes in the head of a man
who flies up and vanishes into the air.

A Big *Almost*

I can almost imagine
what it was like
to be my mother,
with emphasis on *almost.*
Her feelings about being
in this, the only world,
rise up in me
and are turned away
by my personality.
It wants to be itself,
not someone else,
though that someone else
is only a few molecules away.

The Cloud

I should read *The Cloud of Unknowing* again.
It's been fifty years.
I can't remember what it said,
so maybe I don't have to read it again.
Maybe I'm the Cloud!
A wisp of it.

The Ripple Effect

Joe said
"If you paint a tree
that looks exactly like a tree,
no one will believe you."
Likewise anything,
like the million ripples
rippling into each other's glitter:
If I tell someone
about those ripples they'll think
"Uh oh" and look away.
I'm going to anyway.

Ducks

It makes me sad to think
I'm petty—where'd
those ducks go? Off
to the left, I think,
then south, for sure.
I'm starting to get nervous
about following them.
I should leave them alone.
I should leave myself alone.

Chinese Twins

When I was in China
I had the sudden desire
to be in a cabin in Vermont
remembering the moment
when I felt that way

and now I'm here
in the cabin
but without a desire to be in China,
not at this moment, anyway.
I don't need that desire:
the two moments were just connected
like Siamese twins
who have just learned how to talk to each other.

The Triumph of Beavers

Is there any evidence
that a surrealist
ever saw a beaver?
I know it's a trivial question
but I'm wondering.
I imagine the face of a surrealist
and the face of a beaver
as they suddenly see each other.
They turn and run.
That night
the surrealist has horrible nightmares
of the face of the beaver.
The beaver sleeps pretty well.

The Work Force

I was thinking of what
I was going to say
to the workman
who said he'd be here
around 8, how
to explain how writing
is the thing *I* do,
the way he saws and hammers,
but now it's after 9
and he's still not here,
except in this poem.

High Whoosh

When the crowd of Chinese girls
clamored for my autograph
I gave it happily, stunned,
in a calligraphic script
as if I were writing in Chinese
on a long scroll that called for
a long unrolling of my name,
ending with a fluid whoosh across the sky
and up I went
into the stars!

The Field

Every once in a while white
lines appear in my field
of vision, curling sometimes
at the top of it and I
realize once again that there
is an invisible rectangle
around everything.
How do I know it's there?
I just put it there,
that's how.
And those white lines?
Little hairs
straggling from my eyebrows.

A Rowboat of Happiness

Every time I see the expression *mutatis mutandis*
I get grumpy
because
1) It looks and sounds ugly.
2) I can never remember what it means.
3) That makes me feel less intelligent than I like to think I am.
4) It's often used by people who want to sound more intelligent
   than they are
and now a full blast
of sunlight hits the wet grass.

It’s Nice

to end on a spot
marked X
knowing that Y and Z
don’t matter:
Y has become clouds
and Z the sky above,
blue and white, lovely.

Telegram

This morning about 4
I was lying in bed thinking
about how I'd be here
in this cabin scribbling away
and how the lines go
as far as the words make them go.

Finally I got up
and went down and made oatmeal,
toast and tea, jasmine,
to put a little bit of China into me
and wake me up, like
a real human who
does whatever he has to do.
Like stop.

DOT

A Note on the Title

How short can a title be and still be effective? Consider a title consisting of only one letter, as in the film *Z.* Could a title be even shorter than that? Aram Saroyan once published a "book" (in the form of a ream of blank typing paper) that had no title at all, but I'm not sure that having no title qualifies as a title. In any case, for such a small, unadorned word, *dot* has a lot of resonance for me.

When I was a child, Little Dot was one of my favorite comic-book characters. Every issue was devoted to her obsession with dots. It's impressive how much mileage the strip got from that one simple idea.

The first time I heard the term *polka dots* I imagined them dancing around, which, when you think of it, they sort of do.

The French word *dot* (dowry) struck me as disappointingly bare, as one would hope that a bride would bring to a marriage something more opulent.

When Joe Brainard read aloud from his work, he always said "dot dot dot" for ". . ." His doing so reflected the brilliant naivete of the work itself.

Then there's the crisp, pinpoint sound of the dot in Morse code, indicating *o,* which is visually rather dotlike itself.

When the internet arrived, I was struck by the use of the word *dot* in *dot com,* finally speculating that perhaps *period* and *decimal point* were too slow for the information superhighway. On the typewriter or computer keyboard, though, the dot, period, and decimal point look remarkably similar.

The actress June Brown, in the long-running British television soap opera *EastEnders,* portrayed my all-time favorite character, Dorothy Cotton, better known as Dot.

Many years ago, talking with my grandmother, I described a recurring dream I'd had for several decades, in which the only thing in my visual field was a dot that was infinitely far away, a dot that suddenly accelerated toward my head at incredible speed and abruptly stopped only inches from my face, where it was so enormous I could see nothing else, and then quickly began alternating between infinity and my face. My astonished grandmother said, "Why, Ronnie, I used to have that exact same dream! And I've never told a soul!"

Ultimately, though, my affection for this word might come from the moment in 1964 when Kenneth Koch, reading to me a line from one of my new poems—"at one of the numerous lunch counters which dot our city"—laughed and said, "Dot. That's a good word!"

Tea for You, Too

My friends,
I want to tell you
that in general things
are all right with me,
relatively speaking.
Just a second, here's Einstein
asking where the tea is.
I reassure him
it will be ready soon,
relatively speaking,
and he shuffles back
to the room that holds him,
with plenty of space
for that cup of tea,
even though the cup
is twelve feet in diameter,
about the same size
as my thinking of you
this morning.

Presto

Remember the guy
who sold magic tricks
in a small shop
next door to not
much of anything?
Of course you don't.
He made you disappear.

Starry Night

When I was in high school
I went out on a date
with a girl who looked
at the starry night sky
and blurted out
"Isn't nature *wonderful*?"
as if she had realized this
for the first time in her life.
I laughed in her face.
I wasn't wonderful.

Sonnet (Thunk)

In the back of my head I hear Kenneth Koch
saying, "Your poems are becoming simpleminded"
so I am going to let this one be more complex
and deeper than the blue ocean ever thought
of being. You think the ocean can't think?
It is forever making a large decision,
and it's always the same one,
like a bird opening its breast to the air
whose own breast is heaven,
like when something slams shut
with a muffled *thunk* in the dark
and we vibrate and wonder what vibration is
while hurling ourselves out of the fireworks
in the back of our heads where Kenneth isn't.

I Disobey

I look into the distance and see
Mei-mei Berssenbrugge
standing in the desert.
The wheels on her shoes
slowly wheel her away.
Some cardboard stars descend.
They too have shoes (cardboard ones).
"Don't go back!" the stars cry out,
but since my face is mashed
into wet concrete that tastes rather good,
I disobey.

The Long and the Short of It

I was all dressed up with no place to go
so I wandered around the streets for a couple of hours
looking at periods at the ends of sentences.
A long face on a long day.
The rain came down across the French poetry of the nineteenth
    century.
I was in Paris
in a cafe
operating the telephone.
A voice tells me my wife is pregnant.
I tell my wife.
We have a *grand crème*
and a big laugh.
Our child will be Made in France.

He had nothing to do with my long face,
in fact he considerably shortened it
by adding a comma here and there
and striking out across wide fields of parenthetical expressions
as the stars fled before him.

But my face was stuck on the front of my head,
so consciousness stepped forward and blew a bugle,
and soon ideas were jitterbugging
in and out of each other, creating
abstraction, just as the various woes
of the world blend to make me feel abstract,
like a Gorky, maybe, or the feeling you get
when you aren't suffering enough
and *il n'y a plus de Popeye aujourd'hui*
and my friends accelerate up the chimney like sparks.

Taboo

The first time I encountered the word *taboo* was in a book—I think it was in Margaret Mead's *Coming of Age in Samoa*—around the age of fourteen, and though the word's context gave me a vague idea of what it might mean, I wasn't sure, because the idea of something forbidden was in danger of being drowned out by the sound of native drums in the night. That is, the exoticism of the double-*o* ending had a strong effect on me, conjuring up thatched huts, dense trees, bonfires, and a gibbering witch doctor whose painted face and bizarre headdress flickered in the firelight. *Taboo* was from a deep, dark, primitive zone of the human psyche, a demonic version of *forbidden* and *unlawful.* But it smelled good. That is, if it were the same thing as Tabu, a perfume my mother used. Or were taboo and Tabu two entirely different things, like a boat in water and a boat in poker?

Then I learned that Sigmund Freud—I thought his name was pronounced *Frood*—had written a book called *Totem and Taboo.* A few years before that I had seen his name in a comic book that alluded to him in a way that suggested there was something naughty about him, you know, *s-e-x.* (Yes, in those days some people didn't dare say the word, they spelled it out.) Associated with Freud, *taboo* started to take on a sexual connotation, which became stronger when I heard about his theory of the Oedipus complex. I got mad at my father sometimes, but *kill* him? And sleep with . . . my *mother*? Yikes! What an unappetizing idea! But didn't everyone say that Freud was a great genius? It was very confusing, this Oedipus complex. Better to think about his ideas on the interpretation of dreams and his amusing examples of slips of the tongue. I liked the Latin term for it, *lapsus linguae.* I knew that the first word was in the nominative case and the second the genitive. But wait, *genitive* was close to *genital.* Ah, no escape!

Another Thing That Annoys Me

The spelling of *40.* We have *four* and *fourteen,* and then, for no reason I know of, the *u* is dropped and we're left with *forty,* not to mention the schizophrenic *forty-four.* Most annoying, as Sei Shōnagon would say.

Over There

I have always assumed that my body would provide
reliable transportation to carry me through the day
and no I will not extend that metaphor
and if you know what that means
you'll know what I mean.

John Ashbery once said
"I never get up before the crack of noon."
Pope Francis said
"I am Argentinian. You know
how an Argentinian commits suicide?
He climbs up on top of his ego and jumps off."
"That's all, Bruno,"
Fairfield Porter said to his dog.
Does it help to know that Bruno was a golden retriever?
And that Fairfield was invisible?
All of a sudden.

Agreement

I was
You were
He, she, it was

Wait a minute

Why shouldn't *you*
also be followed by *was?*

If I were you
I'd say "was"

But I wasn't you
I never was
nor will I ever be

In class we chuckled
when we recited
"He, *she-it* is"

and the masculine came first
except when going through a door

Then the word *she*
went through a door

and into a new world

You wasn't there

You were “he”
and it kept being “it”

but don’t blame “it”

“It” doesn’t even know it’s there

The Space Heater

The electric heater—
a cylindrical column
about a yard high
with a silver grille on one side
and behind it two vertical rods
that glow a rich orange—
looks like a ray gun
in an old science-fiction film,
the kind a hero would have aimed
at alien invaders and—*zap!*
Buck Rogers was his name,
leaping heroism was his game,
while his cousin Roy made sure
the West was grand and pure,
his six-gun at his side.
Something about it makes me
want to scream, as if
I had touched an electric heater
on at full blast.

The Great Divide

Excellent thrill-waves flood my head
like steam rising from lust
that has become intellectual.
And then you went into the eighth grade,
where the light hurt your feelings
and killing is immoral—
you have just killed yourself,
in a way. So go sit
in the pink traveling jail and brood,
for the girl who glints like a wink in a mirror
is still chewing her gum and looking around
as if everything is a little bit funny.

Philosophy

Think of it as a description of events and actions
rather than an exposition of ideas and substances

though of course ideas are events too
and ideas are what we make of them.

Thus ends my disquisition. I will now
step down and take my place

among the cobblers and their shoes—
if one can call them that, scraps

of leather bound with thongs every
which way. My shoes are nicer

because I live in a later period
in which footwear is said to be

advanced. But what about Mercury
and those little wings on his feet?

Of what substance were they made?
And by whose idea? And when he flew

what was the philosophy
that let him fly?

Start

> *Each time I do just the thought of you*
> *Makes me stop before I begin*
> —COLE PORTER

I want to do something, but I don't know what. Save my country? Of course, but that's impossible. Be young, or at least forget about my decrepit, sick, and dying friends? That sounds good, the being young part. Sell all my possessions and go live in a . . . what? An igloo?

I've never quite accepted the idea that human beings live or lived in igloos. Since childhood I've thought that the last place I'd want to be in a severely cold climate is inside a hut made of—of all things!—ice. Okay, let's assume there were no materials with which to build a warmer shelter. But why didn't they migrate south, where they could find some trees or mud? Why did the Eskimo man arrive on a sheet of ice and say to his female companion, "Honey, this looks like a good place to settle down"?

In 1967 I arrived in a trashed apartment in a slum and said to my wife, "Honey, this looks like a good place to live." She was not an Eskimo, but she grunted and went to work cleaning the kitchen.

But I'm not interested in the past, I'm just mildly obsessed with it, fearing that if I let go of it I will float off into some endless psychic space. And besides, how much of a future could there be, and who would "I" be in it? A sack of bones being shifted in a nursing-home bed? (But listening to Bach!) Or perhaps an old gent being helped off an airliner by an attractive young woman provided by the Ministry of Culture, on my way to give a reading of my poems on French national television? But am I supposed to read them in French or in English? It's a moot point, because I have lost the satchel that contained the poems, left it . . . where? Perhaps I can phone the airport or the taxi company in New York. But I don't have a telephone, and the young woman . . . where is she? She has gone back to China, to the land of her birth, where her village awaits her, in the year 1736, cook smoke rising from the huts and thinning out into the evening air.

It's like what I was saying to an old friend today: "Many writers our age wish they had been in Paris in the early part of the twentieth century, and some younger writers today wish they had been in New York in the 1960s, and the really young ones wish they had been here in the 1990s! The measurement keeps sliding forward." It would be wonderful to . . . I was about to say wonderful to find oneself walking down the street in ancient Athens ("*Kalimera,* Socrates!") but I chastised myself for having this banal thought, and then I realized that what was *not* banal was the full vision I had of momentarily being there among those strange creatures, the Athenians, for that one hallucinatory moment, and how it happened so quickly that I didn't have time to be terrified by its otherness.

A few years before my grandmother (1900–1998) died she told me how clearly she recalled being eight years old, atop a horse and wearing a pretty dress with blue ribbons, riding from the farm into town (Springdale, Arkansas) on a nice Saturday morning, and as she said this I wished I had been the horse or a tree or the road so that I could have been in that moment with her, so beautiful it was.

"Return with us now to those thrilling days of yesteryear!" intoned the voice of the man who led us into another episode of the adventures of that peculiar cowboy, the Lone Ranger, who, it turned out, was not so lone, being accompanied by his faithful sidekick, Tonto. We do not know that *tonto* in Spanish means *stupid,* so we are innocently swept into the black-and-white world on the screen, a world of dust and sunlight and decent, hardworking homesteaders rescued from brutality and injustice by the Lone Ranger, who asks nothing in return, who in fact at the end simply rides off into the distance, going . . . where? To his next adventure, perhaps. Certainly not to lie down and sleep or do anything else ordinary, such as launder his mask. And though the people he saved always wonder, "Who was that masked man?" we do not share their curiosity, for we know that he is the Lone Ranger, and that explains everything.

I would like to be in Paris with the Lone Ranger, walking down the boulevard Saint-Germain in 1920, even though passersby might think he is the clever archcriminal Fantômas in a cowboy costume, but the Lone Ranger and Fantômas no longer exist the way they once did, just like the boulevard and all of Paris itself. Every time I return to that beautiful city I walk down the streets I knew fifty-two years ago, searching for them, even though they are there, but what I am looking for is the feeling of being in those streets back then, and of course that feeling is long gone, as if it too wore a mask and had disappeared over the horizon in a cloud of dust.

Flying Down to Up There

A thought in a brain and *uno,*
there, whale, here, whaleness:
footprints across the top of the world
where I genuflect to the phone
and say hello to South America—
I think it is going to blow up
like a saint who flies not
to make a point but *to* an appointment
with the arriving rays that turn
you into a burning bird whose song
freezes even firemen in their aureoles,
arms and wings of pomp and flame
whiplashed into place.

Geometry of the Sandwich

If you make a sandwich
using two pieces of traditional American sandwich bread
and slice it diagonally
you end up with two right triangles.
Well, technically one of them is not a triangle,
since where its right angle should be
is rounded.
Look at the sandwich:
the two halves look different.

The difference is a very small thing to notice,
so small as to be useless
in the great rush of life.
I feel sorry for its smallness.

Bubble

It’s a very great pleasure
to walk with you in November,
our bodies sleepy in the clarity
falling across the city
and to feel a kiss arrive
from a height of five feet two
and new shadows on my shirt
rising and falling as I live
and breathe with you.

Free at Last

There must have been
some magic in
that old silk hat
they found,
for when they placed it
on his head
he began
to dance around,
he being God,
the Christian God
who in the Bible
was so grumpy
and now
is without a care
in the world.

At Benny the Bungalow

Once upon a time there was a bungalow named Benny. Inside the bungalow were two chairs, each with a little table next to it.

On one table was a vase of red flowers. On the other table was a brown paper bag.

Rabbit and her little boy, Clyde, knocked on the door of the bungalow, then they chuckled and went on in. It was their bungalow!

Rabbit picked up the vase of red flowers and sniffed them, sighing, "Ahhh!"

Clyde reached into the brown paper bag and pulled out a magic wand and a sandwich. The sandwich started to grow bigger and bigger, but when he tapped it with the wand it shrank back to its normal size. Then he took a bite and munched.

There were two knocks at the door. Rabbit and Clyde went over and looked out the window.

Outside were two people who looked exactly like Rabbit and Clyde. Neither pair could tell whether they were looking through a window or into a mirror. But this was the kind of thing that happened at Benny the Bungalow. It happened all the time.

The Sunny Side of the Street

I will never stop being surprised
by the great number of words
in the English language whose exact
nuances and histories I still don't know.
Meanwhile the sunlight is happily battering
the facade of the building across the street
I see through the window and whose windows
look back and see me here
with a little bit of their sunlight
on my suddenly old right arm, and my head
the one big puzzlement it's been all my life
though all along I thought it knew something
it would tell me someday and
all I get is sunlight coming across the street,
but it's better than, say, pitchforks.

I'll Get It

1.

It's quite satisfying
to have a key ring
with a bunch of keys on it
and to pick the right one
and put it in a lock
and turn it till
it goes *click.*

Locking *up*
is *clunk.*

2.

Yesterday my mother
would have been 96,
but she wasn't.
I tried to get her there
but she wouldn't budge.
She's stuck at 75,
younger than me.

3.

I’ve arranged the books by genre
but now I also have the urge
to put labels on the shelves:
Poetry, Fiction, Etc.,
“Etc.” for those books
that leap down off the shelves
because they don’t want to be
in a category.
I jump up and jump
around the room,
boing! boing! boing!
but I can’t catch them.

4.

Walking across the lawn
I was trapped
in the figure of a man
walking across the lawn
and I couldn't get out
and in some funny way
I didn't want to,
though being a human
is probably not the best
thing to be. What is?
You know, everything.

5.

There's a portrait of a Chinese emperor
who looks ugly,
I mean *really* ugly,
in fact so ugly
that all I can think is
that in his day
he *wasn't* considered ugly
or else the artist
would have been chopped up
and fed to the royal pigs.
"Emperor!" they squeal,
"Give us the artist!"
But he will not,
for the portrait has made him
handsome for all time.

6.

At sixteen
I decided to be a poet
forever
and now, sixty-one years later,
I stop writing
and slap my ear,
but the wily mosquito
zooms off in a blur of sound.
At birth he was a mosquito
but in a day or two
he'll wish he had been a poet,
even one like me,
ear throbbing.

7.

I like the way the hair
on the back of my hand looks
when it's gold against tan skin,
but when it's brown against white
it looks ugly as sin,
when sin is ugly,
which it always is,
according to some people.
"As *beautiful* as sin"
would wreck our moral system,
or what's left of it.
I guess we'd better
leave that alone, as is, alas.

8.

Remember those motorcycle daredevils
who rode on the walls
on the inside of a drum
fifty feet in diameter,
parallel to the ground?
You don't?
Well, okay.

9.

The phone rang
and I called out
"*I'll* get it!"
but there was no one
in the house
except me.
I saved my wife
from answering the phone
though she wasn't there.
That's how much
I love her
or am a nut.

10.

In tai chi class
someone mentioned
Taoist tai chi
and I thought
“Ooo, that sounds *really* good.”
This is the thought of someone
who needs to lie down
like one hundred people
in the high mountains,
where the air is all mirth.

11.

The view through
my window never
looked like this—
red, orange, and
light-green leaves
jumping in random
jumps as raindrops
spatter them one
at a time,
all of it
blocking the view
up the path
into the woods,
like the ringing
in my ears
I didn't notice
until just now.

12.

In the 1,136 pages of *War and Peace*
there is only one comic passage,
late in the book, when Tolstoy
summarizes the Napoleonic Wars:
"He conquered everyone everywhere, that is, he killed a great
many people, because he was a very great genius. And for some
reason he went to kill the Africans; and killed them so well,
and was so cunning and clever, that on returning to France
he bade everyone obey him. And they all did obey him. After
being made Emperor he went to kill people in Italy, Austria,
and Prussia. And there he killed a great many."
The passage continues in this vein,
like writing in a children's book,
then switches back to serious.
What made him use this comic tone?
Napoleon wasn't funny. He was horrible.
And the French erected a huge monument
to house his coffin, inside of which
they placed that little piece of shit.

13.

The asters wave their heads and say
"Sorry to be so late, but
we got held up by the weather,
which caused a big traffic jam,
all those daffodils, peonies, and day lilies
ahead of us, just lolling around
and taking up space."

We cut them and bring them inside
and put them in a vase,
and they just stand there
like startled exclamation points
whose heads are exploding,
as if they were flowers.

14.

Lee Crabtree came to my apartment
and sat on the floor.
He said he didn't need a chair.
We talked about what? and then
he gave me the sheet music
for a song he said we wrote.
Then he left.
The next I heard
he waved to someone
straight across from him,
high in an office window,
and jumped. What,
forty years ago?
It's hard to believe
this isn't a story
I made up.
Lee just jumped.

Close Enough

When I told the poet from South Africa
that when de Kooning came to see Frank
in the hospital, Frank all battered and purple
and covered with tubes, Frank opened his eyes
and said, "Oh, Bill, you shouldn't have gone
to the trouble," her eyes filled with tears,
though she didn't know much
of anything about Frank O'Hara's life.
[I didn't think to tell her that he too
could get emotional—ballet could
make him cry or a movie or one drink
too many and a friend to cry with.]
Let's put that in brackets so I can remember
to cut it out the next time I see it. And
now my ankle itches, the cool morning
is flowing into the many windows of this room,
borne by birdsong and the light of the sun
that has come all this way just to help us
find our way around and recognize each other
from the distance we keep until we forget to
and become a part of the perfect space we're in
because we let ourselves just be there. Like Frank
and Bill? Not exactly, but close enough.

The World without John Ashbery

The world without John Ashbery
has lasted for one day
so far. Soon
one week, one century.
Will people look back
and scratch their heads
the way some do now?
I hope not. But
it's out of my hands
anyway, and I
won't care one whit.
But what he did,
his poetry, that is,
is great.
He gave me a conjunction
and I ran away with it,
though it kept turning
me around, so I ran back.
And here I am
with a conjunction
on my hands.
My idea
was to give it back,
but instead
I'm going to move
the forest six inches
to the left and leave it
at that.

Bill Berkson's Obituary

Two weeks ago you and I
walked down First Avenue
a few blocks before good-bye,
and now I'm walking the same way
with the *Times* tucked under my arm
while you go on out into the whole world
like the perfect gentleman
you always will be,
true and loyal friend.
I'll open the paper at home,
not till then.

Sleepyhead

It's hard to describe
how falling asleep I am,
clouds rising around me pink and blue
and I a dot.

The Dream of the Cadillac

I dreamed I was me
writing this poem

and then I was

When I was a child
people in movies
who got shot in the back
always died

So when the bad guy said
"Turn around"
you'd better not do it

There is no such thing as a poem
Only this poem exists

Or that one
and the bullet flew

Becoming human
must have been terrifying
so they found things
to distract them
They dreamed they were they

in a Cadillac

There is only one Cadillac
in the world
The others are dreams of Cadillacs

I saw the water
but could not make it be
anything else

The glass was neither half full
nor half empty the glass
was not there yet

Like how morning is just around the corner
but you can't see it it's
still dark
though you can hear the Cadillac in it
the engine running
the Cadillac not moving

until the dim edge of the corner appears
in the dawn
and everything gets to be there for a moment
before it's there

Elephant Walk

Once when I was asleep
someone tapped me on the shoulder
and a jolt of cold fear went through me
until I saw it was my own finger.
I was relieved
it wasn't some nut
who had gotten into my bedroom
and decided to tap me on the shoulder.

There was a movie about elephants
that rampaged through the jungle,
knocking everything down—I think
it was called *Elephant Walk.*
I don't recall why they wanted
to knock everything down, they
just seemed very unhappy.

There was another movie
in which a tidal wave of voracious ants
came buzz-cutting their way through the jungle,
chewing up everything in their path,
and the hero had to figure out
what to do, as his girlfriend
kept jerking her hands
to the sides of her head in terror.
I remember thinking that the ants
were going to chew off his and her legs
if they didn't get out of there fast, go
to a different continent where the ants weren't so hungry.
I wanted to tap him on the shoulder.

Big Anniversary

It's October 9th,
a day that means nothing
to me. I can't think
of a single thing associated
with it, no birthday
or disaster, no holiday
or date of death.
It will be replaced
by October 10th, another day
with no resonance
other than the resonance of everything,
which, come to think of it,
is a lot.

The Waiting Room

What are you waiting for?
You almost know
what it is,
but still you wait
in a space in which
you think you'll hold back time,
but time has a way
of getting its way,
and there you are,
left behind with your illusion,
in which you wait
for it to disappear
the way Casper the Friendly Ghost did,
though he's waiting for you,
turning the pages of the comic book
you are still reading.

Wait

A second. I mean
a minute. Then a day
or two. Longer,
like years. There
grows a tree
in paradise
and children say things.
What do they know,
those adorable little morons?

Edge Puppet

The puppet dances
all this way and that,
loose-jointed, head
flopping side to side,
in his commedia dell'arte costume,
a song in his heart,
and he is happy to be there
on the outskirts of town,
dancing like a puppet
with tears in his eyes
that see the tears from inside,
where he is pulling his own strings.

Pencils and Pens

Every once in a while when I open my desk drawer, the flat, shallow one right in front of me, my eyes send to my brain the information that the numerous pens and pencils I had arranged so neatly have once again become strewn this way and that, in jumbles and piles crisscrossing the other items in the drawer—erasers, paper-clip boxes, rubber bands, a staple box, a box of small screwdrivers, two pocketknives, a flashlight, picture wire, tape, small screws, a padlock, a shoehorn, three pairs of scissors, two old wristwatches, a staple puller, map tacks, a hole punch, address labels, a photographer's loupe, postage stamps, a bottle of ink, rubber stamps, rubber stamp pads, batteries, a tape measure, and rulers—and I am seized with the desire to sort the pens and pencils into categories and place them in appropriate areas in the drawer again, but today this desire was shunted aside by the sudden realization that the words that might issue from these instruments will never flow forth from most of them, that whatever I might have said with them will remain forever locked inside them, and that I, as a physical body, am a kind of pencil or pen from which whatever I might say will never issue. A sad thought! But then, when you think about it, not so much sad as normal, at least as measured against the behavior of most of humanity, for don't people rarely express the range of what they think or feel?

Many years ago I described myself as a pencil, but I did it only because I liked the word *pencil* itself—the way it looks and sounds—not because I was using it metaphorically. It is too commonplace a metaphor to arouse any interest in me, but today when I stared into my desk drawer and saw the chaos of pencils and pens, the metaphor became uncontrollable and explosive, and I could not count the explosions, and for a moment I felt afraid. Then the urge to rearrange the pens and pencils drove out my fear, allowing me to anticipate the satisfaction of accomplishing something that is so unimportant as to be almost pointless.

Esther's Notebook

On the reverse side of the page that carries *Les Cahiers d'Esther*—these days the only comic strip I read—are real-estate ads that remind me of the life I was never able to give my wife. Here's one for a cream-colored house in Paris in the seventh arrondissement, in its own private alley off the rue de Grenelle, an eighteenth-century gem with thirteen rooms (six bedrooms) on four levels, near shops and excellent schools—the kind of property that rarely comes onto the market. About six million dollars. And a private parking area. On the reverse side of the page Esther is thirteen, learning how to deal with the world.

Reality

Nature is everywhere the same,
In Paris and in Terre Haute.
Dombasle's Triptolemus by another name.
A chlamys is a petticoat.

La Vallière in her coach,
Fancying Mars or the Roi Soleil,
Was as ferocious
As Aphrodite in her shell.

O sons and brothers, O poets,
When a thing is, say it's so.
Be of spirit pure, and then do it.
When the soul is high, nothing's low.

A hiccup escapes Silenus
Among the roses of Paestum.
When Horace gives us Priapus,
Shakespeare may risk Bottom.

Truth has no bounds.
Thanks to bestial Pan, the real
Shows its godly horns
On the blue forehead of the ideal.

—*Victor Hugo*

Apostrophe

To myself

One common error is the misuse of the apostrophe in *its* (or *it's*). Example: The tournament is in it's fifth year.

Now the clatter of pick-up sticks. If small children can learn to play pick-up sticks, surely they can learn how to use the apostrophe, which is, after all, only one stick. Yes, it has two sides, one for forming possessives and one for indicating dropped letters, and it has two edges, one for confusing you and one for confusing you even more.

Not that confusion is all bad. Sometimes I propel myself into the kitchen not sure whether I want coffee or not. The very fact that it doesn't matter and that I am standing there like an apostrophe in the morning light gives me a thrill. Its my thrill. It's my thrill.

Flash Cards

My second-grade teacher would hold up a card with 2 + 2 or some other math problem on it. The first student who called out the correct answer got to take that card. When she had gone through the entire set, the student with the most cards got to take her place, but there was no point in keeping score, since I always won them all. Vain as I was, I couldn't decide whether it was better to be at my seat winning or at the front flashing the cards. It was a few steps from my desk to the front. Since those days, I have been able to take only a few steps away from myself, and when I turn around I can bear only a quick peek between my fingers.

The Uprising of the Beans

The baked beans fly into the living room
where Mom, Dad, and Sis
are locked in a mah-jongg tussle.
Dad is soon covered with beans
that bang against his body, crying
"We want *something*!
We demand *something*!"
"Little beans," he says,
"you can have anything
you want," and the beans
cheer and dance as Mom and Sis
swing into radiant harmony.
Dad is great.

Love Song

It is drifting, the season, it
is bent, like a racetrack

and the memory of you with white lace collar
and black dress bent back, the top part

of you grazing the top part of me
and the rest of you swept into the dark.

Coffee Corner

The large bowls of coffee at breakfast in old France,
the heavy porcelain cups in old American diners,
the brown plastic cups in cheap motel lobbies,

the feeling that you ought to drink the entire cup,
the slight resentment you feel at feeling this,
the wondering why you do it then, you dope,

the gratitude for someone's making the coffee,
the decision not to have a third free refill,
the surprise of a really bad cup of coffee,

the way it used to cost a nickel, then a dime,
and now anywhere up to god knows what
(you brought your credit card, right?),

the brown print drying on the lip of the cup,
the trace left in the bottom,
the rest of it thrumming inside you,

thrumming its stimulation through tubes
in your body, hello, let's go, are we late, do
you have the keys, oh god I can't find my wallet.

Shadows at Noon

One of my college professors told me that when comparing two things (as in "He's as big as a house"), the first *as* should be *so* when following a negative verb ("He's not so big as a house"). Because I respected my teacher, I unhesitatingly accepted this rule, but I have never found it in any grammar manual, so in defending it to others I have had no recourse other than to say "It's what F. W. Dupee told me." One weakness of this defense is that few people now know who he was. He left behind only a few books of nonfiction and a diminishing number of students who might still remember this fine point of his exactitude.

My term paper for his Modern Poetry course discussed what happened at noon in the poetry of Emily Dickinson.

In 1965, one year after college, I found myself living in Paris. One day, in a small shop on the rue Mazarine, I bought a used book called *Ombres chinoises,* a title much more intriguing than its English translation (*Shadow Puppets*). The book focused on the shadow-puppet plays performed in the late nineteenth century at Le Chat Noir, the Montmartre cabaret where other acts included Erik Satie at the piano and a fellow known as Le Pétomane, who was able to blow out a candle by farting. I became so fascinated by shadow-puppet plays that I decided to write a book about their history, apparently something no one had ever done. In the following years I took notes for this endeavor, which I kept in a manila file folder, but the project remained there, a few scraps of paper.

Who

Who is that knocking at my chamber door?
Who is that whose foot is standing on the floor?

It is me mum, come to say one word:
"Ron" in a tone no one can understand

for it is not a name, it is a power
that drove her life up to a point and then

off. The boy at fifty-eight who held her hand
and felt that final squeeze, so strong

for one so near to death, now sits
and puts his Ron foot on the floor.

F

I'm thinking in my sleep about the word *fetal* because I realize that's the position my arms are in, and then the variant spelling *foetal* clicks into place. Was the initial *f* a modernization of *ph*? Or do all *f* words come from Latin and all *ph* words from Greek? *Fantastic* and *phenomenal*—these words start to whirl around, both inside my head and outside my body, then they fly up onto a distant hilltop that is backlit by the sun that will soon rise. I uncurl my arms.

Soft Roll

Last night my wife
bit into a soft roll
and her tooth fell out
just like that,
no warning, no pain,
no nothing and now
no tooth, except
the one she held
in the palm of her hand
as she said
"I'm falling apart"
and laughed.

People Take Pictures of Each Other

You think of the people
you used to know,
relatives and close friends,
and how they got reduced
and sucked onto photographic paper,
living on in a black-and-white world,
which isn't so bad for them
while you're thinking of them,
but when you aren't
they have to stop and wait
for you to bring your mind
back to them
and then they are happy,
almost laughing.

Pipe Dream

1.

I yearned to find the love of my life, never certain that I *would* find her and that someday I would wake up at 5 a.m., fix toast and tea, and realize that without her I am nothing. Before her I was something—a young man yearning for her—and now I'm an old man yearning for her, for me.

2.

There is no song lyric more moving than “September Song”: “And these few precious days I’ll spend with you.” *Moving* is not the right word, it’s more like *gut-wrenching* or *heart-stabbing*—a physical assault. The words fly toward me, but I bat them away and wait for my next breath.

3.

It's the next day and the same raindrops are going *tap-tap-tappity-tap* on my roof, but the idea of a bluebird has landed on my shoulder ever so gently. I have no fear that it will peck me or dig its claws into my flesh, for it is a serene bluebird, even more exalted than the bluebird of happiness. On the other shoulder is an unoccupied space—not even air is there—open for the arrival of something tremendous, such as a smattering of periods in search of sentences to end.

4.

5.

I've never been able to understand an experience I'm in. It's all too everything. That is, a *now-or-never* whose *now* disappears and whose *never* seems forever. I guess that that clarification doesn't help. Let me try it this way: childhood, I had no idea; adolescence, no idea; adulthood, ditto; and now, total ditto. But sometimes—not often—there comes the feeling that everything is all right anyway, that the pipe is having a dream about *you.*

Falling Asleep in Poetry

It's hard to write a poem
when you are on the verge
of falling asleep, but Robert
Desnos could do it, even when
he *was* asleep, or so
the story goes.
There are photos of him
lying on a couch asleep,
but is he writing a poem?
I don't remember any utensils.
Just his heavy eyelids.

"You are standing on my eyelids"
wrote his fellow poet Paul Éluard,
"you" being not Desnos but a woman.
It feels like neither poet
had to work hard
to write their poems,
even Desnos when awake.
I thought writing this poem would wake me up,
but it woke him up instead,
and Éluard has tiptoed away.

In Conclusion

I've come to the conclusion
that humanity is hopelessly stupid,
even more stupid than a raindrop,
but that if we could achieve the intelligence of a raindrop
we would be happy
to be one
and go splat.

Pants

Good morning, pants
of Nature, blue striding
across my visual field,
a hearty hello to you
and a thank-you for striding,
even if you are just a bug
making tiny waves on a pond.
You are still the pants of Nature!

Lunch Bucket

How corny and sentimental
it is to remember the lunch bucket
my grandfather took to work,
black metal with a vaulted lid
hinged to the rectangular box
inside of which was a thermos of coffee
and a sandwich and maybe
a hard-boiled egg. He himself
was anything but hard-boiled,
just a regular guy
though kinder than most
and gentler.
I see him in the big metal shed,
among the metal pipes and grinders,
with a dim light filtering in
as he sits down next to Gomez,
the new guy some people called a "wetback,"
whose English made my grandpa laugh,
and opens the lunch box,
unscrews the plastic thermos cap,
and pours the coffee into it.
He was glad to have a job
and he liked Gomez.

Otter Moment

I just saw an otter,
at first a head moving
just above the surface,
then disappearing underwater
for a while and coming up
near the bank, forelegs pulling him
up onto it, and undulating
across the ground, a shining
and oh dear unattractive
fat tube. In *his* world
he's gorgeous!

Parallel Parallels

Two parallel lines
have two *l*'s in their name
but want to be perpendicular
to each other.
Don't they have anything better to do?
Off they go
into an area called Zen,
where they are welcomed,
the first parallel lines
in Zen!
With an exclamation point
perpendicular to them!

Peppermint Air

Only twenty minutes and
I already don't smell
the peppermint oil
on the cotton balls
I have placed in this room
to keep the mice out.
I sit here in a cube of air,
a big nonmouse.

Ping

The time will come
when the car will stop
and you will get out,
the car will go on
and you will see
all around you
nothing,
absolutely nothing,
then *ping*

Knockouts

Ça a l'air de rimer
—APOLLINAIRE

Do you speak English?
I don't speak Russian.
I am a great poet.
I am a great tennis player.
Where is the bathroom?

The Chinese word for *something*
is *tongshi,*
made up of two characters,
tong (west) and *shi* (east).
That seems to make sense.

When you scratch your head
your fingers curl up
like a question mark.

So he said, "Let's run
and have some fun before I melt away."
Without legs, run?

Like Birnam Wood
to Dunsinane, eh?

That seems to rhyme, eh?

Long ago
I made the mistake of thinking
that life is mysterious.
Life is not mysterious.

It is mysterious
only to those
who think about it too much.
Peasants don't think
that life is mysterious.
They are too busy staying alive.

There is some word
that feels like it should have a *j* in it
but I can't remember what it is

Not *picaresque*

(as in *Don Quixote*)

or *babushka*

A monkey jumped on a buzzard's back

sticks spinning in the air
like "evil"

and that movie theater
in Paris, what was it—
"oriental"
like a cross
between a xylophone and a pyramid
and on the rue de Grenelle, wasn't it?
I lay in bed
in its green jade embrace.

La Pagode!

of course—rue de Babylone

Look, I can't do anything
about it, it being like
Nevada or vanishing

and let the Devil take tomorrow

for it doesn't matter
what you think
but why you think it

and it took me a while
but now I'm inside your face
and I won't leave until I
feel like it, friend,
and I don't mind
giving you the creeps—
in fact,
I kind of like
being made of snow

A young woman
with pink hair
starts across the street
as if she were someone else,
the hair very so what,
but it rides across the street,
a pink cloud
on its own,
so not so so-what.
Electricity

is like the nervous system,
branching and buzzing
inside that pink hair
that is still riding

inside my pink head.
I am a pink snowman.
You don't believe me,
because you don't have pink anything.

In Syria some children
have red hair, red
with blood, that is.
Let's put them all
in a box and fold it
so it vanishes,
like they just did.
Boom boom boom boom,
as the song says.
You knocks me out.
Like Nevada.

So when I wake up
the first thing I do
is nothing.
I just lie there
saturated with myself.
Then I knock myself out
and from all over my body
little points of light
float out into the room.
Boom boom boom boom.

My Early Childhood

My name was Ronnie
and I knew it,
though I had four black lines
that formed a box around me,
not too close, and there
were wiggling lines
emanating from each
of those four black lines,
wiggling and waving
as if craziness lived inside them,
and the great thing
is that I had no idea
they were there.
After all,
they weren't hurting anybody.

In Umbria

Because I have no hope of ever going back
—GUIDO CAVALCANTI

So how *did* Perugino get from Perugia to Florence?
On a donkey?
And who went with him?
Oho!
Here are raindrops falling from the sky
onto his head and shoulders,
and the ears and the mane of his donkey have drops too
because that's what happens
when you can't buy an umbrella on the corner
from the little old Chinese woman
whose ancestors made a screen
that shows us winding our way
through the hills in the now slanting rain.

Pluto

If you have ever wondered what
it's like to be human,
keep wondering, brothers
and sisters, because that's all
you can do
to try to catch
in your hands
whatever it is
that moves away
when you reach for it.
Pluto used to be a planet
and a dog, now
it's a what?

Russian Mountain

I said, "What does *montaña* mean?"
and the kids shouted, "Mountain!"
"Aha. So what does *rusa* mean?"
"Russian!"
"So *montaña rusa* means *Russian mountain.*"
"No!" they laughed.
"What does it mean?"
"Roller coaster, you know, like
the Cyclone at Coney Island."
I didn't tell them
I knew that all along.
They were so happy
on Russian Mountain.

Ticket

A car drives through
the visual patterns
in my brain, the driver
my father
totally at ease
at 110 miles per hour.
All I see
is a blur go by
but I know who
it is.

Both of Me

Paul, the Separated Man / Leaped forward
—KENNETH KOCH

The reasonable part of me knows that the song title "Who Can I Turn To?" would not sound so good if it were "Whom Can I Turn To?" and the pedantic part feels that the more grammatically correct *whom* should be kept alive, to slow its slippage into desuetude, becoming more of a marker of one's education than a useful, if small, tool for communicating well, for I tend to forget that there is room enough in the world for both the formally correct and the colloquial, and that in any case there is nothing I can do to change the course of the history of our language. It is what it is.

In high-school French class, first year, our teacher introduced the rules for the agreement of nouns and adjectives. For example, *cher monsieur* became, when addressing a mature or married woman, *chère madame.* One student raised his hand and asked a perfectly sincere question: "Why don't they just keep *cher* the same, the way we do with *dear sir* and *dear madam*?" The teacher looked at him for a moment and then delivered a crushing truth: "Because they don't."

I don't think she went on to say that although we can trace the changes of a language throughout history, we can't always explain *why* things developed the way they did, and in this case *why* isn't a useful question to raise, because knowing the answer won't make us learn French any faster. She might have pointed out that English has its own puzzlements, and that a language such as Chinese, which Westerners tend to think of as hopelessly complicated, is grammatically much simpler than English, as it has no singular or plural nouns, no agreement of nouns and adjectives, no agreement of subject and verb, no articles, and no past or future tense, at least as we conceive of them, but I doubt that she knew much about Chinese, and besides it probably would not have made the student feel less perplexed. No, when it comes to a language, it is what it is, just as the student was who he was. (Bob Stubblefield.)

Which, believe it or not, brings me to matches. My childish assumption was that they are called that because they look identical. If you spill a box of them onto a table, you cannot tell one from the other, a fact that doesn't worry you, as they look rather beautiful spilled out like that. A few days ago someone asked me about the matches in a poem of mine: perhaps I had written about them because, although rather insignificant objects, they represent reality? My immediate thought was to answer no and let it go at that, but instead I agreed that a match could be an example of reality, as indeed anything can, and that a match has as much reality as a mountain. Of course a match doesn't "have" reality, it is an example of reality, or at least what we commonly refer to as reality. Then it turned out that the word *match* does not derive from similarity of appearance, but rather from an ancient Greek word.

Alex Katz painted a portrait of Allen Ginsberg on six separate aluminum sheets of different sizes and shapes, on each of which is a section of Ginsberg's face—frontal, turned slightly, and in profile—in varying degrees of close-up. Four of the pieces are mounted on a wall and the other two are freestanding in front of them, about four feet from the wall, forming what might be called a highly controlled and frozen cubistic explosion. Faced simultaneously with one fragment zoomed in and another zoomed out, I felt as if I had gotten inside Ginsberg's face! It's like walking down a busy street in Manhattan and realizing that you're actually *in* the street that's *out* there. That is, not only are you alive, you *are* life, and who you are seems, for a moment at least, beside whatever the point might be.

Visible Ink

This is the room
where many years ago
I'd lock myself in
and then lock myself
into myself.
It was as safe
as being in
an invisible safe
and all I had to do
was wait
for the words
that leaped
into my . . . what?
and slid down
inside my pen
and onto where
the paper was.

But now when I walk
into that room I bang
my head on the edge
of the door and blood
falls from my forehead
onto the floor
in a pool
that gets redder
and redder.
I'm surprised
you don't see it.

Encore with Rectangle and Philosophy

I built a house / and had ideas in it.
—RON PADGETT

Initio it was weird,
everything,
Boom!
ribbons and shimmering everywhere,
and this and thisness:
stop, look, and sound too
waiting to come out
as soon as movement said to,
and a bone walked around
as if something had happened to it,
like, an infinity ago.

• • •

Excuse me.
I have to get up
and walk around a little.
My abode
is dark and cozy
but sometimes it turns me
into a bowling ball,
and yes
I weigh sixteen pounds
and am suddenly marbleized
as I hook into the pocket
and decimate all ten pins
in one explosive explosion!
—Wait, *decimate*
is not the *mot juste,*

nor *cave* nor *bowling ball.*
(My soul has just multiplied itself,
in case.)

On second thought,
I don't think
I *can* get up.
Would you give me a hand?
Shakespeare?

What is Shakespeare?
The fellow bound
upon a wheel of fire
and rolled up into the sky?

• • •

I'm stuck to a moment,
then it goes away.

I am not stuck to the world,
I *am* the world,
two feet tall
and zero deep and wide.
Look at the picture
in the dictionary
next to the word *mysticism:*
there's nothing there.
What do you think about
that?
(You're coming out of the wrong side of my head.)

• • •

Pronouns aren't for everybody.

•••

My head went into everybody
the way vowels went into words
and life was a little easier,
then,
the way the Pacific Ocean
was easier than the Atlantic
and *best* was better than *better,*
and the barnyard swung open
in a kind of orchestral majesty
that got sucked into a pile of cow dung,
which caused ancient China to wake up
and be modern China, smiling
and gesturing Oh hello! and everything.
I gave the driver some yuan
and got out of the taxi inwardly,
and then got out outwardly,
the driver went forward
into a pile of cow dung.
I figured there was time,
but for what?
Everybody went into my head
the way harmony went into music.

•••

There are a lot of details in the world
—too many for me, so
I *blur* them, using my ability to *blur,*
except now instead of you
I see invisible ink and it's thrilling
in a different way (for me,
not for you).

•••

In the middle
of the night
What
is the name of that island
we went to
way back when and what
should be done with my ashes?
It had two pronunciations,
one for its citizens, one
for the rest of us. Released
into the stream in Vermont, perhaps.

Aside from the Hague,
how many cities begin (in English)
with *the*?

•••

Antigua.
I wrote it down.

•••

If you think
about the tasks
ahead of you
in the day,
go ahead and turn them
into small rectangles,
sweep them
into your hand
and toss them outside.
Then kill yourself.

•••

The Bronx.
I wrote it up.

•••

Beating so.
You give your hand to me
and then you say hello,
but I can hardly speak
my heart is . . .

. . . like the fork *now*
falling toward the floor and everything
falling as you grab grab grab

•••

O my.
That's what people used to say.
God had left the sentence.
O me.

•••

Coleridge
sat alone under a lime tree,
missing his friends,
and wrote about it—
a bird flew past,
electrifying,
the first time that something happened
during the writing of a poem
and got included.

Okay, first a bat goes by
and then a bee is singing,
and then the bird (a rook)
"(Now a dim speck, now vanishing in light)."
The bat and the bee I forget
but that bird is bang on.

•••

The idea of 1/3
is more appealing
than the idea of 2/3.

•••

I built a house
that had ideas in it.
Am I supposed to be
the something of something?

•••

It's a long way
between love of country
and licking your lips.
You're told to love your country
by people who want you
to obey them but never tell you
that you should lick your lips
before trying to eat or drink something
that might burn them.

•••

.

Don't "go" "there."
(Or the bell will ring.)

• • •

I dreamed there was
an athletic team called
The Tokyo Infinities.
How could there be
more than one infinity?
Like, say, seventeen of them.
Maybe each member
has his own infinity.
Their uniforms were orange and black.

• • •

When Coleridge says "now" in his poem
he means now, whenever that was or is:
Now—a dim concept,
vanished in light
that vanished in the dark.

Inside

Notebook, you,
my friend,
are running out of pages.
It's time to say good-bye
to you, leaving a few blanks
at the end
for you to rest in.
For me there is no rest,
just more words
somewhere else,
my portable prison,
my life sentence
without parole,
surrounded by puns.

Notes

The poems in this book are sequenced according to the year of their first publication in book form, from 1964 to 2011, but this chronology doesn't always reflect the dates of composition; for example, some of the poems in my first collection were written *after* some in my second. My uncollected poems, grouped here as *Poem and Other Poems*, are arranged in roughly chronological order by date of first draft—ranging from 1960 to 2004—and if that date is unknown, by educated guess. Uncollected poems that were drafted after 2004 (and not included here) continue to be what I optimistically call works-in-progress.

I have omitted collaborative works done with artists and other poets.

In a prefatory note for *Poems I Guess I Wrote*, a grab bag of pieces that go back as far as 1965, I offered this explanation of the title:

> Leafing through old notebooks and folders of my writing, I have, from time to time, found certain poems that stop me in my tracks. The evidence that I wrote these poems—the handwriting, the font of the typewriter I was using at the time, the marginal scribbles and revisions, the stylistic gestures, and so on—is undeniable, but I have no memory, or at most a tiny inkling of a memory, of having written them.

This forgetfulness does not apply to any other book I have published.

The Italian translations of the odes in the *Great Balls of Fire* section are by George Schneeman. *Grazie*, Giorgio. Thanks also to Grazia della Terza, Dante della Terza, and Cristina Chetry for a few tweaks.

"I'll Get It": The quotation from Tolstoy is from Constance Garnett's translation of *War and Peace*, Modern Library edition (New York, no date), p. 1103.

"Knockouts": The epigraph can be translated either as "That seems to rhyme" or as "That seems to make sense."
The song referred to is John Lee Hooker's "Boom Boom."

"Reality": This poem is a translation of Victor Hugo's "La Réalité," from his *L'Art d'être grand-père* (*The Art of Being a Grandfather*), published in 1877.

Terre Haute: For the purposes of rhyme, I have replaced Hugo's Gonesse with Terre Haute. Gonesse is a commune about ten miles northeast of Paris. In 1783 the world's first hydrogen-filled balloon flew from Paris and landed in Gonesse, where terrified local peasants destroyed it with pitchforks. In 1923 the largest Klu Klux Klan rally ever held in Indiana attracted a reported 75,000 people near Terre Haute.

Dombasle: Mathieu de Dombasle (1777–1843) was a French agronomist, one of the first French farmers to grow beets to produce sugar. Also, he invented the Dombasle plough.

Triptolemus: In Greek mythology, the goddess Demeter taught Triptolemus the art of agriculture. He flew across the land in a winged chariot while Demeter and her daughter Persephone helped him complete his mission of educating the whole of Greece in the art of agriculture.

Chlamys: The chlamys is a short rectangular cloak originally worn by men in ancient Greece.

La Vallière: Louise de la Vallière (1644–1710), who was seriously in love with Louis XIV, was his mistress for six years. The two had five children. She spent the last thirty-six years of her life as a Carmelite nun.

Silenus: In Greek mythology, Silenus is a satyr, the adoptive father of Dionysus, the god of wine and uninhibited festivity.

Paestum: Paestum was a major ancient Greek city in Greater Greece (now southern Italy). The well-preserved ruins of Paestum are famous for their ancient Greek temples, amphitheater, and city walls.

Acknowledgements

The books of my poetry collected in this volume have been dedicated to my wife Patricia, my son Wayne, my daughter-in-law Siobhán, my grandson Marcello, my father Wayne, and my friends Kenward Elmslie and George Schneeman. To them I happily add my granddaughter Michiko.

I am very grateful to everyone who has published my poems in magazines and books, especially Bill Berkson, Ted Berrigan, Tom Clark, Robert Cornfield, Larry Fagin, Christopher Fischbach, Kenward Elmslie, Richard Hell, Lita Hornick, Allan Kornblum, Mark Polizzotti, Anne Waldman, Lewis Warsh, and Bill Zavatsky, as well as the entire staff past and present of Coffee House Press.

Index of Titles

Index of First Lines

Coffee House Press began as a small letterpress operation in 1972 and has grown into an internationally renowned nonprofit publisher of literary fiction, essay, poetry, and other work that doesn't fit neatly into genre categories.

LITERATURE
is not the same thing as
PUBLISHING

Funder Acknowledgments

Coffee House Press is an internationally renowned independent book publisher and arts nonprofit based in Minneapolis, MN; through its literary publications, Coffee House acts as a catalyst and connector—between authors and readers, ideas and resources, creativity and community, inspiration and action.

Coffee House Press books are made possible through the generous support of grants and donations from corporations, state and federal grant programs, family foundations, and the many individuals who believe in the transformational power of literature. This activity is made possible by the voters of Minnesota through a Minnesota State Arts Board Operating Support grant, thanks to the legislative appropriation from the Arts and Cultural Heritage Fund. Coffee House also receives major operating support from the Amazon Literary Partnership, McKnight Foundation, and the National Endowment for the Arts (NEA). To find out more about how NEA grants impact individuals and communities, visit www.arts.gov.

Coffee House Press receives additional support from Bookmobile; Dorsey & Whitney LLP; and the Schwab Charitable Fund.

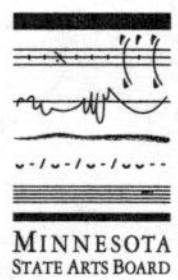

McKNIGHT FOUNDATION

The Publisher's Circle of Coffee House Press

Publisher's Circle members make significant contributions to Coffee House Press's annual giving campaign. Understanding that a strong financial base is necessary for the press to meet the challenges and opportunities that arise each year, this group plays a crucial part in the success of Coffee House's mission.

Recent Publisher's Circle members include many anonymous donors, Patricia A. Beithon, Robin Chemers Neustein, Kelli Cloutier, Theodore Cornwell, Jane Dalrymple-Hollo, Jeremy M. Davies, Mary Ebert and Paul Stembler, Kamilah Foreman, Eva Galiber, Bryan Garrett, Roger Hale and Nor Hall, William Hardacker, Randy Hartten and Ron Lotz, Carl and Heidi Horsch, Amy L. Hubbard and Geoffrey J. Kehoe Fund of the St. Paul & Minnesota Foundation, Hyde Family Charitable Fund, Kenneth & Susan Kahn, the Kenneth Koch Literary Estate, Cinda Kornblum, the Lenfestey Family Foundation, Carol and Aaron Mack, Gillian McCain, Mary and Malcolm McDermid, Daniel N. Smith III and Maureen Millea Smith, Vance Opperman, Mr. Pancks' Fund in memory of Graham Kimpton, Alan Polsky, Robin Preble, Ronald Restrepo and Candace S. Baggett, Elizabeth Schnieders, Steve Smith, Jeffrey Sugerman and Sarah Schultz, Paul Thissen, Allyson Tucker, Grant Wood, Margaret Wurtele, Aptara Inc., The Buckley Charitable Fund, and Dorsey and Whitney Foundation.

For more information about the Publisher's Circle and other ways to support Coffee House Press books, authors, and activities, please visit www.coffeehousepress.org/pages/donate or contact us at info@coffeehousepress.org.

Ron Padgett's *How Long* was a Pulitzer Prize finalist in poetry, and his *Collected Poems* won the LA Times Prize for the best poetry book of 2014 and the William Carlos Williams Award from the Poetry Society of American (PSA). He has also received the Shelley Memorial Award and the Frost medal from the PSA. His translations include *Zone: Selected Poems of Guillaume Apollinaire* and Blaise Cendrar's *Complete Poems*. Seven of his poems were used in Jim Jarmusch's film *Paterson*. New York City has been his home base since 1960.

Very Collected Poems was designed by
Bookmobile Design & Digital Publisher Services.
Text is set in Garamond.